An Image

of *the*

Soul in Speech

Literature and Philosophy

A. J. Cascardi, General Editor

This series publishes books in a wide range of subjects in philosophy and literature, including studies of the social and historical issues that relate these two fields. Drawing on the resources of the Anglo-American and Continental traditions, the series is open to philosophically informed scholarship covering the entire range of contemporary critical thought.

ALREADY PUBLISHED

J. M. Bernstein, *The Fate of Art: Aesthetic Alienation from Kant to Derrida and Adorno*
Peter Bürger, *The Decline of Modernism*
Mary E. Finn, *Writing the Incommensurable: Kierkegaard, Rossetti, and Hopkins*
Reed Way Dasenbrock, ed., *Literary Theory After Davidson*
David Haney, *William Wordsworth and the Hermeneutics of Incarnation*
David Jacobson, *Emerson's Pragmatic Vision: The Dance of the Eye*
Gray Kochhar-Lindgren, *Narcissus Transformed: The Textual Subject in Psychoanalysis and Literature*
Robert Steiner, *Toward a Grammar of Abstraction: Modernity, Wittgenstein, and the Paintings of Jackson Pollock*
Sylvia Walsh, *Living Poetically: Kierkegaard's Existential Aesthetics*
Michel Meyer, *Rhetoric, Language, and Reason*
Christie McDonald and Gary Wihl, eds., *Transformation in Personhood and Culture After Theory*
Charles Altieri, *Painterly Abstraction in Modernist American Poetry: The Contemporaneity of Modernism*
John C. O'Neal, *The Authority of Experience: Sensationist Theory in the French Enlightenment*
John O'Neill, ed., *Freud and the Passions*
Sheridan Hough, *Nietzsche's Noontide Friend: The Self as Metaphoric Double*
E. M. Dadlez, *What's Hecuba to Him? Fictional Events and Actual Emotions*
Hugh Roberts, *Shelley and the Chaos of History: A New Politics of Poetry*
Charles Altieri, *Postmodernisms Now: Essays on Contemporaneity in the Arts*
Arabella Lyon, *Intentions: Negotiated, Contested, and Ignored*
Jill Gordon, *Turning Toward Philosophy: Literary Device and Dramatic Structure in Plato's Dialogues*
Michel Meyer, *Philosophy and the Passions: Toward a History of Human Nature.* Translated by Robert F. Barsky
Reed Way Dasenbrock, *Truth and Consequences: Intentions, Conventions, and the New Thematics*
David P. Haney, *The Challenge of Coleridge: Ethics and Interpretation in Romanticism and Modern Philosophy*
Alan Singer, *Aesthetic Reason: Artworks and the Deliberative Ethos*
Tom Huhn, *Imitation and Society: The Persistence of Mimesis in the Aesthetics of Burke, Hogarth, and Kant*
Jennifer Anna Gosetti-Ferenci, *The Ecstatic Quotidian: Phenomenological Sightings in Modern Art and Literature*
Max Statkiewicz, *Rhapsody of Philosophy: Dialogues with Plato in Contemporary Thought*

An Image
of the
Soul in Speech

Plato *and the* Problem of Socrates

David N. McNeill

The Pennsylvania State University Press
University Park, Pennsylvania

An earlier version of Chapter 7, "Human Discourse,
Eros, and Madness in Plato's *Republic*," appeared in the
Review of Metaphysics 55, no. 2 (2001).

Library of Congress Cataloging-in-Publication Data

McNeill, David N., 1965–
An image of the soul in speech : Plato and the
problem of Socrates / David N. McNeill.
p.   cm.
Includes bibliographical references (p.   ) and index.
ISBN 978-0-271-03585-7 (cloth : alk. paper)
1. Socrates.
2. Plato. Dialogues.
I. Title.

B317 .M395
183'.2—dc22
2009024996

The Pennsylvania State University Press is a member of the
Association of American University Presses.

It is the policy of The Pennsylvania State University Press to
use acid-free paper. Publications on uncoated stock satisfy
the minimum requirements of American National Standard
for Information Sciences—Permanence of Paper for
Printed Library Material, ANSI Z39.48–1992.

This book is printed on Natures Natural,
which contains 50% post-consumer waste.

For my mother and father

Contents

Acknowledgments ix

1 Introduction: Plato's Socrates on the "Problem of Socrates" 1

2 *Republic* Book 1: Philosophy and Cultural Decadence 11

3 Polemarchus, Politics, and Action 46

4 Thrasymachus, Rhetoric, and the Art of Rule 92

5 Gorgias and the Divine Work of Persuasion 123

6 Protagoras, Antinaturalism, and the Political Art 147

7 Tyrannical Eros and the Philosophic Orientation of the *Republic* 178

8 Imitation and Experience 206

9 Poetry, Psychology, and τὸ θυμοειδές 244

10 Psychology and Ontology 280

Conclusion: An Image of the Soul in Speech 302

References 309

General Index 321

Index of Classical Passages 339

Acknowledgments

In the long process of writing and re-writing this book, I have been fortunate enough to come to owe many remarkable individuals a great deal of thanks. The project began, in a significantly different form, as a doctoral dissertation for the University of Chicago's Committee on Social Thought under the supervision of Robert Pippin. I am deeply grateful his for his guidance, advice and support. I would also like to recognize the particular debt that I owe to John Ferrari, who was unfailingly generous with his time, insight, classical learning and friendship from the time when I first appeared as a visitor to the Classics Department at the University of California at Berkeley. The book in its present form first took shape while I was a Mellon Postdoctoral Fellow in Philosophy at Grinnell College. The final chapters were completed while on a study leave from the University of Essex. I gratefully acknowledge the support of these institutions, and the opportunity to pursue philosophy with the exemplary colleagues and students I found there. Thomas Bartscherer, Brian Manning Delaney, Jim Kreines, Jonathan Lear, Paul Ludwig, Chris Marks, Wayne Martin, Mark Sacks, Richard Velkley and Bernard Williams all read and commented on various drafts; conversations with them, Chris Lynch and David Neidorf have contributed greatly to my understanding of the issues broached in this work. My colleague Dan Watts read and commented upon the manuscript in its entirety. Whatever its remaining faults, the finished work benefited greatly from his invaluable contribution. I thank James Rodwell for his excellent work on the indexes, and John Morris for his perceptive copyediting.

My debts to Stewart Umphrey and Michael McShane extend further back, to my undergraduate years at St. John's College, Annapolis, and my first attempts to think with and through Plato. The thoughts expressed in this book are so closely bound up with what I have learned from them that to talk of influence seems manifestly inadequate. Finally, my deepest thanks to Sandra Moog, without whom this book, and much more than this book, would not have been possible.

I

Introduction
Plato's Socrates on the "Problem of Socrates"

I in no way have the leisure for these things; the reason, my friend, is this. I am not yet able, in accordance with the inscription at Delphi, to "know myself." It thus appears ridiculous to me [γελοῖον δή μοι φαίνεται] to consider other things while ignorant of this. Therefore taking leave of these things, I accept what is customarily believed about them and, as I was just saying, I consider not these things but myself, whether I happen to be a wild beast more complex [πολυπλοκώτερον] and puffed up [ἐπιτεθυμμένον] than Typhon, or am I a tamer, simpler animal partaking in some divine and gentle [ἀτύφου] portion by nature.

—PLATO, *Phaedrus* 230e4–a7

Socrates explains in Plato's *Phaedrus* why he doesn't distrust the myth of Boreas's abduction of Orithuia from the banks of the Areopagus, as do the wise (οἱ σοφοὶ). The reason, he suggests, is that before he could take on the burden of inquiring into the legitimacy of the traditional stories of the gods and heroes, he would have to have completed another task that he considers prior, an inquiry into himself which leaves him no leisure for other inquiries.[1] He says that he wants to know what sort of creature he is, whether he is a many-coiled and arrogant beast or a living being (ζῷον) which partakes of something simple and divine. Until he knows the answer to this question, he says, it seems ridiculous to him to inquire into anything else.[2] Socrates says, moreover, that if he were to distrust the myths, if he had time for such

---

*All Greek citations from Plato are from Plato 1967–68. I have largely followed Allan Bloom's translation of the *Republic* and R. E. Allen's translation of the *Protagoras*, though I have freely altered those translations when appropriate. I have noted when I have altered extended translations from those works. All other translations from the Greek are my own unless otherwise cited.

1. The fact that Socrates articulates his search for self-knowledge in opposition to the attempt to find a rationalizing historical origin of myth is significant both for our understanding Socrates' account of the cultural environment in which he pursued his philosophic mission (see §2.1) and, ultimately, for Plato's account of the difference between Socrates and his sophistic opponents. See Ferrari 1990, 9–16. On the role that rationalizing accounts of the mythic tradition played in the thought of the pre-Socratics and the Sophists, see Morgan 2000, 101–6 and context.

2. In the *Philebus,* where Socrates defines the ridiculous (τὸ γελοῖον) as a kind of vice which stands in opposition to the Delphic inscription, he claims that the most common form of ignorance of oneself is ignorance about one's soul, falsely believing oneself to be superior in virtue when one is not (*Phlb.* 48c).

inquiries, he would not be *atopos*, strange or out of place. We have reason to suspect, however, that if Socrates were not *atopos* he would not be Socrates.[3]

Socrates' concern with self-knowledge is more than obvious; it is proverbial. This does not mean, however, that it is obvious in what sense Socrates is concerned with self-knowledge. The above passage from the *Phaedrus* can be interpreted as indicating two different questions about the self or soul that Socrates is said to address in Plato's dialogues. One way of interpreting Socrates' question is to take it as an instance of his familiar inquiry into definitions; in this case he would be asking what sort of thing is the human soul as such, and the two alternatives he canvasses as possible answers to the question allude to the two disparate conceptions of the soul Socrates presents in the dialogues: the tripartite division of the soul of the *Republic* and the *Phaedrus* on the one hand, and the simple and immortal soul of the *Phaedo* on the other. Another way of interpreting Socrates' question, however, is to take it as referring to a personal, ethical inquiry into himself as an individual. On this reading Socrates is asking not "What sort of thing is a human being?" but rather "What sort of thing am I?" And, if we don't simply discount what he says here as ironic, one of the possible answers he confronts is "Something monstrous."[4]

I believe that we have paid insufficient attention to the presence in Plato's dialogues of this latter ethical question concerning Socrates the individual, and, for that very reason, we have obscured aspects of Socrates' answer, as presented in the dialogues, to the former question regarding the nature of the human soul. Moreover, I contend that if we are to understand Plato's portrait of Socrates, we must come to see that these two types of inquiry—one apparently narrowly personal, practical, and ethical; the other apparently broadly universal, theoretical, and ontological—are for Socrates ultimately inseparable.

This book is an attempt to understand Plato's account of Socrates' characteristic philosophical and pedagogical activity—the *pragma* Socrates calls into question and so ambiguously defends in Plato's *Apology*[5]—by focusing on two aspects of that account. The first is Socrates' confrontation with his own problematic ethical status; the second is the central place in Socrates' philosophic practice of a complex moral psychology, a psychology that differs greatly from the one commonly attributed to him. Contrary to what may still be called a standard account of

---

3. On Socrates' *atopia* as the key to his character, see the introduction to Vlastos 1991, and *Symp.* 215a–22c.

4. Compare Griswold 1986, 36–44. Griswold focuses on the ethical dimension of Socrates' question, but argues that "the truth lies somewhere in between the two alternatives [Socrates] sets out here" (41). On Griswold's interpretation we are meant to see that neither the "tame" nor the "hypertyphonic" alternative could apply to Socrates' erotic, philosophical soul.

5. *Ap.* 20d.

Socratic "intellectualist" moral psychology,[6] Socrates' philosophic practice as made manifest in Plato's dialogues is decisively informed by an account of human motivation and action that is acutely sensitive to the role of the imagination in human ethical life, to the psychic structure of the emotions, and to the historical and cultural context of an individual's ethical commitments. This moral psychology not only guides Socrates' dialectical engagements with his various interlocutors in the dialogues, it also crucially informs his understanding of his own hypothetical method of inquiry. Thus, one of my aims is to offer a defense of Socrates' philosophic practice, and Plato's presentation of that practice, against a tradition of criticism going back to Aristotle that attributes to Socrates an illegitimately abstract intellectualist understanding of human psychology.[7] However, this initial defense will involve confronting deeper questions about Socrates' methods, his motivations, and his influence on his contemporaries.

Of course, as the *Apology* makes clear, ethical questions about Socrates' public philosophic practice predate any written justification of that practice and provide, to a great degree, the context for all of Plato's works. Socrates' defense involves, in the first instance, his confrontation with his cultural shadow—a "certain Socrates" (τις Σωκράτης) who contemplates things in the heavens, investigates things under the earth, and makes the weaker argument the stronger. This popular identification of Socrates as a Sophist and natural philosopher is the charge of Socrates' "first accusers," and it provides the basis, according to Socrates, for the later charges of impiety and corruption that Meletus brings (*Ap.* 18a–19d). In the following chapters I will show how Socrates' recognition of and implicit response to such challenges, particularly those involving the identification of Socratic philosophy with sophistry, crucially inform his rhetorical, pedagogical, and dialectical activity as made manifest in the dialogues. I will argue that Socrates' turn away from a direct inquiry into natural beings involves not only a turn to a self-critical examination of our concepts and methods of reasoning but also, necessarily, an ethical and psychological investigation into an individual human inquirer. No less than his examination of his interlocutors, Socrates' inquiry into himself is, in the first instance, an investigation of a particular soul and a concrete human life. In his own case the life he examines is as controversial, enigmatic, and influential as any in the Western tradition.

6. The evidence for the "standard" view of Socratic intellectualism is summarized and critiqued in Kahn 1996, 224–57. See also Christopher Rowe's response to Kahn (2002).

7. As Ronna Burger has shown (2008), Aristotle's own apparently critical engagement with Socrates in the *Nicomachean Ethics* is part of the argumentative strategy of that work, and both this argumentative strategy and the guiding intention of the *Ethics* can be seen to be broadly Socratic. On the role Aristotle plays in the interpretation of Plato presented here, see note 9 below.

In both my initial defense and subsequent reframing of the inquiry into Plato's account of Socrates' activity, I will also draw on a rich tradition of later philosophic engagements with the figure of Socrates. This tradition has been the subject of a number of recent studies whose primary focus has been what we can learn about later philosophers by their interpretation, appropriation, or critique of Socrates as an exemplar of the philosophic life.[8] My interest, however, is in the illumination these later accounts—especially those implicitly or explicitly critical of Socrates—can provide for our reading of Plato. I believe that the philosopher who follows Aristotle's lead and criticizes—even attacks— Plato's Socrates is often more likely to honor not only the spirit, but even the letter, of Plato's dialogues than authors who seek to defend one or another hypothesized stage of Plato's philosophic development.[9] Profound philosophic criticism of apparent deficiencies in Socrates' arguments is a most important first step in revealing more or less subterranean currents in Plato's dialogues, and the philosopher who exposes and explores tensions in the surface of a Socratic conversation can be our best guide toward uncovering deeper levels of analysis guiding that conversation. As the title of this volume suggests, my interpretation has been guided in key respects by the most famous and most penetrating critic of Socrates in the Western tradition, Friedrich Nietzsche. Employing aspects of

---

8. See Long 1988, Kofman 1998, P. Hadot 1995a, and Nehamas 1998. See also Zuckert 1996 and Lane 2001, which treat modern engagements with Plato and Platonism. An exception is Julia Annas's treatment of middle Platonist interpretation of Plato (1999).

9. In Aristotle's case, this may have been part of his intent. In book 1 of the *Nicomachean Ethics,* Aristotle begins his inquiry into and critique of the concept of the "universal good" in the theory of forms with the claim that "such an inquiry may seem arduous, since the men who introduced the forms are dear to us. But perhaps one should deem it better, even necessary, for the preservation of the truth even to abolish what is one's own, especially if one is a philosopher. Both are dear to us, but it is sacred to honor the truth first" (καίπερ προσάντους τῆς τοιαύτης ζητήσεως γινομένης διὰ τὸ φίλους ἄνδρας εἰσαγαγεῖν τὰ εἴδη. δόξειε δ᾽ ἂν ἴσως βέλτιον εἶναι καὶ δεῖν ἐπὶ σωτηρίᾳ γε τῆς ἀληθείας καὶ τὰ οἰκεῖα ἀναιρεῖν, ἄλλως τε καὶ φιλοσόφους ὄντας· ἀμφοῖν γὰρ ὄντοιν φίλοιν ὅσιον προτιμᾶν τὴν ἀλήθειαν, *Eth. Nic.* 1096a11–17). This passage is thought to be the ultimate source of the proverbial "Amicus Plato, sed magis amica veritas," but as Martin Ostwald has noted (Aristotle 1962, 10n19), the sentiment itself seems to be an echo or paraphrase of Socrates' qualms regarding his critique of Homer in book 10 of the *Republic* (595b–c). The fact that Aristotle chooses to evoke and endorse a sentiment expressed by Plato's Socrates at the very moment he initiates his critique of the theory of forms suggests (as does Aristotle's use of the dual number) that rather than simply choosing to honor truth at the expense of honoring Socrates and Plato, he might consider himself to be honoring Socrates and Plato *in* honoring the truth first and foremost. There is a growing body of scholarly literature that focuses on the near consensus of late antiquity that the philosophical views of Plato and Aristotle were closer than is now commonly assumed. Indeed, as George E. Karamanolis argues, Platonists from the third to sixth century C.E. considered Aristotle's philosophy "a prerequisite for, and conducive to, an understanding of Plato's thought" (2006, 4). See also Gerson 2006 and I. Hadot 1991, 175–89. Consonant with these views and the interpretation of Aristotle in Burger 2008, in the chapters that follow I will treat Aristotle's texts as particularly illuminating aids in interpreting Plato.

Nietzsche's critique of Socrates, I will show that Plato presents in the dialogues his own version of what Nietzsche calls in the second section of *Twilight of the Idols* "the problem of Socrates." Despite the well-documented complexity of Nietzsche's intimate engagement with Socrates and Plato throughout his written work, we can provisionally articulate the "problem" Socrates represents for Nietzsche in terms of two questions:[10] (1) Is Socratic dialectic an expression of a thwarted desire for political mastery, a *decadent* manifestation of what Nietzsche calls the "will to power"? and (2) Can human ethical life sustain the kind of self-conscious reflection that seems to be the salient characteristic of Socratic philosophy? Or, to put this second question another way, is the human being who lives the examined life really living? These questions, I will argue, are not foreign to Plato's dialogues— far from being problems that Nietzsche or later commentators impose on the dialogues from without, they are already engaged at the deepest levels within the dialogues themselves.

Despite my invocation of Nietzsche's critique of Socrates, however, it is Plato's, not Nietzsche's, account of the "problem of Socrates" that is my concern. Indeed, what I want to show is how a number of profound questions about and challenges to Plato's account of Socratic philosophy that we associate with modern criticisms of "Platonism" arise from within the context of the dialogues themselves. Thus, in the course of my interpretation of the dialogues I will seek to establish three interpretive strands that bring Plato's presentation of Socrates into contact with recognizably Nietzschean concerns. First, I will show that the image book 1 of the *Republic* presents of the historical context of Socrates' dialogic activity corresponds in important respects to Nietzsche's account of Socrates' age, and, moreover, to Nietzsche's account of his own transitional historical epoch. Second, I will show the presence in Plato's dialogues of a theory of human creative and interpretive activity that corresponds in significant ways to Nietzsche's thoughts about the "will to power." In the dialogues this view is primarily attributed to the Sophists, and, as such, appears as a theoretic orientation opposed to Socratic philosophy. However, I will also argue that Plato's presentation of Socrates' dialectical method gives a pride of place to a kind of persuasive "poetic" activity that renders problematic this putative opposition. Third, I will show how Socrates' inquiries into the relation between the city and the soul in the *Republic* present a view of what we can provisionally call Socratic "political psychology." This political psychology resembles Nietzsche's "physio-psychology" at least to this degree: it focuses on the different internalized ethical narratives and justificatory schemes which inform human souls, and indicates how these different internalized narratives mediate human beings'

---

10. For an overview of the range of scholarly work on Nietzsche's relation to Socrates, see Porter 2005.

perception of their world. This line of inquiry will culminate with a focus on the problematic role of the "spirited" or *thumoeidic* aspect of the soul in Socrates' account. I will argue that Socrates' discussion of *to thumoeides* in the *Republic* engages a similar complex of concepts and questions to the one that Nietzsche explores under the rubric of the will—questions about the relation between conation and cognition; questions about the relation between aggressive drives and moral impulses; questions about representation, interpretation, and the creation of value. It is in this context that we can adequately confront the possibility of something like the "will to power" animating Socrates' philosophic, rhetorical, and pedagogical activity; it is also in this context, I believe, that we can articulate a conception of Plato's thought which can engage with and, to a significant degree, respond to Nietzschean and post-Nietzschean critiques of "Platonism."

In proceeding in this way, I may seem to invite the charge of anachronism in my reading of Plato. The force of such claims will be counterbalanced to some degree by the crucial role played in my interpretation by the historical context of Plato's writing. However, I do not deny that I attribute to Plato an awareness of theoretical possibilities in philosophy and psychology, ethics and politics that are considered characteristically—even paradigmatically—modern. If my arguments are persuasive, they will provide evidence to challenge our current understanding of the opposition between ancient and modern accounts of the self, society, and nature.

1.1 Socrates and the Dialogue Form

There is a growing consensus on the need to take into account some aspects of the dramatic structure of Plato's dialogues when offering an interpretation of them. However, this consensus by no means extends to any general agreement about what it means to take account of the dramatic structure of Plato's dialogues.[11] Therefore, despite my sense that the only genuinely persuasive argument for a particular way of reading the dialogues is given through a persuasive interpretation of the dialogues themselves, a brief word seems called for. In the following chapters I will offer a number of (more or less) novel suggestions for how one might view the relation between drama and argument in Plato's dialogues. I suspect that each of Plato's dialogues has something particular to teach us about how to read Plato's

11. See Ausland 1997. There has been an enormous amount of scholarly work in recent years devoted to the question of the relation between the dialogue form and philosophic content. For overviews of these developments in Plato scholarship, see Ausland 1997; Griswold 1999; Press 1996; and Gonzalez 1995, 2–13. See also the essays in Gonzalez, along with the studies in Press 1993 and 2000; Gill and McCabe 1996; and Klagge and Smith 1992.

dialogues. What this means concretely is that I believe an interpretation of a Platonic dialogue should, ideally, orient itself with respect both to the unity of the individual dialogue and to the multiplicity of Plato's dialogues; that is, an interpretation of a passage in the *Republic* should take account not only the context provided by the *Republic* as a whole but also the place of the *Republic* among Plato's dialogues.[12] While this interpretive ideal will only be dimly approximated in the following chapters,[13] it will, as an ideal, play a crucial role in my interpretation. I will argue, for example, that the representation of eros in the *Republic* should be understood in its relation to and difference from the representation of eros in the *Symposium* and the *Phaedrus,* and that a recognition of the differences in the representation of eros in these three dialogues will help us to better understand the particular character of each of these dialogues individually. I will also argue that Socrates' confrontation with Thrasymachus in book 1 of the *Republic* can be read in conjunction with his confrontations with Gorgias and Protagoras in the dialogues bearing their names, and that these three confrontations between Socrates and a Sophist form something of an ascending series. By comparing Protagoras's characterization of the activity of the Sophist and Gorgias's characterizations of the activity of the rhetorician with Thrasymachus's account of justice as "the advantage of the stronger," I will show how each of these Sophists, with different degrees of skill, different levels of political prudence, and, apparently, greater and lesser self-knowledge, is endorsing the view that what constitutes human excellence is the ability of an individual to impose his interpretation of the world upon others. Again, locating Thrasymachus's account with respect to Gorgias's and Protagoras's will show us something about the *Republic.* In this way my interpretation of the *Republic* will, at times, move freely between Plato's dialogues, but in each instance the move will be motivated by a desire to locate the *Republic* with respect to Plato's intention as disclosed throughout the dialogues.

In addition to this effort to locate the *Republic* with respect to other dialogues, my interpretation differs from most in a manner worth noting at the outset. As I have indicated, I will argue that "problem of Socrates" is presented in the dialogues

12. This is not to suggest that Plato's dialogues form together a comprehensive unity of which the various dialogues are parts; thus, I am not claiming that the dialogues form a "cosmos." While the dialogues each present a partial perspective on the subjects they treat, which partiality can be disclosed as partial by comparing the various dialogues with one another, this does not imply that the sum of the dialogues taken together presents an entirely nonperspectival whole. On the question of the dialogues as "cosmos," see Griswold 1999 and Clay 1987.

13. In this regard, the two most obvious lacunae in my interpretation of *to thumoeides* in the *Republic* will be the lack of any thematic treatments of either the relation between the *Republic* and the *Timaeus* and the *Critias,* to which the *Republic* is narratively tied, or the relation between the *Republic* and the *Laws,* to which the *Republic* is thematically tied.

as a problem with which Socrates himself was deeply engaged. It is in this respect that my interpretation, despite my appropriation of certain aspects of Nietzsche's account of Socrates, is most clearly informed by interpretive assumptions foreign to that account. In contradistinction to Nietzsche's description of Socrates as the "cleverest of all self-deceivers,"[14] I contend that Plato depicts Socrates as the most self-conscious of characters, and this contention decisively informs the interpretation I will offer of Socrates' pedagogical activity as it is represented in the dialogues. In particular, I will argue that a central part of Plato's literary presentation of Socrates is his portrayal of Socrates as the self-conscious, even literary, author of (a) the dialogues of which he is the narrator, such as the *Republic* and the *Protagoras,* and (b) various aspects of those dialogues of which he is not the principal narrator. The fact of Socrates' narration of various dialogues has generally played a relatively minor role in interpretations of those dialogues. In the *Republic,* for example, the fact of Socrates' narration of the dialogue has, for the most part, only been considered in the context of interpretations of the critique of mimesis. However, in my interpretation this fact—the fact that our access to the events of the *Republic* is always mediated by Socrates' narration of those events—will be made to bear a great deal of interpretive weight. Simply put, I will consider the *Republic* a Socratic fiction embedded in a Platonic fiction. In my interpretation of the dramatic significance of key events in the dialogue, I will first consider the "intention" of Plato's Socrates as narrator before I look to Plato's intention as author. This point calls for some clarification. The Socrates that I am putting forth as an author here is, nonetheless, Plato's Socrates and not the historic Socrates per se. My interest is in understanding Plato's portrayal of Socrates as an exemplary manifestation of a kind of philosophic life, and I am suggesting that a crucial aspect of Plato's portrayal of the character Socrates is his portrayal of that character as an author.[15]

Both the character of Socrates' authorship and Plato's intention in portraying this aspect of Socrates' *pragma* in various dialogic contexts resists any easy generalization. Socratic authorship in the dialogues ranges from Socrates' implausible

14. Nietzsche 1988, 6:37.

15. That said, I believe that my own attempts at understanding Plato's account of "Socrates" always involve reflecting upon what the historical Socrates represented for Plato. Furthermore, I believe that an implicit reflection on the historic Socrates plays a role even in those accounts of Plato's Socrates that assert the impossibility of any access to the historic Socrates. Alexander Nehamas, for example, argues that the Socrates we encounter in the dialogues is "to all effects and purposes" a Platonic fiction (1998, 7). Nonetheless, his account of the enigma Socrates represents, both to readers of the dialogues and to Plato as author, focuses on the question of how Socrates came to be. It seems undeniable that if this question was a genuine problem for Plato, it could only have been a problem with reference to the actual historic figure of Socrates and not with reference to the *character* Socrates, of whom, it seems, Plato could only ask whether or not this character was, in fact, a coherent and plausible one.

attribution of certain remarks to Clinias in the *Euthydemus* (290b2ff.) to his account of his conversation with Diotima in the *Symposium*,[16] from the various images, metaphors, and analogies Socrates constantly employs in argument to the myths describing the soul's journeys before and after its sojourn in this world. One aspect of Socratic authorship, however, remains consistent across the dialogues, and provides a crucial insight into Socrates' conception of philosophy. This is Socrates' tendency to *enact* a dialogue *within* a dialogue. Consider the following characteristic move of Socrates in Plato's dialogues. In the course of a conversation with an interlocutor, often at a key juncture in the argument, Socrates attributes some position to himself, to his interlocutor, or to himself and his interlocutor together. Then, rather than asking a direct question, Socrates conjures up a hypothetical figure to question the person to whom the aforementioned position has been attributed.[17] That is, instead of asking his interlocutor "What about x?" or even "What would you say to the question 'What about x?'" Socrates asks something along the lines of "What if someone were to approach you (us) and ask 'what about x?' What would you (we) say to such a person?" Some variety of this maneuver is to be found in every dialogue in which Socrates is the principal speaker, and the hypothetical interlocutors Socrates invokes range from relatively familiar-seeming figures such as the "expert in refutation" of *Theaetetus* 200b–c, the citizens of Athens of *Meno* 71a, or the "common many" of *Protagoras* 353aff. to "interlocutors" as unusual as the laws of Athens (*Cri.* 50aff.), the art of rhetoric and the arguments opposed to that art (*Phdr.* 260d–e), and the pleasures (*Phlb.* 63bff.). Plato's Socrates does not only engage in dialogue with his interlocutors; by invoking these imaginary interlocutors, he ceaselessly gestures toward the "dialogic" character of human thought. To put this point in another way, if we are to maintain that Plato's Socrates seeks to educate his interlocutors in dialogue with them, we should also maintain that he seeks to educate at least some of his interlocutors or auditors about the complex interrelations between character and argument, imagination and thinking, that are disclosed in Socratic conversations.

In this context, I will argue that book 1 of the *Republic* is, among other things, an extended lesson in the art of "Socratic dialogue," and in so arguing I will show how we might begin to make good on two claims Socrates makes at the beginning of book 2: that the arguments in book 1 are a "prelude" (τὸ προοίμιον, 357a2) to the rest of the *Republic*,[18] and that Socrates had already shown in what he said to Thrasymachus that justice was better (ἄμεινον) than

---

16. See Cornford 1981 and Rosen 1987, xxxi.
17. See Longo 2000.
18. See Ausland 1987 and Kahn 1993.

injustice, but that Glaucon and Adeimantus did not accept (or understand) the demonstration he gave them (οὐκ ἀπεδέξασθέ, 368b6–7). The only other occurrence of *prooimion* in the *Republic* is in Socrates' account of the studies prescribed for the guardians who are to become philosopher-rulers. There Socrates calls the study of number, geometry, stereometry, astronomy, and harmony the "prelude" to the "song" of dialectics, and he claims that the principal difference between the mathematical arts and dialectic is that the mathematical arts pursue their inquiries and demonstrations on the basis of hypotheses of which the mathematical arts can give no account. Only with the study of dialectic is one able to give and receive an account (δοῦναί τε καὶ ἀποδέξασθαι λόγον, 531e3) of these hypotheses. On analogy with this division between the demonstrations offered by the mathematical arts and dialectic, I believe that the "prelude" of book 1 is best understood as a dramatic, dialogic demonstration of the superiority of justice to injustice, which demonstration takes as given certain cultural and historical suppositions or "hypotheses," while the majority of the remaining books are devoted to an inquiry into and at least a partial account of those hypotheses.[19] The suppositions in this case are certain "givens" of the fifth-century Athenian ethos, aspects of the ethical and cultural environment in which Socrates pursued his philosophic mission and which decisively informed Socrates' dialogic practice. Thus, book 1 provides an imaginative re-creation of one possible response to a question that will dominate the rest of the *Republic*: what is the relation between the philosopher and the political community? The drama enacted in book 1 supplies one possible image of (according to a later image) the philosopher's descent into the cave, and his contestation with habitual cave dwellers over the shadows of what is just.

---

19. It has often been remarked upon that book 1 resembles the "Socratic" or "aporetic" dialogues, while the rest of the dialogue resembles so-called middle period works such as the *Gorgias*, the *Phaedrus*, and the *Symposium*. This led many commentators to the conclusion, first introduced by K. F. Hermann, that book 1 was originally a separate dialogue which Plato later incorporated into the *Republic*. More recently, a number of commentators have suggested that in book 1 Plato demonstrates certain inadequacies in Socrates' elenctic method that the remaining books are intended to critique and correct. In contrast to these views, I believe that the more "Socratic" book 1 stands in a complementary relationship to the rest of the *Republic*, offering a "demonstration" of Socrates' dialogic method, of which the remaining books offer an "account." In this respect, my interpretation bears some resemblance to Charles Kahn's "proleptic" hypothesis, first put forward in Kahn 1993 and elaborated upon in Kahn 1996. Kahn demonstrates a degree of continuity between the issues raised in book 1 and the rest of the *Republic* which renders implausible the suggestion that book 1 was originally conceived as a separate dialogue. See also Thesleff 1999, 1–6.

2

Republic Book 1

Philosophy and Cultural Decadence

But Socrates guessed even more. He saw through his noble Athenians: he comprehended that his own case, his idiosyncrasy, was no longer exceptional. The same kind of degeneration was quietly developing everywhere: old Athens was coming to an end. And Socrates understood that all the world needed him—his means, his cure, his personal artifice of self-preservation.

—NIETZSCHE, *Twilight of the Idols,* section II, aphorism 12

According to Nietzsche, Socrates' age was an age of disintegration, a time when a collision between different forms of life, together with their characteristic modes of self-justification, brought about an "ironic" self-consciousness and a skepticism about the legitimacy of any adequate justification for a way of life.[1] Without "constant unfavorable conditions," the tyranny and intolerance of the old aristocratic morality were no longer experienced as necessary. At such "turning points in history," Nietzsche tells us, there is an unprecedented proliferation of diverse interpretations of the world and modes of justification that struggle with one another for dominance.[2] In such a moral environment, human beings experience themselves as a war between "opposed . . . drives and value standards." The average human being, the individual of "healthy common sense" who expressly identifies himself with the value standards of the broader human community of which he is a part, can no longer act "instinctively" because the moral order that gave structure to his instincts is no longer experienced by that individual as binding.[3] The felt need to defend one's way of life begins to move the implicit narratives through which these human beings experience their lives as justified toward consciousness; their "myths" are "dying." As Nietzsche writes in his account of the "death" of the Olympian myth world in *The Birth of Tragedy,* "One begins apprehensively to defend the credibility of the myths, while at the same time one opposes any continuation of their natural vitality and growth; the feeling for myth perishes, and its place is taken by the claim of

1. I offer a fuller articulation of Nietzsche's account of Socrates' relation to his age in McNeill 2004. See also Bertram 1985; Dannhauser 1974; P. Hadot 1995a; Kaufmann 1988, 391–411; Nehamas 1998, 128–56; and Zuckert 1996, 10–32.

2. Nietzsche 1988, 5:214.

3. Ibid., 5:120.

religion to historical foundations."[4] It is at this point, on Nietzsche's account, that Socrates, or more accurately, Plato's Socrates, steps in as the principal object of a new kind of myth, a myth which preserves dying Greek culture *as a dying culture*. That is, the very process through which the modes of justification of the old culture had been undermined, the "rationalization" of myth and the attempt to bring to consciousness the implicit narratives through which members of the culture had experienced their lives as "justified," becomes itself a new narrative of self-justification. The search for self-knowledge, the critique of hypocrisy, the exposing of the contradictions in one's soul, and the recognition of one's ignorance become, with this Socratic myth, the new ideals of Greek culture. For those human beings who "imitate" (*nachmachen*) the Platonic Socrates, it seems that the only way to legitimate one's way of life is to bring to consciousness as fully as possible the reasons one lives as one does. Thus, according to Nietzsche, we must understand Socrates' philosophic mission, no less than Nietzsche's own, as specifically historically located. Not only did Socrates' philosophic practice arise out of and orient itself to the degeneration of traditional Athenian morality; it was also, in some sense, a transformation of this very degeneration.

As I have indicated above, I will begin my investigation of Plato's account of Socrates' philosophic activity by offering a reading of book 1 of Plato's *Republic* which appropriates aspects of Nietzsche's interpretation of Socrates. In particular, I will argue that the image book 1 presents of the historical context of Socrates' dialogic practice corresponds in important respects to Nietzsche's account, not only of Socrates' age but also of Nietzsche's own transitional historical epoch. I will argue that the Athens disclosed to us through Socrates' narration in the *Republic* is *decadent* in precisely Nietzsche's sense of that term; an "ironic self-awareness" of one's culture as a culture has led to a debilitating skepticism about the dominant values of that culture.[5] As Plato represents it, Socrates' philosophic activity occurs in a transitional epoch, a moment in history between the "death" of the Homeric gods and the recognition of the consequences of this "death"; that is, the collapse of the traditional values embodied in and supported by those myths. As with Nietzsche's account of the "death" of the Christian God, the controversial claim is not that belief in the Homeric gods had become, for some, "unbelievable";[6] the controversial claim is rather

---

4. Nietzsche 1967a, 10.
5. Other commentators who implicitly or explicitly engage Nietzsche's account of decadence in their interpretation of book 1 of the *Republic* include Baracchi 2001; Brann 1990; and Strauss 1978. See also Eric Voegelin's account of Polus as a representative of the intellectual in a "decadent society" (2000, 79–83).
6. Nietzsche 1988, 3:573.

that even in the case of those individuals who considered themselves exponents of traditional values and religious beliefs, the cultural ground had shifted. The fact of self-conscious reflection on the tradition had made it the case that all that was available was an "ironic" appropriation of the tradition as a source of value. It is in this context, I will argue, that we must understand Socrates' philosophic and pedagogic activity as it is presented in the *Republic,* and, following Nietzsche, I will argue that Socrates' activity is shaped in determinate ways by his engagement with this historical context. However, in contrast to Nietzsche, I will be claiming that it is part of Plato's intention to present Socrates' activity in this light, and, furthermore, that Plato represents Socrates as having this historical understanding of his own activity.

One apparent difficulty with such a reading of Plato's dialogues is that it attributes a kind of historical consciousness to Plato and to Plato's Socrates which is at odds with the generally accepted view of Plato's thought as largely ahistorical. And indeed, one prima facie difference between modern thought and ancient thought is that while much modern thought explicitly focuses on the ways in which our cognitive access to the world is determined by the time in which we live and the historically determined conceptual resources available to us at that time, ancient thought lacks any such explicit focus. Thus, whether it is viewed as a virtue or a vice of the modern world (and Nietzsche, among others, views it as both), we are accustomed to think that history is a problem for us in a way it was not for the ancients. While I believe that there are important differences between Plato's understanding of history and, for example, Rousseau's or Hegel's, it should be clear at the outset that these differences cannot extend to anything like a straightforward denial on Socrates' part of the significance of a particular historical context for human thought. For a principal theme of the *Republic* is the significance of the appropriate cultural environment in the education of a potential philosopher. Moreover, as is shown by Socrates' account of the decline of the regimes in books 8 and 9 (to say nothing of the Stranger's account of the ages of man in the *Statesman* [*Pol.* 269d–274e]), Plato will sometimes present differences in political and cultural environments in terms of an historical progress or regress.[7]

This interpretation of Socrates' self-understanding in the *Republic* will help lay the groundwork for an adequate confrontation with Plato's account of the "problem of Socrates." Prior to that confrontation, however, one of my aims

---

7. Obviously, the suggestion that Plato presents Socrates as self-consciously orienting himself to the particular historical context in which his public philosophic activity comes to be already points to a sense in which his self-understanding is not wholly limited by his historical context.

will be to show how the historical context provided by book 1 contributes to a defense of Socrates' dialogic practice against some recent critiques of that practice, many of which can be viewed as descendants of Nietzsche's critique. I believe that much of what readers find most troubling about Socrates self-presentation in the *Republic,* including the apparent "intellectualism" of Socrates' moral psychology, his critique of poetry, and perceived inadequacies in Socrates' elenctic method, should be reassessed in the light of Socrates' presentation of the historical context of his philosophic mission. What must be seen is that Socrates' exhortation to reflection and self-examination comes to be in a cultural environment which is already shot through with reflection and that Socratic "intellectualism" seems to be, at least in part, a self-conscious response to the "intellectualism" of the time.[8]

2.1 Time and Place

Socrates tells his unnamed auditor or auditors that he went down to Piraeus with Glaucon the son of Ariston to pray to the goddess and because he wanted to see the festival held in her honor. The goddess is the Thracian goddess Bendis, who seems to have been the only non-Greek deity officially recognized by the Athenian Assembly during the fifth century. It has been suggested that Plato chose this setting as a way of indicating that, if Socrates was indeed guilty of introducing new divinities into the city of Athens, he did no more than the democracy itself.[9] While this is undoubtedly right, this event has more immediate significance for the discussion to follow. The Piraeus was the main port of entry into Athens of people, goods, and ideas from foreign cities. It was, to use a modern phrase, a center of cultural diversity in Athens.[10] This point is stressed by the fact that none of Socrates' principal interlocutors in book 1 are Athenian

---

8. Thus, contrary to Nietzsche's account, I will argue that the Socratic "intellectualism" displayed in the *Republic* is not merely a reflection of the conditions of his time, but a self-conscious strategy for responding to those conditions. In this sense, Socrates' narration of the *Republic* is not only as an account, but also a defense of his dialectical *pragma.* See Allan Bloom's interpretive essay in Plato 1991, 307–9. Authors, apart from Nietzsche, who relate "Socratic intellectualism" to an intellectualism implicit in the culture include Michael O'Brien (1967) and E. R. Dodds (1951).

9. Plato 1991, 311.

10. See Roochnik 2003, 69–77. For Roochnik, the contrast between the lack of cultural diversity in *kallipolis* and the evident cultural diversity of the Athenian democracy in which the fictional founding of *kallipolis* takes place argues for reading the *Republic* as a qualified defense of democracy. While I agree with the general claim that we can find such a defense in the dialogue, I believe that Roochnik is not sufficiently sensitive to the degree to which problems Socrates diagnoses in "democratic" culture inform the argument of the dialogue as a whole.

citizens; Cephalus and Polemarchus are *metics,* and Thrasymachus is from Chalcedon.[11] Socrates has gone down to the Piraeus to see and, it seems, welcome the introduction of a foreign god and a foreign cultural tradition into the city of Athens. Socrates and his interlocutors are about to engage in a conversation about justice—what it is, how it comes to be, whether it is better or worse for a human being to be just—and this conversation occurs in the shadow of what we would call "cultural relativism."

The burgeoning awareness on the part of fifth-century Greek peoples of their culture as a culture has been the subject of a number of recent works that deal with the ways Greek identity was constituted in part through its opposition to foreign peoples.[12] This oppositional development of the concept of "Greekness" plays a central role in Thucydides' *History* and is arguably the principal theme of Herodotus's *Histories.* Without speculating on specific historical developments, I want to suggest that Plato saw a relation between the self-conscious reflection on Greek tradition occasioned by Greek confrontation with the fact of "foreign gods," primarily through the Graeco-Persian war, and the "decadence" of fifth- and fourth-century Athenian culture. This is not, however, because Plato (or Plato's Socrates) considers the distinction between Greek and "barbarian" in any way essential;[13] Socrates invokes this distinction in conversation with Glaucon only to undermine it subsequently, and his claim that some necessity may "even now" compel philosophers to rule "in some barbaric place somewhere" (499c) shows how little consequence this distinction holds for Socrates. Instead, what this inaugural festival of a newly authorized deity points to is a level of self-consciousness about orthodoxy and heterodoxy in Athenian public religion, and more generally to the very idea of orthodoxy, of correctness of opinion or belief about the gods. It points to a self-conscious relation to Greek religious and cultural tradition as a source of ethical and aesthetic norms, a self-consciousness that was incommensurate with the continued vitality of Greek "mythic" religion and with it the continued vitality of Greek "tragic" culture.

The self-consciousness demonstrated in the attempt to demarcate between native and foreign gods not only lays the ground for Socrates' trial, it also provides the context in which we must understand Socrates' philosophic mission. I suspect, moreover, that the difficulties surrounding the attempt to assign a dramatic date to the *Republic* arise from the fact that Plato intends the temporal setting of the *Republic* to be not a specific date but rather a period of years roughly contemporaneous with Socrates' "philosophic mission" to the city of Athens.

11. Cf. 562e.
12. See Cartledge 1993; Hall 1989; Hartog 1988.
13. See *Pol.* 262a–e.

Despite the tendency of most commentators to assign one of two dramatic dates, either 411/410 or 422/421, to the *Republic,* it has been argued that the evidence internal to the dialogue resists either classification. This has led some commentators to argue either that Plato intends the *Republic* to stand outside of any particular historical context[14] or that Plato simply didn't care about the dramatic date of the *Republic* and was habitually careless about anachronisms in his work.[15] The first of these alternatives seems possible, although it is difficult to see why an inconsistent date would serve this purpose better than a simply indeterminate one (e.g., the *Lysis*) or an impossible one (e.g., the *Menexenus*). The second alternative is difficult to reconcile with the care evident in every other aspect of the *Republic,* particular in the opening pages of book 1.[16] While I believe that the historic evidence taken by itself is inconclusive on the question of whether or not a single dramatic date for the *Republic* is possible, the hypothesis I have suggested to account for the multiplicity of contradictory clues regarding the dramatic date of the *Republic* is supported by the fact that there exists a strict parallel in another of Plato's dialogues, a dialogue whose dramatic structure mirrors that of book 1 of the *Republic:* the *Gorgias.*[17] In the *Gorgias* there are indicators pointing to dates ranging from Pericles' death in 429 to at least 411 and arguably as late as 405.[18] This is very close to the range of

14. Moors 1987.

15. Nails 1998. Nails provides a very useful summary of the scholarly debate about the dramatic date of the *Republic,* stretching back to August Boeckh's 1874 argument for 411/410, and argues persuasively against the plausibility of any single date for the conversation of the *Republic.* While Nails recognizes that Plato at times constructed dialogues with deliberately indeterminate and even impossible dramatic dates, she argues that some of the anachronisms in the *Republic* are simply too trivial for us to imagine that there was any artistic intention behind their inclusion in the *Republic.* However, the examples Nails cites of trivial anachronisms are not obviously anachronistic. She cites, first, the fact that Ismenias the Theban is used as an example of a corrupt rich man despite the fact that "his iniquities, taking bribes from the Persians" began only after Socrates' death; and second, that Polydamas the pancratiast is described as someone who is stronger than Socrates despite the fact that his victory in the pancratium occurred in 408. It is hardly surprising, however, to find Socrates using someone as an example of a particular quality before that person has gained enough renown for that quality to merit mention in the historical sources (see, inter alia, *Tht.* 142c and *Phdr.* 279a).

16. One aspect of Socrates' narration that is particularly difficult to reconcile with the assertion that anachronisms found in book 1 are merely the result of Plato's carelessness is the fact that he calls attention to the question of time with the second word Socrates utters, Κατέβην χθὲς εἰς Πειραιᾶ μετὰ Γλαύκωνος τοῦ Ἀρίστωνος (I went down yesterday to Piraeus with Glaucon son of Ariston). Socrates' χθὲς (yesterday), when heard against the background of the multiplicity of conflicting chronological references, signals, I believe, not an individual date but an entire historical period now past. For χθὲς used figuratively in this way to refer to an historical epoch distinguished both from the present and ancient times, see *Grg.* 450d1–4. See also Herodotus *Hist.* 2.53.1.

17. See Blondell 2002; Reeve 1988, 35–41; and Natorp 1994, 180.

18. See Dodds 1959, 17–18.

dates suggested by various commentators for book 1 of the *Republic*.[19] In both cases, I believe, the reason is the same. Plato is locating the conversation in a specific historic era, bounded on one end by the death of Pericles and on the other by the Athenian surrender to Sparta in 404, that is, the years in which the Athenians prosecuted the Peloponnesian War without the leadership of the one man who, according to Thucydides, because of his ability and reputation was able to lead the people of Athens rather than being led by them.[20] With Pericles' death, Thucydides suggests, the democracy lost the only leader who could have saved Athens from succumbing to her own internal strife.[21] These years saw Athens's defeat and the passing of the "golden age" of the Athenian democracy. It is this era, a time Plato's readers would recall with a sense of the end soon to come, which provides the historical context for the activity Socrates calls in the *Gorgias* his "true political art" (τῇ ὡς ἀληθῶς πολιτικῇ τέχνη, *Grg.* 521d7). And it is this historical period, and Socrates' dialectical political activity in this period, that is on display in book 1 of the *Republic*.[22]

Book 1 of the *Republic* and the *Gorgias* are unified, moreover, in their presentation of the character of this historic period. It is an era of reflection upon, and potential skepticism about, the sources of human motivation and evaluation. In the *Republic*, the subversive potential of this reflective awareness of one's culture as one culture among many comes dramatically to the fore in Thrasymachus's account of justice as "the advantage of the stronger," but the preconditions which make a Thrasymachus possible are signaled well in advance of his intrusion into the conversation. Socrates' narration in book 1, particularly in its representation of Socrates' interlocutors, provides us with an image of this cultural environment, suggests an etiology for it, and, most significantly, indicates the kinds of misunderstandings about human excellence and the strategies of self-deception it engendered. Socrates' three principal interlocutors in book 1 each represent one such strategy, and by paying attention to the various ways Socrates engages each of them in conversation, we can deepen our sense of the complexity of Socrates' characteristic activity.

19. As Nails recounts, these range from as early as 424, supported by Rankin 1964, to as late as 409/408, supported by Adam 1926. However, at least one reading of the available evidence puts the establishment of the cult of Bendis as early as 429/428. For a briefer synopsis of the range of opinions, see Nails 2002, 324–26.

20. Thuc. 2.65.8.

21. Thuc. 2.65.12. This claim is consistent with Socrates' suggestion that while Pericles may have been better than his successors at preserving the people of Athens from physical harm (511c6) by providing the means for conducting the war, he nonetheless did not make the Athenians better human beings (517b–c). See Strauss 1978, 151–53.

22. For an account of the significance of identifying the dramatic date of the *Gorgias* with the Peloponnesian War years, see Benardete 1991, 7–9.

2.2 Characters

Platonic characters are, with very few exceptions, primarily of interest as ethical and psychological exemplars.[23] This does not prevent, however, many of them from also having symbolic and even allegoric functions in the dialogues. This is the case with Thrasymachus, Polemarchus, and especially Cephalus, whose principal contribution to the argument of book 1 is to be found in his multivalent symbolic role. I will treat the symbolic significance of each character in turn, but I will do so with respect to what I believe is the allegoric structure of book 1 as a whole. As I have suggested, the problem of reflection dominates book 1, and the contours of this problem as presented in book 1 set the stage for the entire dialogue to follow. As I hope to show, Socrates believes that all human desires and aspiration involve some level of self-justification, some implicit claim that the life being led is worth living. He recognizes, moreover, potential dangers involved when, through self-conscious reflection on the sources of ethical justification, these implicit strategies begin to become explicit. The form that Socrates' illustration of these dangers takes is, at least in the first instance, a critique of the specific historical culture in which such reflection first becomes prominent. Cephalus, Polemarchus, and Thrasymachus together provide Socrates' dramatic articulation of the dominant modes of self-conscious relation to and appropriation of the ground of ethical justification in late fifth-century Athens, and the comprehensiveness of Socrates' critique derives from the fact that these three modes correspond to the tripartite division of the soul or, more specifically, to the lives associated with the three parts of the soul. These are the three "most notable kinds of life" Aristotle refers to in book 1 of the *Nicomachean Ethics:* the contemplative life, the political life, and the life of pleasure (1095b13–19).[24]

The particular ramifications of the "decadence" of fifth-century Athenian culture for the self-conscious appropriation of each of these lives as paradigmatically good differ, and to appreciate these differences we must turn to Socrates' conversation with each character. In general, however, this much can be said. The particular conception of the human good with which each of these three characters identifies has been subject to a debilitating abstraction from the

---

23. Cf. the distinction between "ethological" and "doxological" mimes in Klein 1965, 18. A great deal of my argument will concern the ultimate significance of Plato's representation of the ethical psychology of Socrates' interlocutors for our interpretation of Socrates' dialectical *pragma*. On the general issue of Plato's dramatic representation of character, see Blondell 2002, 53–112.

24. I cite Aristotle's classification of the three lives, rather than Socrates' discussion of the philosophic, honor-loving, and profit-loving types of human beings at 581c for reasons I discuss at length in section §2.8 below. On the relation between Aristotle's account of the three lives and the *Republic*'s tripartite division of the soul, as well as an interesting account of the Pythagorean provenance of both, see Stocks 1915.

human experience of that good; in Cephalus, Polemarchus, and Thrasymachus we see, as it were, a human good denatured.

2.3 Cephalus and the "Old Age" of Culture

It has often been suggested that Cephalus—the father of three of the assembled company, very much aged, seated in ceremonial attire, having just sacrificed to the household gods—is meant to represent traditional religion and morality.[25] This, however, is only half right. More precisely, Cephalus represents the moribund state of traditional Athenian religious culture at the close of the fifth century. Cephalus, whose exceeding age and approaching death Socrates comments on with rather disconcerting rudeness, stands in for a dying cultural tradition, a metaphoric "death" which is related to the metaphoric "old age" of Athenian culture. Plato is representing the "decadence" of traditional Athenian piety via the same metaphor of the "old age" and "youth" that Nietzsche uses in his account of the "decadence" of an historical culture in "On the Uses and Disadvantages of History for Life." In that work, Nietzsche describes a "historical culture" as "a kind of inborn grey-hairedness" and claims that "those who bear its mark must instinctively believe in the *old age* of mankind."[26] Members of an historical culture are haunted by an "ironic self-awareness" of their culture, which culture is primarily identified with great human beings and events of that culture's past. While Nietzsche indicates in the history essay that the sense of "lateness" which vitiates his own nineteenth-century "historical culture" is the residue of the Christian eschatological view of history, in *The Birth of Tragedy* and *Twilight of the Idols*, Nietzsche's description of the decline of the "tragic age" of the Greeks invokes the same metaphors of age and infirmity. As we will see, Socrates' representation of Cephalus begins with this conception of cultural senescence, and his conversation with Cephalus reveals the dangers inherent in this kind of cultural self-consciousness. However, insofar as none of these issues is invoked explicitly in the *Republic,* it will be helpful at this point to turn momentarily to the *Timaeus,* the *Critias,* and the *Laws.* These dialogues, obviously companion pieces to the *Republic* in some sense, invoke just these metaphors of youth and age in order to describe Greek culture, and the treatment there will provide some further context for our reading of book 1.

25. On the variety of commentators' responses to the depiction of Cephalus in the *Republic,* see Blondell 2002, 169nn20 and 21, and Beversluis 2000, 189–91.
26. Nietzsche 1983, 101.

The *Timaeus* begins with Socrates expressing a desire to see "in motion" the city he and his interlocutors have described the previous day, a city which resembles the *Republic*'s "city in speech." In response to Socrates' wish, Critias promises to tell a true history which reveals ancient Athens as that very city.[27] It turns out, Critias tells them, that in his youth he heard "an old account from a not young man," Critias's grandfather, also named Critias, who heard it from his father, Dropides, who in turn heard it from Solon, "the wisest of the seven" and Dropides' relative and close friend. Solon had told Dropides that in his travels in Egypt he learned from the Egyptian priests about the ancient history of Athens and about a battle fought between ancient Athens and the barbarian empire Atlantis wherein the ancient Athenians fended off the onslaught of the invading barbarian host and saved the Greek peoples from slavery. Subsequent to the Athenian victory, catastrophic earthquakes and floods sank the great island of Atlantis and overwhelmed the entire victorious Athenian army. As the only survivors of these catastrophes were "unlettered and uncultured" mountain herdsmen, no record was preserved in Athens of these ancient Athenians and their victory over the barbarian nation of Atlantis. Indeed, throughout time there have been periodic catastrophic events that have wiped out all but the most ignorant of Athenians, depriving Athens of any knowledge of its true history. The historical innocence displayed by the Athenians inspires the oldest of the Egyptian priests to say to Solon, "You Greeks are forever children, no Greek is old. . . . You are all young in soul, for you do not have in your souls even one ancient belief heard from ancient times nor one learning grizzled with age" (*Ti.* 22b–c). Critias's account of Solon's encounter with Egyptian historians alludes to the "old age" of late fifth-century Athenian culture in a number of ways. First, by having Athens's great democratic reformer recount a story clearly modeled on the Athenian victory against the invading Persian army at the Battle of Marathon, Critias's account unites the two events that later generations of Athenians would hold up as the defining moments of the Athenian democracy, the instances of Athenian virtue against which later conservatives would measure the present and find it wanting. Second, as Critias emphasizes, many years have elapsed between Solon's time and the setting of the *Timaeus*. Third, insofar as the old Egyptian judges the Greeks of Solon's time as immature because they lack ancient beliefs and learning hoary with age, Solon's recovery of Athens's ancient history must be understood as sowing the seeds of Athens's dotage. Critias offers his listeners a greater and more ancient Athenian victory against which even the tales of Marathon would seem to be pale imitations.

27. See Morgan 1998 and 2000, 261–81. See also Broadie 2001.

The image of late fifth-century Athenian culture as psychically aged is reinforced by a related passage from book 3 of the *Laws,* where the Athenian Stranger invokes "ancient accounts" of periodic catastrophes similar to the ones that Solon supposedly brought back from Egypt. In the Athenian Stranger's version of the story, once again the survivors of these cataclysmic events are illiterate mountain herdsmen. The scope of the Athenian Stranger's account, however, is not restricted to Athens alone, but concerns Greek culture in general, and the focus is not on the lost historical record but rather on the loss of sophistication in the arts, "particularly the contrivances that city dwellers use against one another." However, as Kleinias asserts, the Greeks have accumulated two thousand years of such sophistication. Most significantly for the argument of the *Republic,* the Athenian Stranger contrasts the simplicity (εὐθύς) of those people from earlier times with the skepticism about human beings and gods that characterizes the sophisticated people of his day. "For no one, because of their wisdom, knew to suspect a lie, as people do now, but they believed the things said about the gods and about human beings to be true and they lived according to these things" (679c). While I do not want to suggest that the views the Athenian Stranger expresses in the *Laws,* much less those Critias expresses in the *Timaeus,* are directly revelatory of Plato's views, I do believe these passages make clear that Plato uses the metaphor of the youth and old age of a culture in ways that parallel Nietzsche's use of that metaphor, and that Plato uses it in contexts directly relevant for the argument of the *Republic.* In brief, the image we are offered of the old age of a culture in the *Timaeus, Critias,* and *Laws* is one of (a) self-consciousness about one's own culture extended through a sufficient period of time, and (b) identification of historic events and figures of one's culture as paradigmatic for that culture.

Plato's depiction of Cephalus extends this analysis of the old age of Athenian culture, and the first move in this depiction is an extended pun on Cephalus's name, a striking example of Plato's occasional fondness for low comedy in the service of serious ends. As Eva Brann has pointed out, Socrates describes Cephalus as seated "on a sort of head-pillow and stool" (ἐπί τινος προσκεφαλαίου τε καὶ δίφρου, 328c2), and Cephalus's first remarks are about how the pleasures associated with the body wither away in him (αἱ ἄλλαι αἱ κατὰ τὸ σῶμα ἡδοναὶ ἀπομαραίνονται, 328d3–4). That is, Cephalus is presented as something of a disembodied head. There are two other appearance of disembodied heads in Plato's dialogues: after hearing Agathon's account of eros in the *Symposium,* Socrates fears being turned to stone by a Gorgianic head; and in the *Theaetetus,* while discussing Protagoras's *homo mensura* thesis with Theodorus, Socrates imagines Protagoras's head appearing out of the ground to rebuke them for misrepresenting his theories.

In all three cases the meaning is the same: each represents some kind of separation between thought and experience, between "word" and "deed."[28] In Cephalus's case, however, this separation is quite different from the sophistic abstractions of Agathon's appropriation of Gorgianic rhetoric, or Theaetetus's reception of "Protagorean" relativism, and in order to make clear the character of Cephalus's "abstraction," it will be helpful to turn to Nietzsche's account of the demise of Greek tragedy, aided by some terms from more contemporary cultural anthropology.

2.4 Ethos and World View

In "Religion as a Cultural System" and "Ethos, World View, and the Analysis of Sacred Symbols," Clifford Geertz defines religion as a system of symbols that, through the enactment of religious ritual, unites an *ethos* and a *world view*. In Geertz's account both of these latter terms have a very broad purview. Geertz writes:

> In recent anthropological discussion, the moral (and aesthetic) aspects of a given culture, the evaluative elements, have commonly been summed up in the term "ethos," while the cognitive, existential aspects have been designated by the term "world view." A people's ethos is the tone, character, and quality of their life, its moral and aesthetic style and mood; its underlying attitude toward themselves and their world that life reflects. Their world view is their picture of the way things in sheer actuality are, their concept of nature, of self, of society. It contains their most comprehensive ideas of order.[29]

While there are many questions one could ask about the coherence of these categories as so described, particularly in placing the aesthetic entirely on one side of this divide and the cognitive entirely on the other, some dichotomy between (as Geertz paraphrases) "the world as lived" and "the world as imagined" is recognizably at work in Nietzsche's account in *The Birth of Tragedy* of the

---

28. Compare also Sallis 1999, 14: "One recalls from the *Republic* that when Socrates went down to (the) Piraeus and engaged in the long conversation in Polemarchus' house, the first interlocutor he encountered was named Cephalos (Κέφαλος). If one recalls that the character thus named turned out to be all head, an old man who had lost all the desires of the body, then one cannot but wonder about a discourse such as the one that Socrates is now about to present, a discourse that is *merely head*."

29. Geertz 1973a, 126–27.

opposition between musical "mood" (*Stimmung*) and conscious knowledge (*bewussten Erkenntnisse*) in poetic creation.[30] Moreover, the unifying role Geertz assigns to religious rituals, particular those which he calls (following Singer) "cultural performances," echoes Nietzsche's account of the role of Dionysian tragedy in providing "a unifying mastery" of drives that is the hallmark of every "true culture."[31] As Geertz writes, "In a ritual, the world as lived and the world as imagined, fused under the agency of a single set of symbolic forms, turns out to be the same world."[32]

With Geertz's opposition between "lived" and "imagined" worlds in hand, we are better equipped to state the kind of "abstraction" Cephalus represents, and the role of the "age" of culture in that abstraction. According to Geertz, in religious ritual a way of life and a way of conceiving the cosmos "confront and mutually confirm one another." He writes, "the ethos is made intellectually reasonable by being shown to represent a way of life implied by the actual state of affairs which the world view describes, and the world view is made emotionally acceptable by being presented as an image of an actual state of affairs of which such a way of life is an authentic expression."[33] It is not difficult to see, however, that whatever the power of religious rituals, the ethos and world view that are brought together in ritual performances must be compatible to some degree; that is, there must be some degree of fit between a culture's concepts of "nature, of self, of society" and the lived experience of the culture's "tone," "character," and "quality of life." This is particularly the case with traditional religions, as opposed to those Max Weber called "rationalized," because of the specific and concrete relation between religious concepts and social norms such religions embody. If, however, this is at all right, then insofar as the concrete ethical relationships that constitute the "lived world" of a people change over time, so too must their "imagined world" change; there must continue to be a degree of plasticity in both religious concepts and religious rituals for ritual to continue to have the unifying effect Geertz (and Nietzsche) ascribes to it. It is the failure of this very plasticity that Nietzsche describes as the death knell of religious culture, and his description of this process is worth quoting in this context. He writes: "For this is the way in which religions are wont to die out: under the stern intelligent eyes of an orthodox dogmatism, the mythical premises of a religion are systematized as a sum total of historical events; one begins

30. Nietzsche 1967a, section 12.
31. Nietzsche 1988, 7:430.
32. Geertz 1973b, 112.
33. Geertz 1973a, 127.

apprehensively to defend the credibility of the myths, while at the same time one opposes any continuation of their natural vitality and growth; the feeling for myth perishes, and its place is taken by the claim of a religion to historical foundations."[34] In the *Timaeus* and the *Critias*, we are presented with precisely this kind of effort to provide not only the city in speech but also the "noble falsehood" of autochthony (*Cri.* 109d1–3) with a basis in "historical truth." More generally, the account of the old age of a culture given in those dialogues points toward a strict continuity in the mythic tradition, a preservation and handing down of ancient beliefs and stories. In Cephalus we see the consequences of this rigidity in belief and rituals—as Nietzsche puts it, the feeling for myth has died. As we will see in some detail below, Cephalus, all head and withered body, represents the continuation of an "imagined world" after the "lived world" which it was made to comprehend has ceased to exist.

As I indicated above, I do not want my use of Geertz's terms "ethos" and "world view" to suggest that I endorse Geertz's strict division between aesthetic and cognitive aspects of culture. If Geertz is right in asserting that in still vital religious rituals the lived world and the imagined world of a people "turn[ ] out to be the same world," this implies the possibility of their turning out to be *different* worlds, and in the case of a sufficient separation between lived world and imagined world it is hard to see how this imagined world could be said to function cognitively. At some degree of abstraction from life, imagination ceases to view a world at all. Or, to put the point in more cognitive terms, an "intellectualist" abstraction is, as such, intellectually as well as experientially inadequate; it misunderstands intellect as much as it misunderstands experience. Once again, a better way of characterizing the dichotomy at work here may be in terms of the familiar Greek distinction between *logos* and *ergon,* not only as represented in Nietzsche's censure of "the conservatives of ancient Athens" who "still mouthed the ancient pompous words to which their lives no longer gave them any right."[35] but also in the Platonic sense of an opposition between account and work or function. We could say that because the ancient stories no longer reflected the culture as lived, these stories no longer provided an account which did the work of unifying a culture. In this respect at least, they were now, as Wittgenstein might say, language on permanent holiday. Thus, if, on the narrative level, Cephalus is so preoccupied with the sacrifices because he fears punishment in the afterlife, on the level of the allegory it is because the schism between ethos and world view has become too great to be healed by the therapeutic power of any religious ritual.

34. Nietzsche 1967a, section 10.
35. Nietzsche 1966, aphorism 212.

2.5 Cephalus and the Poets

I have suggested that Cephalus represents a kind of separation or abstraction of the "imagined world" of the Greek poetic tradition from the "lived world" which that tradition was meant to explain, defend, or justify. As I have indicated, such a separation between lived and imagined world indicates, among other things, a misunderstanding and misappropriation of the intellectual or account-giving aspect of the tradition. This misunderstanding and misappropriation of the tradition is clearly evident once we compare Cephalus's interchange with Socrates to the poetic sources Cephalus looks to as authorities. Cephalus begins, as many Socratic interlocutors begin, with a statement that could easily be mistaken for one of Socrates' own.[36] He complains that Socrates does not visit them in the Piraeus often enough, though he should, for as the pleasures associated with the body waste away in him, the desire for and pleasure in speeches has grown the more. This can call to mind Socrates' claim in book 6 that "when someone's desires incline strongly to some one thing, they are therefore weaker with respect to the rest, like a stream that has been channeled off in that other direction" (485d4–7). There are, however, obvious differences between Cephalus's statement and Socrates'. On Socrates' view, it is the strength of the desire for learning that leads to the weakening of the other desires; on Cephalus's view, it is only with the weakening of the other pleasures that his desire for speeches grows strong. The importance Cephalus places on the weakening of bodily desires explains, to some degree, Socrates' rather disconcerting bluntness. Socrates responds to Cephalus by remarking how much he enjoys talking to the exceptionally old, and he wants to know from Cephalus what it is like to be at that time of life the poets call "upon old age's threshold"; that is, fast approaching death. He asks, "Is it a hard time of life, or what have you to report of it?" Cephalus responds in a way which both confirms our impression that the strength of Cephalus's desire for conversation is entirely consequent upon the weakness of competing desires, and which offers the first example of Cephalus's systematic misappropriation of the poetic tradition.

Cephalus says that it is not age itself that is most to blame for the abuse old age receives, but rather the character of the human beings concerned, and he brings up an anecdote about Sophocles to support his case. He says,

> I was once present when the poet was asked by someone, "Sophocles, how are you in sex? Can you still have intercourse with a woman?" "Silence

---

36. See *Lach.* 194c, *Chrm.* 161b. On the apparent similarity of Cephalus and Socrates, see Blondell 2002, 169; and Reeve 1988, 6.

[Εὐφήμει], man," he said. "Most joyfully did I escape it, as though I had run away from a sort of frenzied and savage master." I thought at the time that he had spoken well and I still do. For, in every way, old age brings great peace and freedom from such things. When the desires cease to strain and finally relax, then what Sophocles says comes to pass in every way; it is possible to be rid of [ἀπηλλάχθαι] very many mad masters. (*Resp.* 329b7–d1)

While Cephalus presents his words as a paraphrase of Sophocles', the contrast between original and paraphrase is even greater than the contrast between Socrates' and Cephalus's views on the relation between the strength and weakness of desires noted above. Despite the interpretation Cephalus gives to Sophocles' words, there is nothing in those words that implies that the poet's erotic desires had simply evanesced with his advancing years. Instead Sophocles speaks of an active escape (ἀπέφυγον) from sexual desire, which he likens to a flight from a raging and savage master. Indeed, Sophocles' εὐφήμει suggest an anxiety about the security of this imaginative escape, a fear that his former master may yet reclaim him. Cephalus, on the other hand, describes the slackening of desire as being "released" (ἀπηλλάχθαι) by a multiplicity of mad masters, masters who seem real enough to Cephalus.[37] The distance between Sophoclean and Cephalic piety can be measured by this: where Sophocles spoke of eros with dread and reverence as one dominating passion from which he narrowly won his escape, Cephalus speaks only of one among many "democratic" desires that age and incapacity excuse him from serving.

Socrates responds to Cephalus's anecdote by "setting him going" (ἐκίνουν), a word that can have the connotation of disturbing or profaning the sacred.[38] In the name of the many, he suggests that perhaps it is not so much Cephalus's character but his wealth that has been the comfort of his old age. Cephalus answers with another anecdote, again identifying himself with a famous figure of Athens's recent past, this time Themistocles. Just as Themistocles had maintained that being an Athenian was a necessary but not a sufficient condition

---

37. Significantly in this context, the word ἀπαλλάσσεσθαι can also mean "to die." As we will see in §3.4.2 below, the many masters Cephalus serves should to be understood in relation to Socrates' account of the conflict within the democratic individual's soul between his identification with internalized representative figures of different ways of life. See 561c–e; cf. Benardete 1989b, 13.

38. This connotation is strongest in the proverbial expression κινεῖν τὰ ἀκίνητα, which the LSJ translates as "to meddle with things sacred" (see *Leg.* 684e, 843a, 913b), which expression Socrates uses playfully at *Theaetetus* 181b in his discussion of the doctrines of Heraclitus. However, as Jebb notes in his commentary on the *Antigone,* κινέω can itself carry the connotation of a sacrilegious or profaning act (Sophocles 1900, l.1061).

of his renown, so Cephalus maintains that wealth is a necessary though not a sufficient condition for bearing old age easily; far more important than wealth is good character, without which wealth cannot provide contentment (329e–330a). Despite Cephalus's emphasis on the question of character, Socrates continues his inquiry into Cephalus's wealth, culminating with the question "What do you suppose is the greatest good that you have enjoyed from possessing great wealth?" Cephalus's response once again indicates the limits of his piety and of his understanding of the mythic tradition.[39] Cephalus assures Socrates that "when a man comes near to the realization that he will be making an end, fear and care enter him for things to which he gave no thought before." The myths about Hades and the punishment waiting there for the one who has committed unjust deeds, myths that he had laughed at up to then, now terrify him with the fear that they might be true. Full of terror, he reckons up (ἀναλογίζεται) and considers whether he has done anything unjust to anyone. The man who finds many unjust deeds lives his final days in anticipation of evil, while for the man conscious of no unjust deed, Cephalus says, "sweet and good hope is ever beside him" (331a). In support of his praise of hope, Cephalus invokes Pindar, and despite the fact that the poem he quotes from is now lost, there is reason to believe that Cephalus quotes it without understanding. According to Cephalus, Pindar says that whoever leads a just and holy life,

> Sweet hope accompanies,
> Fostering his heart, a nurse of his old age,
> Hope which most of all pilots [κυβερνᾷ]
> The ever-turning opinion of mortals.

Within the context of this fragment alone, there is reason to question whether Pindar is praising the "pilot" most responsible for the "ever-twisting judgment" (πολύστροφον) of mortals. Moreover, the extant odes indicate a condemnation of hope would be much more characteristic of this poet. "Hope" (ἐλπὶς) is presented in Pindar's odes as a necessary and ineliminable aspect of human striving, but it is also presented as the most dangerous and unreliable of guides. In the Eleventh Nemean, Pindar writes of our limbs as fettered by "shameless hope" (ἀναιδεῖ ἐλπίδι, *Nem.* 11.45–46). Moreover, in the passage from the odes that seems to provide the clearest parallel to the passage Cephalus quotes, Pindar provides a decidedly less comforting view of hope than Cephalus's. In the Twelfth Olympian ode, addressed to the goddess Fortune (Τύχα), who is said to pilot (κυβερνῶνται) swift ships on their journeys, Pindar writes:

39. See Howland 1993, 61–62.

But men's hopes [ἐλπίδες] are tossed up and down
as they voyage through waves of empty lies.
No man on earth has yet found out from the gods
a token of things to come;
man's perception is blinded as to the future. (Verity trans.)[40]

Whatever the status of Cephalus's grasp of Pindar, however, the moral he draws from the poet is impressive. He tells Socrates that his reason for holding the possession of money to be a most worthwhile thing—not for any man but for the decent and orderly one—is that it contributes greatly to "not cheating or lying to any man unwillingly, or again to not having to depart to that place in dread, owing some sacrifices to a god or money to a human being." This account of the virtue of wealth seems, as Socrates says, entirely noble (παγκάλως). The question remains whether Cephalus's understanding of his words is equally noble, and Socrates put this to the test. He takes Cephalus's words and extracts from them a definition of justice, something Cephalus clearly never offered, and his reformulation differs substantially from what Cephalus did say.[41] Socrates asks, "But as to this itself, justice, can we so simply say that it is the truth and giving back whatever one has taken from someone, or is doing these things themselves sometimes just and sometimes unjust?" (331c1–5). The divergence between Cephalus's words and Socrates' reformulation is clear. Where Cephalus spoke of not cheating or lying against one's will (ἄκοντά), Socrates speaks of telling the truth unconditionally (ἁπλῶς); where Cephalus spoke of the obligations one has to gods and human beings, Socrates speaks only of returning those things that one has taken from someone. Despite these seemingly profound differences between Cephalus's assertion and Socrates' paraphrase, Cephalus does not object when Socrates proceeds to pose a counterexample to this putative definition. Before we turn to that counterexample, however, we must ask why Socrates alters the substance of Cephalus's assertion, and why Cephalus fails to observe this alteration.[42] Our answer to these questions will both provide one more crucial example of Cephalus's misappropriation of the poetic tradition and, at the same time, offer us an insight into an aspect of Socrates' dialogic practice.

Cephalus's failure to notice Socrates' intentional misprision is an extreme variety of a common feature of the dialogues. At some point in the discussion,

---

40. Pindar *Ol.* 12.5–10.

41. See Beversluis 2000, 197, and Roochnik 2003, 52–54.

42. Roochnik comments that "Cephalus must be stunned" to hear Socrates' reformulation of his "casual remarks" into a precise definition of justice (2003, 53). As we will see, however, the fact that he does not appear stunned, that he does not offer any objection to Socrates' reformulation, tells us something about Cephalus's own lack of understanding of these "casual remarks."

Socrates' interlocutor will respond to one of Socrates' questions in a way that will strike the reader as odd; it will seem as if the interlocutor has made some slip, through inattention, simple stupidity, or perhaps, as in the case of Callicles' claim about Polus in the *Gorgias* (and Polus's subsequent claim about Gorgias), a failure of nerve. The mistakes of Socrates' interlocutors, however, are never simple, and in reading the dialogues we should always assume that their slips are significant. In these instances, I suggest, we are called upon to ask what is it about Socrates' interlocutor that could account for this apparent lapse, to ask what kind of person we could expect to answer in that way as opposed to some other that we would find more intuitively plausible. In Cephalus's case the question is more pointed. We can ask about the difference between the kind of person we might expect to have offered Cephalus's original formulation and the kind of person who could accept Socrates' reformulation as appropriate to that assertion; the difference between these two kinds of human being corresponds, I believe, to the difference between Cephalus's archaic world view and his late fifth-century ethos. Cephalus's original claim about the value of wealth was perfectly Homeric, or to be more precise, it was perfectly Odyssean. One can easily imagine Homer's Odysseus agreeing that the good of wealth is that it allows one to fulfill one's obligations to gods and men and to avoid cheating or lying against one's will. However, it is clear that Odysseus would never agree that justice, which Socrates will soon equate with "human excellence," is equivalent to telling the truth under all circumstances. One sign of this is the fact that both of the occurrences of the word translated above as "to cheat" (ἐξαπατάω) in the *Odyssey* have an unambiguously positive connotation. In one instance it is applied to the goddess Athena; in the other, Odysseus is reflecting on his subterfuge against the Cyclops and says, "My heart laughed within me that my name and my excellent cunning had thoroughly deceived them" (ἐμὸν δ᾽ ἐγέλασσε φίλον κῆρ, ὡς ὄνομ᾽ ἐξαπάτησεν ἐμὸν καὶ μῆτις ἀμύμων, *Od.* 9.413). We imagine that, if asked, Odysseus would say that if one was forced to lie by circumstance, or if one chose to for one's own reasons, lying well was a form of human excellence, and that the *Odyssey* is the story of a man who excelled all other men in the art of lying. It would then be up to us whether we should believe him.

2.6 Cephalus, Money, and Politics

Cephalus, however, is not Odysseus, and the lived world that could correspond to the imagined world of the Homeric poems is not Cephalus's world. This is the reason that he does not object to Socrates' reformulation: it is truer to the ethical attitudes revealed in Cephalus's concern with punishment in the afterlife.

When asked about what good wealth has brought him, Cephalus all but asserts that he had given no thought to the question of justice prior to approaching the end of life. When he does finally turn to that question, he describes it as a counting up (ἀναλογίζεται) of unjust deeds. He has no positive conception of justice, no conception of the positive obligations one might have to gods or men in the absence of a prior injustice. His ethical world has only two kinds of people: those who find many unjust deeds in their past, and those who are conscious of no unjust deed. And it seems very unlikely that Cephalus places himself in the latter category. Although he has just come from the sacrifices when Socrates arrives at Polemarchus's house, and has spoken to Socrates for a very short time, when he is relieved of the burden of argument by Polemarchus's interruption Cephalus leaves, saying that he should have been tending to the sacrifices before this (ἤδη, 331d7). It seems that his reckoning up of unjust deeds has convinced him he has time left for little else.

More generally, we can see how the difference between Cephalus's statement and Socrates' reformulation corresponds to the difference between the ethical and political world Cephalus inhabits and the disparate ethical and political worlds of the composite poetic tradition to which he clings. Homer's poems depict the alliances and blood feuds of Dark Age tribal chieftains before the rise of the polis; Pindar, whose surviving poems are about victors in the Panhellenic Olympic games, wrote of and for a late archaic cosmopolitan elite; Sophocles wrote for the most important Athenian communal religious festival, and the significance of the polis and citizenship loom large in his Theban cycle. The imagined world of each poet, therefore, corresponds to a different kind of political and ethical world, with different kinds of political association and different positive notions of ethical and political obligation. Insofar as Cephalus looks to this composite poetic tradition as a *direct* source of ethical and political understanding, his understanding abstracts from the particularity of these differing notions of positive ethical obligation, and so is correspondingly abstract and negative.

This abstract and negative sense of political and ethical obligation is reflected in Cephalus's political status as a *metic,* a resident alien with limited political rights.[43] It is also reflected in his wealth—the source of what patriarchal political power he has—and his means of acquiring it. Cephalus is a businessman, a "money-maker" (χρηματιστής), and his limited understanding of political association is appropriate to his role in life. Aristotle claims, in the *Politics,* that the only association that can truly be called a polis is the one that aims at virtue, and that any other community should merely be called an alliance (συμμαχία).

---

43. See Monoson 2000, 214–15n20; and Annas 1981, 18–34.

His demonstration of how this is so, like so many passages in the *Politics,* reads like a commentary on the *Republic.*

> That this is the case may be readily proven. If two different sites could be united in one, so that the city of Megara and that of Corinth were embraced by a single wall, that would not make a single city. If the citizens of the two cities intermarried with one another, that would not make a single city, even though intermarriage is one of the forms of social life which are characteristic of a city. Nor would it make it a city if a number of people, living at a distance from one another, but not at so great a distance but they could still associate, had a common system of laws to prevent their injuring one another in the course of exchange. We can imagine, for instance, one being a carpenter, another a farmer, a third a shoemaker, and others producing other goods; and we can imagine a total number of as many as 10,000. But if these people were associated in nothing further than matters such as exchange and alliance, they would still fail to have reached the stage of a city. (Aristotle *Pol.* 1280b.13–24, Barker trans., rev. R. F. Stalley)[44]

With this analysis, Aristotle provides us with the tools to understand the significance of the fact that the concept of justice first appears in Plato's *Politeia* as injustice (ἀδικήσαντα), spoken by a resident alien businessman in the harbor of the Piraeus.

As we have seen, despite Socrates' claim that he enjoys talking to the very old, it is clear that he isn't interested in talking about what they want to talk about; despite Cephalus's determination to air his views on the character of human beings (ὁ τρόπος τῶν ἀνθρώπων, 329d3–4), Socrates is equally determined to ask Cephalus only about money. One reason for this insistence on Socrates' part is that Cephalus's relation to money indicates the defect in Cephalus's understanding of human character and introduces the role that money will play in the remainder of the *Republic.*[45] The Greek word for monetary currency, νόμισμα, is instructive here. Related to the word for law or custom (νομός), its root meaning is "anything sanctioned by custom." Money is the generically useful, fully fungible, and fully abstract representation of human social capacities. As such, it is the most powerful example of the tendency to think about human social capacities as abstracted from concrete human relationships.[46] Thus, it is both a manifestation of and a contributing cause underlying one of the most

---

44. Aristotle 1995.
45. See Shorey's note 3 to *Republic* 362c in Plato 1969–70.
46. Cf. Aristotle *Eth. Nic.* 1133a27–1134a22.

pervasive misunderstandings that we see Socrates take issue with in the dialogues, the tendency to think about "capacity" or "power" (δύναμις) in abstraction from a purpose or goal of that power. The self-conscious identification with this abstract notion of capacity is the intellectual inheritance Cephalus leaves for Polemarchus;[47] it provides the foundation for Polemarchus's own abstract account of the political animal.

2.7 Fighting with Shadows

New struggles—After Buddha was dead, his shadow was still shown for centuries in a cave—a tremendous, gruesome shadow. God is dead, but given the way of men, there may still be caves for thousands of years in which his shadow will be shown. And we—we still have to vanquish his shadow.

—*The Gay Science,* aphorism 108

The preceding arguments may seem less than fair to Cephalus in at least one respect. While it is true that Cephalus neither notices nor objects to the ways in which Socrates transforms a defensible statement about the benefits of wealth for a decent and orderly man into a problematic definition of justice, Socrates does not make it easy for Cephalus to do so. Hard on the heels of his reformulation, Socrates presents a counterexample that encapsulates in a few words the most profound problems that any account of justice must confront. He says, "I mean something of this sort: everyone would surely say that if someone were to take weapons from a friend who is of sound mind and that friend, becoming mad, demands them back, one must not give such things back, nor would the one who gives them back be just, nor again should one wish to tell the whole truth to a person in this state" (331c, trans. altered). I will return below to the significance of madness, both for our understanding of Socrates' dialogic practice and for the argument of the *Republic.*[48] For now, it is sufficient to recognize that the question of madness brings along with it deep questions about intentionality, objectivity, and responsibility that, if they are answered at all in the *Republic,* are only answered by the *Republic* in its entirety; that is, with this example Socrates already frames the question of justice in terms which, given the resources of the *Republic,* could only be adequately resolved by the introduction of philosopher-rulers and the ascent out of the

47. As Cephalus leaves the conversation to return to the sacrifices, he says to Polemarchus, "I hand down the speech to you" (παραδίδωμι ὑμῖν τὸν λόγον), a phrase whose obvious meaning in this context is that of giving Polemarchus Cephalus's role in the argument with Socrates, but which can also connote a transmission of legends, proverbs, or teachings from one generation to the next.

48. See §7.1.

cave. For, as the account of the decline of the regimes in book 8 indicates, the *Republic* presents degenerate cities as in some sense "pathological." Given this fact, it is not unreasonable to assume that at least some tyrannical regimes will be as "mad" as the tyrannical individual described in book 9. However, from the perspective of such a degenerate regime, it is the philosopher, the just man, and the just action that will appear insane. Consider, for example, Glaucon's claim that the person who is able to do injustice "would never set down a compact with anyone not to do injustice and not to suffer it." To do so, Glaucon claims, such a person would have to be mad (*Resp.* 359b).

It is uncharacteristic of Socrates' practice in the dialogues to explicitly introduce such a difficult question so early in a conversation, and it is also uncharacteristic of him to take an interlocutor's words as a definition (ὅρος) without having asked for such a definition. Moreover, Socrates' persistent questions about Cephalus's wealth, his refusal to engage Cephalus on the question of human character, even the particular way in which he introduces the question of madness, all seem to contribute to Cephalus's hasty departure. For it is likely that there is more than one level on which the aged Cephalus, so concerned with order and decency, finds the possibility of madmen with axes disturbing. In short, despite Socrates' professed eagerness to converse with the very old, his actions indicate the contrary. Why, then, does Socrates proceed in this way?

At one level, we are well advised to follow Cicero's suggestion that Socrates removes Cephalus, as gently as possible, from a conversation which neither his station nor his capacities suit him to participate in.[49] At another level, however, we can look back to Socrates' claim that his questioning of Cephalus was inspired by a desire to "move" or "agitate" (κινέω) Cephalus. According to the interpretation I have been offering, Cephalus represents a kind of metaphoric "old age" of the Greek poetic tradition and an intimation of the "death" of that tradition as a source for popular ethical norms. His views represent the sedimentation of disparate authoritative voices from the tradition, a sedimentation which must be overcome if a genuine inquiry into those questions for which the tradition is supposed to have authoritative answers is even to begin. Indeed, to fully appreciate Cephalus's symbolic role in the *Republic,* I think we must recognize that (at least according to one ancient source)[50] he *should* already be dead, and that, nonetheless, he staggers on. He represents, Nietzsche might say, the shadow of the dead Homeric gods projected on the wall of this particular cave, a shadow as yet unvanquished. As may be intimated by Polemarchus's somewhat unseemly eagerness to remind his aged father that he is "heir of

49. *Att.* 4.16.
50. Cf. Brann 1989, 96n9.

what belongs" to Cephalus (331d), the problem of a moribund religious tradition is not only that it no longer provides individuals with a living sense of what is highest or best, it is also that it inhibits and overshadows attempts to take up anew the question of the highest good for human beings. This is made apparent in Polemarchus's and Thrasymachus's reflections on the problem of justice, which are both implicitly circumscribed by their relations to the dying religious tradition that Cephalus represents. Polemarchus's account is circumscribed in that it simply fails to inquire into and leaves untouched those questions—about human and divine nature, about human origins and the ultimate ends of human action—for which the mythic tradition was supposed to provide answers. Thrasymachus's account, on the other hand, is circumscribed in that the answers it offers are entirely parasitic upon the conventional and traditional accounts of justice that it seeks to overturn.

As I have suggested above, I believe that Socrates' portraits of Cephalus, Polemarchus, and Thrasymachus are meant to correspond to the tripartite division of the soul introduced later in the *Republic,* and his depiction of each character is meant to demonstrate certain deficiencies in that character's way of relating to and self-consciously identifying with the characteristic goods associated with the lives of contemplation, honor, and pleasure, respectively. In the most general terms, we can say that while each character identifies with a particular conception of the best life, his way of representing the content of that life is cut off from the lived experience of the goods associated with it. The separation between "lived" and "imagined" world manifest in Cephalus's conversation with Socrates, however, plays the additional role of providing the preconditions for the quite different kinds of abstractions we will see manifested in Polemarchus's conception of the political life and Thrasymachus's presentation of the tyrannical life.

In the context of Nietzsche's analysis of the degeneration of culture, the fracture between the composite poetic tradition that Cephalus looks to for an account of man's place in the cosmos and the ethical attitudes disclosed in his conversation with Socrates demonstrates that within fifth-century Greek culture the "moral order" that had once been supported by the mythic tradition is no longer "instinctual," that is, it is no longer *experienced* as binding by the members of the culture. Thus, in Nietzsche's terms, the culture on display in book 1 of the *Republic* is no longer characterized by a "unifying mastery of drives" and hence is no longer a "true culture." In Nietzsche's analysis, the loss of a sense of unity in a culture occasions a struggle between individual moral-psychological types, which either had been suppressed under the constraint of the old, intolerant, "aristocratic" morality or had found their place in relation to the order pre-scribed by that morality. In such an environment there is a proliferation of new modes of justification, as each individual moral-psychological type feels the need to defend and explicitly justify its way of living. Nietzsche contends, however, that not all types of morality can be made explicit; on his account, the very attempt to explicitly justify a "noble" mode of valuation undermines the noble.

As I have argued above, Socrates' presentation of his conversation with Cephalus corresponds in a number of ways to Nietzsche's etiology of cultural decadence. Furthermore, as I hope to show, Socrates' presentation of his encounters with Polemarchus and Thrasymachus, when viewed in the context of the *Republic* as a whole, further demonstrates the deleterious consequences for certain modes of implicit self-justification when they become conscious of themselves as such. Polemarchus and Thrasymachus represent, respectively, human beings who attempt to orient and, more significantly, *justify* their lives with respect to the goods associated with the "spirited" and "desiring" aspects of soul in abstraction from (Polemarchus) or opposition to (Thrasymachus) the love of wisdom. In the next two chapters, I will argue that Socrates' conversations with these characters demonstrate the ways that, as in Nietzsche's analysis of cultural decadence, this very attempt to autonomously justify these ways of life—that is, to justify them independently of any reference to something conceived of as higher—can lead to a detachment from the goods characteristically associated with these ways of life.

Before turning to those conversations, however, I will try to show how the *Republic* relates the dangers inherent in self-consciously identifying one's good with "spirit" and "desire" to the attempt to explicitly justify such identifications, and I will do so by turning to book 9 and the second of Socrates' three proofs presented to Glaucon for the superiority of the philosophic life. The general sense of Socrates' argument is that those human beings who are ruled by some aspect of soul other than the philosophic not only do not attain the highest good possible for human beings, they also deprive themselves of the highest goods attainable even for the aspect of soul which rules in them. However, there are peculiarities to Socrates' argument, and these peculiarities point toward the role played by attempts at explicit self-conscious justification of these ways of life in the failure of nonphilosophic rule in the soul.

2.8 Pleasure, Self-Justification, and the Three Lives

Socrates begins his second proof for the superiority of the philosophic life in book 9 by arguing that, corresponding to the threefold division of the human soul, there is a threefold division of pleasures, desires, and kinds of rule. However, in this context he does not call these three parts or aspects of soul the "calculating" (τὸ λογιστκόν), the "spirited" (τὸ θυμοειδές), and the "desiring" (τὸ ἐπιθυμητικόν), as he had earlier in the *Republic*. Instead, he begins to articulate a division between, first, "that with which a human being learns" and, second, "that with which he becomes spirited," but he balks at calling the third aspect "that with which a human being desires." And it is obvious why he must resist naming the third aspect in this way: it is because he is in the process of presenting an account of the desires and pleasures proper to each of the three aspects of the soul. Nor can he, for the same reason, call it "that with which a human being is pleased." Socrates claims in regard to this third aspect of soul that "because of its many forms, we had no peculiar name to call it by, but we named it by what was biggest and strongest in it," but the passage in which Socrates and Glaucon named this aspect of soul *to epthumêtikon* provides no evidence of this sort of qualification. There Socrates opposes the calculating to "that with which [the soul] loves, hungers, thirsts and is moved by the other desires" (439d). Nonetheless, in this context Socrates avoids characterizing this aspect of soul in terms of any particular work or function, and instead substitutes the names the "money-loving" (τὸ φιλοχρήματον) and the "gain-loving" (τὸ φιλοκερδὲς) for this aspect of soul. Socrates claims, in defense of this move, that "we also called it the money-loving, because such desires are most fulfilled by means of money." However, this aspect of soul was never called *to philochrê-maton* when it was said to be playing its proper role in a well-ordered soul. In fact, it is only once *to epithumêtikon* is said to be "put on the throne" in the soul of the oligarchic man that it is also called *to philochrêmaton* (539b–d), that is, *to epithumêtikon* and *to philochrêmaton* are only equated in contexts where this aspect of soul is said to rule.[51] Having renamed the "desiring" aspect of soul the "money-loving" and "gain-loving," Socrates fashions parallel name pairs for *to thumoeides* and *to logistikon*, renaming them, respectively, the "victory-loving" (φιλόνικος) and "honor-loving" (φιλότιμος) aspect, and the "learning-loving" and "philo-sophic" aspect of soul. Once again, with respect to *to thumoeides*, the equation of *philonikos* and *philotimos* first occurs in a context where this aspect of soul is said to rule, in Socrates' account of the timocratic man and regime (545a).

Having completed his terminological shift, Socrates turns to the comparison between the lives of the "three primary classes of human beings," which three classes are now called the "philosophic," the "victory-loving," and the "gain-loving," in terms of the pleasures appropriate to each. The strangeness of Socrates' comparison of the three lives becomes clearer once we compare it to

---

51. The only previous occurrence connecting τὸ ἐπιθυμητικόν and τὸ φιλοχρήματον is 435e–436a, in a passage in which money-loving defines the character of a regime, i.e., a fully politicized context in which money-loving could be said to rule.

Aristotle's discussion of the "three most notable kinds of life" in book 1 of the *Nicomachean Ethics*. According to Aristotle (*Eth. Nic.* 1095b5–1096a10), there are three primary conceptions of the good as exemplified in the lives human beings lead, and these three lives are (1) the life of pleasure, (2) the political life, and (3) the contemplative life. In Aristotle's discussion he explicitly *excludes* the life of the money-maker because wealth is merely an instrumental good—that is, for the very reason that Socrates chooses to call what had been called the "desiring" aspect of soul the "money-loving" aspect. Furthermore, while Aristotle does claim that "men of taste" (οἱ χαρίεντες) conceive of the good as honor because this is, roughly speaking, the end pursued in political life, he also says that people seem to pursue honor in order to convince themselves that they are good. One can see this because they primarily seek to be honored by the more intelligent people among those who know them, and they seek to be honored for their excellence. On this view, honor too appears as an instrumental good, even if it is not conceived as such by the people who pursue it. It is clear, moreover, that on either account they do not seek honors for the sake of the pleasure that comes from being honored per se.

Elsewhere in the *Republic* Socrates makes clear that he is aware of this alternative, and more plausible, way of characterizing the comparison between the three lives. At 505b he claims that in the opinion of the many the good is pleasure, while in the opinion of the "more refined" (οἱ κομψότεροι) it is practical wisdom, that is, the virtue most central to Aristotle's account of the political life. Why, then, does Socrates present the comparison in the way that he does? The reason, he claims, is that "the pleasures of each form, and the life itself, dispute with one another, not about living more nobly or shamefully or worse or better but about living more pleasantly and painlessly" (581e–582a). That is, he presents the comparison in terms of the pleasures appropriate to each of the three lives as *directly* connected to the attempt by representatives of each life *to justify* the superiority of their chosen way of life to the other two alternatives. As opposed to Aristotle's account, which looks to the lives actually led as evidence of the implicit beliefs of the human beings leading those lives, Socrates begins his comparison with an imaginary interview of representatives of each life. Socrates claims that if Glaucon were willing to ask three such men, "each in turn" (ἐν μέρει), which life of these was the most pleasant, each man would praise his own life. However, when Socrates offers the arguments that the money-loving, honor-loving, and philosophic individuals would put forward in defense of the claim that their life was the most pleasant, it becomes clear that their arguments are not essentially about what is most pleasant. Instead, the lover of money and the lover of honor conceive of the difference between the pleasures wholly in terms of the goods they have chosen to direct their lives toward, while the philosophic individual indicates his distance from the experience of the other two pleasures. Thus, the lover of money claims that the other pleasures are "worth nothing" (οὐδενὸς αξίαν) if they do not make money, and the lover of honor decries the pleasure of money as "vulgar" (φορτικήν) and the pleasure of learning as "smoke and nonsense" (καπνὸν καὶ φλυαρίαν), while the philosopher says these other two pleasures are "very far away" (οὐ πάνυ πόρρω).

Framing the comparison between the three lives in terms of a dispute between representatives of these lives has two immediate consequences in Socrates' presentation. First, the ground of the comparison shifts from the goods appropriate to each of the lives to a comparison between the "pleasures" of these lives. Second, the experience of pleasure itself seems to get lost. We can see why this might be so if we consider what role "pleasure" must play in such an argument. The representatives of each of the lives, *ex hypothesi,* do not endorse the goals inherent to the other two lives, therefore these goods must be translated into some kind of "common currency" which the representatives of all three lives will recognize. This "common currency" is pleasure,[52] or more specifically, the "harmless pleasures" (357b) that everyone recognizes as good, even if not everyone is willing to concede that they are constitutive of the good as such. Instead of arguing on the basis of the goods which are constitutive of a given life, Socrates shifts the focus to the subjective experience of the appropriation of these goods—and this subjective experience is described as pleasure. The life in question is now described as one that seeks a particular pleasure, and it is the difference between pleasures that becomes the subject of controversy. However, this attempt to defend a way of life in terms of goods common to all ways of life, however good or bad those lives may be, is inherently suspect. Socrates argues in the *Crito,* for example, that between those who accept and those who reject the claim that it is never right to return injustice for injustice "there is no common basis for decision: when they view each others' counsels, they must necessarily hold each other in contempt" (49d, R. E. Allen trans.).[53] Moreover, as a result of this move the term "pleasure" has been deprived of any positive content; it becomes equated with the satisfaction of desire. Desire, moreover, has been severed from any natural disposition of the body or soul and has been construed as whatever contingent goals an individual identifies as his own. The desires become a set of "preferences," and pleasure becomes the satisfaction of those preferences.[54]

What this means is that the contest between pleasures cannot be decided on the grounds of pleasure itself, for the very reason that we have now redefined

---

52. Cf. *Phd.* 69a–b.
53. Compare Aristotle *Pol.* 1283a3, *EE* 1243.22–23.
54. Cf. Wiggins 1980, 255.

the difference between lives wholly in terms of the divergent subjective experience of the goods of those lives. Socrates shifts the argument, accordingly, to the question of the *authority* of the philosophic, honor-loving, and money-loving individuals to judge the relative merits of the different pleasures, and their *competence* in making arguments in support of their relative judgments. On Socrates' staging of the dispute, each of the representatives of the three lives has made a claim to live the most pleasant life. The question now becomes: how are Socrates and Glaucon to "know which of them speaks most truly" (581d)? The answer, Socrates suggests, comes not from an independent consideration of their respective claims, but from a judgment concerning which of the representatives is most likely to have made the correct assessment. This judgment is to be based upon their relative qualifications in terms of "experience, prudence and argument" (582a), and on each of these qualifying criteria in turn, the philosopher is judged by Socrates and Glaucon to be more authoritative.

The looming circularity of the ensuing argument is shown by the fact that the second criterion, "prudence," is dealt with by means of the simple assertion that only the philosopher will have gained his experience of pleasure "in the company of prudence" (582d). This indicates in one stark gesture the problem with the argument for the authority of the philosopher as a whole: it is only persuasive if one has already accepted the philosopher's viewpoint as authoritative. More specifically, the argument depends on accepting, as Glaucon does, the validity of philosopher's claim to have experienced the pleasure of "knowing the truth as it is" (581d). The philosopher is said to be superior in terms of his experience of pleasure because he has been compelled to experience all three forms of pleasure, whereas the others lives have at best only the most fleeting experience of the pleasure of learning. However, to accept this claim is to deny the prima facie claim made by the other two lives, that the putative pleasure of learning is nothing real; it is "worth nothing" to the money-lover and "smoke and nonsense" for the honor-lover. That is, the money- and honor-lover contend that the philosopher's putative experience of a higher pleasure is nothing but empty words. They are, therefore, unlikely to be persuaded by the philosopher's putative superiority in terms of the final criterion of "argument." Nor, it seems, should they be. Socrates contends that since what is to be finely judged must be judged by means of arguments, and "arguments are especially the instrument of the philosopher" (582d), what the lover of wisdom and the lover of argument praise would necessarily be most true. This bit of reasoning seems to imply that whoever has more experience in arguments will make better arguments, and whoever makes better arguments will lead a better life—conclusions that are no doubt congenial to Thrasymachus, who would appear on these grounds to be the second-best human being in the *Republic*. This is an example of what

Aristotle calls "philosophy as the many practice it"—thinking that "by taking refuge in arguments" they are practicing philosophy and thereby becoming more excellent human beings (*Eth. Nic.* 1105b13–15).

The final step in Socrates' demonstration of the superiority of philosophic pleasures concerns the difference between pleasure conceived positively and pleasure conceived merely as the absence of pain. This argument is quite complex, and it would take me too far afield of my present inquiry to explore it in depth. Focusing, therefore, only on the issues that we have seen arise in the earlier stages of Socrates' argument, we can see how Socrates recasts the problem of judging the pleasure-claims of the philosophic individual in the context of the dialogue as a whole, and how, at the same time, this argument indicates the ways that the philosophic life is misunderstood when it attempts to defend itself primarily in terms of the pleasure associated with it.

Socrates begins by arguing that alongside pleasure and pain there is a third thing, a repose of soul, which is neither pleasant nor painful, but which lies in between the movement that is pleasure and the movement that is pain. This repose can appear to an individual either pleasant, when it is contrasted to an experience of pain, or painful, when it is contrasted to an experience of pleasure. Socrates argues, however, that this appearance is illusory. To make this point clearer, Socrates compares the three states to "up, down, and middle" and argues that if a human being who had no experience of the "upward region" were brought from "the downward region" to the "middle," he would falsely assume that he had come to the "true up" (584d–e). Analogously, Socrates argues that if a person who had not experienced true pleasure were brought from a state of pain to a state of repose, he would falsely assume that that he was "nearing fulfillment and pleasure" (584e–585a).

By presenting an account of illusory pleasure, Socrates makes concrete the inadequacy of his previous arguments concerning the authority of the philosopher's judgment of the respective merits of the three ways of life. For the substance of the money-lover's and honor-lover's implicit arguments against the philosopher was that his putative experience of a higher pleasure was just such an illusion. To reiterate, the success of the argument depends entirely on Glaucon's accepting the claim of the imagined representative of the philosophic life that the pleasures of knowledge far outstrip those of honor or wealth. He does so either because he simply accepts the imagined philosopher's viewpoint as authoritative, or because he assumes himself to have experienced just these pleasures. In the first case, the argument *for* the authority of the philosopher's judgment becomes an argument *from* that authority; in the second case, the putative argument for the authority of the judgment of the philosopher collapses into an assertion of the superiority of intellectual pleasures. In either case, an argument meant to establish the authority of the philosopher's judgment becomes entirely dependent upon the authority of the judgment of the individual (Glaucon, in this instance) who assesses the philosopher's claims to authority.

The conclusion of Socrates' argument with Glaucon, however, shows the latter's judgment to be lacking the authority to validate the pleasure-claims of the imagined philosopher precisely in that he does not see the inadequacy of "pleasure" as a standard. At the turning point of Socrates' argument he asks Glaucon, first, whether, as hunger and thirst are emptiness of the body's condition, ignorance and imprudence are emptiness of the soul's condition, and whether the man who gets intelligence becomes full. While Glaucon enthusiastically agrees, this argument proves to be an artifact of the attempt to defend the philosophic life in terms of an abstract and generic concept of pleasure. It makes the wisdom-loving part of the soul analogous to *to epithumêtikon,* "the companion of certain replenishments and pleasures" (439d). However, as Glaucon should remember, Socrates went out of his way in book 7 to deny that knowledge is analogous to filling up of the soul's empty state. He claimed there, contrary to the assertions of certain men, that learning is not a process in which knowledge is "put in" to the soul, but a turning of the eye of the soul from that which is coming into being toward that which is (518b–e). Despite Glaucon's enthusiastic approval of Socrates' "oracular" condemnation of those "who have no experience of prudence or virtue, but are always living with feasts and the like," glutting themselves "like cattle" (586a–b), his view of the difference between philosophic and nonphilosophic pleasures reduces, in the end, to the preference for fine dining he asserted at the beginning of the *Republic* (357d).

We will return below to the relevance of Glaucon's misapprehension of the goods inherent in a philosophic life for our understanding of the broader argument of the *Republic.*[55] In the present context, Socrates' staging of an imagined defense of the philosophic life in terms of an abstract conception of "pleasure" points toward the inevitable problems that arise for any argument attempting to defend a way of life in terms which abstract from the ends toward which such a life is directed. Furthermore, it suggests an intimate connection between the attempt to self-consciously justify one's way of living in such terms and a misapprehension of the very goods that make such a life worth living. The problem with the imagined philosopher's defense of the philosophic life is not that he claims that the philosophic life is the most pleasant, it is rather that this defense seeks to conceive of philosophic pleasure in terms that are discursively accessible to individuals who are, *ex hypothesi,* foreign to the very experiences being described as most pleasant (582c). Socrates' conversation with Glaucon

55. See chapter 9.

about the pleasures inherent in the philosophic life suggests that, in striving to justify a philosophic life in terms which can be accepted by even that individual who is supposed to be wholly foreign to philosophy, one runs the risk of alienating oneself from the very experiences one seeks to defend.

2.9 Heteronomy

In Socrates' three-step argument for the superiority of the philosophic life in terms of the pleasures appropriate to the three parts of the soul, we can discern an example of another aspect of Socrates' dialogic practice, analogous to what Gregory Vlastos called "complex irony"; it is an argument which manifestly fails to support its conclusion on the surface, but one which defends the same conclusion at a deeper level. Socrates argues that when the entire soul follows the love of wisdom the entire soul will gain pleasures which are both the truest and most its own, and that when "one of the others" has mastery of the soul "the result is that it can't discover its own pleasure and compels the others to pursue an alien and untrue pleasure" (587a). As I have tried to demonstrate, the arguments he explicitly offers in defense of these conclusions are riddled with problems. However, these very problems point to another way of understanding the conclusion that when something else other than the love of wisdom "rules" in the soul, the soul pursues desires that are not its own. The word translated above as "alien" is *allotrios*, literally "belonging to another." I believe that Socrates is gesturing here to what we would now call the problem of "heteronomy" and the "politicization" of the desires. The "other" implicitly referred to in *allotrios*, I suggest, is not simply the other parts of the soul, but the other human beings before whom one must give an account of one's way of life. Socrates' entire argument indicates the way in which the attempt to self-consciously justify a certain way of life to others can alter the experience of that very way of life. Judgments about better and worse lives become confused with judgments about the ability to defend a given way of life. The proper goods of the three aspects of soul have a tendency to be replaced, first by the subjective experience of those goods, and second by the public manifestation of those experiences. The question of our ability to represent to others that which we perceive as good tends to displace and transform those very perceptions, and that which is incapable of public representation—intellectual insight as opposed to public argument, the privacy of soul in contradistinction to either public character or philosophic-literary "voice"—has a tendency to be denied or forgotten. In modern terms, both the intelligible and the personal become wholly "political."

As we will see, both Polemarchus and Thrasymachus, in very different ways, offer visions of human political activity which treat the human social and political world as self-enclosed; they abstract, not only from any account of the intelligible order of the world, but also from the private experience of individual human beings. Abstracting both from the nature of the cosmos and from human nature, Polemarchus and Thrasymachus depict human intentional action isolated from considerations of any natural or universal end for those actions, and from considerations of bodily desires or affects. I will argue below that this circumscribed view of the human social and political world, itself a consequence of and response to the waning of the tradition, provides the point of departure for the argument of the *Republic* as a whole.

Before turning to Polemarchus's account of the political life, however, I will respond to two potential objections to the foregoing account. I have suggested that Socrates' narration of the *Republic* points toward possible dangers in what we might call the "democratic" culture of explicit, intersubjective self-justification in terms of goods that are common to all lives—and in this sense all of the characters on display in book 1 are "democratic" souls, whatever the content of their positive views about which regime is best.[56] The two objections can be phrased in terms of, first, a general characterization of Socrates' dialogic practice, and second, a specification of this more general characterization. Contrary to the implications of my argument, one might object, Socrates himself is presented in the dialogues as a paradigmatic case of someone who seeks to engage all sorts of souls and all kinds of lives in philosophic arguments about their lives and the goods which characterize those lives; moreover, he tries to show each of these individuals that, in terms of the very goods which they espouse, the philosophic life is the best life, and the life they truly desire. So runs the general characterization. More specifically, Socrates is shown in the dialogues defending the philosophic life to representatives of the life of pleasure. Therefore, it cannot be the case that Socrates thinks there is something wrong with the idea of defending philosophy to these individuals, or in these terms. These objections would be powerful if the claims they made about the dialogues were true. I believe, however, that they are not.

I will respond to the specific objection before turning to the more general characterization. This objection claims that in Plato's dialogues Socrates defends the life of philosophy to representatives of the life of pleasure in terms appropriate to such a life. This claim is wrong in two respects. First, Socrates is never presented in the dialogues as arguing with someone who is anything like

---

56. This point will become clearer once we have discussed Socrates' account of the democratic individual in §3.4 below.

an adequate representative of the life of pleasure. In general, when Socrates is presented as arguing against someone who appears to espouse pleasure as the end of human action, that individual is really espousing the freedom from conventional opinions that the life of pleasure seems to exhibit. In what is, in effect, a response to the problem of heteronomy explicated above, these individuals praise not pleasure itself, but rather the noble independence of that human being who will not be turned aside by the opinions of the many from the pursuit of pleasures conventionally considered base. In a move reminiscent of some contemporary theorists of desire, in Plato's dialogues it is spirit and not desire that motivates the turn to the body, and it is not pleasure itself but freedom from societal constraints that is the principal good espoused by pleasure's defenders. Callicles comes to mind as the best example from the dialogues. His admiration for "the young lion" whom he imagines breaking the bonds of convention and trampling underfoot "our" laws and codes, the "natural justice" he sees in this "slave," "our slave," rebelling and proving himself "our master"—these are not views inspired by his experience of the good of pleasure; rather, these claims are inspired by his experience of his own enslavement to convention, and the self-loathing he feels because he is not "man" enough to overcome this enslavement. In fact, the only individual who has any claim to being a representative of the life of pleasure in the dialogues is Philebus, but, of course, Socrates is not shown arguing with Philebus in the *Philebus*. It is rather the honor-loving Protarchus who engages Socrates in the long, complex, and abstract arguments that make up the dialogue. Philebus simply can't be bothered.[57] Moreover, in those places in the dialogues where Socrates argues with someone who *seems* to espouse the life of pleasure, such as Socrates' conversation with Callicles in the *Gorgias* or his conversation with Thrasymachus in book 1 of the *Republic,* the public setting of these conversations and Socrates' mode of argument suggest that in these cases Socrates may be more concerned with seeming to convince or convict his opponent than in actually persuading them. I will return to this aspect of Socrates' conversation with Thrasymachus below.

Turning now to the more general characterization of Socrates' dialogic practice, we can see that this objection is also wrong in two respects. First, as I have attempted to show with regard to Cephalus, there are individuals with whom Socrates only appears eager to engage in philosophic discussion.[58] There are, I believe, a variety of reasons for Socrates' reticence to attempt to engage everyone in philosophic discussion, and I will postpone a discussion of these issues until later. However, this much should be immediately apparent: despite Socrates' claim

57. See Klein 1985.
58. See Ausland 1997, 383–85.

in the *Apology* that he seeks to engage every Athenian citizen and stranger whom he should meet, that the dialogues never show Socrates' discussing philosophy with an Athenian craftsman, nor do they provide any evidence of him discussing piety, for example, with anyone who could be considered a representative conventionally pious Athenian.[59] Second, even with those individuals whom Socrates does choose to engage in a discussion of the superiority of the philosophic life, the above general characterization of Socrates' dialogic practice abstracts from the pervasiveness of Socratic irony in the dialogues. It confuses the fact that Socrates is willing to speak with a variety of individuals regarding their lives and the philosophic life with the claim that Socrates is attempting to make plain to those individuals the grounds upon which he himself philosophizes; that is, in the terms Socrates uses in the *Euthyphro,* it confuses Socrates' "philanthropy" with a "pouring out" of himself in speech to every human being who will listen to him.[60] Most of all, it ignores the radically ad hominem character of Socrates' arguments, the fact that Socrates' conversations often, if not always, start from the premises espoused by his interlocutor and his refutations proceed by showing the internal contradictions of the interlocutor's conception of what is best.

---

59. Consider, in this context, the fact that in the *Laches* Socrates is known to Laches and Nicias, prominent political men, and to the sons of Lysimachus and Melesias, but not to Lysimachus and Melesias themselves. Cf. *Euthphr.* 2d–3a.

60. Ἐγὼ δὲ φοβοῦμαι μὴ ὑπὸ φιλανθρωπίας δοκῶ αὐτοῖς ὅτιπερ ἔχω ἐκκεχυμένως παντὶ ἀνδρὶ λέγειν . . . εἴ τίς μου ἐθέλει ἀκούειν. *Euthphr.* 3d8–9; cf. *Symp.* 175d. It is this confusion, Socrates fears, that is most responsible for the Athenians' belief that Socrates corrupts the young.

3

Polemarchus, Politics, and Action

In the previous chapter, I suggested that Socrates' narration of his encounter with Cephalus is intended to exhibit a metaphoric cultural "death" of the poetic and religious tradition in late fifth-century Athens. In this chapter, I will argue that Socrates' conversation with Cephalus's son, Polemarchus, explores the ramifications of the waning of the tradition for the ethical and political environment in which Socrates pursued his public philosophic activity. I will treat Socrates' conversation with Polemarchus with three goals in mind. First, I will try to show how Polemarchus's account of justice as "helping friends and harming enemies" discloses a vision of the human political world which attempts to abstract wholly from the extrapolitical, and in so doing abstracts from the very goods he hopes to achieve in political action and the political life. Second, I will argue that Socrates' arguments with Polemarchus point to a conceptual division between intellectual and dispositional components of human action, both of which seem to stand outside the abstractly political world Polemarchus envisions. This conceptual division, I will argue in the next chapter, becomes the basis for two opposed visions of the autonomy of the political world whose interrelation crucially informs the "psychopolitical" argument of the *Republic*. Finally, I will look to Socrates' conversation with Polemarchus as an exemplar of Socrates' characteristic dialectical *pragma*. The last of these three goals will most directly influence the way that I proceed in this chapter, and calls for some preliminary clarification.

As I suggested in §1.1, I take Socrates' narration of book 1 as an extended lesson in the art of Socratic dialogue. Each of Socrates' three principal inter-locutors in the opening pages of the *Republic* becomes in his narration a repre-sentative of a human type characteristic of the cultural environment in which Socrates pursued his public philosophic mission. Cephalus, Polemarchus, and Thrasymachus each represent a type of misunderstanding about the human good and an allied type or strategy of self-deception. Moreover, differences in the ways that Socrates engages, or fails to engage, each of the three should be seen as illustrative of different *typical dialogic strategies* Socrates employs with different types of interlocutors. I have argued in §2.9 that, despite Socrates' apparent claims to the contrary in the *Apology,* Plato's Socrates does not engage all interlocutors in the same way or with the same aims and intentions. Indeed, as we have seen, one among Socrates' conversational aims when speaking to Cephalus seems to be removing him from the conversation. We have also seen why this might be so; Cephalus's age, talents, and station all tend toward making him an inauspicious participant in a conversation which will include the most radical of revisions to the traditional moral and political order. Socrates' conversation with Thrasymachus, on the other hand, is informed throughout by Socrates' response to Thrasymachus as a potential threat to the emerging community formed by the participants in the dialogue. As we will see in the next chapter, the closing interchange between Socrates and Thrasymachus makes two things evident. First, Socrates does not succeed in persuading Thrasymachus by means of the arguments he puts forward in book 1. Second, Socrates does not *intend* to persuade Thrasymachus directly by those arguments; if Socrates persuades Thrasymachus, he does so indirectly. At least initially, we can say that Socrates is less interested in persuading than in taming or, as Glaucon puts it, "charming" Thrasymachus. Thrasymachus apparently diverts the course of Socrates' conversation with Polemarchus, and provides the impetus for Glaucon and Adeimantus's joint framing of the question concerning whether the just or unjust life is superior. For the *Republic,* Thrasymachus's intervention is essential. But Socrates treats Thrasymachus more like a problem to be solved, or a resource to be tapped, than a joint inquirer in any sense.

Then we have Polemarchus, whose conversation with Socrates is exceptional in the extent to which it is nonexceptional. While Polemarchus, like all of Socrates' interlocutors in Plato's dialogues, is depicted as a particular individual whose individual personality decisively informs Socrates' conversation with him, he also appears to be what we might with some caution call a "normal" Socratic interlocutor. He is an ambitious young man who shows some familiarity with and appetite for intellectual debate, but he is neither set in his ways beyond the possibility of instruction (Cephalus) nor a professional intellectual with his own rhetorical agenda (Thrasymachus). He is neither the best nor the worst of the young men with whom Socrates converses in the dialogues, neither the most nor the least intellectually talented. More significantly, even the particular misconception about the human good that characterizes Polemarchus as an individual is to some extent typical. As we will see in detail shortly, Polemarchus exemplifies the broad tendency shared by many of Socrates' interlocutors to think about "capacity" or "power" (δύναμις) in abstraction from a purpose or goal of that power. Consonant with this brief sketch of Polemarchus as a "normal" or "standard" interlocutor, I will try to show, by following quite closely the warp and weft of Socrates' conversation with him, how this conversation is particularly illustrative of Socrates' dialogic practice.

Polemarchus, I have suggested, inherits from his father a notion of human political capacity abstracted from the end or purpose of that capacity. While this conception of bare or brute political capacity remained implicit in Cephalus's account of the benefits of wealth for a man of character, it becomes explicit in Polemarchus's account of justice as helping friends and harming enemies. The account given above of the decadence of Greek religious culture provides us with a sense of why this might be so. While the poetic and religious tradition as represented by Cephalus is, so to speak, absent as a living source of ethical norms, it is still very much present as a source of political authority—this much Socrates' prosecution should make clear. Polemarchus, who boldly interrupts to assume his father's place in the argument, clearly wants to appropriate the authority of his patrimony, both literally and figuratively. Unfortunately, he cannot find within the conflicting dictates of the composite poetic tradition the resources or justification for the life of political action which he so clearly desires, and, unlike his father, he is not willing to spend his life the slave to a multiplicity of antagonistic desires waiting for the release that age and infirmity bring. Therefore, in his continuation of the argument with Socrates, Polemarchus attempts to appropriate the tradition simply as a bearer of authority, and this attempt is signaled by the way in which he first invokes the authority of the poet Simonides in defense of his father's putative definition of justice.[1]

When Socrates' interchange with Cephalus leads to the conclusion that "speaking the truth and returning what one has taken" cannot be the definition of justice, Polemarchus interrupts to say that it most certainly is, "if, indeed, one should be persuaded by Simonides" (εἴπερ γέ τι χρὴ Σιμωνίδῃ πείθεσθαι, 331d5). As opposed to his father's implicit identification with authoritative figures from the tradition, Polemarchus begins with an explicit assertion of the authority of one such figure and phrases his first assertion about justice in the form of a conditional. If Simonides is to be believed (and the εἴπερ γέ in Polemarchus's conditional indicates his assumption that Simonides is to be believed), then, Polemarchus maintains, "It is just to give to each what is owed." What Polemarchus does not do, however, is offer any argument as to why Simonides, or any other authoritative figure from the tradition, *should* be believed.[2]

---

1. On the general issue of the appropriation of the poetic tradition as a source of authority in fifth-century intellectual culture, see Morgan 2000, 91–132.

2. Polemarchus's invocation of Simonides is another indication of aspects of the tradition being cut loose from their original contexts. Simonides, like Pindar, wrote for a cosmopolitan aristocratic elite and is presented in both the *Protagoras* and the (questionably Platonic) *Hipparchus* as an associate of tyrants.

Socrates responds by focusing, not on Simonides himself, but on Polemarchus's interpretation and understanding of Simonides. He says that while it is "not easy to disbelieve a Simonides," who is "a wise and divine man," neither is it easy to understand what Simonides has said. Perhaps Polemarchus understands what it is Simonides meant, for surely he did not mean that it was just to return anything to anybody regardless of that person's soundness of mind when the demand was made. Polemarchus is willing to assert that he does in fact know what Simonides meant—he meant "friends owe it to friends to give something good and nothing bad." In coming to this conclusion, Polemarchus does not adduce any evidence from Simonides,[3] and in the argument that follows Polemarchus shifts almost imperceptibly from explicitly being a spokesman for Simonides (332c5–d1), to stating his opinions about what Simonides meant (332d7–9), to simply stating his own opinions (332e5). This replacement of the authority of the tradition with the authority of an authoritative *interpreter* of that tradition is a fundamental component of the abstraction characteristic of Polemarchus, an abstraction which attempts to view the human political world as self-enclosed and self-sufficient.[4]

The decadence of the traditional poetic and religious culture, and the shadow that it still casts over any attempt to inquire into the question of what is highest and best for human beings, provides the background for Polemarchus's attempt to defend and justify a wholly autonomous conception of the political. Polemarchus's understanding of the political is deficient, I will argue, in that it attempts to do without any reference to any extrapolitical conception of human nature or the good for human beings; it represents, we might say, politics for politics' sake. If Aristotle is right to assert that while the polis comes into being for the sake of life, it *exists* for the sake of living well (*Pol.* 1252b27–32), this abstraction of politics from the extrapolitical is, as such, a degrading of the political. By turning briefly to the image we are given of Polemarchus in the opening scene of the *Republic,* we can come to see more clearly the abstractly political character of Polemarchus's understanding of human social relations.

Polemarchus, whose name means "military leader" (the "Polemarch" was one of the seven Archons of the Athenian democracy), first appears in the *Republic* not *in propria persona* but as the unseen source of a command, conveyed through a slave, that Socrates and Glaucon wait. When he does arrive on the

---

He seems a singularly inappropriate authority figure for Polemarchus, who seems to equate justice with patriotism and whose activity in support of the democratic faction in Athens (along with his wealth) led to his murder at the hands of the Thirty.

3. Cf. *Prt.* 339a–347a.

4. Cf. Hobbes, *Leviathan* 26.21–25, 33.21–25.

scene, his first act is a playful, but none too tasteful, gesture toward the possibility
of using force to compel Socrates and Glaucon to stay in the Piraeus. Even after
Adeimantus gently intervenes with the mention of a novel religious ceremony and
contest to entice Socrates to remain, Polemarchus continues to adopt the role of
commander. The force Polemarchus gestures toward is "democratic" political
power reduced to the brute fact of numerical superiority; he tells Socrates, "Either
prove stronger than these men or stay here." However, as Adeimantus's intervention indicates, it is not clear that Polemarchus has any reason to assume that he
has the authority to speak for these men. When Socrates suggests that there is
another possibility—that he and Glaucon could persuade rather than overpower
Polemarchus's group—Polemarchus doubts that this is possible. All that he and
his group need do is simply refuse to listen. Glaucon, not Socrates, agrees that in
this case persuasion would be impossible. However, it is one of the central implications of the "musical" education of the guardians that Socrates will explicate
later in the *Republic* that Polemarchus and Glaucon are mistaken in their agreement. Persuasion comes in many forms, not all of them spoken or sung, and it
seems entirely possible to become persuaded of something by someone without
becoming aware of that fact. Unconscious persuasion, however, is not something
that Polemarchus is likely to recognize; as we will see, an overestimation of the
significance of the explicit and the public character of human social relations
marks his entire conversation with Socrates.

Polemarchus's initial defense of his father's argument shows that the same
tendencies that became evident in the opening scene of the *Republic* inform
Polemarchus's understanding of justice and the just man. In his account of
what is "owed to each" (τὸ τὰ ὀφειλόμενα ἑκάστῳ), Polemarchus expressly
denies that the just human being owes to a friend that which the friend has left
in his keeping if "the giving and the taking turn out to be bad" (332a–b). He
replaces Cephalus's traditional notion of returning what one has taken with
the idea that the just man owes to each what is "fitting" (τὸ προσῆκον)—good
to his friends and harm to his enemies—without any apparent compunction
about overturning this conventional understanding, and this despite Socrates'
urging that "what [any man has] deposited is surely owed to him" (332a1).
Polemarchus's initial confidence in his interpretation of Simonides is all the
more striking given Socrates' great emphasis on his own failure to understand.
This initial confidence is mirrored in Polemarchus's failure to question the
ability of the just man to ascertain what is fitting for both friends and enemies.
At the same moment that he assumes for himself the authority to interpret
Simonides' gnomic utterance concerning justice, he appropriates for the just
man the authority to determine what is good for his friends regardless of what
those friends may think about the matter.

3.1 Human Being and Citizen

Polemarchus's characterization of justice as an obligation to do good to friends and harm to enemies makes clear what I have called the abstractly political character of his orientation. As Seth Benardete notes, it is only in an unqualified political context that the world easily divides into friend and enemy.[5] In particular, the notion that one "owes to one's enemies that which is fitting—some harm," that is, that one is *obliged* to harm an enemy, makes clear that Polemarchus's notion of justice is directly tied to a particular understanding of the common good which equates it with the good of the polis rather than any independent conception of the good of the individuals who make up that polis. For the idea of an *obligation* to harm one's enemy only makes sense in the context that one's enemy is "the enemy" and a failure to attempt to inflict harm is a shirking of one's patriotic duty. Polemarchus goes further than this, of course. His account of justice as "the fitting" quickly moves, with Socrates' help, from an obligation to help friends and harm enemies to the simple fact of such help or harm—justice helps friends and harm enemies. With this move Polemarchus appears to equate justice with military or political success narrowly defined. This appearance is consistent with the fact that the first assertion Polemarchus makes on his own behalf, rather than as an interpretation of Simonides, is that the just man is the man most able to help friends and harm enemies in waging war and being a military ally. Notice, moreover, that Polemarchus does not make the justice of harming one's enemies dependent on the justice of helping one's friends; that is, he does not present the harm one does to one's enemies as a necessary, and perhaps lamentable, consequence of helping one's friends. Harming enemies is not an indirect consequence of certain actions that can be described as just; it is, rather, constitutive of their justice.

Before we turn to the details of Socrates' explicit refutation of Polemarchus's account of justice, and in particular, before we deal with the analogy between justice and *technê* which dominates that refutation, it will be useful to reconstruct as accurately as we can the perspective on justice Polemarchus wishes to express by means of the formula "justice is helping friends and harming enemies." We can do this by turning to moments later in his conversation where Socrates seems to be directed appealing to, or obviously conflicting with, Polemarchus's strongest intuitions about justice. This will help us to see more clearly Polemarchus's overarching vision of the political world. By locating the

---

5. Benardete 1989b, 16. Cf. Carl Schmitt's discussion of friend and enemy as the essential terms of political discourse in *The Concept of the Political* (1996).

vision of the political which underlies Polemarchus's responses to Socrates' arguments we will be in a better position to understand the significance of those arguments. We will be better prepared to understand both Socrates' dialogic intent vis-à-vis Polemarchus and his apodeictic intent vis-à-vis the assembled company and/or the auditors of his narration. We will also be prepared to appreciate the relations between these two levels of intent.

As we have seen, Polemarchus claims that harming enemies is categorically just. A strict consequence of this view is that in any military conflict both sides are *ex hypothesi* just, insofar as they are harming or seeking to harm their enemies. Therefore, according to this definition, to inflict harm on enemy combatants in war is *always* to harm human beings who are acting justly. As extreme as these claims may sound, it is easy enough to imagine someone believing something analogous to this claim. The heroes of the *Iliad,* for example, recognize the excellence of their foes, and the excellence they recognize is, first and foremost, excellence in the conflict in which they are presently engaged. Indeed, if these heroes were not fighting against men who were "good men" in the requisite sense, that is, if their enemies did not exhibit *aretê,* there would be nothing particularly admirable about a victory over these enemies.[6] However, later in the conversation, when Socrates presents the conclusion (albeit arrived at by a much more circuitous route) that, according to Polemarchus's definition, it is just to "treat badly men who have done nothing unjust," Polemarchus emphatically rejects this conclusion. Indeed, he says, "the argument seems to be bad" or "corrupt" (πονηρὸς γὰρ ἔοικεν εἶναι ὁ λόγος, 334d7). Polemarchus's unconditional rejection of the conclusion that it is just to treat badly men who have done nothing unjust is among his most remarkable contributions to the argument. For, if one is to consider participation in war just in any sense, it seems that the only reasonable response to Socrates' conclusion is: "Yes, even in a just war it is sometimes necessary to harm human beings who have done nothing unjust." That Polemarchus does *not* respond this way shows that, prior to Socrates' probing, he implicitly considers the distinction between friend and enemy to be perfectly aligned with the distinction between good and bad men. It would seem, however, that this could only be true if friend and enemy were natural kinds, or if one's status as friend and enemy were constitutive of one's

6. This, of course, points to something paradoxical underlying the ethical situation of these heroes. The nobility of a warrior elite must strive to combine two quite opposed modes of ethical identification and ethical distinction. On the one hand, one is a warrior only insofar as one fights in the service of some larger community with which one identifies. A group of individuals who engage in conflict without any implicit identification with a broader political community are, in the context of the Homeric poems, simply pirates. On the other hand, one is noble only insofar as one distinguishes oneself on the battlefield against similarly situated nobles, in contradistinction to that broader political community, and in particular, in contradistinction to those who are unable or unwilling to fight.

status as a good or bad human being. That the former of these two alternatives is not Polemarchus's view should be obvious, if for no other reason than the absence of any form of the word "nature" from the discussion. Nor, however, does Polemarchus seem conscious of the latter possibility. Instead, Polemarchus's vision of the political community seems oblivious to any distinction between natural and political kinds; the political distinction between "us" and "them" is the only essential distinction operative in Polemarchus's original conception of good or bad human beings.

By equating one's ethical status as a human being wholly with one's political status as friend or enemy, Polemarchus seems to be taking the self or soul as wholly congruent, indeed identical with, the role one plays in the political community. That this is, indeed, Polemarchus's implicit assumption can be seen not only in his unqualified endorsement of the claim, at 335c3, that "justice *is* human excellence," but most particularly in his responses to Socrates' questions in the argument leading up to this claim. After Socrates has pointed out to Polemarchus the difficulties presented by the fact that human beings make mistakes about whom they consider friends and whom they consider enemies, and has rephrased Polemarchus's original formulation as "it is just to do good to the friend, if he is good, and harm to the enemy, if he is bad," Socrates asks whether harming any human being whatsoever is proper to the just man ("Εστιν ἄρα, ἦν δ' ἐγώ, δικαίου ἀνδρὸς βλάπτειν καὶ ὁντινοῦν ἀνθρώπων, 335b2–3). When Polemarchus responds that "bad men and enemies ought to be harmed," Socrates persuades Polemarchus that it is not proper to the just man to harm anyone, by arguing (1) that to harm a human being is to make that human being unjust, and (2) the just cannot make others unjust by means of justice.

These two claims can seem unremarkable in this context, for, as many commentators have noted, they seem to be similar to claims Socrates makes elsewhere in the dialogues. A passage in the *Crito* is often cited, in which Socrates argues that it is never right to return injustice for injustice, and that the greatest harm that can come to a human being is to be harmed with respect to "whatever it is of ours to which justice and injustice pertain" (47e–48a). However, in the *Crito* Socrates explicitly contrasts this more serious harm to the harm that can come to the body, and appears to argue that life is not worth living with a body that has been sufficiently harmed (47d–e). It is therefore by no means clear that Socrates is persuaded of the claim that to harm a human being is always to make him more unjust; for it is by no mean clear that Socrates believes bodily harm makes a person unjust.[7] Why, then, is Polemarchus persuaded? The reason, I

---

7. The point is complicated by the fact that Socrates sometimes appears to deny that harm to the body is genuine harm. In the *Apology*, for example, Socrates claims that neither Meletus and Anytus can

suggest, is that he does not recognize the significance of the distinction between harm to the body and harm to the soul, and he does not recognize the significance of this distinction because the only "soul" or "self" that concerns him is the self expressed in political action.

Consider in this context the arguments Socrates uses to persuade Polemarchus that harming a human being is to make him worse with respect to human virtue. Socrates asks whether horses and dogs that have been harmed are made better or worse, and whether they are made worse with respect to the species-specific virtues of each animal; that is, he asks whether dogs who have been made worse are made worse with respect to the virtue of dogs or that of horses. Polemarchus contends that horses and dogs that have been harmed *are* made worse, and they are made worse with respect to the virtues of their respective species. It is, moreover, not difficult to see why Polemarchus might accept this much of Socrates' argument. For an animal such as a horse, it is at least plausible to suggest that what it is to be an excellent horse is more or less an immediate expression of the natural characteristics of the species; that is, excellence (ἀρετή) in a horse is the strength, speed, physical beauty, and, perhaps, spiritedness of the animal. From this perspective, what it means to harm a horse is to harm it with respect to these excellences. A sick, lame, or disfigured horse—or a horse that has had its spirit broken rather than tamed—is a worse horse.[8] However, the case with human beings seems quite different. However much one may be persuaded that human excellence requires something like a distinctive human nature, life for a human being is not and cannot be an immediate expression of that nature. Lives must be led, which is to say that a human being has, for good or ill, a conscious, and implicitly self-conscious, relation to his own life-activity.[9] The good for human beings must be determined or discovered, and for the Socrates of Plato's *Apology* at least, any account of

---

harm him in any way, for it is not permitted for a better man to be harmed by a worse man (Ap. 30c8-d5). Socrates apparently moderates this claim immediately thereafter, claiming that death or banishment is not "great harm" (μεγάλα κακά, 30d3) and that doing something unjust is a "far greater" harm (πολὺ μᾶλλον, 30d4). However we are to understand Socrates' claims in the *Apology*, however, there is no evidence in the present passage of the more radical claim that bodily harm is not genuine harm, nor could it plausibly be the basis for Polemarchus's assent.

8. It is, of course, a question whether and in what sense a tamed horse is better or worse than an "unbroken" horse.

9. As Marx puts it, "The animal is immediately identical with its life-activity. It does not distinguish itself from it. It is *its life-activity*. Man makes his life-activity itself the object of his will and of his consciousness. He has conscious life activity. It is not a determination with which he directly merges. Conscious life-activity directly distinguishes man from animal life-activity" (1978a, 76). In more contemporary contexts, consider John McDowell's response to Philippa Foot's neo-Aristotelian account of "natural normativity" (McDowell 1998).

human excellence must include an account of each individual's excellence in the discovery or determination of the good for human beings.

Socrates' awareness of this difference between human beings and animals is not only obvious in general, it is also made manifest by the tentative way in which Socrates asks if he and Polemarchus should assert that human beings are the same as animals in this respect, that when they are harmed, they become worse with respect to human virtue.[10] Polemarchus eagerly asserts that the human being is the same as the animal in this respect, because unlike Socrates he takes a human being to be essentially determined by that human being's participation in the political community. To put this point in another way, Polemarchus abstracts from human interiority and simply equates "human being" and "citizen."[11] On the basis of this identification, Polemarchus's assumption that a human being who has been harmed is made worse with respect to human virtue begins to makes sense. If a human being is entirely or essentially identical to his participation in the activity of his political community, and most particularly to his participation in the aggressive or defensive military actions of his political community, then, as would be the case with a (cavalry) horse or a (guardian) dog, physically harming that human being is harming him in the most essential respect.

Consider in this context Socrates' description of Asclepius's "statesmanlike" prescription of a regimen designed "so as not to harm the city's affairs" at 407d–e. Asclepius, according to Socrates, only prescribed a regimen suited to curing the occasional illnesses of people who were basically healthy; regarding those with chronic illnesses, Asclepius "didn't think he should care for the man who's not able to live in his established rounds, on the grounds that he is no profit to himself or to the city." Now compare this description to Socrates' claim at 496b–c that, were it not for the "sickliness" of his body, "our companion Theages" would likely have been "exiled from philosophy." On Socrates' account, Theages' sickliness (which Socrates compares to a horse's bridle) restrained him from entering politics, and hence made possible a great good, perhaps the greatest good, for Theages' soul—the potential "to keep company with philosophy in a way that is worthy." However we are to understand Socrates' ultimate views on the relation between the individual and the political community, this much should be clear: Socrates recognizes, as Polemarchus does not, a fundamental distinction between human being and citizen.

---

10. The use of μή with the present subjunctive ('Ανθρώπους δέ, ὦ ἑταῖρε, μὴ οὕτω φῶμεν, βλαπτομένους εἰς τὴν ἀνθρωπείαν ἀρετὴν χείρους γίγνεσθαι; 335c1–2) indicates Socrates' doubt about the assertion. See Smyth 1920, §1801.

11. See §9.2 below.

The final argument in Socrates' refutation of Polemarchus's definition of justice is an argument that purports to demonstrate that it is not the work of the just man to harm either a friend or anyone else (335c–e). This argument reveals a corollary to Polemarchus's equation of the individual with his role in the political community, a corollary that will be very significant for our understanding of the dialogue as a whole. If an individual is entirely or essentially constituted by his participation in a political community, that is, if there is no meaningful distinction to be drawn between the role an individual plays in the community and the individual playing that role, that is, if there is no privacy of soul or human interiority, then there is no meaningful distinction to be drawn between just action and just intention; more generally, there is no meaningful distinction to be drawn between the relationships between members of the political community and the significance of those relationships for the individuals involved. On this view, a relationship between two members of the community cannot have divergent meanings for each individual; if it appears as if a relationship means different things to different people in the community, it can only be that one or more parties to this relationship is mistaken. The only meaning a relationship between different people in the community can have, the only true interpretation of that meaning, is the meaning given to it by "the people" as a whole. There is, in Polemarchus's vision of community, no space for questions concerning the possibility of communication between individuals. If the community as a whole, rather than the individuals making up that community, wholly determines the significance of relationships between individuals, there can be no problem of other minds. There is only community-mindedness or public-spiritedness. Consider, in this context, Polemarchus's assumption that he can speak for the dialogue's *mute personae*, and his arrogating to the just man the authority to determine what is good for his friends. The name we would give to the meaning or interpretation present in a "people" as a whole, as opposed to the interpretation of separate individuals, is the "political culture" of a people. In Polemarchus's vision of the political, it is the human being most at one with the dictates of this political culture who is most just.

Now consider Socrates' claim that the just man cannot harm, that is, make others unjust, by means of justice. The argument Socrates gives for this claim has two steps, and we will look as each in turn. In the first step Socrates asks Polemarchus two questions that are difficult to translate into English. Bloom translates these two questions as "Are musicians able to make men unmusical by music?" (Ἆρ' οὖν τῇ μουσικῇ οἱ μουσικοὶ ἀμούσους δύνανται ποιεῖν; 335c9) and "Are men skilled in horsemanship able to make men incompetent riders by horsemanship?" (Ἀλλὰ τῇ ἱππικῇ οἱ ἱππικοὶ ἀφίππους; 335c11) However, this translation tends to assimilate *hoi mousikoi* and *hoi hippikoi* too closely to the other craftsmen such as doctors and builders that Socrates invokes earlier in the discussion with Polemarchus, and it obscures the strict parallel between *amousos* and *aphippous* essential to Socrates' argument. What the translation does not make clear is that, unlike the arts of medicine and piloting, "music" and "horsemanship" were considered aspects of the aristocratic *culture* with which a well-bred gentleman was expected to have familiarity, and that "the musical" (ὁι μουσικοὶ) and "the horsemen" (ὁι ἱππικοὶ) were, in certain contexts, roughly synonymous with "gentlemen" (καλοὶ κἀγαθοί). So too, the terms *amousos* and *aphippous* do not primarily mean "bad at music" and "bad at riding," but rather "inexperienced with the Muses" and "inexperienced with horses." If, in particular, we translate the first of Socrates' questions as "Are the cultured able to make others uncouth by culture?" we can see more clearly why Polemarchus would deny that this is possible.[12] As Socrates argues in book 3, simple contact and familiarity with the right kind of rhythms, harmonies, and artifacts were thought to make a human being "graceful" (εὐσχήμων) and "a gentleman" (καλός τε κἀγαθός, 401e–402a).

We are now also prepared to see the relation between Polemarchus's denial that "the musical can make others unmusical by music," and his denial that the just can make others unjust by justice, or that the good (ὁι ἀγαθοὶ) can make others bad by virtue. Polemarchus implicitly believes that justice is synonymous with conformity to (one's own) political culture, as expressed by the laws and customs of the city and embodied in the citizenry as a whole. One becomes just, on this view, simply by assimilation to the dominant culture. In the dialogues, this belief is expressed most clearly by Meletus in the *Apology*. When Socrates asks Meletus who makes the youth of Athens better, as opposed to Socrates, who, Meletus claims, corrupts them, Meletus responds first by saying simply "the laws." When Socrates points out that his question was not what, but *who* makes the youth better, that is, who knows these very things (thus making clear that *hoi nomoi* refers here to both laws and customs), Meletus responds, under pressure of Socrates' questioning, by claiming that all Athenians know the law and all make the youth better with the sole exception of Socrates. The essence of Socrates' response to Meletus is also worth remembering at this point. Socrates argues that, just as all men are not able to make horses good, but rather it is one man, or at most a very few, who are able to make horses better, it is hardly possible that one person alone corrupts the youth while all the others make them better. As the rest of the *Apology* shows, it is the contrast

---

12. Without this understanding of ὁι μουσικοὶ and ὁι ἱππικοὶ, i.e., if we took Polemarchus simply to be denying that the musician can make others inept at music by means of the (technical) art of music, then his denial would seem to conflict with his apparent admission that the arts provide their possessors with the capacity for opposite effects (333e–334b). On this argument, see §3.3 below.

between, on the one hand, the body politic as a whole, a body constituted by the laws and customs of the city, and, on the other hand, the individual who is willing to inquire into what makes a human being good that is essential here.

We can now see the significance of the second step in Socrates' argument that the just man cannot make others unjust by justice. In this final step, Socrates compares the "work" of the good man to the "work" of the abstract properties of "heat" and "dryness," and argues that just as cooling is not the work of heat but its opposite, and wetting not the work of dryness but its opposite, so too harming is not the work of the good but of its opposite. Thus, Socrates concludes, it is not the work of the just man to harm either a friend or anyone else, but of his opposite, the unjust man. The problem with this argument is that Socrates here equates the natural causal power appropriate to explanations of changes in phys-ical bodies with the effects of human ethical action on the ethical character of human souls; as Julia Annas puts it, the problem with these examples is "that they leave out the element of agency altogether."[13] However, where Annas takes these examples as "not seriously meant" and merely intended "to make vivid the idea that no power can produce its opposite," it must be seen that Socrates would never casually or unintentionally allow for examples which blur the dis-tinction between natural causal explanations and explanations concerned with the orientation of human intentional actions toward the good. For this is to blur the distinction between "second sailing" and first (*Phaedo* 96a–100a).[14] What, then, is Socrates' intent in invoking these examples, or rather, deferring for the moment the question of Socrates' dialogic intent vis-à-vis Polemarchus, what is Socrates' apodeictic intent, that is, what does he wish to demonstrate to the assembled company or the auditors of his narration about Polemarchus's view of the political? I believe, as Annas's observation should suggest, that Socrates is pointing toward the inability of Polemarchus's view of the political to account for the possibility of human agency.

In the passage from the *Phaedo* just cited, Socrates distinguishes between what could be called the physical "cause" (αἰτία) and intelligible "cause" of his sitting in jail waiting to be executed by the order of the Athenian demos. He contends that it is an absurd misuse of language to call any of the relevant facts about the physical world the *aitiai* of his situation, a misapplication of a name founded on what Ryle would later call a "category mistake." To claim that facts about Socrates' body or physical environment could be blamed or held responsible (the root meanings of αἴτιος) for this state of affairs is, he claims, to fail to make a crucial distinction: the distinction between that which

---

13. Annas 1981, 33.
14. See the next paragraph and §3.4.3 below.

"in actuality" is responsible (for something) and that without which that which *is* responsible could never *be* responsible (for anything). To consider these physical conditions, rather than Socrates' "choice of what is best," responsible for what Socrates has done is, Socrates says, a very careless way of speaking. There are two things we should note about this passage before interpreting its significance for Socrates' discussion with Polemarchus. First, contrary to the dialogue's apparent dismissal of the body as a mere prison hampering a soul that would otherwise be free, Socrates' mere flesh and bones are explicitly presented here as necessary conditions for the possibility of Socrates doing anything at all. Second, despite Socrates' clear preference for the account which says that it is Socrates' choice, rather than the state of his body, which is responsible for his actions, he does not explicitly endorse the idea that his choice is that which is "in truth" responsible. He only makes clear that it is a much better candidate for responsibility than bones, sinews, and the like. The reason for his reticence in this regard is likely due to the fact that his choice of what is best depends on what seems to him good, and this depends in turn, Socrates seems to believe, on the good itself.

We must defer until a later chapter a discussion of the relation between an individual agent's choice and his perception of the good. For now, we can say at least this much about Socrates' account of agency in the *Phaedo:* on that account, despite the fact that any adequate account of human action must involve reference to physical facts as necessary conditions, such physical facts cannot be given explanatory priority. Explanatory priority must be given to the agent, his choice of what is best. Why should we accord explanatory priority to the agent and his choices? On this point, Socrates' account is less clear. But the context, particularly Socrates' concern with the problems of accounting for the unity and identity of generated things (96e–97b), suggests the following explanation. To describe something as an action, rather than an event, is to unite a series of states of affairs with respect to the individual whose action those states of affairs are said to instantiate; it is to say these states of affairs belong together *because* they all play a role in describing the intentional activity of an agent, and in our explanation it is the agent who is ultimately responsible for their belonging together. To identify an action is to see its unity and identity as dependent upon the unity and identity of an agent, and to attempt to understand what constitutes an action *as* an action (as opposed to an event) is, at least in part, to inquire into the conditions for that unity and identity.

For Socrates, this latter question, the question of the unity and identity of the human agent, is proximally a question of ethical psychology, that is, a question of what is or seems good for a human individual, and ultimately a question of the good itself. Deferring until our later discussion a further justification of these claims, we can nonetheless see how the above account of human action provides us with a context in which to understand the significance of Socrates' equation of the "work" of the just man with the "work" of the physical properties of heat and dryness. Polemarchus, I have argued, implicitly identifies the virtue of justice with conformity to political culture and with action in service of the polis. On Socrates' view, these two aspects of Polemarchus's vision of the political are in contradiction to one another. By allowing the city to interpret the significance of his actions, Polemarchus disavows his own agency and attempts to replace it with the agency of the city. Instead of the polis being understood as a necessary condition for the possibility of the ethical action of the individuals who participate in that polis, the individual citizens become, in effect, "members" of the body politic, whose interaction is understood as the necessary condition of the action of the city. But it is the city itself, not the members, which is ultimately responsible. On this view, justice, that is, the political culture of the polis, moves through the body politic like heat transferred from member to member without, so to speak, anyone being the wiser for it.

3.2 Disposition and Knowledge

I will now turn to the details of Socrates argument with Polemarchus, particularly focusing on his invocation of an analogy between justice and *technê*. I will allude to some general facets of the problem of justice raised by Socrates' use of the analogy between justice and the arts, but in so doing I will largely restrict myself to commenting on the work of other commentators on this passage.[15] My principal aim will be to show how Socrates' deployment of this analogy is part of an attempt on his part to demonstrate problems with Polemarchus's conception of political action. I will argue that Socrates is indicating the difficulties presented for a wholly political theory of human action and motivation; that is, a theory of human action and motivation that attempts to do without reference to any extrapolitical ends or goals for human action. More specifically, I will argue that Socrates' arguments and examples point toward an apparent difference in kind between ethical dispositions on the one hand, and knowledge

---

15. The most comprehensive treatment of the limitations of the *technê* analogy is Roochnik (1996). Commentators who claim that the Socrates' dialogue with Polemarchus is intended to show the problems with equating justice and art or craft include Annas 1981, Cross and Woozley 1964, Irwin 1995, and Reeve 1988. Beversluis argues, to the contrary, that "we are compelled on neither textual nor philosophical grounds to read the exchange between Socrates and Polemarchus as a criticism—much less, as a rejection—of the *technê*-analogy" (2000, 206). On Beversluis's interpretation, see note 7 below. For a recent defense of the craft analogy, see Parry 2003.

of ethical universals on the other, both of which seem to stand outside Pole-marchus's abstract vision of the political world and political action. In subsequent chapters we will see this conceptual division between ethical dispositions and ethical knowledge reflected in a series of oppositions which structure the argu-ment of the *Republic* as a whole, most centrally in the opposition between the "mathematical" and "musical" education of the guardians. For now, however, we must turn to Socrates' analogy between justice and *technê*, a dubious analogy in itself, but one well suited to demonstrating the inadequacies of Polemarchus's vision of the political world.

There are, it seems, two principal objections to Socrates' apparent character-ization of justice as a *technê*. First, the arts are each directed toward a particular end, the goodness of which is taken for granted in the practice of that art. Ques-tions concerning the worth of a given art must remain external to the practice of the art itself. Contrary to Socrates' suggestion in his account of Asclepius, if a doctor decides not to treat certain chronic illnesses because he deems it better for individuals having such illnesses to die than to live, this decision cannot be considered an aspect of the medical art as such.[16] The medical art, as such, is directed toward the goal of providing health to bodies or maintaining health in bodies; the question whether striving toward this goal is best for the overall welfare of the individual patient, while an important question concerning the practice of medicine, is not a question for which the medical art itself provides the resources to answer.[17] Unlike the art of medicine, which is conceived as good relative to a given end, if justice is a virtue, it is conceived as something unqualifiedly good. Second, as Aristotle argues, the arts insofar as they are conceived of as capacities directed toward a given end seem to be also capacities for the opposite of that end.[18] The art of medicine provides its possessor not only with the capacity for providing or maintaining health in bodies, but also with the capacity for producing illness in bodies. However, in describing a human being as just, we are attributing to that human being not merely a capacity for the kind of activity we would characterize as just, but also a *dispo-sition* to that kind of activity and the *intention* to engage in it *because* it is just. As Aristotle also argues, the virtuous human being, to be virtuous, must choose the right course of action for the right reasons (*Eth. Nic.* 1105a25–b10).

It has been noted by a number of commentators that these two objections can also be directed against Polemarchus's conception of justice as helping friends and harming enemies. What has not been made sufficiently clear by

16. Cf. Adeimantus's suggestion that such a decision belongs instead to the political art (407e).
17. See Annas 1981, 26; and Plato 1991, 322.
18. Cf. Reeve 1988, 8; and White 1979, 63–64.

these commentators, however, is the way that these two objections point to two distinct limitations on Polemarchus's account of justice—limitations on either side, so to speak, of Polemarchus's conception of the political and of human action. In the first objection the arts are seen as disanalogous to the virtues because the arts remain at the level of technical or "instrumental" reason and do not reflect, as ethical deliberation must, on the ethical status of the ends toward which our actions are directed. The arts seem to be unacceptable as analogues for the virtues, according to this objection, because they are insufficiently rational. The problem, we could say, is that the arts do not reach beyond the determinacy of a given practice or institution to the place of that practice or institution in a more comprehensive account of the good. In the second objection, by contrast, the arts are seen as disanalogous to the virtues because the arts, viewed as cognitive capacities, do not seem inherently limited with respect to the use that is made of them by the possessor of that capacity, nor do the arts seem to provide within them a source of motivation ensuring that they will be used well. The problem with the arts in this case, we could say, is that they do not reach down into the soul of the person possessing facility in the art. Seen in this light, these two objections allude to the horns of a dilemma concerning ethical deliberation and action familiar from dialogues such as the *Laches* and the *Charmides:* on the one hand, if the virtues are primarily understood as states or dispositions, they seem insufficiently reflective; on the other hand, if the virtues are understood primarily as varieties of knowledge, they seem insufficiently emotive.[19]

This dilemma recapitulates on the level of political action, that is, on the level appropriate to Polemarchus, the division between *logos* and *ergon* we first encountered in our discussion of "world view" and "ethos" in relation to Cephalus and the decadence of the Greek poetic and religious tradition. As I have argued, the decadence of the Greek religious tradition, coupled with the persistence of this tradition as a source of political authority, is the background against which we must view Polemarchus's attempt to understand human ethical life as wholly originating from and oriented to the autonomously conceived political community. That Socrates believes, to the contrary, that human ethical life must be directed toward something beyond the political as such is, perhaps, the one substantive issue upon which almost all interpreters of the *Republic* agree. Most interpreters also agree that such is the main upshot of Socrates' arguments with Polemarchus. I am also a party to this consensus. The main difference between my interpretation of this aspect of the dialogue and most

19. See R. E. Allen's introduction to the *Laches* (Plato 1996, 55–59).

other interpretations is the focus I want to put on the significance of Socrates' argument for the problem of human action.

I will argue that Socrates' analogy between justice and *technê* is meant to indicate the ways in which Polemarchus's conception of the virtue of justice is subject to both of the horns of the dilemma adumbrated above.[20] In particular, I will argue that insofar as Polemarchus orients his understanding of human ethical life entirely with reference to a given political community, and lacks both an extrapolitical conception of human nature and an extrapolitical conception of the end or goal of human action, his conception of justice can provide neither an account of what distinguishes justice as intrinsically, rather than instrumentally, good nor an account of the human motivation to be just. I will also argue that Socrates' argument gestures toward a specific *technê* which, if not wholly immune to the force of Socrates' objections, could at the very least go a long way toward responding to the putative deficiencies of the analogy between justice and *technê*. This art is the art of politics, or more specifically, the legislative branch of that art. I will argue that Polemarchus's failure to consider the art of politics indicates inadequacies in his self-conscious relation to the good with which he most closely identifies, the good of ethical and political action.

3.3 Means and Ends

I have suggested that Socrates' deployment of the analogy between justice and *technê* gestures toward a dilemma concerning our way of understanding the virtues, a dilemma whose horns are (1) an understanding of the virtues as dispositions or states of character, which seems to unacceptably limit the role of reason in the exercise of the virtues; and (2) an understanding of the virtues as cognitive capacities, which seems unable to account for the motivation to be virtuous. That Socrates' introduction of the analogy between justice and *technê* gestures toward the first horn of our dilemma we can see both by the examples he uses and the way in which he introduces these examples. He begins his comparison between justice and the arts with the art of medicine and the putative art of cooking, and asks Polemarchus, here standing in for Simonides, to say to what each of these arts gives that which is owed or fitting. Polemarchus responds

20. Compare Annas's contention that Socrates' invocation of the *technê* analogy is directed at Polemarchus's implicit belief that justice is the skill of helping friends and harming enemies (1981, 27). Beversluis claims, in response, that "the text provides no good reason for believing that this is true" (2000, 210). However, one will find Beversluis's argument persuasive only to the degree one accepts his rather restricted conception of how one might attribute beliefs to Platonic characters.

that medicine gives drugs, food, and drinks to bodies and that cooking gives seasonings to meats. It is clear, however, in each case that these answers are incomplete without the addition of the specific end toward which each art or pseudo-art is directed. The art of medicine, we would say, gives drugs, foods and drinks to bodies *for the sake of health,* and the art of cooking gives seasonings to meats *for the sake of pleasure.* While Polemarchus considers drugs, in the case of medicine, and seasonings, in the case of cooking, to "belong" to their respective objects, this belonging must be understood with respect to that for the sake of which each art is constituted as an art; that is, it is only with respect to the goal of producing or maintaining health in bodies that, in giving drugs to bodies, the medical art gives what is fitting or belongs to bodies. Furthermore, by choosing medicine and cooking as his examples of putative arts, Socrates makes clear both that it is open to question whether the goods internal to a given art are simply good and that it is open to question whether the goods internal to different arts are even compatible.

Socrates continues his *elenchus* of Polemarchus's instrumental conception of justice by arguing that for each kind of technical advantage or disadvantage the just human being could hope to effect (for friends and enemies respectively) there exists someone with a technical competence in a given field of endeavor more able to help and harm than the just man. Thus, with respect to disease and health, the doctor is more able to help and harm, with respect to danger at sea the pilot is more able to help and harm, and so on. Socrates does not invoke this same argument, however, in response to Polemarchus's suggestion that the just man is most able to help friends and harm enemies in "making war and being an ally in battle," though his subsequent mention of the soldier's art (336d6–8) makes clear that he could argue that it is the professional soldier who is most able to help friends and harm enemies in war (cf. 374a–d, 422b). Instead, he accepts Polemarchus's assertion that the just man is the most capable or powerful (δυνατώτατος) ally in battle, and asks whether justice is useful (χρήσιμον) only in times of war. Polemarchus maintains, to the contrary, that the just man is most useful at acquiring contracts (τὰ συμβόλαια), that is, partnerships (τὰ κοινωνήματα), in particular those concerning money (εἰς ἀργυρίου). Pursuing the same argumentative strategy that he had with regard to the just man's capacity to help friends and harm enemies, Socrates brings Polemarchus to the conclusion that whenever money is to be used in partnerships, someone with some particular knowledge or capacity *other* than justice will be the most useful partner, and in the course of this argument justice is relegated to the role of guarding those possessions which are not currently in use. Socrates argues that, according the view Polemarchus is defending, justice is useless when each thing is to be used and useful only when each thing is useless. If it is analogous to the arts, Socrates concludes, justice isn't anything very serious.

We are now prepared to see the ways in which Polemarchus's conception of justice exhibits the same kind of inadequacies as the "instrumental" reasoning inherent in the arts. Like the conception of justice as an art, Polemarchus's definition of justice suffers from the defect that it is entirely relative to preexisting institutions, in this case political institutions, or rather, one political institution, the polis, the goodness or justice of which Polemarchus simply takes as given. His initial conception of the just man is of a man who actively and successfully participates in a political association or community (κοινωνία). He seems not to have considered, however, the question of the justice of a given community as constituted.[21] He seems indifferent to the difference between regimes and, as we have seen, equates the excellence of the good citizen with the excellence of the good man.[22] As Aristotle argues, however, the excellence of a citizen qua citizen is relative to the constitution of the regime. Since there are several different kinds of constitutions, there cannot be "a single absolute excellence of the good citizen." But, Aristotle continues, "the good man is a man so called in virtue of a single absolute excellence" (*Pol.* 1276b30–33).[23] Nor does Polemarchus seem to have considered any extrapolitical ends for the sake of which a given political association may be constituted. As we have seen, Aristotle argues that the only community that deserves the name of polis, that is, the community that is political in the highest sense, is one that is constituted for the sake of virtue. While Polemarchus conceives of justice not only as a virtue, but as the whole of virtue, his understanding of virtue is limited to what have been called the "executive" virtues, or more precisely, his initial understanding of virtue is limited to the executive function that has been attributed to certain virtues.[24] He thinks of justice as a capacity to make commitments, and stand by those commitments once made, without having bothered to think too much about what kind of commitments could qualify as justly engaged in and justly honored.

Socrates does not directly address either the question of the difference between the excellence of the good citizen and the excellence of the good human being or the question of the end toward which a political association is directed

21. Cf. Benardete 1989b, 16–17; and Strauss 1978, 70.

22. For Polemarchus's equation of justice with human excellence *tout court*, see 335c4. See also Aristotle *Eth. Nic.* 1129b20–30.

23. Aristotle's argument depends on the unstated assumption that constitutions differ in a respect which is relevant to the excellence of the citizen. However, elsewhere Aristotle makes clear that the roles assigned to citizens vary in different constitutions, and that, moreover, there are degenerate forms of constitution. Cf. R. F. Stalley's note (Aristotle 1995, 352).

24. On "executive virtues," see Pears 1978.

in his refutation of Polemarchus. In fact, in Socrates' entire dialogue with Polemarchus he avoids mentioning a putative art which, if not immune to the
force of the objection that any art lacks the reflective resources necessary to
stand in as a sufficient analogue for the virtue of justice, at least could go much
further in this direction than any of the arts Socrates explicitly mentions. This
putative art is the art of politics (ἡ πολιτικὴ τέχνη), which Socrates contends
in the *Charmides* is the "knowledge of the absence or presence of knowledge of
justice" (170b), and which he contends in the *Gorgias* comprises legislation
(νομοθετική) and justice (δικαιοσύνη) as its parts. The legislative function of
the art of politics, which will so dominate Socrates' conversation with Glaucon
and Adeimantus—his fellow "lawgivers" to the city in speech—is pointedly
absent from Socrates' argument with Polemarchus.

Moreover, Socrates' grouping together of medicine, cooking, and justice
seems designed to call to mind the above-mentioned passage from the *Gorgias,*
and with it the absence of the legislative function of the art of politics. In this
passage Socrates elaborates and explains (to Gorgias) his claim (to Polus) that
rhetoric is not art, but rather a form of flattery that imitates the part of the art
of politics called justice. Socrates claims to recognize two genuine arts concerned with caring for the good condition of human beings, which arts are
each subdivided into two parts. The two genuine arts are one unnamed art,
comprising gymnastic and medicine, which cares for the good condition of the
body, and the political art, comprising legislation and justice, which cares for
the good condition of the soul. The genuine sub-arts, Socrates contends, are
each imitated by a form of flattery, with cosmetic imitating gymnastic, cooking
imitating medicine, sophistry imitating legislation, and rhetoric imitating justice.

If we can take this passage from the *Gorgias* as context for the *Republic*—
and I have already suggested reasons for believing that we can—it seems that,
by having Socrates compare justice to medicine and cooking, but not to
gymnastic or cosmetic, Plato seems to be pointing to the significance of the
absence of the legislative function of the art of politics from the conversation.
On Socrates' account in the *Gorgias,* each pair of sub-arts is composed of a
member which is remedial or rehabilitative and a member which is productive or constitutive. Elsewhere in the *Gorgias* Socrates makes clear that, in this
dialogue at least, (1) he takes gymnastic to be productive of strength and
beauty in bodies (452b), (2) he takes medicine to be rehabilitative of a body
which has acquired some illness or defect (478b–d), and (3) he takes justice to
be rehabilitative of a soul which has acquired some illness or defect (478bff.). If,
then, the analogy between these four sub-arts holds in this regard, as medicine
rehabilitates a body that has acquired some defect, while gymnastic is originally
productive of the good condition of bodies, insofar as justice is considered

rehabilitative of a soul that has acquired a defect, legislation must be considered as originally productive of the good condition of souls.[25]

Clearly this understanding of the function of the legislative branch of the art of politics as productive of the good condition of souls is consonant with much of Socrates' explicit argument in the *Republic*. As such, it provides a powerful contrast to the instrumental reasoning involved in the arts Socrates mentions here. It remains an open question, of course, whether or in what sense legislation is an art. However, it is telling nonetheless that neither Socrates nor Polemarchus mentions it, or the political art in general, in their discussion of the "art" of justice. Obviously, as both the *Republic* and the *Gorgias* demonstrate, Socrates' silence here cannot be because he is unaware of the possibility of conceiving politics and legislation as *technai*. The reasons for his failure to explicitly address the art of politics must wait, however, until we turn to our discussion of the aspects of Socrates' dialogic *pragma* revealed in his conversation with Polemarchus. In Polemarchus's case, however, it is clear that he fails to mention the art of legislation because this alternative simply doesn't occur to him. This is most telling because it is the art of politics, and in particular its legislative function, which provides the best candidate for an art which could correspond to Polemarchus's original definition. It is the laws, we could say, if they are well constituted, that benefit good men, that is, friends of the polis and harm bad men, that is, enemies of the people. And it is the (sub-)art of legislation, if any art at all, that would ensure that the laws are well constituted.

Despite the fact that the legislative function of the art of politics would have provided the best candidate for an art which could support the manifest content of Polemarchus's original definition, it is in no way surprising that Polemarchus does not make this suggestion. The notion of an art of legislation points immediately toward the historical contingency of the most sovereign laws of the polis and hence raises the question of whether the laws which constitute his polis, and not some other polis, are best. Polemarchus's strict identification of the common good with the good of the polis itself does not allow him to look beyond the determinacy of the polis to the question of whether its laws are good or bad. Moreover, the notion of an art of legislation points toward the possibility that some one individual, or a very few, might have the requisite knowledge to truly benefit good human beings, or at least avoid harming them. Polemarchus's democratic political sympathies, and more so, his willingness to relinquish his individual responsibility for judgment about good and bad in favor of the judgments of the city as a whole, make this latter suggestion most disquieting.

25. On the relation between the art of medicine and the legislative art, see Moes 2001.

Most significant, however, for the reading I want to offer is the implicit consequence of the absence of the art of legislation for Polemarchus's conception of political action. Polemarchus, as we have seen, equates excellence with political action, but he wants to leave the prescription of the ends of ethical action entirely up to the body politic. Returning in this context to Socrates' analogy between the excellence of horses and the excellence of human beings, just as the excellence proper to these animals can be seen as an immediate expression of their nature, Polemarchus wants the excellence proper to ethical action to be an immediate expression of one's status as a citizen. However, insofar as the animal is an immediate expression of its nature or life-activity, it is not the individual animal that is *responsible* (in the explanatory sense used above) for its actions, but rather the species to which the animal belongs. That is, we do not in general explain the purposive activity of animals with regard to ends proper to the animal as an individual, but rather with regard to the natural character of the species; the individual animal cannot for this reason be conceived of as an agent, precisely because its activity belongs in the relevant sense not to the individual animal but to the species as a whole. Polemarchus, in aspiring to an excellence which would be the immediate expression of one's status as a citizen, wants to be, in Marx's terms, identical to his "species-being" (*Gattungswesen*), but in this case the relevant "species" is "Athenian citizen" and not "human being" *tout court*.[26] However, on Polemarchus's conception of the political, it is not the individual human being to which we should attribute agency, but rather the relevant "species."

To be considered an agent, a human being must be considered responsible, in the relevant sense, for his actions. But we can only ascribe that kind of responsibility to a human being if that human being *takes up* that responsibility, and the way a human being takes up responsibility is by "legislating" proximal ends with respect to her perception of what is best, by "deciding" (αἱρέω, in the *Phaedo* passage), that is, "resolving upon a purpose" (προαίρεσις, in both Plato and Aristotle). It is these decisions or purposes or intentions, resolved upon by the individual human agent, that allow us to ascribe her actions to him, and it is only in this sense that they can be conceived as *her* actions, as opposed to the movements of her body or the expression of the political culture in which she participates. Both Plato and Aristotle suggest that insofar as one acts, that is, insofar as one is responsible in the relevant sense, one acts within the context of some sort of political community.[27] However, Polemarchus's mistake is to confuse or conflate "that without which one cannot be responsible"

26. Marx 1978a, 114–16.
27. See §§9.7 and 9.8 below.

with "that which is responsible"; he mistakes the fact that participation in a political community is necessary for ethical action with the idea that such participation is sufficient for ethical action. By so doing he deprives himself of the very good with which he identifies, the good of political action, for in the end it is not he, but the polis, which "acts," using Polemarchus merely as an instrument for "purposes" that are not truly his own.

3.4 Use and Abuse

In the next stage of Socrates' argument, he turns to the second horn of the dilemma concerning ethical action cited above, in which the virtues are conceived of as cognitive capacities, and thereby seem to be unable to account for an individual's motivation to be virtuous. Socrates now focuses not on the arts themselves but rather on the native capacity or cleverness (δεινότης) of the human being proficient in the arts. With an odd four-step argument Socrates brings Polemarchus to the conclusion that proficiency in the arts is entirely value-neutral and that the art of justice is a much an art of stealing as it is an art of guarding against theft. Despite its oddity, many commentators take Socrates' argument concerning the value-neutral character of capacity in the arts to be relatively straightforward in intent,[28] and the tendency to take it at face value is no doubt fostered by the fact that Aristotle makes a similar claim in *his* refutation of the supposition that justice is an art. However, once we look to the details of Socrates' argument, we will see it is anything but straightforward. In short, the individual claims that Socrates and Polemarchus agree upon are highly questionable, and even under the most charitable of interpretations the inferences are invalid. I will first catalogue these defects in the argument before turning to an interpretation of their significance.

Socrates begins his argument by offering three examples of a capacity that putatively comprehends opposite ends. First, he asks Polemarchus whether the man who is cleverest (δεινότατος) at landing a blow, either in boxing or some other kind of fight, isn't also the cleverest at guarding against it. Second, he asks whether the person who is cleverest at guarding against disease is also the cleverest at getting away with producing it unnoticed. Finally, he asks whether the one who is a good guardian (ὁ αὐτὸς φύλαξ ἀγαθός) of a military encampment is not also the person who can steal the enemy's "plans and other dispositions" (βουλεύματα καὶ τὰς ἄλλας πράξεις). On the basis of these three examples, Socrates concludes that whenever someone is a clever guardian he is

28. Cf. Adam's appendix II to book I (Plato 1963).

also a clever thief, and thus, if the just person is clever at guarding money, he must also be clever at stealing it. This is a conclusion with which Polemarchus is understandably uncomfortable, and one he could have avoided had he objected to either Socrates' questionable claims or his questionable logic.

The movement from the first example to the last is also a movement from the least to the most plausible candidate for a supposed capacity for opposites. Despite Polemarchus's quick assent, the claim that the man most skilled in landing a blow in a fight is also the one most skilled at guarding against a blow is, I believe, simply false, and is at the very least highly questionable. Not only do different highly skilled fighters seem more or less apt at offensive and defensive maneuvers, but different styles of physical combat focus more or less on one or the other capacity.[29] Nor does Socrates seem generally insensitive to or inexperienced in the difference between various forms of physical combat.[30] Both differences in physical constitution and different kinds of training and experience are necessary for being the most skilled at either offensive or defensive maneuvers. Moving to Socrates' second example, even if we were to grant that the man with knowledge of health and sickness is both the most able to guard against disease and to introduce it into the body, the addition of producing it "without being noticed" (λαθεῖν) seems to bring in a quite different capacity than that which comes with knowledge of medicine, one which is at least as extraneous to the medical art as the earning of wages (cf. 346b). That is, we have very little reason to suspect that the human being with the most skill in caring for the sick has either the character or the experience necessary to make him the most skilled at surreptitiously introducing illness. Socrates' final example, the guardian, while the most likely candidate for a capacity that must comprehend opposites, gains its credibility as a claim at the expense of making Socrates' argument totally invalid; it is a complete non sequitur. It differs radically from the previous two examples both in the way it is phrased and in the content of the example. Whereas in the previous two examples Socrates spoke of a cleverness or native capacity (δεινότης), here Socrates describes the guardian simply as good (ἀγαθός) without gesturing toward any particular capacity that constitutes the goodness of the guardian. In this case Socrates does not argue, most implausibly, that the man who is best at staying at his sentry post is also the man most skilled at infiltrating the enemy camp without being noticed. Instead he makes the quite different, and quite plausible, claim that the good guardian of an army is the very man who can steal the enemy's plans. This example gains its force from the fact that Socrates has shifted from relative judgments related to an

29. Beversluis 2000, 216.
30. See *Lach.* 191a–c.

individual's dispositional capacities (i.e., artifacts of constitution, character, or training) to an absolute judgment related to the end toward which an activity is directed. However, once he has secured Polemarchus's agreement to this claim, he immediately shifts back to speaking of the cleverness or native capacity of the guardian, concluding that the argument shows that "of whatever a man is a clever [δεινός] guardian, he is also a clever [δεινός] thief."

Thus, Socrates' inferences are invalid and the individual claims to which Polemarchus agrees are at least arguable, and probably false.[31] What, then, is Socrates trying to demonstrate with this argument? He is trying to demonstrate, I believe, the problem of the relation between dispositions to act and the ends of action. If we compare Socrates' three examples, we can see that they form something of an ascending series, each dealing with quite different kinds of ability, indeed quite different senses of what we mean by "ability." He begins with the art of hand-to-hand combat, in which training in the art expresses itself in physical capacities of the individual. He then moves to the art of medicine, but with the addition of what seems to be a capacity of psychological or ethical character, the ability to deceive. He then ends in the "art" of guarding, which seems in his example not to be a determinate capacity of any kind, but to comprehend whatever will result in ensuring the preservation of the military camp. Moreover, as the argument of books 2–5 shows, it is by no means clear that everything that is required for guarding an army or a city can be characteristic of any one individual.

Polemarchus does not recognize the difference in level between these three examples. Nor does he notice the radical difference between the kinds of "training" required for the forming of the individual who is most adept at guarding against blows, the individual who is most able to do *anything* "unnoticed," and the individual who is a "good guardian." Polemarchus's failure to recognize these distinctions is, I believe, the complement to his failure to consider the legislative branch of the art of politics. If, as I have suggested, human agency requires

31. By shifting the key term in his argument between "clever" or "adept" (δεινός) and "good" (ἀγαθός), Socrates invalidates his argument, unless we are to assume that these words can be taken as functionally synonymous. Elsewhere in the dialogues, however, Socrates shows exactly how strange any easy transition between *deinos* and *agathos* should sound to an attentive listener. The adjective *deinos* is etymologically related to *deos*, a word that means "fear," "awe," or "terror," and the original meaning of *deinos* was "fearful," "awesome" or "terrifying." It came to mean "clever," in somewhat the same way that the English word "terror" spawned the adjective "terrific." Unlike that English adjective, however, *deinos* maintained a much closer relationship to the original signification of something to be feared. Thus, Socrates can say at *Protagoras* 341a–b that Prodicus has instructed him not to say that Protagoras is an "awfully wise man" (σοφὸς καὶ δεινός . . . ἀνήρ), for by "awful" (δεινός) we generally mean something bad, and at *Laches* 198d Socrates comes very close to defining *deinos* as that which is to be feared. Thus, it is not only at a formal level that Socrates invalidates his argument by shifting from "clever" to "good"; the semantic range of these two terms differs significantly.

"legislating" proximal ends with respect to our perception of what is best, and taking up individual responsibility for our actions, this is by no means all that human agency requires. It is also necessary, obviously, for us to be able to carry out or enact the purposes we have set for ourselves, for no one, it seems, would call an action something that we have decided to do but were not actually able to do. The necessity of enacting our decisions presents three problems for the prospective agent, one practical, one psychological, and one epistemic, which correspond to the three levels of Socrates' examples, and I will treat each problem in turn. While I believe that Socrates considers the epistemic problem to be, finally, the deepest and most interesting of the three, I will focus primarily on the psychological problem. One reason for this is that, while the practical and epistemic problems must be faced by any account of human agency, the psychological problem only arises for a particularly robust conception of human agency such as the one Socrates apparently holds. In addition to discussing the significance of the practical, psychological, and epistemic problems facing the prospective agent, I will show how these three problems gesture toward, respectively, the gymnastic, the musical, and the philosophical educations that Socrates lays out for the guardians/philosopher-rulers of the city in speech.

3.4.1 The Practical Problem and Gymnastic

The practical problem facing a prospective agent who wants to enact the proximal ends she has set for herself is that she must take into account her physical capacities, her temperament, and her character and consider whether those capacities, temperament, and character are suited or unsuited to the projected goal of her actions. If she decides that her capacities, temperament, and character are unsuited to her projected goal, she must either reassess the proximal ends she has set for herself or undertake to train her capacities and reform her character in such a way that she is up to the task she has set herself. If her capacities, temperament, and character are manifestly unsuited to the task she sets for herself, and she does not train her capacities or reform her character, not only is she unlikely to achieve the result she desires, even if she were to achieve that result, it would be open to question whether we can ascribe that result to her agency.[32]

Socrates' account of the gymnastic education of the guardians seems primarily directed at addressing the practical problem of agency, though, of course, at this

---

32. If, for example, I were to attempt to break the world record in the high jump, and somehow crossed the bar without knocking it down, any sane person should look for some other causal factor (bizarrely directed hurricane-force winds?) responsible for that state of affairs, and not ascribe it to my successfully enacting my intention.

stage of their education the guardians are not legislating ends for themselves, but instead seek to enact the ends decided upon by the "lawgivers" of the city in speech, or later, the philosopher-rulers. Socrates' account of gymnastic begins as a training directed toward the body (376e, 403c–404e), but changes to an education of the soul (410b–d), an education whose principal function seems to be habituating the characters of the guardians so that they exhibit the "executive" functions associated with the virtues of courage and temperance. That is, an appropriate training in gymnastic will prevent the guardians from being "softer than they ought" and will allow them to exhibit what Socrates calls "political courage," that is, "the preservation, through everything, of the right and lawful opinion about what is terrible, and what not" (430a–b). As this description indicates, even when gymnastic is treated as an education directed at the soul and toward the cultivation of character, "character" is here conceived in quasi-physicalist terms, as "mettle" that needs to be appropriately "tempered" if the guardians are to be able to perform their assigned roles in the city. A correct gymnastic education will not help the guardians, or anyone, Socrates seems to suggest, know what the best thing to do is, but once they have decided—or been told—what they must do, the correct gymnastic education will make it more likely that they persevere in the face of those pleasures and pains, fears and desires, which would otherwise have turned them aside from their appointed task.

3.4.2 The Psychological Problem and Music

The psychological problem is not only more complex, there is more room for controversy over the question of whether it represents a genuine problem for human agency. I think it can hardly be doubted, however, that it represents a problem for the theory of human agency Socrates seems to hold in the dialogues. The problem can be stated in the following way: to consider a decision and the action arising from that decision as genuinely our own, not only does it seem necessary for us to legislate proximal ends with respect to what seems best to us, but we must also be able to *experience* those ends as our own. Otherwise we experience ourselves as divided, as in conflict with ourselves. If that conflict remains present to us, we can find ourselves pursuing some goal that seems, in some sense, foreign to us. In such a case we might consider not ourselves but rather something "in us" which is nonetheless "external" to ourselves as really responsible for our doings.[33] This aspect of mental conflict is the flip side of the phenomenon known as *akrasia* (Plato's term is ἀκράτεια) or "weakness of the

---

33. See Watson 1987; cf. Velleman 2008.

will," wherein *despite* our legislation of proximal ends for ourselves we find ourselves doing something which conflicts with that legislation. In either case we have reason to doubt whether the relevant actor is the individual agent and not some sub-agential drive or desire or aspect of soul.

It is often claimed that Socrates denies the phenomenon of *akrasia*. If this is supposed to mean that Socrates denies that people are disposed to say of themselves that they acted against their knowledge of what is best for themselves, this claim is obviously false, for if that were the case Socrates would have no position to argue against. Nor, for that very reason, could Socrates deny that people do things for which they *believe* they have less good reasons than they have for another course of action, for if someone believes that he acted against his knowledge of what is best for himself, he clearly believes he did something for which had less good reasons for doing than not doing. What is it that Socrates denies, then? Socrates denies that the person who says that he acted against his knowledge of what is best for himself is correct in attributing to himself knowledge of what is best for himself. Moreover, while in most other contexts we would be very ill-advised to substitute "justified true belief" for "knowledge" in characterizing Socrates' views, I believe in this case we can say that Socrates would deny that such an individual would be wrong in attributing to himself justified true belief about what is best for himself. This is due to the fact that the very presence of psychic conflict undermines the claim to have adequately justified belief about what is best for oneself. Socrates would argue that if a person pursues one course of action while telling himself that he knows another course of action would be better for himself, the conviction favoring the "better" course of action must be experienced by that person as less than adequately justified. As G. R. F. Ferrari has argued, the argument of the *Protagoras* shows that on Socrates' view the phenomenon of *akrasia* demonstrates that the akratic would-be agent is both ignorant of what is best for himself, and ignorant of that very ignorance.[34]

Clearly, the account Socrates gives in the *Republic* of the rule of the philosophic aspect of the soul is meant to address the problem of the soul divided against itself. For Socrates contends that it is only with this kind of rule in the soul that the different aspects of the soul are said to be in harmony with one another; any other kind of rule in the soul requires the forcible repression of other aspects of soul. On Socrates' view, in an individual who is psychically divided against himself, it is not that individual but merely some aspect of that individual which is the relevant actor here. This is one sense is which our "legislations" or life-projects can be experienced as foreign to us, or heteronomous.

---

34. Ferrari 1990a; see also Ferrari 2007b.

This characterization becomes more plausible once we recall the account of the heteronomy of the desires given above (§2.9) and the relation, demonstrated in Socrates' account of the decline of the regimes, between the individual's legislation of proximal ends for himself and the political and cultural context in which an individual legislates ends for himself. What must be recognized is the way that the argument of the decline of the regimes depends on the process by which an individual internalizes and identifies with a variety of different kinds of lives and life-projects and modes of social justification. In this account, it is only the philosophic individual who is not internally conflicted, both about what he wants and, more significantly *who he wants to be*.

Consider, in this context, Socrates' description (at 561a–e) of the democratic man who lives according to the maxim that all desires "are alike and must be honored on an equal basis," the man committed, as Adeimantus says, to "the law of equality." Particularly in the case of the democratic man, Socrates' "analogy" between city and soul seems to be no mere analogy. The democratic man is said to be "filled with the greatest number of characters [πλείστων ἠθῶν μεστόν] and beautiful and many-colored, just as that city [ὥσπερ ἐκείνην τὴν πόλιν]."[35] What it means for the democratic man to be "filled with" different "characters" is made clear in Socrates' previous statement about him. Socrates says, "Sometimes it is as if here were spending his time in philosophy. Often he does politics, jumping up and saying and doing whatever comes to him. Should he at some time emulate warriors, he turns he turns that way; and if it's money-makers, he turns in that one" (561d, trans. altered). As this description indicates, the conflict within the democratic individual's soul is not a conflict simply between object preferences but between his identification with and admiration of different ways of life, ways of life that have, or should have, radically different modes of justification. This conflict within the democratic man indicates that he possesses no unified sense of self, no reasonably well-integrated identity with respect to which his actions can be justifiably considered his own and not the effect upon him of the competing claims to the best life offered by his internalized representatives of the "philosophic," "honor-loving," and "money-loving" lives. Thus, Socrates intimates, his actions are never his own, his various sayings and doings come to him by chance (τύχῃ).

I have argued that to address the practical problem facing a prospective agent, she must assess her physical capacities, temperament, and character to see if these are likely to enable her to perform the task she had set for herself,

---

35. As opposed to the timocratic man, who is said by Socrates to *correspond to* the timocratic *regime* (κατὰ ταύτην τὴν πολιτείαν, 548d6) and by Adeimantus to be like that regime, or the oligarchic man, who is said by Socrates to be *similar to* the oligarchic regime and *correspond to* the oligarchic city, the democratic man is said to be "just as" the democratic city.

and if she finds they were not, she must either reformulate the proximal ends she has set for herself or appropriately train her capacities and habituate her character with these ends in mind. So, too, it seems that addressing the psychological problem facing a prospective agent can involve a kind of assessment, training, and habituation. In this case, however, the assessment must be directed toward recognizing conflict in the soul. Perhaps this conflict is easily detected and fairly easy to understand, for example a conflict between a newly chosen course of action and a desire to cling to the comfort and familiarity of an old habit, in which case the training necessary can be as simple as habituating oneself to this new course. However, conflict in the soul can be much more difficult to detect, and once detected even more difficult to understand. Before one can seek to reeducate his desires, he must understand those desires. He must know what it is he wants, and what a human being wants, it is safe to say, is not always coincident with what he says to himself he wants.

Consider, for example, an imperfectly "oligarchic man" who slips and indulges one of his "unnecessary" desires (558d–559d). It is likely that such a man would call himself *akratic* and say that his desire for pleasure won out over what he knows or believes to be best, that is, the accumulation of wealth. But looking back to Socrates' account of his generation (553b–d), a more likely hypothesis is that this man is not entirely convinced that the single-minded accumulation of wealth is what is best for him. (Indeed, Socrates' description makes clear that he believes that no one could be truly "single-minded" about the pursuit of wealth.) Recall that this man had emulated as a youth his timocratic father, and it is his father's ruin at the hands of his political enemies and his own subsequent poverty and humiliation that inspires his turn to money-making, a turn Socrates describes as motivated and maintained by fear, not by desire. His pursuit of wealth and the ruling status he accords it in his soul is pathologically conditioned; he holds down the other aspects of his soul, Socrates says, "not by persuading them that 'they had better not,' nor by taming them with argument, but by necessity and fear, doing so because he trembles for his whole substance" (554d). The pathological character of his pursuit of wealth is most clearly demonstrated by the way he is said to humiliate the calculating and spirited aspects of his soul, as he was once humiliated because of his father's failed pursuit of glory, and by the fact that he is said to let the calculating aspect consider *nothing* but where he is likely to make more money, and the spirited aspect honor *nothing* but wealth and the wealthy. If such a pathologically conditioned character should slip in his restricting himself to the necessary desires, it would hardly be surprising. However, before he was in any position to try to reeducate his desires in such a way that he would not have to forcibly repress the greater part of his soul, he would have to understand much better than he does the source of his conflict. This man does not just need rehabituation; this man needs therapy. Before he can attempt to construct for himself a reasonably well-integrated identity, he needs to understand the ways in which he has been lying to himself about what he knows and doesn't know about what is best.

It is, of course, much easier to see the way that Socrates' account of the musical education of the guardians correlates to the kind of habituation required in the simple case, the case of a conflict in the soul that is readily detectable and easily resolvable. Unlike gymnastic, which was primarily directed at the "executive" functions of virtue, the musical education is directed to an education of the desires, designed first and foremost to prevent conflicts of desire among the guardians as a class and in the individual souls of each guardian. In the first instance, this means providing models for admiration and aspiration that bind the young guardians to their city. These models and the rhythms and harmonies that follow from them are meant to bind the guardians to the city and to one another by establishing "a community of pleasure and pain" (462b) whereby each of the guardians is disposed to call the same things "my own" (462c). Thereby, the city in speech is made to conform to one of the two divergent principles Socrates sets down as the greatest good for a city: "that which binds it together and makes it one" (462b). Famously, one of the "musical" devices the founders of the city use for the sake of unity among the citizens in general is the "noble" or "well-born" lie, which claims that all of the citizens were born of the land itself and that "they must think of the other citizens as brothers and born of the earth" (414e). Moreover, with regard to the guardian-auxiliaries in particular, "a community of pleasure and pain" will be achieved to the highest degree possible by instituting the "community of women and children" wherein no child will know his parent or parent his child. The only way this community of women and children can be maintained, however, is by means of "a throng of lies and deceptions" practiced by the rulers for the sake of the ruled.

However, the musical education is also said to educate the desires of the guardians in a quite different way, and to inculcate a different, and seemingly contradictory, capacity in the souls of the guardians. Socrates says that the man who receives the finest musical education and has been properly reared among the products of craftsmen "whose good natural endowments make them able to track down the nature of what is fine" will have "the sharpest sense for *what has been left out* and what isn't a fine product of craft or what isn't a fine product of nature" (401c–e, emphasis added). That is, the best students among the guardian-auxiliaries will have the capacity to see beyond the limits of the education that they have received. It is from their ranks that the next generation of rulers will be chosen, and however we are to understand the latter stages of the education of the philosopher-rulers, one thing is clear. The next generation of rulers will have to confront the fact that they have been systematically lied to by the previous generation. They must come to learn, at least, that they had individual fathers and mothers, because they must be the ones implementing the program of breeding, and using a throng of lies and deceptions to maintain it. Moreover, if the philosopher-rulers are imagined to have ascended beyond the cave of their musical education altogether, they will see that all the lies that they have been told are lies, not least the "well-born lie" of autochthony which originally bound them to the city and their fellow citizens.

3.4.3 The Epistemic Problem and Philosophy

The mention of the philosopher-rulers' putative ascent out of the cave brings us to the last of our three problems facing a prospective agent. The epistemic problem for a potential agent who wants to enact her intentions is simply stated: to consider an agent responsible for her action in the relevant sense, she must be actually doing what she thinks she is doing. This is not only to raise the question of whether she is dreaming, or mentally ill, it is also to raise the question of whether and to what degree any particular doing corresponds to the description under which that doing was intended as an action. In Aristotle's terms, it is to raise the question of the relation between the major premise and the minor premise of the practical syllogism. And even should we be relatively sanguine about the connection between such Aristotelian major premise/minor premise pairs as "it is pleasant to eat something sweet" and "this is something sweet," the case seems quite different when considering the major premise "it is good to help my friend" and the minor premise "this will help my friend." If, along with Socrates and a reformed Polemarchus, we want to help our friends and harm no one, and if we have ever thought that we had helped a friend and later come to believe that we may have harmed that friend unintentionally, we have reason to believe that, for intentions such as "to help a friend," the problem of knowledge can seem both unavoidable and insurmountable.

Even more fundamentally, to consider an agent responsible for her actions, we have to consider her not to be laboring under profound illusions about who she is and the world in which she wants to act. That is, to know whether she is truly acting, we have to ask whether she is "dreaming" in the sense that Socrates applies to dreaming in the *Republic:* dreaming, Socrates says, consists in believing a likeness of something to be not a likeness but rather the thing itself to which it is like (476c5–7). Of course, according to Socrates' cave analogy, it would seem that the only person who is not *always* dreaming in this latter sense is the philosopher-ruler who has risen out of the cave. The prisoners in the cave look at the shadows they cast upon the wall of the cave and think they see themselves; they look at the shadows of artificial objects and think they see their world. Moreover, the very fact that they are described as prisoners makes the point that I am trying to stress. According to this image, to dwell in the cave is to be rendered incapable of action; it is to mistake the clash of shadows on the wall of the cave for a recognition that one is acting in the world, when in truth, one is bound and helpless. It is only those human beings who have once seen the truth of the things that are by rising out of the cave and contemplating the *idea* of the good, and have descended again to the shadows—those who are "most able to participate in both lives" (520b)—who could truly be said to be act. According to Socrates, neither those "without experience of the truth" nor those "who are allowed to spend their time continuously in education" could be said to act in the strong sense which we have been pursuing here, "the former because they don't have any single goal in life at which they must aim in doing everything they do [πράττειν ἃ ἂν πράττωσιν] . . . , the latter because they won't be willing to act [ἑκόντες εἶναι οὐ πράξουσιν]" (519b–c).

When stated in this way, however, Socrates' putative solution to the epistemic problem seems only to serve to make the problem more acute; it only serves to radicalize the division between ethical dispositions and ethical knowledge we saw arise in our discussion of the *technê* analogy. On the one hand, Socrates presents the attainment of the knowledge necessary for genuine action as coming at the cost of *any* disposition to act. On the other hand, the claim that the philosopher-ruler is most able to "participate in both" (ἀμφοτέρων μετέχειν) the political and the theoretical life apparently deprives the philosopher as ruler the requisite "single aim" (σκοπὸν . . . ἕνα) toward which she must aim in all her actions. Thus we can see that the much-discussed question of the philosopher's motivation to return to the cave, or rather her motivation to allow herself to be *compelled* to return, presents problems not only for the explicit political project of the *Republic*.[36] It also presents problems for a coherent conception of human action. So, too, the duality of the philosopher-as-ruler not only appears to contravene the founding dictate of the city in speech that each individual should practice one art (370b). It also appears to threaten the very psychic integrity that the dialogue suggests defines the philosopher's justice and is essential to the philosopher's happiness.

These apparent consequences of Socrates' account of the philosopher's ascent out of the cave are, I contend, neither unintended nor peripheral to Plato's

---

36. See Gill 1996, 287–307, for a useful survey of contemporary attempts at addressing the problem. I agree with Gill's conclusion that Plato does not intend "to close the motivational gap between the desire for postdialectical knowledge and the desire to rule" (306) but rather seeks to highlight this gap. Unlike Gill, however, I believe that Plato seeks to highlight this gap as a philosophical *aporia*, and not simply because he seeks "to underline the status of post-dialectical knowledge as the highest human activity" (307).

concerns. They are, rather, fundamental both to Plato's presentation of "the problem of Socrates" and to the broader argument of the *Republic*. Indeed, I believe that much of Socrates' presentation of image of the cave is an artifact, first, of what I will call the "philosophic orientation" of the *Republic*, and second, of the "therapeutic" function of Socrates' dialogue with Glaucon in particular. I will explain what I mean by the "philosophic orientation" of the *Republic* in chapter 7, and what I mean by "therapeutic" in the section immediately following this one, which deals with Socrates' "alliance" with Polemarchus. However, before proceeding to that section, I will turn again to Socrates' account of his "second sailing" in the *Phaedo* to provide an alternative interpretation of the significance of the epistemic problem facing the prospective agent and its relation to an alternative account of the philosophic life Socrates presents in the dialogues.

The description of the character and goals of the philosophic life presented in Socrates' image of the philosopher's ascent out of the cave and direct contemplation of the *idea* of the good is, to say the least, difficult to reconcile with the image he uses to describe his own "second sailing in search of the cause" in the *Phaedo*. In the former case, Socrates imagines the potential philosopher-king being compelled to stand up and being dragged by force up the steep incline out of the cave and forced out into the light of the sun. Once there, the potential philosopher-king gradually accustoms himself to the upper region, first looking at shadows and images in water, later looking at the things themselves of which these are shadows and images, and finally gazing upon the sun itself, Socrates' likeness for the *idea* of the good. This image of the philosopher looking directly at the sun is not only strange in itself, it contrasts strongly with the image Socrates uses in the *Phaedo* passage to explain his own turn away from a direct contemplation of the beings and toward contemplating the truth of the beings "in arguments" or "accounts" (ἐν λόγοις). He claims there that it seemed to him that he needed to take care lest he experience what happened to those who tried to directly observe an eclipse of the sun, rather than its reflection in water or something similar. He feared that if he tried to observe the beings directly with his eyes or other senses, his soul would become altogether blinded. Therefore, he says, he took refuge in accounts and sought to investigate the truth of the beings in them.

Socrates' turn to an investigation of the truth of the beings *en logois* is usually understood to simply mean a turn to an investigation of *concepts* or *propositions* and much in the *Phaedo* passage seems to point in this direction. However, Socrates immediately qualifies his presentation of his "second sailing" in a way which points to another sense in which Socrates could be said to investigate the truth of the beings "in accounts," a sense which more closely accords with his practice as revealed in Plato's dialogues. He says, "Perhaps my likeness is in a certain way not right [or not alike, ἔοικεν], for I do not in any way agree that the one who contemplates the beings in accounts is [contemplating them] in images [ἐν εἰκόσι] more than the one who contemplates them in deeds [ἐν ἔργοις]" (*Phd.* 99e5–100a2). There is now a fair degree of consensus among commentators that what is called the Socratic *elenchus* is not an examination primarily directed toward propositions but an examination of people's lives.[37] Surprisingly, this consensus has not had much impact on interpretations of Socrates' account of his "second sailing."[38] However, Socrates' qualification of his original formulation suggests that we can find in both human speeches and human actions "images" in the relevant respect, images of the good in which one can contemplate the "truth of the beings."

Much of the rest of this book will deal with what it means to say that Socrates investigates the truth of the beings as they are imaged in the souls of his inter-locutors, but for now I would like to point out two more aspects of the above quotation from the *Phaedo* and interpret its significance for the epistemic prob-lem concerning human action. First, the initial phrase of the above quotation, which I have translated "Perhaps my likeness is in a certain way not right," could be translated more literally as "Perhaps that which I liken (to something) is in a certain way not alike." This suggests that Socrates is indicating that the reflections or images of the beings he contemplates in human speakings and doings could be less than adequate images of the beings themselves. Second, insofar as Socrates sees human speakings and doings as reflections or images of the beings, that is, as less than entirely real, he must see his own speakings and doings in this same light—as potentially inadequate representations of those things that most truly are.

Having considered these possibilities, and in the context of Socrates' account of his "second sailing" in general, we can offer this alternative account of that philosophic education which is described as "an art of turning" in book 7 of the *Republic,* and its relation to the epistemic problem confronting a potential agent. The first thing that the soul can come to recognize, by turning away from the shadows cast on the wall of the cave and toward the things that are, is that the shadows are shadows of artifacts, of human constructs, which bear some indeterminate relation to the "beings that most truly are" of which they,

---

37. See especially Brickhouse and Smith 1994, 12–14.

38. One reason for this (or perhaps a sign of it) is the tendency of most commentators to take *en ergois* (literally "in works" or "in deeds") to mean "in facts" or "in concrete." However, neither is this interpreta-tion suggested by the other uses of *ergon* in the dialogue, nor is it easily reconcilable with the passage as a whole. For if by "concrete" we mean something like concrete physical objects, then their status as "images" would, it seems, have made them appropriate objects of contemplation and obviated the need for Socrates' "second sailing." A notable exception to this tendency is Stanley Rosen's treatment of the passage (1993).

in turn, are said to be likenesses. This turning can make us see these shadows
and images, as it were, in a new light, but they cannot prevent them from being
shadows of artifacts. If we replace "artifact" with "my legislation of proximal
ends with respect to what is best," and "shadows" with "the doing that I believe
furthers this proximal end," we can see that, in terms of the image of the cave,
all of our "actions" are, at best, reflections of what Socrates calls a hypothesis about
who we are and what is best for us. And if we cannot, with the philosopher-king,
ascend out of the cave entirely, at least we can be mindful of the hypothetical
status of our own agency. We can recognize the possibility that our legislations
of proximal ends are poor images of the goods they point toward: at least then
we will not be dreaming, that is, taking these images not to be images but the
very things of which they are meant to be images.

3.5 Socrates' Alliance with Polemarchus

Throughout my treatment of Socrates' conversation with Polemarchus I have
suggested that Socrates is willing to use arguments that he does not wholly
endorse, arguments that mean something different for Socrates, and for the
perceptive auditor, than they do for Polemarchus. I have also suggested that,
were Socrates' only object to refute Polemarchus's claim that justice is helping
friends and harming enemies, he could have done so without the extraordinarily
complex and problematic arguments he uses. The clearest example of this latter
claim is the easily exposed contradiction noted above between Polemarchus's
contention that the just man helps friends and harms enemies and his belief
that the just man never harms those who are acting justly. Nonetheless, in contrast to his treatment of Cephalus, as we have seen, and of Thrasymachus, as
we will see, Socrates seems genuinely interested in persuading Polemarchus.
Furthermore, in contrast to his conversations with Cephalus and Thrasymachus, Socrates gives Polemarchus more than ample opportunity to take the
conversation in another direction than the direction it eventually takes. In the
previous sections of this chapter, I have focused, for the most part, on what I
have called Socrates' apodeictic intent in his conversation with Polemarchus,
that is, what Socrates attempts to demonstrate about Polemarchus's view of
the political to the assembled company in the Piraeus, or to the auditors of
his narration. In this section I will focus on Socrates' dialogic intent, that is,
what Socrates hopes to achieve vis-à-vis Polemarchus in particular. I will try to
make plain some features of Socrates' dialogic practice which play a role in the
vast majority of his conversations in Plato's dialogues.

By reviewing Socrates' arguments, we will see that his conversation with Polemarchus has three distinct phases, which I will refer to using terms borrowed from the Greek. In the first, the "zetetic" or inquiring phase, Socrates inquires into Polemarchus's understanding of justice as "the fitting," and his questions are relatively open ended. While they suggest that Socrates has a particular interpretation of Polemarchus's understanding of justice, they leave Polemarchus plenty of space to correct Socrates' interpretation if it is wrong, and lead the conversation down a quite different path. When Polemarchus's responses in the first phase tend to confirm Socrates' initial supposition, Socrates initiates the second, the "elenctic" or cross-examining phase. In this phase Socrates asks questions specifically with the intent of examining Polemarchus's ability to see beyond the limitations of his original formulation. Polemarchus's failure in this regard leads Socrates to the third, the "therapeutic" or reformative phase. In this phase Socrates seems to simply lead Polemarchus in a particular direction in an attempt to begin to reform Polemarchus's implicit conception of justice "from the inside," so to speak. That is, Socrates' arguments draw upon what I have called Polemarchus's "vision" of the political to redirect that "vision" without explicitly calling it into question. Thanks to Thrasymachus's interruption, of course, we can only guess what this reformation of Polemarchus's views would eventually have led to. These three stages are, I believe, characteristic of most of Socrates' conversations in the dialogues. In particular, they are characteristic of Socrates' conversations with the politically ambitious young men who are his most frequent conversation partners.

3.5.1 Stage One: Zetesis

As we have seen, Socrates' initial inquiry into Polemarchus's definition of justice as helping friends and harming enemies takes the form of an analogy between justice and *technê*. As we have also seen, the character of their conversation would have been entirely different had Polemarchus considered legislation to be a part of the "art" of justice. Despite the fact that Socrates does not explicitly introduce the art of politics or the sub-art of legislation, we can see that he gives Polemarchus more than ample opportunity to do so. In fact, he gives Polemarchus some hints which would suggest these as candidate arts to someone who was open to these suggestions. Consider these possible answers that Polemarchus could have given to crucial questions in the first, zetetic, phase of Socrates' argument which would have pointed toward the art of politics, and directed the conversation to a deeper level than any that is reached in the manifest content of book 1. In response to Socrates' question "And what about the just man, in what action and with respect to what work is he most able to help friends and harm enemies?" Polemarchus could have responded, in somewhat Aristotelian fashion, "In the action of ruling and being ruled in turn with his fellow citizens, and with respect to the work of guiding the polis toward virtue." Instead, Polemarchus responds, "In my opinion, in making war and being an ally in battle." Socrates is even more generous with his hints when he asks, just as the skilled player of draughts is a better partner in "setting down" (θέσιν) draughts, and the house builder is a better partner when "setting down" (θέσιν) bricks, in what partnership a just man is a better partner. Polemarchus does not respond, as he might have, "The just man is a better partner in setting down laws," (νό μων θέσιν)," the most common use of the word θέ σις in the dialogues and the one most appropriate to the context. Instead, Polemarchus offers that the just man is the better partner "in money matters." Finally, when Socrates objects that the just man is not a better partner in using money in buying horses or building ships or any other specific use of it, Polemarchus does not respond that the arts which deal with horses or the building of ships are subordinate to the art of generalship, which is in turn subordinate to the art of politics, which is, as such, the art of correct use.[39]

That Polemarchus does not even consider these alternative answers to Socrates' questions indicates that, in his attachment to the Athenian polis, he is not only committed to democratic politics, that is, politics in which the only requirement for participation in rule is free birth, he is also committed to the ideology of the "democratic soul" Socrates will describe in book 8: he conceives of no hierarchy of ends. More significantly, his acceptance of the analogy between justice and *technê*, coupled with his failure to consider the art of politics as a candidate art, shows his unwillingness to consider the polis as one among many possible poleis, and hence his unwillingness to fundamentally question whether this polis is itself just. It shows his inability to look beyond this polis and this culture to those things against which the justice of the actions of the polis could be judged. These limitations suggest that Polemarchus is not someone with whom Socrates can inquire, in any straightforward sense, into the question "what is justice?"

3.5.2 Stage Two: Elenchus

However, Socrates is not yet convinced. He moves, therefore, into the second, or elenctic phase of his argument; he tests Polemarchus's ability to see beyond

---

39. Both the art of politics as an art of correct use and a hierarchy among the arts are central aspects of the account of the art of politics presented in the *Euthydemus*. Cf. Aristotle *Eth. Nic.* 1094a1–a17, and Burger 2008.

the limitations of his original formulation. Socrates poses directly to Polemarchus the essential difficulty with any notion of justice that posits a strict identity between justice and the opinions of any group, no matter how authoritative. He points out to Polemarchus that people make mistakes, and in particular, that they make mistakes about who is good or bad, useful or useless; they make mistakes about whom they choose to call friend and whom they choose to call enemy. Polemarchus is duly impressed with the force of this objection, enough so that he proposes that he and Socrates change one of the definitions they have been working with. However, his proposal shows that even if he is impressed with Socrates' objection, he has not really understood its significance. He has not understood the radical consequences that accepting the distinction between seeming and being should have for his account of justice. For he does not propose that he and Socrates revise their definition of justice as helping friends and harming enemies. Instead, he proposes that they revise their definition of friend and enemy. As opposed to calling friend whoever seems good to an individual, and calling enemy whoever seems bad to an individual, Polemarchus suggests that they change their definition to "The man who seems to be, and is beneficial [χρηστόν], is a friend . . . while the man who seems beneficial and is not, seems to be but is not a friend," and he suggests that they take the same position with regard to the enemy. However, a moment's reflection reveals that this redefinition merely covers over the problem of seeming and being that Socrates' objection revealed. If, as Socrates suggests, human beings make mistakes about who is good and who is bad, useful or useless, changing the definition of friend and enemy in this way will not help anyone decide whom they should benefit and whom they should harm.

If Polemarchus had understood the significance of Socrates' objection, he might have argued as follows. If it is possible to be mistaken, and think that a good man is bad, and take him as an enemy, and that a bad man is good, and take him as a friend, it may be the case that one can never truly know whether the friend or enemy one (tries to) help or harm is a good human being or a bad human being. Therefore, one must decide whether it is more unjust to benefit a bad human being or to harm a good human being. If one decides, *ceteris paribus*, that it is more unjust to harm a good human being that to benefit a bad human being (as it seems Polemarchus, and indeed most of us, would; cf. 334d3), then one would have reason to think that one should strive to avoid harming anyone unnecessarily, and only harm someone who seems bad if one has to choose between harming someone who seems good and harming someone who seems bad. Indeed, one might argue that the just human being in a imperfect world, a world where human beings make mistakes, would never act with the guiding intention of harming someone, but would only act with the intention of helping her friends and those who seem good to her. Of course, in that imperfect world, it is likely that helping one's friends in this way will sometimes entail harming those who are not one's friends, but we can imagine that the most just human being would strive to help her friends in such a way that she would not be likely to harm (or at least seriously harm) those who seem to her good. Thus, by reflecting on the significance of the distinction between seeming and being for the problem of justice, Polemarchus could have arrived at an understanding of justice similar to the one he is eventually persuaded of by Socrates: that the work proper to the just human being is helping one's friends and not harming anyone at all.[40]

However, Polemarchus does not respond to the distinction between seeming and being Socrates introduces into the conversation in this way. Instead he proposes that he and Socrates redefine friend and enemy, as we have seen, to allow for four possibilities: (1) the real friend (the man who seems and is good), (2) the apparent friend (the man who seems good and is not), (3) the apparent enemy (the man who seems bad and is not), and (4) the real enemy (the man who seems and is bad). I have suggested that Polemarchus's attempt to solve the problem that the distinction between seeming and being poses for the just man by redefining friend and enemy shows that he has not understood the significance of this distinction. Socrates, it seems, suspects as much. Therefore, Socrates tests Polemarchus to see whether he has, in fact, understood the distinction. He offers Polemarchus in succession two propositions that he presents as reformulations of Polemarchus's fourfold distinction between real friend, apparent friend, apparent enemy and real enemy. These supposed reformulations, however, turn Polemarchus's distinction on its head. Socrates' first response to Polemarchus's suggestion is, "Then it seems that the good man will be, by this argument, a friend, and the bad man an enemy?" To which Polemarchus should respond, if he had understood his own formulation, "No, Socrates. Only the good man who also *seems* good will be a friend. The other good men, those who do not seem good, will either be apparent enemies, if they seem bad, or neither friends nor enemies, real or apparent, if they seem neither good nor bad." Instead, he simply responds, "Yes." Socrates then interprets Polemarchus as having said, "It is just to do good to the friend, if he is good, and harm the enemy, if he is bad." Here Polemarchus could have responded, "Wrong again, Socrates. We said that the friend is by definition good and the enemy is by definition bad.

---

40. Even in the case of retributive justice, one can strive to ensure that the punishment of criminals is either intended with the end of reform or, at the very least, understood as enacted with the guiding intention of helping those who seem good, rather than the guiding intention of harming anyone.

You must be thinking of the apparent friend and the apparent enemy." The fact that Polemarchus does not make these or similar responses clearly indicates that he did not understand his proposed redefinition, and has failed to grasp the significance of the distinction between seeming and being for the problem of justice.

3.5.3 Stage Three: Therapeia

Socrates began by inquiring, in a relatively, if not entirely, open-ended way, into what Polemarchus understood by the formula "justice is helping friends and harming enemies." He assumed that Polemarchus probably meant something along the lines "justice is preserving the regime and destroying or conquering the enemies of the city," but he left open the possibility that Polemarchus meant something more interesting. In particular, by the way in which he framed the analogy between justice and *technê*, he gestured toward a more elevated notion of the art of politics, an art directed toward the cultivation and maintenance of the good condition of the souls of the members of the polis. Polemarchus, however, could only think of war and money and harming bad men. Next, Socrates took a more direct approach and introduced the distinction between seeming and being, and argued that the fact that human beings make mistakes about who is good and who is bad should pose significant if not insurmountable problems for a definition of justice which considered the harming of enemies categorically just. Socrates introduced this distinction with the dialogic intent of testing Polemarchus's ability to see beyond his regime-dependent ideas of justice to the fundamental philosophical issues that surround the intention to act justly. When Polemarchus accepted the distinction between seeming and being but deployed it in a way that indicated that he didn't really *get* it, Socrates quickly introduced two supposed reformulations of Polemarchus's new definition of friend and enemy, reformulations that Polemarchus would have objected to had he begun to grasp the significance of this distinction for the problem of justice. Polemarchus has failed the test; he has shown his inability to see beyond his abstractly political vision of the human world and human ethical action.

The fact that Polemarchus cannot see beyond his manifestly inadequate conception of the political world indicates that he is, so to speak, a danger to himself and others. I have argued above that conflict in an individual's soul can be hard for that individual to detect and even harder for that individual to understand. In Polemarchus's case, he does not even detect, prior to Socrates' intervention, a conflict between his commitment to the justice of helping one's friends and harming one's enemies and his commitment not to harm a human being who has done nothing unjust. However, had he actually tried to act on his commitment to harming the enemies of the city of Athens in the Peloponnesian War, for example, the people of Melos, he would have come to confront in a radical way the possibility of conflict between these two commitments. Moreover, if we assume that his commitment to not harming those who have done nothing unjust is deeply felt, it is more than likely that he would not only confront this possible conflict, he would suffer from it. We have seen that Polemarchus implicitly identifies justice with conformity to the culture of the polis. He considers just men and friends to be those who conform to that culture, and bad men and enemies those who do not. We can also now see the danger that someone like Polemarchus might represent for someone like Socrates, someone who is decidedly unlike the other men of the city and who asks troubling, undemocratic questions about law, and justice, and about the one man who knows. We must not allow ourselves to forget the numerous references Plato makes in book I of the *Republic* to Socrates' trial and death. In this context, we can now see the significance of Polemarchus's first gesture in the dialogue, his pretense, in the name of "these men here," of forcefully preventing Socrates from an ascent. Polemarchus seems, in general, to be something of a loose cannon, and more than a tad too eager to harm "bad men." In summary, Polemarchus has shown himself to be actually conflicted, potentially dangerous, and, perhaps, not even potentially a philosopher.[41] Therefore, Socrates does not explicitly show Polemarchus the limits of his vision of the political, but instead undertakes to reform that vision, not by attacking it directly, but by transforming it from within.

Now, at this point, a few words need to be said about what I mean by Polemarchus's "vision" of the political and my claim that Socrates transforms that vision from the inside. We can take a first step by turning to Jonathan Lear's work on the relation between Platonic and Freudian accounts of the soul. In an essay on the concept of transference, Lear argues that alongside our shared contributions to a communal social world, each of us is also "attempting to create and inhabit an idiosyncratic polis—an *idiopolis*—the peculiar lineaments of which are largely unconscious."[42] He interprets the psychoanalytic phenomenon of transference as an unconscious attempt on the part of the analysand to draw the analyst into this idiopolis, and have the analyst play a role which confirms the idiosyncratic world of meaning the analysand has constructed. On Lear's account, Plato's description of the reciprocal relationship between a shared cultural world and the psychic structure of the individuals who inhabit that world shows his recognition of a political correlate of transference phenomena. I will

41. Cf. *Phdr.* 257b.
42. Lear 1998, 70.

return to Lear's discussion of these issues when discussing Socrates' account of the relation between the soul of the philosopher-king and the structure of the best polis.[43] However, Lear contends that it was Freud's unique discovery that "even when a person participates in shared cultural activities, those activities will tend also to have an idiosyncratic, unconscious meaning for that person." Moreover, Lear thinks that Socrates was insensitive, both to the phenomenon of transference in general and to the idiosyncratic unconscious meanings that define an individual's idiopolis.[44]

I suggest to the contrary that Socrates is presented throughout Plato's dialogues as being extraordinarily, almost supernaturally, prescient about the unconscious world of meaning constructed by individuals. He is sensitive, not only to the fact of unconscious meanings, but also to their symbolic and imagistic character. It is this unconscious world of meaning, to which Lear gives the fitting name of "idiopolis," rather than any abstract proposition, that Socrates examines when he contemplates the truth of the beings as they are imagistically represented in the words and deeds of his interlocutors. Moreover, Socrates is not only sensitive to the imaginary character of these unconscious meanings, but he is peculiarly adept at confronting these images on their own terms. He confronts the imaginary with the imaginary.[45] When an individual such as Polemarchus shows himself to be incapable of or resistant to meeting Socrates on the ground of argument, Socrates is capable of meeting that individual in the clouds of fantasy. He can speak the language of an individual's illusions. Thus, when Polemarchus shows an incapacity for or psychic resistance to confronting the consequences of the fragility of our grasp on the knowledge of who is a good and who is a bad human being, when he is unable or unwilling to confront his own responsibility for ethical action and wants to have the assurance of being a member of the body politic whose ethical judgments are necessarily right, Socrates reforms Polemarchus's unconscious vision of the political world by using the tools appropriate to this unconscious symbolic world. He draws an analogy between human beings and the most spirited and the most loyal of animals, horses and dogs, an analogy that Polemarchus finds persuasive because he aspires to a vision of uncomplicated excellence like the

43. See §10.4 below.

44. Lear 1998, 69. Lear's views on this issue have developed over time. In Lear 1998, he contends that Socrates' blindness to transference rendered him a therapeutic "disaster," and he points to the fact of Socrates' prosecution and execution by the Athenian *demos* as evidence of this therapeutic ineptitude. See, however, Lear 2006a and especially Lear 2006b.

45. Adeimantus, who is himself quite sensitive to the power of the imaginary, even pokes fun at Socrates for his habitual use of images in argument (487c).

excellence exhibited by those animals. He draws an analogy between justice and the physical property of heat, which Polemarchus finds persuasive because he wants to believe that justice comes to individuals merely by their participating in the political community and passes between them like heat suffusing the body politic, and does not want to have to confront the consequences of the fact that justice, even justice expressed in communal action, requires an individual assuming responsibility for his own actions.

We have seen some of the reasons for Socrates' choosing to therapeutically intervene in Polemarchus's psyche. Polemarchus is wedded to a notion of justice which, even if he is not presently aware of it, indicates a conflict in his soul between his aspiration to act as an individual and his aspiration to conform wholly to his culture, his desire to do whatever the city wants him to do, and his desire that his actions be just in some sense which transcends the city. Moreover, Polemarchus's vision of the political seems to embody the most dangerous aspects of the Athenian democratic political culture, those aspects which were responsible for Socrates' accusation by Meletus, Anytus, and Lycon. With Socrates' guidance, Polemarchus has moved from a notion of justice as helping friends and harming enemies to the claim that the "work" of the just man is helping the good and harming no one. Again, it is worth stressing that this does not necessarily entail that the just man will never harm anyone in any situation; it only entails that whatever harm he might do be in the service of some greater benefit.

Nonetheless, we must confront the deeply troubling aspects of Socrates' intervention into Polemarchus's soul. The "help" he has given Polemarchus seems to be at least as much in his own interest as in Polemarchus's, and as was the case with Polemarchus's account of the just man, Socrates is willing to give this "help" without Polemarchus asking for it, or even knowing how exactly he is being helped. This is the darker side of Socrates' invocation of helping and harming horses and dogs in what I have been calling the "therapeutic" phase of Socrates' arguments. Horses and dogs are paradigmatically "spirited" animals not only because that they exhibit fierceness to strangers and gentleness toward friends (376a–b), or because they sometimes exhibit a "courage" which will lead them to fight on without regard to their physical safety (375b). Horses and dogs are also paradigmatically spirited animals in that they are the animals most susceptible to training; they can accept as their own "good" the "good of another" (cf. 343c), and can be the instrument of a work which benefits not themselves but their master (342e). The "alliance" Socrates forges with Polemarchus, like the alliance between the philosopher-rulers and the guardian-auxiliaries, ultimately seems to depend on a kind of lie, a willingness on Socrates' part to deceive Polemarchus—perhaps for Polemarchus's own good. Whether this lie is a "well-born" lie or not is unclear.[46]

It is perhaps due to the fact that Thrasymachus perceives, on some level, these implications of Socrates' analogy between horses, dogs, and men that he can finally no longer contain himself and bursts into the conversation brimming with indignation, real or apparent. And it is to Socrates' conversation with Thrasymachus that we now turn.

---

46. Nietzsche, at least, would deny that it was. Cf., inter alia, *Beyond Good and Evil* 212, *Twilight of the Idols* 2.2.

4

Thrasymachus, Rhetoric, and the Art of Rule

Socrates' conversation with Polemarchus remains incomplete due to Thrasy-machus's interruption. This fact seems to provide grounds to ameliorate the force of the critique of Socrates' practice begun in the final paragraph of the previous chapter. Despite the obvious similarities between book 1 and the so-called aporetic dialogues, there is a crucial difference between Socrates' "therapeutic" work in those dialogues and the therapeutic aspect of his conversation with Polemarchus: Socrates' therapeutic work is cut short by the presence in the assembled group of someone like Thrasymachus, that is, someone who is willing to exploit the most troubling implications of Socrates' argument and attempt to manipulate them to his own less than laudatory purposes. One might argue in Socrates' defense that, if Thrasymachus had not been there, Socrates would have been free to pursue a course similar to the ones he takes in the "aporetic" dialogues. He could have continued to pursue the question "what is justice?" with Polemarchus until they had reached an impasse in the argument, an *aporia* that would have cast doubt on the adequacy of the conclusions they had reached in the course of the argument. We can imagine such a dialogue ending, as book 1 does, with an exhortation to take up the inquiry anew.

It is not difficult to see, however, that this defense of Socrates' treatment of Polemarchus only goes so far. Socrates' move from inquiry to therapy was predicated, I have argued, on his recognition of Polemarchus's limitations as a philosophic inquirer. There is little in Socrates' presentation of him to suggest that Polemarchus would have had much luck in trying to disentangle the intricate threads of Socrates' argument on his own. If Polemarchus's alliance with Socrates is to yield for him any further insight, if he is to make any progress in his under-standing of justice, it would seem he could do so only in conversation with Socrates. But if this appearance is correct, we can ask whether Polemarchus has merely replaced his implicit dependence on the guidance of the political community with a more explicit dependence on Socrates' guidance. More starkly put, if, prior to Socrates' intervention, Polemarchus implicitly understood himself as a vehicle or instrument for the decisions of the democratic political community, we can ask whether after Socrates' intervention he has become a vehicle or instrument of Socrates' political purposes. These questions point us toward the issues we will begin to explore by examining Socrates' confrontation with Thrasymachus.

Thus far in our investigation of the "problem of Socrates" we have been given ample reason to doubt the adequacy of views that criticize Plato's Socrates for ignoring or marginalizing the significance of the emotive, desiderative, and volitional aspects of human psychology. We have also seen reasons for doubting Nietzsche's apparent claim that Socrates' dialectical inquiries were a more or less unconscious reflection of the cultural degeneration of his time. We have thereby reframed, if not yet answered, the second of the two questions I associated with Nietzsche's account of the "problem of Socrates" in the opening pages of this book. We have begun to see the ways in which Plato's Socrates framed his public philosophic activity in conscious recognition of the dangers a kind of self-conscious reflection pose for human ethical life. We are now prepared to confront more directly the other side of Nietzsche's critique of Socrates, the claim that Socratic dialectic is a decadent manifestation of what Nietzsche called "the will to power," and we will begin to do so by looking to Plato's presentation of Socrates' public contestations with the "Sophists" Thrasymachus, Gorgias, and Protagoras.[1] At the same time, we will look to Socrates' narration of his encounter with Thrasymachus as a further articulation of the cultural environment in which he undertook his public philosophic activity.

Socrates' dialogue with Thrasymachus takes up almost two-thirds of book I of the *Republic* and is, to say the least, quite complex. The length and complexity of this portion of book I make it impossible for me to give as thorough an account of Socrates' portrait of Thrasymachus as I have attempted to offer of Socrates' presentations of Cephalus and Polemarchus. Moreover, much of what I want to show about Thrasymachus's position, in particular its relation to a broader sophistic theory of human creative activity, can be more clearly and persuasively illustrated by turning, in the next two chapters, to Socrates' conversations with Gorgias and Protagoras in the dialogues bearing their names. Therefore, rather than attempting to interpret the whole of Socrates' conversation with Thrasymachus, I will begin by looking at Socrates' depiction of Thrasymachus leading up to his first definition of justice as "the advantage of the stronger." I will argue that this depiction shows a conflict within Thrasymachus's soul that prepares us for, and is mirrored in, the conflict between his two divergent accounts of justice and injustice. I will then treat these two divergent accounts in turn, and I will argue that the first account corresponds

---

1. As we will see, the term "Sophist" acquires a technical sense in the *Gorgias,* according to which a "Sophist" is contrasted with a "rhetorician." In this sense, of the three only Protagoras merits the appellation "Sophist."

to Thrasymachus's self-conscious relation to his own art of rhetoric as an art of rule and the second account corresponds to his self-conscious relation to the ethical psychological matter of that art. I will conclude by discussing Socrates' implicit analysis of the conflict in Thrasymachus's soul, and the significance of this analysis for the argument of the *Republic*. For reasons that will become clear in that discussion, I will then turn to Gorgias's account of the art of rhetoric and Protagoras's account of the art of sophistry to complete my sketch of the view of human creative activity presented by the Sophists in Plato's dialogues.

Socrates likens Thrasymachus's entry into the conversation to the attack of a wild animal, but makes clear at the same time how tame a beast Thrasymachus really is. Thrasymachus, Socrates says, had moved to take over the argument many times before his eventual outburst, but had been restrained by those sitting near him who wanted to hear the rest of the argument. He was even obliging enough to wait for a natural break in the argument. When he does erupt, moreover, the dominant emotion he expresses throughout his tirade is the uniquely human and distinctly ethical emotion of indignation.[2] Despite Socrates' claim that he and Polemarchus were terrified by Thrasymachus descending upon them, Socrates' narration of Thrasymachus's intermittent abuse presents a figure that is anything but terrifying. He seems oddly impotent. In striking contrast to the immediate physical threat gestured toward in Socrates' simile, Thrasymachus seems to be all talk. A certain degree of self-consciousness about this fact seems to be at least one source of Thrasymachus's apparent indignation; he desires to distinguish his way of speaking from the "foolishness" spouted by Socrates, while recognizing a degree of kinship between the two. Thrasymachus claims to recognize that Socrates practices a version of his own art of "precise speech" (340e), and he seems to think that Socrates is giving precise speakers a bad name. In particular, he is offended by how mannerly and compliant Socrates' brand of precise speech seems (336b8). He seems to think that the right kind of precise speech should really *do* something.[3] An indication of this is the fact that the harshest invective he heaps upon Socrates always has at its base an accusation of idle talk (φλυαρία, ὕθλος, κόρυζα), the same accusation that Callicles directs toward Socrates in the *Gorgias* (489b, 490d–e). However, it is Thrasymachus, and not Socrates, who is shown by the dialogue to be ineffective, at least insofar as he seems unable to get any of his designs accomplished. He is manhandled by Socrates in argument, and compelled (ἠνάγκασαν, 344d4) by the others

2. See Lycos 1987, 40–41.
3. Cf. C. D. C. Reeve's claim that Thrasymachus's attack on Socrates "is the cry of every substantive theorist against the destructive critic" (1988, 10). Reeve's preference for substantial theorizing over Socrates' aporetic questioning is no doubt responsible for his zealous prosecution of the case against Socrates and his relatively unqualified admiration for the philosopher-king (see 3–28, 191–95).

against his will to stay and defend himself when he wants to leave after his most spectacular rhetorical flourish.

The contrast between the animal ferocity that Socrates ascribes to Thrasymachus and the intellectualism of his "precise speech," between his distaste for idle talk and his own apparent impotence, prepares us for the bifurcate character of Thrasymachus's argument for the superiority of the life of injustice. The difficulty of reconciling Thrasymachus's first definition of justice as "the advantage of the stronger" with his later account of justice as "doing the good of another" has been the subject of a great deal of scholarly scrutiny, the main thrust of which has been to determine whether (and to what degree) Thrasymachus's contrasting accounts of justice indicate a fundamental incoherence in his views.[4] However, even those commentators who want to champion the underlying consistency of Thrasymachus's position on justice do so by attempting to explain away the prima facie conflict and, like Cleitophon later in the dialogue, attribute it to some casual error on Thrasymachus's part occasioned by Socrates' elenctic pressure. The manifest tension between his various formulations has been considered, at best, a stumbling block in our endeavor to reconstruct Thrasymachus's views. It has seemed to many readers not much more than a piece of defamatory rhetoric, part of Plato's attempt to show up Thrasymachus (and the Sophists in general) as confused and incompetent.

Contrary to these views, I will suggest that an explanation of the surface conflict between Thrasymachus's divergent accounts of justice is essential to our understanding his conception of human political activity and the vision of human creative activity that underlies and supports it. What has been missing, I will suggest, from most previous attempts to interpret Thrasymachus's intervention into the conversation in book 1 is an adequate consideration of his status as a theorist and practitioner of the art of rhetoric. The key to comprehending his various assertions about justice and injustice lies in understanding their relation to his conception of the art of rhetoric itself as an art of political rule. Furthermore, I will suggest that Socrates' refutation of Thrasymachus depends, in the first instance, on Thrasymachus's failings as a rhetorical artist; Thrasymachus's inadequacy as a *political* theorist will be revealed to be inseparable from his inadequacy as a theorist of *rhetoric*. However, prior to turning to the apparent conflict between Thrasymachus's views on justice, I would like to point out a different way in which Thrasymachus seems to be conflicted, a conflict which will be significant for our understanding of his character.

4. The course of the contemporary debate was in many ways set by G. B. Kerferd (1947). Kerferd provides a useful overview of earlier scholarship, as does W. K. C. Guthrie (1971). See also Hourani 1962, and Kerferd's "reply" (1964); Henderson 1970; Maguire 1971; Cross and Woozley 1964, 38–41; Harlap 1979; Annas 1981, 50–56.

Thrasymachus begins his contribution to the evening's conversation by what is in effect an elaborate accusation of Socrates' dishonesty and injustice, an accusation that appropriates the language of the law courts. He accuses Socrates of being motivated by a love of honor,[5] and does not want to let Socrates get away with asking and refuting without having to be called to account for his own views about justice. He demands that Socrates tell him "clearly and precisely" what Socrates thinks justice is, hoping, it seems, to be able to best Socrates at his own game and refute Socrates' definition of justice. In addition, he rules out of court any such answer as "the needful" or "the helpful" or "the advantageous" as "inanities," that is, as idle talk. When Socrates responds that whatever mistakes he and Polemarchus have been making are unwilling mistakes, Thrasymachus scoffs at this response and puts it down to Socrates' "habitual irony" or "dissembling" (εἰωθυῖα εἰρωνεία); that is, he suggests that Socrates is lying in order to avoid having to answer for himself. However, when Socrates suggests that he might offer, on reflection, one of the answers that Thrasymachus has forbidden, Thrasymachus does not ask what Socrates' answer is. Instead, he asks Socrates, "What if I could show you another answer about justice besides all these and better than they are? What punishment do you think you would deserve to suffer?" (337d). This response is telling, and sets the stage for the rest of Socrates' conversation with Thrasymachus. Unlike Socrates, who, ironically or not, adopts a position of ignorance, Thrasymachus cannot help but indicate that he thinks he has, as Socrates says, a very fine answer. Despite his apparent desire to have Socrates answer, and despite what seems to be his better judgment,[6] Thrasymachus cannot prevent himself from speaking. We will return to this facet of Thrasymachus's personality after we have seen what his "very fine answer" amounts to.

One final thing we should note about Socrates' dialogue with Thrasymachus before proceeding, however, is that in Thrasymachus's case Socrates' dialogic intent seems to coincide with his apodeictic intent.[7] That is, as Thrasymachus fears, Socrates seems more interested in putting Thrasymachus on display as something of a cautionary tale than in directly persuading Thrasymachus by means of his arguments (347a–b). However, the very fact that Socrates is able to do this so easily and so thoroughly is the means he uses to teach Thrasymachus about the inadequacy of his account of the just and the unjust man. As we will see, Socrates makes quite clear that he is using against him the fact that Thrasymachus cannot say certain things in public safely. However, this prudential lesson

5. See §6.5 below.
6. He seems to know that Socrates will refute him once he chooses to speak. See 337d–e.
7. See §3.1 above.

is the first step in a much deeper lesson about the kind of "legislation" which would be necessary if Thrasymachus's "tyrannical" project were to have any hope of succeeding, a lesson whose point we will only see once we have left Thrasymachus behind and turned toward Gorgias and Protagoras, more theoretically sophisticated exponents of the putative art he practices.

4.1 The Advantage of the Stronger

I have suggested in the previous chapter that Thrasymachus's two accounts of justice and injustice can be seen as extensions of the dichotomy between virtues conceived as dispositions and virtues conceived as cognitive capacities which we first encountered in Socrates' conversation with Polemarchus. To be more precise, each of Thrasymachus's divergent accounts of justice is a transformation of and implicit response to the two sides of Socrates' critique of Polemarchus's vision of the human political world as self-enclosed and self-sufficient. I do not mean to suggest by this claim that Thrasymachus conceives of his two accounts in this way. Rather, what I am claiming is that these two divergent accounts of justice and injustice are representations, at the level of the socially and politically constructed soul, of those aspects of human experience which Socrates implied in his conversation with Polemarchus stood outside the wholly political realm. In his deployment of the analogy between justice and *technê,* Socrates implicitly suggested that Polemarchus's view of the political could account neither for the ends toward which human actions are directed nor for the human capacity to take up those ends. Polemarchus's view abstracted from both our capacity to legislate ends for ourselves with respect to our perception of what is best and our capacity to experience emotively those ends as our own; it replaced mind with "community-mindedness" and body with the "body politic." The consequence of this communitarian vision was to replace individual agency with the agency of the polis. This is a consequence that, for obvious reasons, Thrasymachus cannot abide, for he wants to assert the absolute superiority of the tyrannical individual, the individual who can "subjugate cities and tribes of men" to himself (348d). Therefore, he attempts to represent both reason and volition in terms that abstract from anything outside the realm of human discourse and its political consequences. He does so only at the cost of presenting two conflicting visions of that world, one corresponding to a wholly technical conception of reason, the other corresponding to a wholly politicized conception of desire. The first results in what has been called Thrasymachus's "legalism" or "conventionalism," the second in what has been called his "immoralism." We begin, as the dialogue does, with the "legalistic" Thrasymachus.

If we were to present Thrasymachus's initial explication of his claim that "justice is the advantage of the stronger" in rough rather than precise speech, we might say that he is presenting a *nominalist* account of justice. On this view Thrasymachus would be saying that justice is the name that the ruling faction in any city gives to obedience to the laws, which laws they set down with a view to their own interest. And, in a rough sense, this is obviously true—insofar as the ruling faction in a government is more or less representative of some particular group, they will have a tendency to pass laws that reflect the interests of this group, and they will call those laws, and obedience to those laws, just. However, if we were to look at the issue more precisely, we would see that, as opposed to what this view implies, the laws cannot be considered directly expressive of the private interests of the members of the ruling faction, for two reasons: first, the ruling faction itself represents some kind of compromise between the private interests of its individual members, and second, the very form of law is a gesture toward some form of legitimacy separate from the will of the ruler or rulers.[8]

These problems are not problems for Thrasymachus's view, however, because Thrasymachus's first definition is not imprecisely *nominalist,* but precisely, and somewhat bizarrely, *legalist* or *nomothetical.*[9] The compromise of the private interests of members of the ruling faction and the gap between the form of law and the will of the ruler are not problems for Thrasymachus's account of the "advantage of the stronger" because his view of the art of rule abstracts entirely from private interests and individual wills. Consider his curious way of phrasing his first argument for the claim that justice is the "advantage of the stronger." He says that "each ruling power [ἡ ἀρχὴ, as opposed to the rulers [ἀι ἀρχαί] sets down laws for its own advantage; a democracy sets down democratic laws; a tyranny, tyrannical laws; and the others do the same" (338d). The odd thing about this formulation is that in it, Thrasymachus seems to identify the "ruling power" with the regime or regime type, rather than the individual rulers of that regime, and to present the regime itself as the source of legislation. This identification is shown most clearly by Thrasymachus's claim that a tyranny sets down tyrannical laws (Τίθεται δέ γε τοὺς νόμους . . . τυραννὶς δε τυραννικούς).

---

8. Cf. the argument against the claim that Thrasymachus holds a "nihilist view" of justice in Cross and Woozley 1964, 32–36.

9. Kerferd, Annas, and Strauss all identify Thrasymachus's first position as "legalist." Unfortunately, as the divergent interpretations these three authors give of Thrasymachus's "legalism" demonstrate, the term can have a range of meanings, which tends to obscure the precise character of Thrasymachus's account. Thrasymachus's implicit understanding of legislative activity, on the interpretation I offer, is close to that espoused by the Chinese legalist tradition. He conceives of the art of rule as essentially an expertise in legislative control of the passions of the many. However, the limitations inherent in his articulation of the art of rule show that he is also "legalistic" in the sense of being ultimately dependent on abstract formal principles in the exercise of his art.

While the identification between the ruling power and the regime makes a degree of sense with regard to *dêmokratia*—though certainly less sense with the Greek notion of *dêmokratia* than it would with our notion of a representative democracy—it seems to make little sense in the case of an oligarchy and no sense at all in the case of a tyranny. A *tyranny* does not make laws, we would say, a *tyrant* does—if, that is, we are right to call the formal expression of the tyrant's wishes "making laws" as opposed to "giving commands" or "issuing edicts."[10] It is Thrasymachus's failure to distinguish between the "that which rules" in a regime and the laws or the constitution of that regime that is our initial clue to the first of Thrasymachus's two complementary abstractions, and it is from here that Socrates' examination of Thrasymachus proceeds.

Socrates' first question seems to be merely a restatement of Thrasymachus's position, but notice that Socrates does not speak about the ruling power, as Thrasymachus does, but rather about those who rule. He asks, to overtranslate a bit, "Do you not, however, also say it is just to obey those who rule?" (οὐ καὶ πείθεσθαι μέντοι τοῖς ἄρχουσιν δίκαιον φῂς εἶναι;) This question points to the distance between the individuals who make up a ruling faction and the laws they enact or the constitution they found. Socrates then asks whether the rulers (οἱ ἄρχοντες) in their cities are infallible or such as to make mistakes. When Thrasymachus responds to Socrates that those who rule do, indeed, make mistakes in laying down laws, and that an incorrect law is one which is disadvantageous to them, Socrates draws the implication that justice as Thrasymachus has defined it is both to the advantage and to the disadvantage of those who rule—an implication enthusiastically endorsed by Socrates' new ally Polemarchus.

At this point in the argument, and in response to Polemarchus, Cleitophon steps forward in defense, as he thinks, of Thrasymachus's position. Thrasymachus, Cleitophon suggests, merely made a verbal slip when he identified justice with the advantage of the ruling power *simpliciter;* what Thrasymachus *really* meant is that justice is doing what the stronger, that is, the ruler, *believes* to be in his advantage. That is, Cleitophon wants to attribute the success of Socrates' refutation of Thrasymachus to exactly the kind of casual slip on Thrasymachus's part that I have suggested (§2.5) that we as readers are likely to wrongly attribute to Socrates' interlocutors. So too, Cleitophon is wrong in attributing this kind of mistake to Thrasymachus; in fact, Cleitophon has it backwards. In Thrasymachus's opinion, his mistake was not that he identified justice with the ruling power; his mistake, rather, was to accede to Socrates' suggestion that it is just to obey whomever happens to hold the position of ruler. Thrasymachus instead

---

10. See Xenophon *Mem.* 1.2.43–44, Thuc. 3.62.3, and Aristotle *Pol.* 1292a1–35 for clear statements of the ancient conception of tyranny as essentially opposed to law.

reaffirms his original position; it is just to obey the ruling power; or, as he restates it, justice is the advantage of the ruler *qua* expert craftsman, the ruler "in precise speech" (κατὰ τὸν ἀκριβῆ λόγον).

Before continuing with Socrates' examination of Thrasymachus, we need to ask why, exactly, Cleitophon's suggestion seems so plausible and Thrasymachus's so counterintuitive. One reason, I believe, is that we have a tendency to find plausible, or at least *familiar,* a position Polus voices in the *Gorgias,* in short, that a substantial part of what one imagines would be desirable about despotic rule is simply the capacity to do whatever he thinks best, regardless of its consequences for him; that is, part of what is desirable about the prospect of rule is the freedom from external constraint. This freedom, or the pleasure that comes from its exercise, the pleasure associated with willful self-assertion, is entirely lacking in this half of Thrasymachus's account, though we will see it return with a vengeance, so to speak, in the second half. Here, however, instead of adopting the "common-sense" notion suggested by Cleitophon that focuses on the unenlightened desires of the individual in a position of power, Thrasymachus radicalizes the separation between the ruling power or art and the individual who happens to rule.

By arguing that the ruler "in the precise sense" is only a ruler when he is exercising his craft perfectly, and not a ruler when he is not practicing his craft perfectly, Thrasymachus is claiming, in effect, that it is not a particular human being but rather the art of rule itself that is "the ruling power." Socrates demonstrates that this is Thrasymachus's implicit claim by a series of questions which isolate the function of a particular art, not only from other aspects of the practitioner's daily life but from any experience or natural talent which might seem necessary supplements to the principles of the art of rule itself. First he asks whether a doctor in "the precise sense" is one who cares for the sick or a money-maker, a question to which Thrasymachus quite reasonably responds "One who care for the sick." Socrates' next question is more telling, however. He asks whether, speaking correctly (ὀρθῶς), a captain is a sailor or a ruler of sailors (ναυτῶν ἄρχων), and he presses the point by saying, "I suppose it needn't be taken into account that he sails in the ship, and he shouldn't be called a sailor for that. For it isn't because of sailing that he is called a captain but because of his art and his rule over sailors." While Thrasymachus responds that the captain in the precise sense is a ruler over sailors and not a sailor, we should see his response as an artifact of the abstract sense he gives to the notion of an art of rule. For while it is true that a captain is not merely a sailor but also a "ruler" over sailors, it is also the case that his being a sailor—and a good one—is essential to his being a good ruler over sailors. That is, knowledge of seamanship is not only necessary for him to pilot the ship correctly, it is also an essential aspect of his authority over the men in his crew. Consider, for example, Socrates' image of the democratic "ship of state" at 488a–e. In that image, it is due to the fact that the shipowner-demos is somewhat deaf and shortsighted and is also defective in his knowledge of the sailor's art (γιγνώσκοντα περὶ ναυτικῶν) that the sailors quarrel among themselves over who should captain the ship.[11] Thrasymachus's notion of the art of rule would have us imagine a Caesar, Napoleon, or Alexander "in the precise sense" whose rule over his subjects bears no essential relation to his capacity as a general in the field.

We can, of course, imagine something along these lines, for example a dictator whose authority springs not from his demonstrated capacity as a general but rather from his rhetorical gifts in rousing the masses. However, the abstractness of Thrasymachus's account separates the art of rule from such "gifts" as well. He not only divides proficiency in the art of rule from any other experience or knowledge which might serve as a basis for the authority of the ruler, he also separates it from any natural talents or capacities of the person proficient in the art. Socrates demonstrates this aspect of Thrasymachus's account when he asks whether medicine or any other art, considered in the precise sense, is defective (πονηρά) and whether it is in need of some additional virtue beyond the art itself. Thrasymachus replies, tentatively, that arts are in no way defective, nor are they in need of any supplementary virtue. This claim, which is dubious enough in the case of the art of medicine, is extraordinarily suspect when we consider the art of ruling. It would seem that to be a good ruler—in any sense of "good" we might choose: effective, powerful, domineering—would require some particular excellence beyond the ruling art, some talent or capacity, some experience or force of character, that not everyone is going to have.[12] We can still, of course, imagine a case wherein a ruler, despite being ineffective and talentless in other ways, nonetheless exercises relatively unquestioned authority over his subjects. But this appears to be possible only in cases where the ruler is exercising either what Max Weber calls "traditional authority" or what he calls "legal" authority, rather than what he calls "charismatic authority"; that is, we can only imagine it in cases where the source of the authority of the ruler stands outside the ruler himself.

For Thrasymachus this authority is entirely vested in the "ruling art," an art abstracted from any other knowledge, capacity, or disposition in the ruler. It is

---

11. In that image Socrates is also abstracting from the relation between the knowledge of seamanship and the authority the captain exercises over the sailors, but Socrates' abstraction is diametrically opposed to the abstraction Thrasymachus is guilty of in this passage. Socrates' image of the true captain is one who is *only* concerned with the ship's relation to its natural environment and not at all with his relation to the sailors under his command. I will try to make explicit both the character of Socrates' abstraction and the reasons for it in chapter 6.

12. Cf. Isocrates *Antid.* 15.187.

this infallible art, rather than the fallible individual who happens to hold the position of power in the regime, that Thrasymachus sees as that which is truly the "ruling power." Hence the turn in the argument at 342c, where Socrates says, "But, Thrasymachus, the arts rule and are masters of that of which they are the arts." This turn, which seems so strange, is, I believe, a strict consequence of Thrasymachus's notion of the ruler "in the precise sense" as he has developed it to this point. By isolating the art of rule entirely from the talents, experiences, dispositions, and capacities of the individual who holds a position of rule, Thrasymachus is considering ruling a function of what we might call a formal or pure science (ἐπιστήμη) of rule (343c). Indeed, Thrasymachus introduces the notion of rule as an "epistêmê " (its first occurrence in the *Republic*) at exactly the moment that he introduces the notion of the ruler in the precise sense (340e). However, by conceiving this pure science of rule in opposition to its fallible practical application, Thrasymachus must also accept the consequence that such a pure science is directed toward pure or formal objects, and not toward the practical analogues of these pure objects. Just as a pure mathematics deals not with this or that triangular-seeming object but with the formal character of a given kind a triangle, so too, it would seem, the pure science of ruling subjugates not this or that particular individual but the formal character of a given kind of "political subject." That is, it seems that Thrasymachus's "ruler in the precise sense" could only rule over a "subject in the precise sense," the legally defined "person" rather than the imprecise, and perhaps indefinable, individual human being. Moreover, if we are to understand the relation between a pure science and its objects in terms of "advantage" at all, we could say either that it seeks the advantage of the science itself, that is, it seeks to complete and perfect itself as a science—an alternative that Thrasymachus rejects—or we could say that it seeks the advantage of its formal object, that is, it seeks to give complete and perfect expression to the formal character of its object—the alternative Thrasymachus is forced into by his rejection of the claim that an art is imperfect and seeks its own advantage. What we cannot say, and what *Thrasymachus* cannot say, is that the formal art as such seeks the advantage of any such impure object as the person who happens to be proficient in that art.[13]

At one level, and not the deepest we will explore, Thrasymachus's presentation of the pure art of rule could be ascribed to his role as a *teacher* of the art of rhetoric *as* an art of rule. His denial that the arts as such stand in need of a supplementary virtue could then be explained by the fact that were he to

---

13. It is, of course, also true that the formal science of medicine does not look to the advantage of the impure and unlucky individual who happens to be a patient of the doctor qua scientist, but this objection could hardly be used to Thrasymachus's advantage in his argument with Socrates.

admit that the art of rule is not sufficient in itself but needs to be supplemented by natural capacities in the craftsman-ruler, this would make manifest the fact that the art of rule is not entirely teachable. Thrasymachus, however, may want to say it is entirely teachable, because he teaches it. Under Socrates' questioning, Thrasymachus describes the individual in a position of power as an imperfect oppressor, one who makes mistakes, and Thrasymachus presents himself as the purveyor of the art of perfect oppression. He may want his students to believe that his art will enable them, without any extraordinary excellence of their own, to become tyrants. As I have suggested, however, there are deeper reasons for Thrasymachus's commitment to the abstract art of rule, reasons that have to do with the limited sense in which he is able to conceive himself and his art as *good*. But before we can explore those issues, we must attempt to understand his second formulation of justice: "justice and the just are, in reality, the good of another" (ἡ μὲν δικαιοσύνη καὶ τὸ δίκαιον ἀλλότριον ἀγαθὸν τῷ ὄντι, 343c3–4).

4.2 The Good of Another

At first, Thrasymachus claimed that "justice" is a mechanism of the formal science of rule, embodied in the regime and expressed in the formal principles of legislation. Now, after being forced to admit that when one abstracts entirely from the individual who exercises the art of rule, the ruler *qua* artist of rule doesn't look to his personal advantage, Thrasymachus appears to reverse his position entirely. Where he had first claimed that justice is the name "the ruling power" in any city gives to obedience to the laws that it sets down with a view to its own interest, he now compares the just and the unjust man in a variety of situations, including the situation of rule, and says the unjust man is going to get the better of the just man. But in that case, how could he be identifying justice with the legislation enacted by a competent or scientific ruler? For the "perfectly" unjust man to be identified as unjust while occupying the throne in a tyranny, he has to be contravening or transgressing something other than laws set down in the interest of the ruling power, that is, himself. In Thrasymachus's new formulation, it is as a consequence of this transgression that the unjust man gets more than the just man. Injustice, the most perfect injustice, Thrasymachus says, makes the one who does it most happy.

It will turn out that Thrasymachus has not, in fact, reversed his position. His two accounts of justice both find their source in a common conception of the political world, and their prima facie incompatibility arises from a shift in perspective. As we will see, Thrasymachus has adopted, for the sake of his argument, a radically opposed perspective from the one he adopted in his initial presentation of justice and injustice. With this new perspective, the legalistic and amoral Thrasymachus has apparently given way to Thrasymachus the "immoralist." In the first case, Thrasymachus denied that there were any moral facts about the world; there was only power and exploitation, advantage and disadvantage, arts exercised well or poorly. In the second case, on the other hand, not only *are* there moral facts, but these are the most important facts about the world. For it is only by transgression of what is just, by "taking what belongs to others," that the unjust man is the unjust man, and it is only insofar as he is unjust that he is said by Thrasymachus to be most happy. This point, while perhaps obvious, needs to be stressed, because it will follow us throughout the rest of our discussion of the *Republic*. Both Thrasymachus, in his second definition of justice, and Glaucon, in his "restoration" of Thrasymachus's argument, argue that the unjust man is happy precisely *in virtue of* his injustice. They do not argue, as Adeimantus does, that to be happy an individual must sometimes—perhaps often—do things that are held to be unjust (364a).[14] Rather, they claim that injustice is in itself constitutive of the greatest goods. Consider, for example, Thrasymachus's claim that "the most perfect injustice," that is, the conquest of a people and the establishment of a tyranny, makes the one who does injustice "most happy" (344a). What is significant here is that Thrasymachus does not say that the establishment of a tyranny makes the tyrant as happy as, for example, the great king, a "traditional" authority, and one whom Socrates, at least, is willing to consider possibly just.[15] According to Thrasymachus's second account, this kind of traditional rule just isn't good enough. This account presents injustice and transgression as essential, rather than accidental, to the happiest life.

In order to understand Thrasymachus's intent in expounding his second definition of justice and injustice, we need to keep the following three points in mind. First, while Thrasymachus's first account appeared to be a reductive account of what we call justice and injustice—one which defined away the conventional ethical meaning of justice and injustice—his second account seems to depend upon the most conventional of understandings of justice and injustice. According to this account, the most perfect injustice is that which "by stealth and force takes away what belongs to others." Second, Thrasymachus the "immoralist" is no less abstract a thinker than Thrasymachus the "legalist." It is still tyranny, not the tyrant, which is said to take away what belongs to others. It is injustice that is called mighty and free and masterful, not the unjust man; the unjust man is said to be happy. Third, just as Thrasymachus presents injustice and transgression as essential to the happy life, he presents those who are just and

14. See §10.6 below.
15. *Grg.* 470e.

obedient as essentially, rather than accidentally, wretched. By the very fact of their obedience they make "him who they serve happy but themselves not at all" (343d). He appears to present political rule as a "zero-sum" game (or, as we will see, a less-than-zero-sum game), where to be unjust is, by definition, to win and to be just is, by definition, to lose.

There is a manifest problem with this vision of the political world, however, a problem that is, once again, indicated by a peculiarity in Thrasymachus's language. Near the beginning of his tirade, where he attempts to define justice and injustice for Socrates, there is a puzzling lack of symmetry between his presentation of justice and his presentation of injustice. He says:

> You are so far off [πόρρω] about the just and justice and the unjust and injustice, that you are ignorant that justice and the just are, in reality [τῷ ὄντι], the good of another, the advantage of the stronger and the ruler, and a personal harm to the one who obeys and serves. Injustice is the opposite, and rules the truly innocent [εὐηθικῶν, literally "person of good character"] and just, and those ruled do what is the advantage of him who is stronger, and they make him who they serve happy and themselves not at all. (343c–d, trans. altered)

What makes this passage so confusing is that instead of juxtaposing the action of the unjust man and the just man, or the ruler and the ruled, it juxtaposes two different ways of conceiving the actions of the just men who are ruled. It compares justice, which is "the good of another, the advantage of the stronger and the ruler" with injustice, which is *that which rules* those who "do what is the advantage of him who is stronger." The unjust man is nowhere to be found in this opposition. What Thrasymachus does *not* say here, and *never* says, is that the unjust man *qua* unjust man rules. He also never says that the unjust man does "his own good"; rather, the most he can say is that the unjust is "what is profitable and advantageous for oneself" (ἑαυτῷ λυσιτελοῦν τε καὶ συμφέρον, 344c8).[16]

The asymmetry between Thrasymachus's claim that the just man does "the good of another" (ἀλλότριον ἀγαθὸν) and the absence of any claim that the unjust man does his own good (ἑαυτὸν ἀγαθὸν) points to the significance for Thrasymachus's account of what I have been referring to as "the problem of heteronomy." Thrasymachus's second, "immoralist," account of justice is wholly, and pathologically, other directed. The happiness he conceives for the potential tyrant comes entirely from his rejection and transgression of the "good of another," but includes no independent conception of the good for oneself.

16. Cf. 367c.

Simply put, Thrasymachus cannot conceive of any moral or immoral good—nor, in fact, any emotive or ethical content whatsoever—to the life of political rule. He is unable to assume the psychological perspective of the ruler, and can only conceive of the individual's ethical-psychological relation to rule from *below*. From that perspective, he presents two alternatives: an individual can either transgress the conventions or laws, the implicit or explicit claims others make upon him, or be bound by those claims and do "the good of another." In the first case, the fact of transgression makes the individual happy; in the second, the fact of submission makes the individual wretched.

Thrasymachus never says that the just man serves the unjust man, or that the just man makes the unjust man happy, or that the just man does what is advantageous for the unjust man. Instead, consistently, he says that the just man serves, makes happy, and does the advantage of the *stronger*. Nor does Thrasymachus *ever say* that the unjust man *is* the stronger, however much he seems to imply it. As I have pointed out above, it is injustice which Thrasymachus represents as "mightier, freer, and more masterful" than justice. We are now prepared to see how the apparent contradiction between the two versions of Thrasymachus's account is only apparent. In the second version of Thrasymachus's account, it is only in *becoming* a tyrant that the tyrant is unjust in the relevant sense, that he takes what belongs to others; once rule is achieved, the injustice of the successful tyrant is in the past (344c2). So too, it seems, is his distinctive happiness. Once he is a ruler, the man who holds the position of rule can continue to accrue "profit" at the expense of his subjects, but his distinctive "happiness," the happiness that comes from transgression, is lost to him.

The reason for these peculiarities in Thrasymachus's presentation is that, in moving from his first account to his second, he has moved from the realm of "being" to the realm of "becoming"—from the realm of the pure science of rule to the realm of ethical psychology. In his panegyric to the might, freedom, and mastery of injustice, Thrasymachus is representing the psychology of transgression, and it is from this psychological perspective that the tyrant is said to take what belongs to others and be unjust. When he is no longer taking, no longer actively transgressing what *he sees* as belonging to another, there is no longer any ethical content for him to his injustice.[17] He can now only reap material benefits like a shepherd harvesting wool from his sheep. Correspondingly, in his tirade

---

17. The fact that the injustice of the unjust man is constituted by his transgression of what *he perceives* as the restriction placed upon him from without, and the pathological character of his desire for transgression, is most clearly shown by Thrasymachus's claim that tyranny, in taking what belongs to others, takes all of what is "both the sacred and the profane." What could it possibly mean, in positive terms, to take *all* of what is "sacred"? Moreover, what, outside of a pathological desire for transgression, could motivate someone to *try?*

about the "good of another," Thrasymachus is representing the psychology of what Nietzsche calls *ressentiment*. It is from this perspective of *ressentiment* that one is always serving the strong, always making the ruler happy, and always being ruled by injustice. From this perspective, there is no positive content to political relations, no good in either rule or service; there is only the misery of serving the stronger, the relief of freedom from service, and, once again, the advantage of material goods.

In both these psychological portraits Thrasymachus can give no positive content to the ethical-psychological relations between human beings. In either case, one can reap material benefits from the work of another, but the only ethical-psychological alternatives are transgression and service. This explains Thrasymachus's way of presenting the contrast between the just man and the unjust man "holding some ruling office"—and it is clear from the content of this contrast that this "ruling office" cannot be a position of absolute rule. Thrasymachus says that the just man will "see his domestic affairs deteriorate from neglect while he gets no advantage from the public store, thanks to his being just; in addition to this, he suffers the ill will of his relatives and his acquaintances when he is unwilling to serve them against what is just" (343e). Thrasymachus then says that "the unjust man's situation is the opposite in all of these respects" (τῷ δὲ ἀδίκῳ πάντα τούτων τἀναντία ὑπάρχει, 343e7). If we take the precise-speaking Thrasymachus at his word, this means that the unjust man will get advantage from the public store, and will not incur the ill will of his relatives and acquaintances (notice that neither the just or the unjust man has any friends) because *he is willing to serve them* against what is just. It is still the case, even for the unjust man, that the only meaningful relation between individuals is one of servitude. One can either choose to deny the claims others make upon him or he can choose to be their servant; that is all. This also makes clear why the game of politics, from the perspective of *ressentiment* psychology, is a less-than-zero-sum game. Materially, one person's loss is another person's gain. However, once rule is established, the "stronger" accrue no ethical-psychological benefit, because they are no longer transgressing and are no longer actively unjust. The ruled, on the other hand, are always suffering the brute injustice of the fact of rule, the fact that there is another who is stronger.

4.3 Wage-Earners and Tyrants

As we have seen, Thrasymachus attempts to leave after finishing this speech but is compelled by the others to stay and give an argument in support of what he has said, and it is unsurprising, if a little ominous, that they should so compel him. Thrasymachus has been less than prudent in giving voice to the repressed inner monologue of *ressentiment* and speaking aloud his panegyric to transgression. Socrates is careful in his narration not to present himself as party to the compulsion, however, and instead presents himself as *entreating* Thrasymachus to speak (note the string of particles emphasizing Socrates as a particular individual: καὶ δὴ ἔγωγε καὶ αὐτὸς πάνυ ἐδεόμην τε καὶ εἶπον, 344d5). Socrates, moreover, is careful to make clear to Thrasymachus the dangerous ground upon which he is treading. He urges Thrasymachus to stay and "teach us adequately," saying that it is "not a small matter" that Thrasymachus is attempting to define, but the leading of a complete life, and how "each of us" (ἕκαστος ἡμῶν) can live a life most profitably. And when Thrasymachus asks in reply, "Do I believe otherwise?" Socrates says, "You seem to . . . or else you don't care for us and are in no way concerned whether we will live worse or better for our ignorance of what you say you know." He reminds Thrasymachus that it "wouldn't be a bad investment for you to do some good work for as many as we are." That is, he reminds Thrasymachus that this kind of service to the common good, even if it is merely lip service, is in his own best interest.

We should also note in passing a similarity in the way that Socrates and Thrasymachus metaphorically characterize what I have been calling Thrasymachus's "tirade." They both describe this piece of bombast as something quasi-material that Thrasymachus attempts to put inside his listener's soul. Socrates says that Thrasymachus tried to leave "after having poured a great shower of speech into our ears all at once" (344d1–2). And when Socrates says that he is not persuaded by what Thrasymachus has said, Thrasymachus replies, "If you are not persuaded by what I have said, what more shall I do for you? Shall I give your soul a forced feeding?" (345b4–6). This is quite the opposite of "precise speech"; it presents Thrasymachus's rhetorically charged praise of injustice as something amorphous and mass-like transferred from speaker to listener through the medium of words. We will have occasion to return to these "material" qualities of the rhetorician's speaking below.

For now, however, we turn to Socrates' response to Thrasymachus's second account of justice and injustice. As we have seen, neither in Thrasymachus's account of the pure science of rule nor in his representation of the ethical psychology of obedience and transgression did he describe any goods internal to the activity of ruling for the individual exercising rule. The only "advantage" of the pure science of rule turned out to be, on Thrasymachus's account, the "advantage" directed toward the formal objects of that science. In his second account, on the other hand, while Thrasymachus was able to ascribe an ethical psychological benefit to the process whereby an individual *becomes* a tyrant, the only benefits he could ascribe to the actual practice of rule were the material advantages reaped from the "sheep" in the tyrant's flock. That is, as a consequence of Thrasymachus's inability to assume the ethical psychological perspective of the ruler, Thrasymachus is not able to represent any ethical or psychological content of the life of rule. Leaving aside, for the moment, a consideration of any ethical psychological content which finds value in the happiness of *others*, the problem is that Thrasymachus's tyrant cannot see his polis as his *own* in any deeper sense than he would his shoes or cloak (to use the examples Socrates uses against Callicles' representation of the tyrant in the *Gorgias*). He cannot see the polis as an extension of himself and a reflection of his own magnificence. Nor does he see his rule as a platform for world-historical ambitions; to repeat, this man is no Caesar. Thrasymachus's tyrant cannot see ruling the polis as his "work" in any grander sense than his job, his means to material advantage.[18] He is, to anticipate Socrates' argument, a glorified wage earner.

Socrates refutation of Thrasymachus's second definition hinges on this inability of Thrasymachus to represent any loftier benefit to an achieved tyranny than wages. Tyrannical rule seems, under this description, to be a second-order instrumental good, itself in the service of the instrumental good of wealth. To demonstrate this, Socrates introduces a distinction between different arts on the basis of the different benefits each provides: medicine provides health to the body, the captain's art safety in sailing, and so on. Among the arts, he distinguishes the art of wage-earning as the art which furnishes the particular benefit of wages. He then argues that each craftsman, considered in the precise sense, does not accrue wages insofar as he practices his particular art, but rather by his practice of the additional art of wage-earning—an art all the craftsmen share. They must practice this additional art due to the fact that the primary art they practice, Socrates reiterates, looks to the benefit of that over which it rules. Socrates then concludes this brief refutation by asking Thrasymachus whether the craftsman would receive any benefit from the art that he practices if pay were not attached to it. When Thrasymachus says, "It appears not," Socrates can conclude that no one willingly chooses to rule, but rules only for the sake of wages—either money or honor or the avoidance of a penalty. The penalty he means, as he explains to Glaucon, is the "greatest penalty" of being ruled by someone worse than oneself, if one is not willing to rule.

Now, if Thrasymachus were not in a rhetorical bind, he should have cried foul at Socrates' introduction of the "art of wage-earning."[19] With this art, Socrates seems to have introduced an art which, in its precise sense, looks to

---

18. Cf. Kojève 1991, 140–43.

19. Thrasymachus's οὐ φαίνεται may suggest that he recognizes the problem with Socrates' assertion of the art of wage-earning, and his own inability to take rhetorical advantage of it.

the advantage of the individual who practices the art. That is, it is a counter-example to the very principle upon which Socrates is drawing: that no art or rule, taken in its precise sense, looks to the advantage of the individual who practices the art.[20] However, this is not an argument to which Thrasymachus can appeal. For if he did point out this apparent flaw in Socrates' argument, it would make all too clear the kinship between the supposedly magnificent art of rule and the banausic "wage-earner's art" on his account. On the other hand, if he denied there was an art of wage-earning, it would imply that material benefits as such are not the product of a precise art, and therefore not simply an artifact of the art of rule. That is, it would imply that "excellence" in wage-earning depended on the very capacities—natural talents, force of character, and so on—that we saw Thrasymachus exclude from his account of the precise science of rule. Even more significantly, if Thrasymachus denied that "wage-earning" was a precise art wholly responsible for the accruing of material wealth, he would have to admit what he most wants to deny—that wages depend, in some sense, on being valued by others.

Thrasymachus does not get the opportunity to reply directly to Socrates' claim to have shown by this argument that "the one who is to do anything fine by art never does what is best for himself . . . , but rather what is best for the one who is ruled" (346e–347a). Instead, Socrates shifts the focus of the discussion from the definition of justice to the "far greater" claim that the life of the unjust man is more profitable than the life of the just man. I will not attempt here to give a complete account of Socrates' argument for the superiority of the just life, but will instead focus on the ways that discussion is directed toward the conflict in Thrasymachus's self-conscious relation to his own art of rhetoric as it is manifested in his two divergent accounts of justice and injustice.

4.4 Rule-Following, Justice, and Art

We can best begin by looking briefly to Socrates' description of Thrasymachus in the *Phaedrus*. In that dialogue Socrates ridicules those rhetoricians who think they have captured what is essential to the art of rhetoric by giving technical rules for producing long speeches or short speeches, speeches that excite or subdue a particular emotion, and among them he singles out Thrasymachus for especially rough treatment. Judging from Socrates' account, Thrasymachus seems to have written treatises where he laid out principles for "enraging the many," and for "charming" them once they have been enraged (*Phdr.* 267d–e). He is

---

20. Cf. Reeve 1988, 19.

also said to have a special proficiency for slandering others and responding to slander, proficiencies very much on display in the *Republic*. However, according to Socrates, the person who knows these things knows only "the necessities preliminary to the art of rhetoric" (269b8–9) and not the art itself. Before an individual had any claim to possess the art of rhetoric, Socrates and Phaedrus agree, he would have to know not only these preliminaries, but also know when and to whom they ought to be applied (268b6–7). As we have seen, there are very good reasons to doubt that Thrasymachus knows when and to whom his speeches ought to be applied. We can express the distinction Socrates is drawing in terms of a distinction between two sense of the Greek word *technê*, a distinction roughly captured by the opposition between the English words "art" and "technique." Socrates is saying, in effect, that as a rhetorician Thrasymachus is no artist, but merely a technician. He has no more command of his *technê*, and no more claim to be considered an artist of rhetoric, than someone who stumbled across a book of medicine and learned how to induce vomiting would have to be considered a doctor (268a–c). The distinction between rhetorician-as-artist and rhetorician-as-technician will be crucial to our understanding of Socrates' critique, not only of Thrasymachus's vision of the nine-to-five tyrant, but to the conception of the art of rhetoric which underlies it. However, before we can understand the full significance of this distinction, we need to see more clearly one of its consequences—Thrasymachus's failure to rise above the "matter" of his art.

As I have attempted to show, Thrasymachus's two accounts correspond to (1) the pure science of rule and (2) a representation of the ethical psychology of subjection to rule. These two accounts also correspond, I suggest, to a problematic distinction Thrasymachus draws between the "form" and the "matter" of his art. Thrasymachus's first account corresponds to the formal principles of his own "science" of rhetoric, and his second account to the content of that science, a content which, as we have seen above, both Thrasymachus and Socrates characterize in quasi-material terms. The pure science of rhetoric lays out the formal principles whereby one rouses a crowd to anger, or charms it to complacency. The content of that science, on the other hand, corresponds to the ethical opinions of "the many," upon which opinions Thrasymachus must draw to produce his effects. To understand Thrasymachus's character, we must recognize that, simply put, he believes in the principles of his art, but does not believe (or, rather, *thinks* he does not believe) these opinions. Despite his capacity for drawing upon the suppressed psychologies of transgression and *ressentiment*, and the views of justice and injustice implicit in them, Thrasymachus believes himself to be beyond these ethical-psychological considerations—to be, in effect, too precise a thinker to be moved around by the quasi-material ethical content of these psychologies. He believes himself to be merely using these opinions in order to obtain the one real good he self-consciously recognizes, the good of wealth.[21] As we will see, he is mistaken in this belief.

To see that Thrasymachus does not self-consciously endorse the ethical-psychological view of justice presented in his second account, we need to look at certain details of his defense of the superiority of the unjust life. At 349c–d, when Socrates asks him whether he considers "justice virtue and injustice vice," Thrasymachus's first response is to say that he believes "the opposite." However, when Socrates tries to get him to be more precise, it turns out that Thrasymachus flatly denies that injustice is virtue and justice vice.[22] The reason, as his reply makes clear, is that he denies the applicability of virtue and vice to ethical categories, that is, to questions of "mores" or "character" (ἦθος). When Socrates asks, "Is justice vice?" (Ἡ τὴν δικαιοσύνην κακίαν;), Thrasymachus responds, "No, but an entirely gentlemanly innocence," or more literally, "a very well-born goodness of character" (Οὔκ, ἀλλὰ πάνυ γενναίαν εὐήθειαν) Socrates then asks, "Do you then call justice wickedness?" or, more literally, "badness of character?" (κακοήθειαν). To this, Thrasymachus responds, "No, rather good counsel" (Οὔκ, ἀλλ᾽ εὐβουλίαν).[23] Thus, in Thrasymachus's view, to have "character" at all, that is, to be concerned with ethical categories as such, is to be "ill-advised" (κακόβουλος)—in short, to be subject to a stupidity for which Thrasymachus thinks himself much too clever.[24] Significantly, soon after this exchange Socrates remarks that Thrasymachus is no longer "joking" but now "speaking the truth" as it seems to him (349a).[25]

However, Socrates quickly shows that Thrasymachus is not as clever as he thinks, and is still subject to the ethical categories that he believes he has seen beyond. He places both the just man and the unjust man in hypothetical competition with others, and asks Thrasymachus whether the just man would be willing to "get the better of" the just man, or the just action. Thrasymachus responds, "Not at all . . . for then he would not be the civil [ἀστεῖος] and innocent [εὐήθης] fellow he is." Socrates then asks whether the just man would "believe he deserves [ἀξιοῖ] to get the better of the unjust man, and believe it to be just." Thrasymachus says that the just man would believe this, but would be unable to get the better of the unjust man—and thus far, Thrasymachus's answers, while certainly debatable, seem relatively unproblematic. Next, Socrates

21. Cf. *Phdr.* 266c.
22. See Shorey's footnote to 348c in Plato 1969–70.
23. Cf. 400d–e.
24. Accordingly, Thrasymachus will not himself use the terms ἀρετή and κακία until after he claims to have ceased responding in earnest (350d–e).
25. Literally, Socrates says, "Now you seem to me . . . to be artlessly (ἀτεχνῶς) not scoffing," implying, perhaps, that Thrasymachus is no longer speaking in the voice of his art.

asks whether the *unjust* man would "believe he deserves" to get the better of both the just man and the unjust man, the just and the unjust action. Thrasymachus responds by saying that the unjust man "would believe he deserves to get the better of everyone." At this point, however, we must ask why Thrasymachus doesn't respond to this question of Socrates by claiming that the unjust man doesn't think he deserves anything—he simply takes what he wants? What basis can Thrasymachus give for the unjust man's claim to *deserve* anything? What can this claim even *mean* for Thrasymachus or for his unjust man?

As we have seen, throughout his bifurcate presentation of the science and psychology of justice and injustice, Thrasymachus studiously avoids attributing any positive value to the claims human beings make upon one another in an "ethical" community. The art of rule did not depend, in Thrasymachus's first account, on that authority which could come from demonstrated competence or personal charisma, but on the objective science of legislative exploitation. The unjust man holding "a ruling office" in Thrasymachus's second account did not reap the benefits of the awe with which he was held by his relatives and acquaintances, he just did not incur their ill-will by being unwilling to serve them. In both accounts, any ethical claim made upon one by another, "the good of another," is always either labored under or transgressed. Now, however, Thrasymachus's unjust man is revealed to make implicitly—and unbeknownst to himself—an ethical claim on everyone; he makes an implicit claim about what is just, albeit an incoherent one. He believes he deserves, by virtue of his injustice, more than everyone—even the other unjust man.

It would, of course, be a mistake to take this implicit appeal to justice on the part of Thrasymachus's version of the unjust man to be intended by Socrates, as narrator, or Plato, as author, to be a demonstration that the unjust man as such makes this kind of implicit appeal. The *Republic* as a whole goes a long way toward making a case that everyone, however good or bad, makes some implicit appeal, at some level, to the justice of what they do. However, it is clear that we can imagine someone being a lot more hardheaded in this regard than Thrasymachus, and we can be confident that Plato could as well. What it does suggest, however, is that *Thrasymachus* is making such an implicit appeal, and if we look back on the course of Thrasymachus's argument with Socrates, we will find plenty of evidence that he is, in fact, implicitly making claims about what is just. Or rather, in accordance with the psychology of *ressentiment* he so eloquently portrays, Thrasymachus implicitly makes claims about injustice, specifically, claims about the injustice of Socrates.

From the very beginning, Thrasymachus contends that Socrates doesn't play fair in arguments. Socrates is selfish. While he himself is unwilling to teach, he goes around learning from others and doesn't even thank them for their trouble

(337b). He won't answer himself, but when someone else answers he refutes him even though he himself knows it is easier to ask than to answer (336c).[26] Thrasymachus accuses Socrates of dissembling (337a), of villainy (338d) and of secretly plotting to do him harm (341d). Thrasymachus even apes the role of prosecutor presenting the case against Socrates. However, the charge on which Thrasymachus seeks to convict Socrates is the opposite of the one for which Socrates was tried and convicted by the Athenian demos.[27] He seeks to expose Socrates as a collaborator with an "aristocratic" (εὐήθης) conspiracy of silence regarding the truth about the laws, a collaborator who will deserve to suffer punishment when Thrasymachus speaks that truth (337d). He even goes so far as to accuse Socrates of acting as a "συκοφάντης" in arguments, that is, an informant for the city of Athens. This is what most arouses Thrasymachus's indignation at Socrates' "innocent" portrayal of the good and just man helping his friends and harming no one. Thrasymachus experiences the community of the "good" and the "just" not only as an ideological fiction, but as one from which he suffers exclusion. As in his psychological portrait of rule, he can only experience this community from below. From this position below and outside the ethical community, however, Thrasymachus still makes claims upon that ethical community. Unlike Socrates, who "gratifies his love of honor" from within the ethical community, Thrasymachus desires to be held in esteem for speaking out the truth (ἐπιθυμῶν εἰπεῖν ἵν᾿ εὐδοκιμήσειεν, 338a6), and it is this desire that compels Thrasymachus, against his better judgment, to press the case against Socrates.[28]

Thrasymachus, as we have now seen, is mistaken in his belief that he does not participate in the psychology of *ressentiment* which he depicts in the practice of his art. Moreover, despite his self-conscious contempt for the just man, Thrasymachus implicitly appeals to some notion of justice other than the "art of rule" in his attempted prosecution of Socrates. Given these facts about Thrasymachus, we might think that Socrates would appeal to these implicit notions about justice in his refutation of Thrasymachus's defense of the superiority of the unjust life. He might have tried, that is, to get to the bottom of what Thrasymachus *really*

---

26. These accusations should be compared to *Euthyphro* 3d, cited in §2.9 above. See also the following note.

27. The anger Thrasymachus apes, and participates in more than he knows, is not the anger of the polis, but rather the anger of the individual who feels repressed by the polis. Cf. Strauss 1978, 78.

28. In the *Parmenides,* Zeno distinguishes the love of controversy (φιλονικία, which Socrates applies to Thrasymachus at 338d) from the love of honor (φιλοτιμία, which Thrasymachus applies to Socrates 336c) by indicating that young men are lovers of controversy while older men are lovers of honor (128b–e). The context indicates that the distinction depends upon whether one is attempting to disrupt accepted hierarchies to improve one's position, or attempting to preserve a position of superiority; the first applies to younger men (and Thrasymachus, in Socrates' view) while the second applies to older men (and Socrates, in Thrasymachus's view).

thinks about justice. He does not do so. In fact, he explicitly denies it mattering to his refutation what Thrasymachus really thinks (349a–b), and continues his refutation long after Thrasymachus has said that he is merely playing along with Socrates "so as not to be hated by these men here" (352b). Nonetheless, Socrates clearly persuades Thrasymachus of *something* in the course of his argument.[29] As Glaucon later says, Thrasymachus seems to have been "charmed" like a snake (358b). Moreover, after Thrasymachus has given his argument, he is under no compulsion to stay. Yet stay he does, and becomes so fully integrated into the little community formed by the members of the dialogue that he acts as their official spokesman (450a). He even denigrates "prospecting for gold" as a waste of time in comparison to listening to arguments (450b). He becomes, as Socrates says, Socrates' friend (498d). If, then, he is not persuaded by Socrates' explicit arguments in book 1 concerning the superiority of the just life—and it is clear that he is not and should not be persuaded by those arguments[30]—of what is he persuaded? What does he hope to learn from Socrates? The answer to this question will return us to the issue with which I began this chapter, Thrasymachus's self-conscious relation to the practice of his art. The key to understanding Socrates' refutation of Thrasymachus's claim that the unjust man lives a superior life lies in the fact that the "unjust man" he is now referring to is Thrasymachus himself,[31] and the issue they are debating is Thrasymachus's understanding of the art of rhetoric, his own supposed art of rule.[32]

As we have seen, Thrasymachus is characterized by Socrates in the *Phaedrus* as a mere rhetorical technician, someone who conceives of the art of rhetoric as a system of formal rules for enraging a crowd and then making it docile. In this regard, Thrasymachus is very much like the individual who rules in his first account; his capacity to "rule" his audience does not ultimately derive from the authority he possesses among them due to demonstrated abilities in some relevant activity, nor, obviously, from his personal charisma, but from his mastery of formal or quasi-formal principles of persuasion. Thrasymachus has recognized that saying certain things about justice in certain ways makes people very angry, and saying other things about justice in other ways calms them again. But his "art" is *merely* imitative, not in any way creative. He produces

29. Compare Blondell 2002, 183–87.

30. See Beversluis 2000, 228–42.

31. Consider Socrates' implied substitution of Thrasymachus for Thrasymachus's unjust man at 345a–b, where Socrates says that "he [the unjust man] does not persuade me that this [injustice] is more profitable than justice. . . . So persuade us adequately, you blessed man, that we do not deliberate correctly."

32. Thrasymachus, no doubt, is also impressed with Socrates' own sophistic rhetorical powers, in particular his ability to represent justice as no more than instrumental self-restraint in the service of unjust aims without raising the ire of the assembled company. Nonetheless, as I will argue below, Socrates has more to teach Thrasymachus than this.

affects in his audience by sedulously aping those affects. He is, as Socrates also says in the *Phaedrus*, like someone who presents himself to Sophocles and Euripides and says that, because he has learned how to compose tearful speeches or threatening speeches and the like, he is a tragic poet, and that "he thinks that by teaching the same he is handing down [to his successors] the making of tragedy" (καὶ διδάσκων αὐτὰ τραγῳδίας ποίησιν οἴεται παραδιδόναι, *Phaedrus* 268d1–2). However, as Sophocles and Euripides clearly knew, one is not a tragic poet (or, at least, not one of *the* tragic poets) merely by imitating the work of others. If one is to "hand down" (παραδιδόναι) the art of composing tragedy, one must contribute to and, to some degree, transform that art.[33] One must see the "principles" of composition from above those "principles," and see the mastery of those principles as "the necessities preliminary to the art" (τὰ πρὸ τῆς τέχνης ἀναγκαῖα, *Phaedrus* 269b8–9) and not the practice of the art itself.

We can now see the significance of the alternative interpretation, suggested by Socrates, of the "advantage" toward which a precise art is directed. Recall, first, that Socrates asked whether there is any other advantage for each of the arts than to be as perfect or complete (τελέαν, 341d) as possible. When Thrasymachus did not understand this question, Socrates explained by asking whether any art was lacking something (προσδεῖταί τινος), and among the alternatives he presented if it were lacking something was that each art "considers its own advantage by itself" (αὐτῇ τὸ συμφέρον σκέψεται, 342a6). As we have seen, Thrasymachus rejected the notion that any art, considered in the precise sense, was defective or lacking in any way. However, we can now see that Thrasymachus could have, indeed should have, argued that the precise art seeks its own perfection. For if he had, Socrates would not have been able to conclude that each art only looks to the advantage of that over which it rules. The reason Thrasymachus does not allow for the possibility that the arts are in any way defective or lacking something is that he is not enough of an artist to see the formal principles of his art from above. As a mere rhetorical technician, Thrasymachus needs the assurance that the rules are enough to ensure the perfection of his art.[34] Moreover, as a mere technician, he resembles his picture of the tyrant in that he cannot see the art as his *own* in any profound sense; he cannot see it as an extension of himself and a reflection of his own excellence. Like his tyrant, he can only see his art as a means to the accumulation of wealth. This is the reason that Socrates can force him to

---

33. Cf. Aristotle *Poet.* 1449a8–30.

34. Of course, Socrates contends in the *Phaedrus* that any merely human practitioner of the art of poetry who is not inspired by divine madness will always produce poetry that is incomplete or imperfect (ἀτελής, *Phdr.* 245a5–9). I will argue in chapter 7, however, that this is an alternative that the philosophical orientation of the *Republic* excludes.

concede that the artist would derive no benefit from the practice of his art if wages were not attached to it (346d–e). It is safe to say that Socrates could not get such a concession from Euripides or Sophocles (nor, as we will see, from Gorgias or Protagoras).

Thrasymachus's dependence on the formal principles of his art also explains the purchase that Socrates' argument about whom the just and unjust man will want to "get the better of" has on Thrasymachus. As we have seen, Thrasymachus asserts that, while the just man will want to "get the better" of the unjust man, but not the just man, the unjust man will want to "get the better of" everyone. On the basis of this assertion, Socrates presents what seems to be a blatantly fallacious argument which purports to show that the "just man has revealed himself to us as good and wise, and the unjust man unlearned and bad" (350c). Rather than attempting to analyze this argument in full, I will focus only on what seem to be its most problematic aspects: the claim that "the musical man" will not attempt to "get the better" of another musical man, and the claim that "each is such as the one he is like."[35] In his attempt to show the similarity, and hence (according to this argument) identity in all relevant respects between the man who is just and the man who is wise, Socrates asks Thrasymachus whether "any musical man who

---

35. Socrates' argument (349c–350c) is roughly as follows:

1. He generalizes Thrasymachus's assertion and presents it in the form: the just man gets the better of what is unlike (ἀνόμοιος) but not what is like (ὅμοιος), while the unjust man gets the better of both like and unlike. To this generalization Thrasymachus agrees.

2. He secures Thrasymachus's assent to the claim: the unjust man is prudent (φρόνιμος) and good (ἀγαθός), while the just man is neither.

3. Therefore, he and Thrasymachus agree, the unjust man is like (ἔοικε) the prudent and the good, while the just man is unlike them. Note that this claim is unqualified, i.e., the unjust man is not said to be like the prudent and the good "in the relevant respect."

4. Socrates generalizes this claim as: "each is of the same sort as the one he is like" (τοιοῦτος ἄρα ἐστὶν ἑκάτερος αὐτῶν οἷσπερ ἔοικεν). Generalized in this way, the claim seems to be obviously false. It states that similarity in one respect entails identity in all relevant respects. Nonetheless, Thrasymachus agrees.

5. Socrates asks Thrasymachus (to use the most significant example) whether "any musical man who is tuning a lyre is, in your opinion, willing to get the better of another musical man in tightening and relaxing the strings." Thrasymachus denies this.

6. Socrates generalizes this denial as: in any kind of knowledge (ἐπιστήμη) the man who knows will not voluntarily choose to get the better of the other man who knows. Thrasymachus agrees.

7. Therefore, the man who knows, i.e., the wise man, i.e., the good man, will not want to get the better of the like, but the unlike. And the man who is ignorant will want to get the better of both like and unlike.

8. But then the good and wise man is like the just man. And the ignorant man is like the unjust man.

9. But, by 4 above, each is of the same sort as he is like.

10. Therefore, the just man is good and wise and the unjust man "bad and unlearned."

is tuning a lyre is, in your opinion, willing to get the better of another musical man in tightening and relaxing the strings" (350a). Thrasymachus, reasonably enough, denies this. Socrates then takes this denial as grounds for the claim that "for every kind of knowledge or lack of knowledge" the "one who knows" will not choose voluntarily to say or do more than another man who knows, but rather will choose to do "the same as the man who is like himself in the same action" (350b). However, as almost every reader of the *Republic* will have noticed, it is an extraordinarily large jump from the claim that a "musical man" will strive to tune a lyre in the same manner as any other competent "musical man" to the claim that he will choose to do "the same" as another "musical man" in all aspects of his art. Indeed, if we use the three great tragic poets as our exemplars, innovation seems essential to "handing down" the tradition. Nonetheless, we have seen why Thrasymachus can be brought to agree to this implicit comparison between tuning an instrument and writing a tragedy. He equates a mastery of formal principles, "the necessities preliminary to the art" of rhetoric, with that art itself. To repeat, he sees the formal principles of his art from below.

We are now prepared to see the deepest consequence of Thrasymachus's status as a mere technician of rhetoric, and, at the same time, see why Thrasymachus agrees to one of the most obviously questionable premises in all of Plato's dialogues: the claim that "each is such as the one he is like"; i.e., that similarity in one respect entails identity in all relevant respects. At one level, Thrasymachus is disposed to accept this claim by his assumption that he is essentially the same as the tyrant he portrays. He imagines that, like his successful tyrant, he is beyond the "innocence" of the ethical psychologies he depicts in his second account. Like his tyrant, he manipulates the masses by his knowledge of the formal science of exploitation, without participating in anything so foolish as a belief in ethical virtues. However, at a deeper level, we can see that insofar as he views the principles of his science from below, insofar as he participates in his art by blank imitation rather than anything that could be considered genuinely creative activity, he is as much "ruled" by the principles of his art as anyone in his audience. That is, in slavishly following the principles of his formal science to "liken" himself to his audience, he becomes "of the same sort" as that audience; he becomes the servant rather than the master of his art. Lest this seem too abstract an argument, the same point can be made in the following way. Thrasymachus participates in the art of rhetoric by imitating the ethical psychologies of transgression and *ressentiment*. He produces affects in his audience by blankly imitating those affects. But it is the presence of those affects in his audience that is the ground upon which he assumes a position of superiority vis-à-vis that audience; he despises them for their "innocent" participation in those ethical psychological viewpoints. The reason he despises them, of course, is because he believes that their ethical commitments correspond to nothing real—they are *mere affects,* the "passions" conceived purely in quasi-material terms. This, however, presents a real problem for Thrasymachus insofar as he is only a rhetorical technician and not an artist. Thrasymachus does not, as Socrates does, seek to understand the ethical psychologies of the individuals (such as Thrasymachus) whom he imitates. Indeed, Thrasymachus seems to believe that there is nothing to understand in those affects, no even moderately well-defined intentional object that corresponds to the *pathos* of the many who suffer the rule of the strong. Nor does Thrasymachus use his own imitative participation in this *pathos* in service of some greater creative activity, as would, for example, a tragic or comic poet. The affects that Thrasymachus participates in are, for him as for his audience, *mere affects,* and in aping those affects, he is "moved" by them as surely as they are. Therefore, there is nothing to distinguish him in principle from the people, such as the wealthy Polemarchus, whom he presumes to despise. Even if he were to claim (falsely) that he suffers these affects voluntarily, in the end that would only mean (truly) that he was willing to become despicable for the sake of monetary gain. Insofar as Thrasymachus despises the "innocent" for their participation in the ethical psychology of *ressentiment,* Thrasymachus despises himself.

Socrates, of course, comes very close to saying as much in the closing moments of book 1. He argues that any common enterprise, just or unjust, among citizens or thieves can succeed only if the members of that community do not act unjustly toward one another. It is injustice, he says, that produces faction, hatred, and strife among them, while justice produces unanimity and friendship. Not only will injustice produce factions in a city, or a clan or a tribe; "wherever it comes to be," Socrates says, "it is the work of injustice to implant hatred" (351d). If it comes to be between two men, they will "differ and hate and be enemies to each other" (351e). Even within one man, he says, its power will be the same; it will cause that one man to be "at faction" and "not of one mind" and "an enemy to himself" (352a), and despite the fact that Socrates does not explicitly say it, the implication of his argument is clear and unavoidable: the unjust man hates himself. Again, it is premature to consider this argument of Socrates to be meant to apply to the unjust man as such. That it applies to Thrasymachus, however, should by now be evident. We have seen that Thrasymachus implicitly appeals to the very notions of justice that he despises, and that he unknowingly exhibits the psychology of *ressentiment* that he displays in his art. We have also seen that his own self-conscious understanding of his practice of that art points the way to the conclusion that Thrasymachus despises some part of himself. Nor do I believe that most readers would deny that the way Thrasymachus acts—his anxious self-aggrandizing, his petty attacks on Socrates, his sullen compliance when he is bested by Socrates in argument—indicates someone who has, so to speak, a problem with self-esteem.

The conclusions we have reached in our analysis of Socrates' conversation with Thrasymachus point in two very different directions, toward two very different issues. First, insofar as we have seen the inadequacies in Thrasymachus's conception of the art of rhetoric as an art of rule originate from his status as a mere rhetorical technician, they point toward the possibility of a higher conception of rhetoric, and a nobler practitioner of that art. Second, insofar as we have seen the inadequacies in Thrasymachus's account originate from the conflict in his soul, they point toward the role that self-hatred plays in Socrates' account of the mental conflict, and the soul divided against itself. For reasons that will become clear as we proceed, I will defer a discussion of the second of these two issues until after I have explored the first by turning to the arts of rhetoric and sophistry as they are presented in the *Gorgias* and the *Protagoras* respectively. However, before I leave Thrasymachus for higher ground, it is worth noting one relative obvious way in which these two different perspectives on the inadequacy of Thrasymachus's attempted defense of the unjust life are two sides of the same phenomenon. In his rhetorical tirade, Thrasymachus presented justice as "the good of another," but was unable to present the unjust life as "one's own good." So, too, with respect to his art, he was unable to claim any value for its practice other than the monetary value placed on it by others. The only "goods" he could conceive, either for himself or his tyrant, were material goods. He could find nothing to value but what everyone values to some degree, even if they don't value it very highly. It seems that neither he nor his tyrant thinks himself good enough to be able to keep his own counsel when deciding which good to call his own.

4.5 Fact, Value, and Nature

In this chapter I have, for the most part, focused on Thrasymachus's failings and failures: his unsuccessful attempt to get the better of Socrates in argument, his inadequacy as a rhetorical artist, his inability to conceive of any goods internal to human social and political activity, and, ultimately, his profound lack of self-knowledge. In order to understand Thrasymachus's significance for our understanding of the *Republic,* however, we need to recognize an important sense in which he succeeds. Thrasymachus's conception of a divide between the precise science of rule and the inchoate ethical opinions this precise science governs provides one possible theoretical account of the distinction between "lived" and "imagined" worlds manifested in Cephalus's misappropriation of the poetic and religious tradition. Thrasymachus implicitly articulates a dichotomy between what he sees as facts about the political power relations that define human communities and the ethical values that are the medium through which those power relations are expressed. His conception of the precise science of rule also begins to provide an account of the foundation of those ethical values. They are, Thrasymachus suggests, imposed upon the members of the political community by the form of legislation that defines the "ruling power" in each regime type. While Thrasymachus thinks that sentences expressing moral valuation are either false or have no determinate truth-value—he is what is now called an "error theorist" about ethical valuation—he does not think that ethical discourse can or should be eliminated. Rather, he thinks that the existence of political communities depends upon the fiction of ethical values. What Thrasymachus does not provide, of course, is any account of what power, capacity, or excellence allows a human being to ascend to the status of one who imposes values on a political community. Nor does he provide any account of the value of political life as such.

Moreover, these views do not seem to be original to Thrasymachus. It has been suggested that Antiphon is the original source of the doctrines Plato attributes to Thrasymachus.[36] If this is correct, it seems likely that Plato is implicitly offering an indirect analysis of Antiphon's views. For in the existing fragments *On Truth* (DK 88 B 44), Antiphon's explicit statements exhibit the same prima facie incoherence we have seen in Thrasymachus's two definitions of justice. Antiphon begins with the claim that "justice is not transgressing the laws [νόμιμα] of the polis in which you are a citizen."[37] Later in the fragment, however, he avers that if one testifies truthfully against another, he must necessarily do injustice to the other somehow (ὅμως ἄλλον πως ἀδικεῖν), even though he does what is reputed (νομίζεται) to be just.[38] Consonant with the interpretation I have offered of Thraysmachus's implicit views, Antiphon presents a bifurcate account where an apparent conventionalism about *justice* conflicts with his apparent endorsement of a claim about the reality of *injustice*.[39] If Plato intended his contemporary readers to recognize the similarity between Thrasymachus's views and Antiphon, as seems likely, this suggests the possibility that Plato interprets Antiphon's bifurcate account of justice and injustice as predicated upon the same dichotomy between "fact" and "value" exhibited in Thrasymachus's speeches in book 1.

36. See Barney 2004.
37. DK 88 44, A, col1, ll. 5–11.
38. DK 88 44, C, col1, ll. 1–21.
39. See Barnes 1989, 515–16.

If Thrasymachus derives his view of justice and injustice from Antiphon, this further confirms the impression of him as a mere technician, incapable even in his theorizing of anything creative. But it leaves us with a question about a salient distinction between Thrasymachus's views as presented in book 1 and Antiphon's views as presented in *On Truth*. Thrasymachus makes no mention of the distinction between *nomos* and *phusis*, a distinction that is central to Antiphon's entire account. Indeed, as Rachel Barney notes, Thrasymachus makes no use of the concept of nature.[40] More generally, in marked contrast to the rest of the *Republic*, Socrates' conversations with Cephalus, Polemarchus, and Thrasymachus do not explicitly invoke any substantive concept of nature.[41] In one sense, this seems to be another indication of the political abstraction I have claimed characterizes the cultural environment Socrates represents in his narration of book 1. I will argue, however, that the abstraction from nature we see at work in book 1 provides the context through which we must understand the invocation of nature in later books of the *Republic*. More specifically, I contend that we must understand Socrates' references to nature against the background of a sophisticated anti-naturalist theory of human creative activity espoused by the Sophists Gorgias and Protagoras. The articulation of this theoretical position will be the principal task of the next two chapters.

40. See Barney 2004.
41. The only references to the "natural" in any sense in book 1 occur at 341d7, 347d5, and 352a6. In each case, Socrates uses these terms to refer to the specific or essential character of something, without thereby suggesting that it is *natural entity*. In the first occurrence, for example, Socrates asserts that an art (as such) is naturally directed toward what is advantageous to another. I owe this observation to Stewart Umphrey. See his *Natural Kinds and Genesis* (forthcoming).

5

Gorgias and the Divine Work of Persuasion

In the preceding chapter I argued that Socrates' examination and refutation of Thrasymachus's account of justice and injustice is also an examination and refutation of Thrasymachus's conception of himself as a practitioner of the art of rhetoric as an "art of rule." In particular, I argued that Socrates exposes Thrasymachus as a mere technician who is as much subject to the "rules" of his art as the audience he hopes to persuade. In delineating the limits of Thrasymachus's self-conception, however, Socrates has also sketched out in negative, as it were, the way in which a "true" artist of rhetoric might conceive of herself. Unlike Thrasymachus, she would consider mastery of the formal principles of speaking merely a necessity preliminary to her art. While she would wish to act exactly as another true artist would with regard to these formal principles, she would seek to exceed the accomplishments of other artists with regard to the practice of the art itself. She would see her art as an activity in the highest sense and an end in itself, even if she would also expect to receive material benefits as a consequence of its practice. She would, moreover, consider the art as *her own* in the relevant respects; she would see the excellence of her art as reflecting and manifesting her own excellence, and the authority she derives from its practice as originating in her own talents and capacities. Finally, and more disturbingly, she would consider her own good, the good she derives from the practice of her art, as independent of and different in kind from the goods she represents within her rhetoric. Indeed, insofar as her art expresses itself through her capacity to move her audience at her will, she would posit a chasm between herself as artist and the merely human material she molds in her art.

I will argue that Socrates encounters in Gorgias of Leontini a man who conceives of himself and his rhetorical art in more or less these terms. In the dialogue bearing his name, Gorgias seeks to reveal to Socrates the full extent of his artistic prowess, and attributes to his mastery of the rhetorical art a power that Socrates calls "supernatural" (δαιμονία, 456a5). The main task of this chapter will be to clarify how, on Plato's presentation of him, Gorgias conceives this "daimonic" power. On the interpretation I will offer, Gorgias conceives of himself, in his role as a teacher of the rhetorical art, as responsible for the creation of political *actors,* human beings who speak with *authority* in their political communities. Gorgias attributes supernatural power to his rhetorical art because he believes that one's existence as an individual is inseparable from one's recognition within the community as one who speaks with authority. Insofar as Gorgias conceives of himself as responsible for that authority, he conceives of himself as responsible for the existence of his "students" as individuals. They are, in his eyes, his creatures. Moreover, while he conceives of his creative activity as fashioning political *actors,* the authority they speak with is Gorgias's alone; he considers himself the *author* of their actions.

A crucial aspect of Gorgias's self-conception, I will argue, is the strict divide he posits between his own activity as an artist of persuasion and the merely human political activity of the individuals on whom he practices his art. In so doing, he posits a radical form of what Marx refers to as the first true division of labor: the division of mental from manual labor.[1] Gorgias does not, however, posit it in these terms, for the notion of "mental labor" assumes precisely what he wants to deny—the essential continuity of all human activity as varieties of "labor." Instead, he posits a distinction between "action" and "material production," between the mastery of "persuasion" and the subjection of "manual labor." That is, Gorgias posits something more like the distinction Hegel represents and critiques in the "Lordship and Bondage" section of *The Phenomenology of Spirit.* Moreover, in the manner of a Hegelian critique of what Kojève calls "the existential attitude . . . of the Master," Socrates' refutation of Gorgias turns on the ultimately groundless presumption of independence inherent in Gorgias's position.[2]

Before we turn to the text of the *Gorgias,* it will be helpful to consider, first, the place Thrasymachus's separation between the formal principles of his science and its ethical psychological content has in Plato's account of the teaching of the Sophists in general, and, second, some of what we know of Gorgias from other sources. As the *Apology* and book 10 of the *Laws* clearly demonstrate, Plato presents it as a matter of common opinion that those men who were called the "Sophists" posited a strict divide between *nomos* and *phusis.* According to this common opinion, the Sophists argued that only the material elements of fire, water, earth, and air can be said to exist unqualifiedly, and these material elements owe their existence to nature (φύσις) and chance (τύχη). The secondary physical bodies, both animate and inanimate, owe their existence to the random combination of these material elements. Art (τέχνη) was later "thought up" by living beings, but the things they were able to produce by means of art were, for the

1. Marx 1978b, 159.
2. Strauss 1991, 140.

most part, "mere amusements that are hardly real at all." The only arts held to be of any real worth are those such as medicine or gymnastic, which minister to and tend natural bodies. In contrast to the cultivation of these natural goods, the largest part of the political art and of legislation deals with "mere images" which correspond to nothing in nature; the gods, the ethical virtues, and, most particularly, justice are nothing but legal fictions, untrue artifacts of *nomos* (*Lege*. 889a–890a, *Ap*. 26c–e).

In apparent contradiction to this account of the teaching of the Sophists in general, Gorgias is known to have written a treatise named *On What Is Not or On Nature*, in which he argues (1) that *nothing* is, (2) that even if *something* is, human beings cannot know it, and (3) that even if human beings could know it, they could not express it in speech (λόγος).[3] Central to his argument for the third thesis is the positing of a radical divide between "the things which are" and speech, and while he denies existence to "the things which are," he does not explicitly deny existence to speech, but merely says speech differs from all other things. Moreover, in his most famous display piece (ἐπίδειξις), the *Praise of Helen*, Gorgias presents persuasion through speech as all-powerful, capable of "the most divine works," and it is on this ground that he seeks to exculpate Helen for her apparent betrayal. According to Gorgias, the responsibility falls entirely on "the one who persuaded"; it is he who compelled Helen through speech who is unjust, while she who was compelled is wholly blameless.[4]

While it is disputed among scholars whether Gorgias's *On What Is Not or On Nature* is intended as a serious philosophic work or as a parody of the arguments of the Eleatic philosophers, it is clear, at least, that he was intimately familiar with those arguments. Moreover, as G. B. Kerferd and Richard McKirahan, among others, have argued, the treatise as a whole demonstrates a consciousness of a range of problems in the philosophy of mind and the philosophy of language that compares favorably to any philosophic author before Plato.[5] Thus, whether Gorgias was a philosopher or not, whether he considered himself a philosopher or not, Gorgias was not merely concerned with questions of formal composition. He was a thinker, and was treated as such by later authors in the tradition, such as Sextus Empiricus and the pseudo-Aristotelian author of *On Melissus, Xenophanes, Gorgias,* in whose works the arguments of Gorgias's treatise are preserved. We must keep this fact in mind as we turn to Plato's *Gorgias*.

3. DK 82B3, in Diels 1952, vol. 2.
4. DK 82B11.
5. Kerferd 1981a; McKirahan 1994, 382–86.

5.1 The Power of the Art of the Man

In the following four sections, I will argue that Socrates' conversation with Gorgias reveals that Gorgias's self-conception corresponds to the portrait of the artist of persuasion sketched at the beginning of this chapter. In order to see this aspect of Gorgias's account of the art of rhetoric, however, we must assume that Plato's representation of Gorgias corresponds to the historical picture we have of Gorgias in two respects: first, we must assume that he is a more than merely competent orator—that he is capable of a kind of "precision" in speech which ultimately eludes Thrasymachus; second, that he is capable of, and predisposed to, a far greater degree of rhetorical and literary complexity in his speech than is traditionally assumed in interpretations of the dialogue.

As a number of recent studies have argued persuasively, Gorgias's extant rhetorical works, the *Encomium to Helen* and the *Defense of Palamedes,* are more than merely practical guides to the art of forensic persuasion. Instead, a careful reading reveals that Gorgias's account of rhetorical persuasion in these works is intimately related to, indeed dependent upon, his theoretical reflections on the relation between nature and speech.[6] I will try to show that Gorgias's theoretical commitments similarly inform his contribution to the *Gorgias.* However, to see this, we must pay very careful attention to the specificity of what Gorgias says in the dialogue. Indeed, we must attend not only to what Gorgias says, but also to what he chooses *not* to say.[7] Given the enormous weight that the historical Gorgias placed on the power of words, I contend that we must take the character "Gorgias" in Plato's dialogue *at his word* when he uses phrases such as "apparently" (φαίνεται) or "so to speak" (ὡς ἔπος εἰπεῖν) in opposition to phrases such as "you speak the truth" (ἀληθῆ λέγεις). It is only once we recognize that Plato's "Gorgias" is as subtle a speaker as the historical Gorgias was an author that we can see the full implications of his account of rhetoric in the dialogue.

The subtlety of Gorgias's style is more than matched in the dialogue by Socrates' own subtlety in speech. As was also the case in Socrates' conversation with Thrasymachus, but to a much greater degree, crucial aspects of Socrates' communication with Gorgias occur indirectly. Indeed, much of the conversation between the two of them occurs, so to speak, over the heads of the other participants in the dialogue. Alongside Socrates' manifest critique of rhetoric as a mere "knack" (ἐμπειρία) and no true art, Socrates imparts a subtler message

---

6. See Morgan 2000, 119–39; Porter 1993; Wardy 1998, 6–47; Romilly 1992, 59–73, 95–97.

7. Compare Leo Strauss's remarks in his lectures on the problem of Socrates concerning the "Orator Xenophon," of whom he writes, "He expects the reader of his praises to think as much of the virtues he mentions as of those virtues about which he is silent because of their absence" (1989, 128).

to Gorgias about the limitations in his self-conception as an artist of persuasion.[8] We will return to this facet of Socrates' communication, his willingness to engage in a form of esoteric speech in his public confrontations with Sophists, when considering the significance of these confrontations for our understanding of the "problem of Socrates." For now, however, we should note the extreme demands their intricate *pas de deux* places on the readers of the dialogue. The significance of many of Gorgias's utterances early in his conversation can only be properly understood within the context provided by the arc of that conversation as a whole. For this reason, many of the specific interpretations I offer of those utterances early in this chapter will only appear persuasive once I have been able to fill out this broader context.

In the opening scene of the *Gorgias,* Socrates says that he has come to the home of Callicles to hear Gorgias and to find out from Gorgias himself "what is the power of the art of the man" (τίς ἡ δύναμις τῆς τέχνης τοῦ ἀνδρός, *Grg.* 447c1–2). By phrasing his initial query in this way, Socrates indicates his awareness of a decisive difference between Gorgias, as revealed in this dialogue, and Thrasymachus as portrayed in book 1 of the *Republic.* As the ensuing discussion will make apparent, while Gorgias conceives of the power he deploys as belonging to his art, he conceives of the art and its power as his own. Unlike Thrasymachus, Gorgias thinks of his power in "matters rhetorical" as primarily originating in his own goodness or excellence, not in his mastery of formal rules of rhetoric. As we will see, Gorgias conceives of his rhetorical power as first and foremost *his* power, and only secondarily attributable to his art.

Socrates begins his inquiry by asking Gorgias in what art he is knowledgeable, and what he should be called. Gorgias responds that he is skilled in "matters rhetorical" (τῆς ῥητορικῆς, 449a5). When Socrates next asks whether this means he should be called "an orator" (ῥήτορα, 449a6), Gorgias's brief response is telling. Donald Zeyl's translation of Gorgias's words is fairly standard: "Yes, and a good one, Socrates, if you want to call me 'what I boast myself to be,' as Homer puts it."[9] In the Greek text, however, the words that correspond to "Yes, and a good one" are Ἀγαθόν γε, that is, "Good, at any rate." In point of fact, Gorgias never applies the word "orator" to himself in the dialogue. The closest he comes is at 456b–c, where he describes his own rhetorical power and then attributes a similar power to "the rhetorical man" (ῥητορικὸν ἄνδρα; ὁ ῥητορικὸς). The reason Gorgias does not refer to himself as an orator, I suggest, is that he

---

8. I owe my understanding of this aspect of the argument of the *Gorgias* to a transcript of a course on the dialogue given by Leo Strauss.

9. Plato 1987. Compare R. E. Allen's translation in Plato 1989.

thinks of himself primarily as a *teacher* of rhetorical persuasion. As we will see, however, he has a radical and idiomatic conception of what it is to be a teacher. Similarly, Gorgias responds affirmatively to Socrates' question concerning whether he has "the power to make others" (δυνατὸν εἶναι ποιεῖν, 449b1), *before* Socrates reformulates this claim as "you make others orators" (449c9–d1). It remains to be seen precisely in what sense Gorgias conceives of himself as good, and in what sense he conceives of himself as making others.

The next step in Socrates' interrogation is an attempt to get Gorgias to define the art of rhetoric more precisely. In so doing, Socrates asks what seems to be a very loaded question. He says that he wants to know "with which of the things that are" rhetoric concerns itself (ἡ ῥητορικὴ περὶ τί τῶν ὄντων τυγχάνει οὖσα, 449d1–2, cf. 449d7–8). The polemical character of this question becomes evident once we recall that Gorgias apparently wrote a treatise that explicitly denies that speech is capable of representing "the things which are." Moreover, rather than leaving his question open, Socrates tries to lead Gorgias toward a particular answer, an answer which Gorgias, significantly, does not give. Socrates says that he wants to know what rhetoric concerns itself with, "just as weaving, for example, is concerned with the manufacture [ἐργασίαν, 449d3] of cloaks; is it not?" When Gorgias replies that it is, Socrates follows up with the question: "So, too, music is concerned with the making [ποίησιν, 449d4] of melodies?" Again, Gorgias agrees. Socrates then asks Gorgias to "answer in the same way" (ἀπόκριναι οὕτως, 449d8) about rhetoric. Now obviously, given the paradigms Socrates has so generously provided, one might expect Gorgias to respond that rhetoric is concerned "with the production or making of speeches." Not only does it follow nicely from Socrates' examples, it would seem to be the most obvious response. However, Gorgias does not respond this way; instead he answers, simply, that rhetoric is concerned "with speeches" (περὶ λόγους, 449e1).

One reason Gorgias does not respond that rhetoric is concerned with "the making of speeches," as soon becomes evident, is that he wants to posit a strict distinction between the other arts and rhetoric. Gorgias expresses the basis for this distinction as follows: "The entire knowledge of the other arts concerns manual labor [χειρουργίας] and those sorts of activities [πράξεις], so to speak. With the rhetorical art there is none of this sort of manual labor; all of its activity [πρᾶξις] and authority [κύρωσις] is through speech. Because of this I deem [ἀξιῶ] the rhetorical art to be about speeches, correctly speaking [ὀρθῶς λέγων], as I say" (450b–c).[10] I believe that, as Gorgias indicates, his words are carefully chosen, most particularly his qualification of his claims about the other

---

10. Dodds notes that the key words in this passage, χειρούργημα and κύρωσις, are not colloquial Attic and should be identified as particularly related to Gorgias. See Dodds 1959, 196.

arts with "so to speak" (ὡς ἔπος εἰπεῖν).[11] Gorgias so qualifies his claims for two reasons. First, as we will see below, he believes that it is imprecise to consider instruction in the other arts "knowledge" (ἐπιστήμη). Second, and it is this point that will concern us here, he contends that only those activities that have all their "authority" through speech truly deserve the appellation "activity." Gorgias does not claim that rhetoric is about the "making of speeches," because he believes that it is not "making" (ποίησις) but "doing" (πρᾶξις) that is authoritative. Or rather, there is one particular kind of "making" which is "authoritative" (κυρίως) and a "doing." This "making" is the "making of others" which we have already seen attributed to Gorgias in his role as a teacher of rhetoric.

The distinction between "making" and "doing" that I suggest Gorgias is proposing is nearly identical to the distinction that Critias—leader of the Thirty, and a student of Sophists—draws (or attempts to draw) in the *Charmides*. There, Critias defends an account of temperance as "doing one's own" (τὸ τὰ ἑαυτοῦ πράττειν). Critias denies that this is equivalent to saying that temperance is "making one's own" (τὰ ἑαυτοῦ ποιεῖν). Contrary to Socrates' apparent assumption that the words "to make" and "to do" are practically synonymous (as they were, for the most part, in imprecise speech), Critias argues that one should distinguish carefully between them, for only in those cases where a "making" is good should it be called a "doing." "Making," he claims, is a matter of reproach whenever it is not accompanied by the noble (μετὰ τοῦ καλοῦ), but a "doing" is never a cause for reproach (*Chrm.* 162d–163c). Nor does the connection between Critias's explicit use of this distinction and Gorgias's implicit use seem to be merely accidental. Socrates suggests in his narration of the *Charmides* that Critias's contributions to the dialogue have been appropriated from the Sophists.[12]

Gorgias's understanding of the distinction between real and merely apparent "activities," however, goes much deeper than what Critias is able to make out of it. Indeed, the very kind of political activity that Critias would consider the highest activity is, for Gorgias, the merely human "matter" of the art of persuasion; in

11. It is standard to take ὡς ἔπος εἰπεῖν merely as restricting the scope of πᾶσα, and to translate the phrase as "almost the entire knowledge of the other arts." This translation, however, does not take account of the contrast between ὡς ἔπος εἰπεῖν and the "correct speaking" Gorgias here attributes to himself. The relevant context is supplied by *Republic* 341b5, where Socrates makes explicit the contrast between statements qualified by "so to speak" and those made in the "precise speech" of the Sophists. See also Euphemus's use of ἐς τὸ ἀκριβὲς εἰπεῖν at Thuc. 6.82.3.8.

12. The similarity between Critias's account of temperance and Socrates' use of the same phrase as a definition of justice in the *Republic* raises questions of direct relevance for our inquiry. The *Charmides* passage also suggests that Aristotle's argument distinguishing between *technê* and *phronêsis* on the basis of a distinction between *praxis* and *poiêsis* draws upon and is meant to engage arguments we can associate with the Sophists. This can help explain Aristotle's claim in *Nicomachean Ethics* 6.5.1140a1–4, that in drawing this distinction "we trust exoteric *logoi*." See Burger 2008, 117. Cf. the discussion of the passage in Broadie 1991, 181–87.

comparison to the art of persuasion, politics itself is mere manual labor. To see how this is so, we must return to the questions which lead up to Gorgias's distinction between the other arts and rhetoric. After Gorgias has claimed that rhetoric concerns itself "with speeches," Socrates wants to know with what sort of speeches rhetoric is concerned. All arts, Socrates suggests, insofar as they are *taught* as well as *practiced,* concern themselves with speech. In particular, Socrates contrasts the teaching of rhetoric with the teaching of medicine and gymnastic, which arts in their teaching function, Socrates and Gorgias agree, make men able to speak about their respective subject matters. Thus, according to Socrates and Gorgias, medicine and gymnastic have two levels at which they operate: a functional level, at which they are a knowledge about human bodies, and a pedagogical level, at which they are a knowledge of how to make someone knowledgeable about human bodies.

It is worth noting, first, that medicine and gymnastic are precisely the arts which, according to the Athenian Stranger in the *Laws,* the Sophists held to minister to some natural good. Here, however, while Gorgias seems to think that the benefits of medicine and gymnastic are real enough, he clearly does not rate these benefits very highly. When Socrates asks if medicine makes human beings able to think and speak about the sick, Gorgias replies, "Of necessity" (Ἀνάγκη). Note, too, the loaded term Socrates uses to refer to the sick in this context, οἱ κάμνοντες, a word whose root meaning is "those who labor." It is only "of necessity," Gorgias implies, that one must be mindful of and speak about illness, the sick, and, by extension, those who labor. Nonetheless, Gorgias does admit that the medical and the gymnastic arts are also concerned with speeches, in particular, speeches concerning illness and the good and bad condition of bodies.

Socrates' next step is to generalize the conclusions they have reached about gymnastic and medicine to all the arts. In particular, he wants to attribute the divide between functional and pedagogical levels of discourse to all the arts. He asserts that "each art is concerned with those speeches [at the pedagogic level] which happen to be concerned with the things [at the functional level] of which it is the art" (450a7–b2). Gorgias responds, "Apparently so" (Φαίνεται), and the reason for his reservations about Socrates' claim have nothing to do with its complex syntax. The reason, I suggest, is that Gorgias believes that only those arts concerned with mere necessities, arts such as medicine and gymnastic, are primarily determined by their objects at what I have been calling the functional level. Medicine and gymnastic, Socrates and Gorgias agree, are primarily concerned with knowledge about bodies, and only secondarily concerned with the transmission of that knowledge. That is, medicine's concern with producing health in bodies is what defines it and makes it the art it is, whereas medicine's concern with producing *doctors* is derivative of its primary concern—in Socrates' words, it only "happens to be" (τυγχάνον) concerned with producing doctors. Gorgias's power, to the contrary, is primarily the art of persuasion; that is, it is primarily concerned with producing human beings who have certain beliefs. It is only secondarily concerned with the "matter" of that persuasion: justice and injustice, the freedom of human beings, and rule in the cities. Moreover, those "functional-level" beliefs, beliefs about justice, for example, are derived from and dependent on its "pedagogic level." This pedagogic level is, in turn, dependent on the power (δύναμις) of the man with knowledge of the rhetorical art.

To see that these are Gorgias's implicit claims, we can begin by noting the subtle contrast between two of Gorgias's explicit characterizations of what it is he does. Socrates, still seeking an account of rhetoric's concern at the "functional level," contrasts the arts of arithmetic and calculation, on the one hand, and rhetoric, on the other. Arithmetic and calculation, Socrates says, also have all of their activity and authority through speech; however, they are also *about* something particular: the odd and the even.[13] Socrates says that he is sure that Gorgias would not say that rhetoric is arithmetic and calculation, but what he wants to know is what differentiates rhetoric from these arts. Therefore, Socrates asks Gorgias again what rhetoric is about at the "functional" level, but the way he phrases his question is significant.

Instead of asking "with which of the things that are" rhetoric itself is concerned, Socrates asks "of the things that are, which is the one that the speeches which rhetoric *uses* [χρῆται] are concerned with" (451d5–6). That is, Socrates seems to accept, for the moment, Gorgias's claim that his proper work is not determined at the functional or object level; Socrates implies that rhetoric merely uses those speeches instrumentally in the service of its real work. Gorgias responds by saying that rhetoric *uses* speeches about "the greatest of human works . . . and the best." Note that Gorgias does not say "the greatest *good*" but rather "the greatest of human *works*" (Τὰ μέγιστα τῶν ἀνθρωπείων πραγμάτων, 451d7). Socrates ignores this distinction, for the moment, and objects that a doctor, a physical trainer, and a money-maker would all claim for themselves the distinction of being the craftsman (δημιουργός) of the greatest good for human beings, and asks Gorgias, "What is this that you say is the greatest good for human beings and of which you are the craftsman?" To this question Gorgias responds, "That which is in truth the greatest good, and cause (αἴτιον) of freedom for human beings themselves, and rule over others in the cities of each" (452d5–8). Note, again, that Gorgias does not say that the

---

13. See Dodds 1959, 198–99. For an in depth account of the difference between arithmetic and logistic as it is presented in the passage, see Klein 1968.

greatest good *is* freedom for human beings and rule over others, rather he says that the greatest good is the (or a) *cause* of freedom and rule.

If, however, rhetoric *uses* speeches about the greatest of human actions, and is a *cause* of freedom and rule for human beings, but is not constituted by those actions, this would seem to imply that its real power, its greatest good, is more than merely human. This is, of course, exactly what Gorgias claims to be true of the persuasive power of speech in the *Encomium to Helen,* where he writes that "*logos* is a great lord [δυνάστης μέγας], which by the smallest and most imperceptible body achieves the most divine works [θειότατα ἔργα]."[14] Moreover, this is exactly what Socrates will suggest later in the dialogue. As we have noted above, right after Gorgias says that he will attempt to "reveal clearly [to Socrates] the whole power of rhetoric" as the art of persuasion, Socrates replies, "Seeing it this way, the power of rhetoric becomes manifest to me as something supernatural [δαιμονία] in its greatness," an assessment with which Gorgias enthusiastically agrees (456a–b). This supernatural power is, as I have suggested, the power of persuasion, which Gorgias claims "encompasses and subordinates to itself all powers." In order to understand why Gorgias attributes this more than human power to rhetoric (or, more properly, to himself) we must recognize how Gorgias characterizes the power of persuasion, on the one hand, and the human subjects of persuasion, on the other.

5.2 Knowledge and Persuasion

Perhaps the most striking claim Gorgias explicitly makes in the course of the dialogue is the claim that teaching—which he understands as furnishing knowledge to the student—is itself a form of persuasion. This claim first arises when Socrates is trying to determine what sort of persuasion rhetoric concerns. However, before asking Gorgias this question directly, Socrates characteristically prepares the way with an interesting example, to which we will return below. Socrates says that if he had asked "who Zeuxis is among the figure painters [τῶν ζωγράφων]" and Gorgias had responded, "a painter of figures," Socrates would have been justified in asking, "what sort of figures does he paint and where does he paint them" (453c). The reason this question would be justified, Socrates says, is that there are other figure painters who paint other sorts of figures. Therefore, Socrates concludes, if there are other sorts of persuasion than rhetoric, one is justified in asking a similar question about it.

14. DK Bıı 8.

With this example providing the context, Socrates asks Gorgias, "Whoever teaches something, does he persuade in that he teaches, or not?" To this question Gorgias replies that he who teaches "persuades most of all" (πάντων μάλιστα πείθει, 453d11). For example, Socrates and Gorgias agree, the arithmetical man and arithmetic produce persuasion "of the instructive kind" concerning the quantities of the odd and the even. Therefore, Socrates says, he will ask the same question he did concerning the figure painter: what sort of persuasion is rhetoric and about what does rhetoric persuade? Of course, as is frequently the case when Socrates claims to be repeating himself, this does not seem to be exactly the same question as the one Socrates posed about the figure painter. In the first case Socrates asked what sort of *subject matter,* that is, what sort of *figures,* the figure painter painted, and *where* he painted them. That is, the distinction he drew between painters was not framed in terms of the sort of representation being used in the painting, but rather in terms of (1) the kind of objects being represented, and (2) where those objects were being represented. However, Gorgias treats the two questions as if they are the same, and answers Socrates' second question about rhetoric in terms of the first question about painting; that is, he describes what *sort* of persuasion rhetoric is by telling Socrates *where* it occurs. He says that "it is the persuasion in the law courts and in other gatherings of the masses [ἐν τοῖς ἄλλοις ὄχλοις] and it concerns that which is just and unjust" (454b5–7). The reason Gorgias can answer in this way is that, for him, the distinction between teaching and rhetoric is primarily determined by where and upon whom persuasion is practiced. This strange distinction, a distinction merely of context and not of kind, will determine the difference in subject matter that is used in persuasion.

Socrates and Gorgias isolate two species (εἴδη) of persuasion: teaching, which "provides knowledge [or science, ἐπιστήμη]," and rhetoric, which provides "belief without knowledge" (πίστιν . . . ἄνευ τοῦ εἰδέναι, 454e3–4). In the dialogue between them, however, this distinction does not depend on what we might call the general field of study—Gorgias claims that the orator will be able to produce belief on *any* subject when speaking before "the crowd." It depends, instead, on whom the persuasion involved is being practiced, whether it is practiced on a single individual or practiced on "the masses" (ὁ ὄχλος), or "the crowd" (τὸ πλῆθος). Gorgias *always* uses one of these two terms when he is describing the power of rhetoric to persuade and produce belief; the "rhetorical man" is always seen speaking to "the masses" or "the crowd."[15] Teaching, on the other hand, Socrates and Gorgias agree, is not something that is practiced before the masses. Note, first, that the distinction Gorgias is making is *not* the

15. Dodds 1959, 215.

traditional aristocratic distinction between "the many" (οἱ πολλοί) and "the few" (οἱ ὀλίγοι); that is Callicles' distinction, not Gorgias's (cf. 488d–e). Gorgias claims that he can teach *anyone* to become "rhetorical man," that he can pluck any one of "the many" out of the crowd and make him a "rhetorical man." The distinction Gorgias wants to draw is much more radical than any distinction based on noble birth or economic class; it is, as we will see, an *ontological* distinction between what we might call two human modalities, two different ways in which human beings could be said to exist.

5.3 Ἀπειρία and Ἐμπειρία

Ὁ ὄχλος and τό πλῆθος are examples of what have been called "mass nouns" as opposed to "count nouns." Unlike the plural οἱ πολλοί, they are singular terms for an undifferentiated multitude: the crowd or mass or mob conceived as an indefinite whole. To be an individual or to be simply a member of the moving throng—this is the distinction that matters for Gorgias, and this is what defines the difference between teaching, which produces knowledge, and rhetoric, which produces belief. Socrates puts it this way: for Gorgias, to speak "to the crowd" *means* to speak "to the ignorant" (459a3–5). The reason "the crowd" and "the ignorant" are equivalent for Gorgias is that what it means to have knowledge, according to his conception, is to distinguish oneself as an individual—to be distinct from the crowd. Consider, in this context, Gorgias's strange claim that if a physician and an orator were to contend in front of the assembly about which of them should be chosen as the city's physician, "the physician would appear nowhere" (οὐδαμοῦ ἂν φανῆναι τὸν ἰατρόν, 456b8–c1). When contending against an orator, the orator would so thoroughly deprive the physician of his "reputation" (τὴν δόξαν), that the physician *as* physician would not *be* there in the public gathering at all. His public identity as one who knows about medicine would have been stripped from him. No longer a distinguished public figure, the doctor would disappear in the crowd.

In *On What Is Not or On Nature*, Gorgias is reported to have argued that "the unlimited [or indefinite, ἀπειρία] is nowhere [οὐδαμοῦ]," and if it is nowhere, it is not.[16] Significantly, ἀπειρία is also the homonymous term that Polus uses to mean "lack of skill" or "lack of experience" when describing the benefits of Gorgias's art. Polus claims that the arts have been discovered by human beings "through experience" (ἐκ τῶν ἐμπειριῶν), and that experience (ἐμπειρία) makes us lead our life according to art, while lack of experience (ἀπειρία) makes us

16. Sextus Empiricus *Math.* 7.69.

lead our life according to chance (τύχη). Gorgias participates, Polus concludes, in the noblest of arts (448c). This noblest of arts is, for Gorgias, the means through which an individual becomes an individual, the way in which one acquires an identity and separates himself from the crowd. Prior to being distinguished from the masses, the individual as such does not exist, "he" is merely part of the indefinite human "matter" that the power of persuasion forms.

We can now see that Gorgias implicitly supplies a hylomorphic ontological basis for the dichotomy between the "formal science of rule" and the "ethical-psychological matter" we saw at work in Thrasymachus's two accounts of justice and injustice. What I referred to as the "matter" of Thrasymachus's second account, Gorgias self-consciously conceives in precisely that way. He conceives of the mass of human beings, and their passions, as the indefinite "stuff" that receives the form (λόγος) given it by the power of persuasion. Moreover, like Aristotle and Plato's Timaeus, he believes that matter, considered in abstraction from the form it receives, can only be said to exist in a qualified sense. It is only as a composite of form and matter—as Aristotle would say, as a "this" (τόδε τι)—that one can be said to exist unqualifiedly.[17] For Gorgias, one becomes an individual, one has an identity, when one is distinguished from the mass of humanity. One is so distinguished when one possesses authority of one kind or another, and one possesses authority, as Socrates and Gorgias both seem to agree, to the degree that one has knowledge. As Socrates' example of those who can give advice to the assembly and Gorgias's response to this example show, there are two ways in which one can distinguish oneself from the crowd and speak with authority. One either can be defined as a possessor of an art, and speak to the assembly on one's authority as a doctor, shipbuilder, or general, or one can be authoritative in one's own name, and speak to the assembly as a Pericles or a Themistocles (455b–456a). In Gorgias's view, as we will see, it is only in the latter case that the individual can be considered responsible for his individual existence, that is, for his power to distinguish himself from the crowd. In the former case, it is rather his teacher, and ultimately the founder of the art, who is responsible for this composite of form (λόγος) and human matter. It is the teacher who is able to "impart knowledge" to the student, the teacher who says: you are "this" (τόδε τι—a doctor, a physical trainer, a "rhetorical man"—who brings this individual into existence as a distinct individual, separate from the mass of humanity.

We are now in a better position to understand Gorgias's claim that teaching is a form of persuasion. To put it simply, for Gorgias, knowledge *is* authority, and to teach is to use authority to transmit authority. The "one who knows" in

---

17. *Meta.* 1028a10–31, 1029a8–34; cf. *Timaeus* 49c–52b.

a given subject is the one who possesses the authority to teach a given subject, and the "art" that he teaches is the vehicle of his authority. But this teaching is not "an art of turning" the eye of the soul toward that which is (*Resp.* 518c–d); it is itself persuasion. Returning to Gorgias's claim that he who teaches "persuades most of all" (453d), we can now understand why Gorgias was so happy to affirm that "arithmetic *and* the arithmetical man" teach and persuade, but when Socrates asks if "arithmetic is, then, a producer [δημιουργός] of persuasion," Gorgias responds, "Apparently." For Gorgias, the arts themselves are merely vehicles, the public raiment for the persuasive power of the individual who possesses the *authority* to teach that art (hence Gorgias's reference to "unveiling" of the power of rhetoric; ἀποκαλύψαι, 455d7). This understanding of knowledge as authority (κύρωσις) explains why Gorgias is never shown admitting that the orator will be unable to persuade *the doctor* on matters of health. What Socrates asks, and Gorgias concedes, is that the orator will not be more persuasive than the doctor "to those who know" when speaking on matters of health. Furthermore, Gorgias concedes that if one is to be more persuasive than the doctor (to those who know), he must become more persuasive than "those who know" (459a). What Socrates does not ask, and what Gorgias does not admit, is that the orator must, in this case, acquire the science of medicine. Indeed, the notion of the orator studying this science does not arise at all. Instead the entire discussion is framed in terms of "becoming more persuasive." No doubt Gorgias believes that he could convince your average doctor of anything.

As we have seen, Gorgias does not identify himself as an orator in the dialogue. The reason he does not is that he considers himself primarily a teacher—"he who persuades most of all"—and a teacher, in Gorgias's view, is someone who transmits authority to others. In arts such as medicine or gymnastic, the transmission of authority from doctor to doctor is only incidental to their primary activity of caring for sick bodies. In Gorgias's case, the transmission of authority *is* his primary activity. He considers himself not primarily an orator but primarily a maker of "rhetorical human beings," human beings who have the capacity to distinguish themselves from the crowd. However, this primary activity is one that Gorgias does not seem to share with others. While he claims that he can teach anyone to be able to persuade "the crowd," Gorgias never claims to be able to teach his students his own particular power, that of making rhetorical human beings. He does not, because he believes that the "rhetorical art" is merely the vehicle for a persuasive power that originates from himself. As his martial metaphors make clear (456c–457c), Gorgias conceives of questions of authority in strictly competitive terms, and he clearly believes that at the top of any chain of authority, behind any practice, there is someone who is the ultimate source of authority. Gorgias conceives of himself as the source of the most authoritative of "arts," and considers himself the source and ultimate standard of the activity of those who practice it. His students are, like his art, merely vehicles for his authority. This explains Gorgias's response to Socrates' question "So we should call you an orator " with "Good, at any rate," and its connection to the claim immediately following that Gorgias has the power "to make others." It shows us the profoundest sense in which Gorgias is unlike Thrasymachus; Gorgias considers *himself* the good that others, his students, do.[18]

5.4 Justice, Authority, and Self-Persuasion

The recognition that Gorgias considers teaching to be the form of persuasion whereby one transmits authority to another enables us to understand the most puzzling aspect of Gorgias's claims about rhetoric. Recall that Gorgias claimed both that rhetoric "concerns what is just and unjust" (454b) and that it enables the rhetorical man to speak more persuasively to the crowd than any other craftsman on any subject whatsoever (456b–c). We can now resolve, to some degree, the contradiction between the specificity of the claim that rhetoric concerns what is just and unjust and the universal power Gorgias attributes to it. All of the speeches that come under the province of the rhetorical art, as Gorgias understands it, concern "what is just and unjust" in the specific sense of the fundamental question of political justice; that is, who should rule? That is, Gorgias considers all areas of public life to be determined by the question "Who has the authority to decide?" and he promises to produce human beings who are able to appear to the crowd to have the authority to decide on any subject they speak about. The persuasive ability that the orator learns from Gorgias is the ability to produce in the crowd the appearance that the orator has a justified claim to do what he wants to do; he receives from Gorgias the power to appear just. Moreover, for Gorgias, *to appear to have* the authority to do something *is to have* that authority, to *appear* just is to *be* just. However, as

---

18. We can compare this implicit claim of Gorgias's to the "position maintained for the sake of discussion" Aristotle alludes to at *Physics* 1.185a5–11, the "thesis . . . that what is is one man." While Aristotle discounts this argument as not worthy of refutation, the fact that he classes it with the positions of Heraclitus, Parmenides, and Melissus indicates that this is not an ad hoc absurdity that he has constructed for the occasion, but rather a position held by some figure or figures to whom Aristotle is alluding. Moreover, one obvious (but neglected) possible reading of Protagoras's *homo mensura* fragment is to take it as claiming that it is *one man* (rather than each individual or man as a species) that is the measure of what is and what is not, a possibility explored in chapter 6.

we have seen, this appearance and this authority do not belong ultimately to those "rhetorical human beings" that Gorgias has produced, but rather to Gorgias himself. It is he who decides what is it is to appear just.

Or so Gorgias thinks. However, the fact that Gorgias reduces all questions of justice to questions of political justice shows, to say the least, a rather one-sided view of justice, and it is this view that is the fulcrum upon which Socrates' refutation of Gorgias turns. Insofar as he equates justice with political justice, Gorgias all but ignores the question of retributive justice—the theme which will dominate both Socrates' conversations with Polus and Callicles and the elaborate myth of divine punishment which closes the dialogue. In Gorgias's one reference to the law courts (454b), he refers only to the authority with which the rhetorical man will speak, but does not say anything about what sort of things should be held to be justly done or unjustly done. His lack of concern for issues of retributive justice is consonant with the strict divide Gorgias posits between the authority of speech and mere manual labor. Like the medical art, retributive justice seems to have very little noble about it. It is, as Gorgias says about medicine, a matter of necessity. Indeed, Socrates will assert in his conversation with Polus that even the just executioner is unenviable (ἀζήλωτον, 469b2). While Gorgias considers the orators he produces to be able to get whatever they want in the political arena, Gorgias does not himself engage in politics. He has his sights set on what he conceives to be a more divine good: the creation of individuals. Gorgias's distance from the "merely political" also explains his apparent lack of concern about whether some of his students do things that are conventionally considered unjust. However, this distance presents a problem for Gorgias's views about his activity. In fact, more than one problem.

In his longest speech of the dialogue (456b–457c), Gorgias appears to defend himself against the charge that some of his students might misuse the power of rhetoric to commit injustice. Prior to this defense, however, Socrates has not made any suggestion that Gorgias is being irresponsible in teaching an art that could be misused in this way.[19] Indeed, shortly before this point, Socrates speaks in the voice of an imagined potential student of Gorgias who wants to know on what matters *besides* justice she will be able to advise the city if she associates with Gorgias (455d). It is to this question that Gorgias replies, and his putative defense is merely part of his advertisement for the art he teaches. He is suggesting to a potential Polus or Callicles that he will be able to use the authority of Gorgias's art to do whatever he feels like. However, Gorgias is careful to disassociate himself from the (conventionally understood) injustice his students might commit.

19. Cf. *Grg.* 448e.

If such a student orator should use the power of Gorgias's art to do something unjust, it is the orator who is to blame, and not the teacher who imparted this power to be used with justice.

It is this claim of Gorgias's that Socrates focuses on his refutation. As we have seen, Gorgias concedes that it is not necessary for the orator to acquire the knowledge of the medical art for him to be more persuasive on matters of health to the crowd. Following this admission, Socrates asks Gorgias whether the same is true of the orator with regard to what is just and unjust. He wants to know: Is it necessary for the orator to know the just and the unjust in order to persuade "those who do not know," or is he able to persuade them without himself knowing these things? And if it is necessary for the orator to know these things, will Gorgias be able to teach them to his students, if those students happen not to know these things already? Gorgias responds without hesitation that if a student should happen to come to him not knowing these things, he will teach them to the student. Socrates then purports to show that this admission is in contradiction with Gorgias's earlier implication that his students have the capacity to do things that are unjust.

Before turning to that demonstration, however, we should recognize something about Gorgias's claim to teach his students about what is just and what is unjust. Polus and Callicles both think that Gorgias is forced into this admission because he would be ashamed to admit that the orator does not know and cannot teach what is just (461b–c, 482c–d).[20] The reader should recognize, however, that this cannot be the case. Neither what we know of the historical Gorgias nor what we learn about him in the dialogues would lead us to the conclusion that this is a man who is timid about making outrageous claims. Elsewhere in the dialogues, Gorgias is represented as someone who ridiculed those Sophists who claimed to teach virtue; he believes, on the contrary, that his proper business is "making clever speakers" (ἀλλὰ λέγειν οἴεται δεῖν ποιεῖν δεινούς, *Meno* 95c3–4).[21] Moreover, soon after Polus suggests that Gorgias has been shamed into his answer, Gorgias explicitly denies that Socrates is shaming him in saying what he thinks about rhetoric (463a5); what Gorgias deems shameful for himself is if he were unwilling to follow out the argument (458d7–8). Finally, in this instance, before whom exactly is Gorgias supposed to be ashamed to admit that he cannot teach justice? Polus? Callicles? They are, rather, embarrassed for Gorgias only when he allows himself to be refuted. Just as Cleitophon was wrong in thinking that Thrasymachus had merely made a verbal slip when he did not say "the just is

20. Cf. Kahn 1996, 134–35.
21. Cf. Irwin 1995, 98, 368n8.

whatever the stronger thinks is to his advantage," so too, Polus and Callicles are wrong to attribute Gorgias's concession to timidity. But, of course, they have very little idea of what Gorgias really thinks about his power of persuasion.

If, as I have suggested, Gorgias is not shamed into the concession that he will teach his students justice if they come to him not knowing what it is, why does he concede this point? Furthermore, why does he concede Socrates' further point that the rhetorical man will always *be* just? To see why he does, it will be easiest to begin with this second question—why the "rhetorical man" must of necessity be just on Gorgias's account—and then move back to the question of what it means for Gorgias to "teach" them about what is just.

As we have seen, Gorgias believes that teaching is essentially that kind of persuasion which transmits authority, and his own teaching is the most authoritative persuasion, not least because it takes as its subject matter the question of authority itself, that is, the question of who should rule. As we have also seen, Gorgias claims that the rhetorical man will enjoy absolute authority on any subject he speaks about "to the crowd." However, if one were to enjoy absolute authority before a crowd, one's actions would *always* appear justified to that crowd; whatever one did would appear just.[22] Consider again, in this context, Callicles' paean to the "natural justice" of the revolt and tyranny of the "man of sufficient nature" (484a–b). Callicles believes (or thinks he believes) that such a man would not only be able to do whatever he wanted to do, he would be *justified* in doing it, and this includes, presumably, whatever he wanted to do to Callicles. Such a man, if he were possible, would possess *absolute authority* for Callicles, and whatever he did would be just for no other reason than the fact that *he* was the one who did it. For Gorgias, to appear to have authority is to have that authority, and to appear just is to be just. Therefore, it seems, by Gorgias's own lights, the rhetorical man will always be just.

More significant for Gorgias himself, however, is the claim that he will teach whatever student should come to him about what is just and unjust "if by chance [τύχη] he does not know" these things already. As I have suggested above, Gorgias does not believe that he is the only source of authority. Some individuals, such as Pericles or Themistocles, possess the authority to speak in their own names before the assembly. What distinguishes Gorgias from these "orators" (456a) is his suprapolitical art of "making others," of producing individuals whose emergence from the crowd depends on him and his power. For his "students" the authority they display is not their authority, but Gorgias's own. Prior to the work of

---

22. "For that which in speaking of goods and possessions is called an *owner* (and in Latin *dominus,* in Greek *kurios*) speaking of actions is called author. And as the right of possession is called dominion, so the right of doing any action is called AUTHORITY" (Hobbes, *Leviathan* 16.4).

Gorgias's "art" they will have been part of the indefinite mass (ἀπειρία); they will lack experience (ἀπειρία) of the art and be merely products of chance (τύχη). On Gorgias's account, he alone remains the ultimate source of the authority of the "art" his students practice; he is the "author" of their actions. This explains the peculiar character of Gorgias's responses to Socrates' questions about the justice of the newly educated orator (460b–c). When Socrates asks Gorgias if "the one who has learned justice is just," Gorgias responds, "Entirely" (Πάντως δήπου). And when Socrates asks, "Then the just man, I suppose, does what is just?" Gorgias responds, "Yes." But when Socrates asks, "Therefore, the orator is necessarily just, and the just man will decide [βούλεσθαι] to do what is just?" Gorgias responds, "Apparently, at least." Finally, when Socrates asks, "Then the just man will never decide [βούλεσθαι] to do injustice?" Gorgias responds, "Necessarily" (Ἀνάγκη). Why is it that the just man, Gorgias's student, will *be* entirely just and will *do* what is just, but will only apparently *decide to do* what is just? Because Gorgias does not believe that the student who has "learned" justice from him will "decide" or "will" (βούλομαι) anything.[23] The reason why it is "necessary" that the just man will never "decide" to do injustice is that it is not the just man, that is, the student who is the product of Gorgias's authoritative art, but rather Gorgias himself whose will is expressed in his students' actions.[24]

This argument implies that even when the "just men" who are formed by Gorgias's art do "that which seems best to them" (ἃ δοκεῖ αὐτοῖς βέλτιστα, 467b3), they do not do what they "decide upon" or "will" (βούλονται). This, of course, is the very claim that Socrates makes concerning all practitioners of the rhetorical art in his conversation with Polus, when he argues that orators and tyrants "have the least power in their cities" (*Grg.* 467bff.).[25] As this deliberate echo of Gorgias's implicit argument indicates, Socrates' conversations with both Polus and Callicles seem to be, among other things, an elaborate refutation of Gorgias's claims. To demonstrate in any detail how this is so would

23. Compare Hobbes's claim at *Leviathan* 16.7: "When the actor doth anything against the law of nature by command of the author, not he, but the author breaketh the law of nature; for though the action be against the law of nature, yet it is not his [action, but the author's]."

24. Note also Gorgias's response to the explicit conclusion that Socrates draws from the argument, that the *rhetorical man* will never decide to do what is unjust: "Apparently not, at least" (οὐ φαίνεταί γε). This claim can be understood in two complementary ways, corresponding to the two ways one can be a "rhetorical man." First, the conclusion Socrates draws depends upon the apparent identity between (1) the orator who "at first" (πρότερον) knows the just and the unjust, and (2) the student who must learn these things from Gorgias. But this identity is only apparent; it is only is the first case that one truly decides. Second, in the case of orators such as Pericles or Themistocles, or Gorgias when adopting the role of a rhetorical man, Gorgias would claim that they truly decide. In such cases, however, whatever the intent of the orator, whatever he decides will appear just.

25. See Kahn 1983.

take me decidedly too far afield of my stated aim, which is to demonstrate the presence of a radical theory of human interpretive and creative capacity, attributed to the Sophists, in Plato's dialogues. However, this much can be seen: Socrates' conversations with Polus and Callicles demonstrate quite clearly that, contrary to Gorgias's implicit claims, the "material" he is working with in the case of these two students is far from pure.[26] In their arguments with Socrates, Polus and Callicles each demonstrate deeply held convictions about what is and what is not just. Polus's are rather conventional. He believes that he knows, for instance, that Archelaus the tyrant is unjust, and he clearly finds what Archelaus has done quite shocking (470d–471d).[27] Callicles' views, on the other hand, are rather conventionally anticonventional—though, one must say, his masochistic fantasy of the young lion crushing "our laws" under his feet is extraordinarily powerfully expressed. But, as we have seen, this anticonventional view is clearly a view about justice, indeed "natural justice," a phrase first coined by Plato's Callicles. Both their expressed views and, as we will see, their attitudes toward Gorgias indicate that Polus and Callicles have opinions about what is just that do not derive their ultimate authority from Gorgias.

Unlike Gorgias, Polus and Callicles do not think of the power of speech and persuasion as something more than human, but as a tool human beings use to get what they want. Whatever they have "learned" from Gorgias has not gone very deep; they are not, in fact, *persuaded* of Gorgias's authority. This is one level of the significance of Socrates' claim in his argument with Polus that "the good orators" are in no way "considered" or "esteemed" (νομίζεσθαι) in the cities. Polus and Callicles think of Gorgias, essentially, as someone *useful* to them, and this is demonstrated by the way they comport themselves toward him in the dialogue. Polus is eager to step in for Gorgias, who he thinks "must be quite undone" (πολλὰ γὰρ ἄρτι διελήλυθεν, 448a7) from having answered so many questions. Furthermore, he is willing to assert to Socrates that he knows everything Gorgias knows (462a). Callicles, on the other hand, treats Gorgias almost as a servant; he offers Gorgias's services to Socrates whenever he should choose to call (448b).[28] Moreover, both Callicles and Polus think that Gorgias foolishly allows himself to be shamed by Socrates into a false step in the argument, and Socrates points out to both of them that this is an insult to

---

26. Cf. *Ti.* 50e with *Resp.* 501a–b.

27. In both these regards, Polus is in marked contrast to Socrates, who is willing to say, despite the fact that he is aware that Archelaus is a tyrant, that he does not know if Archelaus is happy, because he has never met him. Since Socrates also claims that the unjust man is wretched (471a), this clearly implies that Socrates does not know if Archelaus is unjust. It is Polus, not Socrates, who asserts Archelaus's injustice.

28. Note the ambiguity of Callicles' "παρ᾽ ἐμοὶ γὰρ" (447b7–8), which could mean "because he is staying with me" or "because he is mine."

Gorgias (461c–d, 487b–c). Of course, after Socrates has made this lack of "consideration" manifest, Gorgias reasserts his authority over Callicles and forces him to submit to Socrates' elenctic punishment long after Callicles has made clear he is no longer willing to continue (497b).

The first indication that Polus is not so entirely Gorgias's creature as Gorgias thinks is, as we have seen, Polus's interruption on Gorgias's behalf immediately following the latter's claim that he can and will "teach" his students about what is just and unjust. This interruption is also the occasion for Socrates' own account of rhetoric. Socrates denies that rhetoric is an art at all, but claims that it is, rather, a part of "a practice . . . of a courageous and speculative soul, and one by nature conversant in cleverly dealing with human beings" (ἐπιτήδευμα . . . ψυχῆς δὲ στοχαστικῆς καὶ ἀνδρείας καὶ φύσει δεινῆς προσομιλεῖν τοῖς ἀνθρώποις, 463a6–8). According to the interpretation I have offered here, this much of Socrates' description mirrors Gorgias's own implicit account of the "art" of rhetoric.[29] However, Socrates continues by calling rhetoric "flattery" (κολακείαν) and a false image of the (sub-)art justice rather than justice itself. Clearly this is a claim that Gorgias might dispute, if, as I have suggested, he conceives of those arts which are not concerned with caring for "necessities" of the body to be merely the public manifestation of and vehicle for the power of the persuasive artist. However, even if Gorgias were to believe that Socrates' distinction between genuine and counterfeit arts is groundless when applied to those arts which have all their authority "through speech," this would not exhaust the significance of Socrates' critique for him.

In his critique, Socrates claims to recognize two genuine arts concerned with caring for the good condition of human beings, each of which is subdivided into two parts. These two genuine arts are one unnamed art, comprising gymnastic and medicine, which cares for the good condition of the body, and the political art, comprising legislation and justice, which cares for the good condition of the soul. As I have argued in §3.2 above, each of these pairs of sub-arts seems to be composed of a member which is remedial or rehabilitative and a member which is productive or constitutive. According to Socrates' presentation in the *Gorgias,* gymnastic is originally productive of a good condition in the human body, while medicine is required to rehabilitate a body that has acquired some defect. Moreover, the account of justice Socrates gives in the *Gorgias* is restricted to retributive justice, which he presents as rehabilitative of a soul that has acquired some defect. Although Socrates does not say it explicitly, the clear implication is that legislation is taken to be originally productive of the good condition of human souls. These

---

29. A notable exception is Socrates' reference to nature. On the significance of Gorgias's failure to invoke nature, see the following chapter.

four genuine sub-arts, Socrates contends, are each imitated by a part of the practice of flattery, with cosmetic imitating gymnastic, cooking imitating medicine, sophistry imitating legislation, and rhetoric imitating (retributive) justice.

Now, if, as I have suggested, Gorgias does not accept the distinction between genuine and counterfeit arts when this distinction is applied to those "arts" which have their authority through speech, the opposition between sophistry and legislation and the opposition between rhetoric and justice will collapse. Sophistry will be identical to legislation and rhetoric will be identical to justice. There will remain, nonetheless, Socrates' distinction between productive and rehabilitative arts, with sophistry/legislation being responsible for the formation of souls and rhetoric/justice responsible for the rehabilitation of souls. This distinction is not one with which Gorgias should be happy, for, as we have seen, Gorgias thinks of himself, through his art, as responsible for the production of human beings with certain beliefs and/or knowledge. Socrates' dialogues with Polus and Callicles demonstrate, however, that Gorgias's students come already formed with many and deeply held beliefs about what is just and unjust, beliefs which the rhetoric of Gorgias's art barely seems to have touched. The most it can do is use these beliefs and draw upon them to achieve certain political ends. Moreover, to have this effect, the orator or teacher of orators must *flatter* the preconceived notions of those whom they hope to persuade. As Socrates argues of the Sophists in general in the *Republic,* the orator must, to exert his persuasive power, become a student or a slave of conventional opinion; he must tutor himself to the "angers and desires of the great, strong beast he is rearing" (*Resp.* 493a–b). That is, he must flatter the convictions of "the crowd" (πλήθους, 492b7).

If Gorgias wants to be truly a "maker" of human beings, it seems the very least he must do is contend with the city and the laws of the city over the souls of his students. He must do more than take an individual from the "crowd" in the city and give him the authority of an orator. He must undertake to form that "crowd," and be responsible for its fundamental convictions about justice. According to the argument of the *Gorgias,* and in many ways the argument of the *Republic,* it is the laws which are primarily responsible for the original formation of these convictions. Consider, in this context, Socrates' claim to Adeimantus that, to do their work well, the philosopher-rulers must "take the city and the dispositions of human beings as though they were a tablet . . . which in the first place they must wipe clean" so that the city and the souls of human beings can best receive the "image of man" that the philosopher-rulers would inscribe there (501a–b). If he is to have any role in the "divine" activity of forming human beings, Gorgias must practice something analogous to the art of legislation so conceived. That is, according to his understanding of Socrates' analogy, he must become more of a

Sophist than an orator or teacher of orators. As we will see in the next chapter, he must become more like Protagoras.

However, before we turn to the *Protagoras,* let me suggest the possibility of another level at which Socrates' critique of Gorgias's self-conception might operate, a level which more closely approximates the significance of Hegel's critique of the abstract self-consciousness (the "Lord") which attempts to posit itself as wholly independent by opposing itself to the determinacy of particular existence.[30] I believe that Socrates suggests this deeper level by a strange comment, apparently made in passing. Right after Gorgias has agreed to Socrates' definition of rhetoric as wholly concerned with producing persuasion in the souls of those who hear it, Socrates says, "Listen then, Gorgias. For know well that, as I persuade myself [ὡς ἐμαυτὸν πείθω], if ever someone speaks with another wanting [βουλόμενος] to know that about which [the] argument is, I am one of them. And I deem you one also" (*Grg.* 453b). Not surprisingly, Gorgias seems confused by this strange comment, and there is little indication that he interprets Socrates' comment as having any deep significance. However, I believe that he should, and *we* should, interpret it as significant.

I have argued that Gorgias's self-conception depends on a radical opposition between his own "daimonic" activity of persuasion and the merely human necessities of caring for the body. I have also argued that Gorgias would describe the majority of political activity as being concerned with "mere necessities." The greatest good is to be the ultimate source of persuasion, to see your own "decision" about what is just and unjust, what is authoritative and lacking authority, reflected in the activities of your students. We have already seen, of course, that Gorgias is mistaken in his assumption that the opinions of his students about what is just and what is unjust derive ultimately from him. However, let us imagine that this wasn't so, or at least less obviously so than it is in the cases of Callicles and Polus. Let us imagine more deferential, more thoroughly indoctrinated students. It is nonetheless the case, Socrates suggests, that Gorgias's putative independence from the political activities of his students is, at the very least, highly problematic. For (and this is what I think Socrates' strange comment is suggesting) if all knowledge is merely a form of persuasion, and if the greatest good for Gorgias is to see his authority reflected in the activity of his students, he must be *persuaded* that their activities do, in fact, reflect his authority. The final subject of Gorgias's persuasive power must be himself, his "knowledge" must be self-persuasion. This self-persuasion, however, must *necessarily* be mediated through the activity of his students. Without this mediation,

---

30. Hegel 1977, 111–19. See also Hegel's own, quite similar characterization of Gorgias in *Lectures on the History of Philosophy* (1983, 1:378–84).

Gorgias's "daimonic" persuasive power, and his self-persuasion, are nothing more than so much wishful thinking.[31]

One may ask, of course, why it is that Gorgias is so blind to the inner convictions of his students and to the fact that his rhetorical power only reaches to the surface of their souls. For whatever we may say about the ultimate failings of Gorgias's theoretical perspective, he is shown in the dialogue to be an extremely subtle and complex thinker. Moreover, in contrast to the import of Socrates' account of rhetoric as a form of flattery, Gorgias appears capable of asserting an authority over his students that does not depend upon any immediate gratification of their psychic pathologies. For as we have seen, it is only under Gorgias's influence that Callicles submits to Socrates' lengthy elenctic chastisement (497b8–10). Instead, if Gorgias is limited as a rhetorical artist, it seems as if this is because he is subject to a failing complementary to that we saw at work in Thrasymachus's account of justice as "the good of another" (§4.2). Thrasymachus is unable to assume the psychological perspective of the ruler; he can only conceive of the individual's ethical-psychological relation to rule from perspective of one subject to that rule. Gorgias, by contrast, imagines the power of his art as wholly transcending the merely political realm. Consonant with his distaste for politics as mere manual labor, Gorgias seems unwilling to get his hands dirty with certain unenviable but politically necessary tasks. If we can take Socrates' conversation with Callicles as a paradigm, these tasks might appear to include a willingness to engage in demagogic rhetoric to publicly humble certain refractory human beings (494a–495a). Gorgias seems unable, because unwilling, to descend into the depths of a soul such as Callicles' and enact the rhetorical counterpart of retributive justice. As we will see in the next chapter, Protagoras is not hampered by a similar fastidiousness.

31. For an alternative account of the significance of Socrates' reference to self-persuasion, see Benardete 1991, 17–19.

6

Protagoras, Antinaturalism, and the Political Art

They say that doing injustice is naturally good, and suffering injustice bad, but that the bad in suffering injustice far exceeds the good in doing it; so that, when they do injustice to one another and suffer it and taste of both, it seems profitable—to those who are not able to escape the one and choose the other—to set down a compact among themselves neither to do injustice nor to suffer it. And from there they began to set down their own laws and compacts and to name what the law commands lawful and just. And this, then, is the genesis and being of justice; it is a mean between what is best— doing injustice without paying the penalty—and what is worst—suffering injustice without being able to avenge oneself. The just is in the middle between these two, cared for not because it is good but because it is honored due to a want of vigor in doing injustice. The man who is able to do it and is truly a man would never set down a compact with anyone not to do injustice and not to suffer it. He'd be mad. Now the nature of justice is this and of this sort, and it naturally grows out of these sorts of things. So the argument goes.

—*Republic* 358e–359b (Bloom trans.)

At the beginning of book 2 of the *Republic,* Glaucon claims that he wishes to hear for the first time an adequate proof of the claim that it is always better to be just than unjust. Believing that Socrates, if anyone, will be able to provide him with such a proof, he famously offers to restore Thrasymachus's argument to the effect that injustice is always superior to justice. In his supposed restoration of that argument, however, Glaucon introduces a distinction between nature and convention that was absent from the surface of Thrasymachus's account. As we have seen, Thrasymachus pursues his defense of injustice and his account of the art or science of despotic rule, without the slightest mention of φύσις or any of its cognate forms. We might be tempted to ascribe the discrepancy between Glaucon's argument and Thrasymachus's, following Shorey, to the fact that Glaucon's presentation of the case for injustice is more "systematic" than Thrasymachus's, were it not the case that we see a similar discrepancy occurring in the *Gorgias.* Here we find Gorgias pursuing an account of the art of rhetoric devoid of any reference to nature, while the chief concern of his aristocratic patron and supposed student Callicles is an extended account of the superiority of nature to convention. What these two examples jointly suggest is a bifurcation in Plato's account of the role that nature plays in the teaching of the Sophists. More precisely, it suggests that despite the central role that nature plays in the *popular reception* of the teaching of certain Sophists, a deeper understanding of their teaching may assign a more problematic and ambiguous status to the concept of nature.

As we have seen, Plato clearly indicates that according to the popular opinion of his time, the Sophists took the opposition between *nomos* and *phusis* to be fundamental and were proponents of nature over convention.[1] The Sophists, on this account, maintained that only the material elements, and the adventitious bodies which arose from their random combination, could truly be said to exist. The only products of human activity which they held to be of any value were those arts, such as medicine and gymnastic, which tended natural bodies. In contrast to those arts that cultivate these natural goods, political art and legislation deals with "mere images" which correspond to nothing in nature. This uncompromising combination of an eliminative materialism with regard to most ethical categories, and a reductive naturalism with regard to those remaining, is also offered by Socrates in the *Theaetetus* as the popular interpretation of Protagoras's *homo mensura* thesis in its most defensible form. After rejecting a wholly subjectivist reading of Protagoras's doctrine as self-refuting, Socrates asks Theodorus whether it is not more likely that Protagoras would have been willing to concede that in matters of physical health and sickness, or political advantage and disadvantage, there exists some natural basis for better and worse judgments. "But it's in the former case, I mean in the just and unjust, holy and unholy things, that [Protagoras's defenders] are willing to insist that none of them is by nature with a being of its own, but the opinion resolved on in common, this becomes true at that time, whenever it's resolved on, and for as long a time as it's so resolved."[2]

Yet at the very moment Socrates offers this apparently plausible popular interpretation of Protagoras's teaching, he indicates that it is somehow less than accurate. This is substantially the view held, Socrates says, by those who do not "altogether speak the speech of Protagoras" (μὴ παντάπασι τὸν Πρωταγόρου λόγον λέγωσιν, *Tht.* 172b6–7). Indeed, earlier in the *Theaetetus* Socrates indicates even more strongly that the popular interpretation of Protagoras's views on nature and convention somehow misses the mark, and he wonders aloud to Theaetetus whether Protagoras might not have uttered his enigmatic dictum for "the rabble [συρφετῷ] such as ourselves" while "speaking the truth in secret to his pupils" (τοῖς δὲ μαθηταῖς ἐν ἀπορρήτῳ τὴν ἀλήθειαν ἔλεγεν, *Tht.* 152c8–10).[3]

---

1. See the introductory remarks to chapter 5.
2. *Tht.* 172b (Plato 1984).
3. Roughly the same phrase, ἐν ἀπορρήτοις λεγόμενος, is used in the *Phaedo* (62b) to refer to the secret doctrines of the Pythagoreans. See also *Cra.* 413a.

Most contemporary commentators now agree that the attempt to assimilate Protagoras's views to those of his relative contemporary Democritus is mistaken. However, they do not take seriously Socrates' suggestion that the esoteric content of Protagoras's teaching is neither the broad relativist doctrine Socrates sketches out with Theaetetus nor the materialist naturalism he attributes to Protagoras's popular defenders. Insofar as Protagoras is considered to diverge from the general portrait of the Sophists presented above, it is not that he contests the terms of the *nomos/phusis* debate, but rather that he is held to be a proponent of convention as a necessary corrective to the miserly provision of a stepmotherly nature.

Contrary both to the opinion of most commentators and to the common opinion in Plato's time, I will suggest in the following chapter that Protagoras's teaching on nature is more complex, more philosophically interesting, and a greater challenge to Platonic philosophy than either of the positions commonly attributed to him. I will argue that at the deepest level of Protagoras's teaching is a radically *antinaturalist* theory of human creative and interpretive activity. Protagoras, on this reading, is not merely antinaturalist in the weak sense of claiming that human social life cannot be adequately explained solely in terms of our animal nature; that is, I am not making the relatively uncontroversial claim that Protagoras is a *humanist* of some sort. On the contrary, I will argue that, on Protagoras's account, human nature is not merely subordinate to convention or culture, but is, in the final analysis, itself an artifact of a kind of poetic activity.[4]

This is not to say that Protagoras's public teaching is without any appeal to nature. Essential to his success as a teacher of political excellence is an implicit appeal to a "natural aristocracy" which might best benefit from his instruction. However, at the deepest level what defines better and worse "natures" on Protagoras's account is their receptivity to either the forming influence of the laws and myths of the city or the exceptional influence of the *artist* of culture. Among the artists of culture Protagoras includes the poets, the founders of cities, and wise men such as himself; this is, in fact, Protagoras's conception of sophistry, the "divine" task of forming human beings.[5] This deeper teaching, therefore, resembles in certain key respects Nietzsche's account in *The Birth of Tragedy* of the great Attic tragedians as "Dionysian artists" who struggle to create meaning in the face of a Dionysian insight into what Nietzsche calls the "true

---

4. In this respect, the interpretation of Protagoras's teaching closest to the one offered here can be found in Ferrarin 2000. However, Ferrarin does not recognize the full complexity of Protagoras's antinaturalism, nor the specific literary character of Protagoras's esoteric self-presentation. See note 27 below.

5. As we will see, Protagoras will offer a metaphysical foundation for the ontological distinction we saw at work in the *Gorgias* between human beings conceived of as individuals and human beings conceived of as part of the indefinite "masses."

but fatal" doctrines of ceaseless becoming and the fluidity of all concepts, types, and species.[6] However, as in some of Nietzsche's early musings on the "Titanic" artist of culture, Protagoras views most human beings as no more than raw "material" upon which the artist of culture works; they are, in a sense, no more than the product of his art.[7]

Let me be clear, then, about my interpretive strategy. A number of commentators have suggested that the tensions in Protagoras's public presentation of his teaching arise from his attempt to simultaneously appeal to an aristocratic elite and assuage the fears of the Athenian demos.[8] This suggestion, as far as it goes, I believe to be correct, and my interpretation of Protagoras's "great speech" will provide ample evidence to support this contention. However, I will also suggest that Protagoras has a third audience in mind, an audience of potential disciples or initiates (μαθητάς), and it is to this audience of potential initiates that Protagoras directs his more radical antinaturalist teaching. Clearly, then, I am attributing a great deal of literary complexity to Protagoras's self-presentation, and the greater part of this chapter will concern itself simply with offering an interpretation of that self-presentation in all its complexity.[9] However, as I have suggested above, my goal is to provide a framework to reconsider the place of nature, and the distinction between nature and convention, in Socrates' response to the challenge of the Sophists in the *Republic*. I will therefore conclude this chapter by briefly indicating the ways in which Protagoras's account of human creative activity raises questions about the status of nature in Socrates' account of the education of the philosopher-kings, and even more significantly, the ways it casts a troubling light on Socrates' own mimetic activity in the *Republic*.

As we proceed, it will be important to keep in mind a number of items concerning Protagoras, garnered from other Platonic dialogues and from sources other than Plato, when considering Plato's representation of him in the *Protagoras*. First, in marked contrast to Gorgias and Thrasymachus, who presented themselves as teachers of rhetoric and who seem to have abstained from conventional political activity, Protagoras presented himself as a teacher of political virtue and was himself active in political affairs, most notably as the author of the constitution of Thurii, a city in south Italy which drew its citizens from all

---

6. See Nietzsche's interpretation of the *Prometheus Bound,* in section 9 of *The Birth of Tragedy.*

7. See Nietzsche 1988, 7:417.

8. See Adkins 1973; Coby 1982; Ferrarin 2000, 303–4; and Strauss 1953, 114–17.

9. I will, for the most part, abstract from the significant fact that we are not given unmediated access to Socrates' encounter with Protagoras, but rather are presented with Socrates' narration of that encounter, but see §6.6.

parts of Greece. That is, Protagoras himself practiced the legislative part of the art of politics.[10] Secondly, among Protagoras's writings were the *Antilogies,* in which he claimed that there are two mutually opposed arguments on any subject, and *On the Gods,* in which he claimed: "Concerning the gods I am unable to know either that they are or that they are not, or what their appearance is like. For many are the things that hinder knowledge: the obscurity of the matter and the shortness of human life."[11] There are reports that he was tried and convicted in Athens for the apparent agnosticism of this claim. Third, Protagoras is most famously associated with the dictum "Human being [or: A human being] is the measure of all things [χρημάτων]—of the things that are, that they are, and of things that are not, that they are not."[12] In the *Theaetetus,* Socrates associates this dictum with Theaetetus's claim that "knowledge is nothing other than perception" (οὐκ ἄλλο τι ἐστιν ἐπιστήμη ἢ αἴσθησις, *Tht.* 151e). On the basis of this association, Socrates develops Protagoras's dictum into the full-blown relativistic theory that has come to be called Protagorean relativism. According to this theory, whatever any individual perceives is true for that individual. However, and this is our fourth point, Socrates suggests, as we have noted above, that Protagoras's most famous dictum has been disseminated for the uninitiated many, and does not represent the real core of his teaching. Moreover, as Thomas Szlezák has shown, the possible esotericism of the teaching of the Sophists is an incessant theme in Plato's dialogues, and this theme is nowhere more pronounced than in the *Protagoras.*[13] Indeed, Socrates' "interpretation" of Simonides' poem begins with a lengthy comic interlude on Sparta as a land populated entirely by esoteric philosophers (342a–343b). It seems that here, if anywhere in Plato's dialogues, we are entitled to look for an esoteric meaning in the public pronouncements of the Sophists.[14]

10. Cf. *Grg.* 464b–e.

11. DK 80B4, translation by McKirahan (1994, 364).

12. DK 80B1.

13. Obviously, I strongly disagree with the Tübingen School's views on the correct hermeneutic approach to the dialogues. Nevertheless, I believe one can appropriate Szlezák's positive arguments about the esotericism of the Sophists for a quite different interpretive project than the one he recommends. Once we recognize that many of Plato's contemporaries maintained that the poetic tradition contained esoteric doctrines, we are afforded a new prospective from which to consider the literary character of Plato's dialogues. The question becomes, not simply whether Plato wrote esoterically or ironically, but rather, how Plato's dialogues work with the assumed esotericism of the poetic tradition. On the assumed esotericism and "allegorical" reading of the poetic tradition among figures associated with the sophistic movement, see Morgan 2000, 98–131. On the Tübingen School's rejection of Schleiermacher's interpretive principles, see the first appendix to Szlezák 1985; on the ubiquity of references within the dialogues to the esotericism of the sophists, see Szlezák 1993.

14. We should, moreover, not be too surprised if this esoteric teaching goes beyond an articulation of the superiority of *phusis* to *nomos,* for we see Hippias proclaiming precisely this thesis and publicly

6.1 Protagoras and the Poets

I have suggested that Plato's portrayal of Protagoras resembles in certain respects Nietzsche's account of the tragic poets. However, we do not need to look to Nietzsche to find grounds for connecting Protagoras and tragedy. Allusions to poetry, and to tragedy and comedy in particular, suffuse the *Protagoras*. First, there is Protagoras's claim that "the greatest part of education for a man is to be skilled [δεινὸν] in poetry" (339a1).[15] Second, there are numerous allusions to the *Symposium,* the dialogue that represents Socrates in conversation with the poets. All of the speakers from the *Symposium* except Aristophanes are present; Alcibiades arrives late (though apparently sober, 316a); Socrates even makes reference to the two kinds of *symposia,* those dominated by the "alien" (ἀλλοτρίαν) voice of the flute, and those where gentleman associate with one another in "their own voices" (τῆς ἑαυτῶν φωνῆς, 347c–d). Third, there is the explanation (one explanation) for Aristophanes' absence: he is, in a sense, the author of the piece. In his narration of the dialogue, Socrates mirrors the structure of Aristophanes' *Clouds* to a remarkable degree, with Protagoras playing the role of Socrates and Callias's house standing in for Socrates' "thinkery."[16] Moreover, like the *Clouds,* the *Protagoras* deals with the potentially dangerous teachings of a Sophist who speaks enigmatically and spends most of his time indoors among students (311a).[17] Nor is the *Clouds* the only Aristophanic source Plato is drawing on; Socrates' narration also seems to use elements from Aristophanes' *Frogs* and *Archanians.*[18] Finally, in addition to these more or less subtle dramatic allusions linking Protagoras to the tragic poets, Socrates is much more blatant when he

---

denouncing the tyranny of convention before all assembled. Hippias, however, is presented by Plato as the least philosophically interesting representative of sophistic in the dialogues. Socrates seems to treat even the buffoonish pair of Euthydemus and Dionysodorus with more respect than he does Hippias.

15. Socrates' claim shortly thereafter (341a–b) that Prodicus has instructed him that it is incorrect to call Protagoras an "awfully wise man" (σοφὸς καὶ δεινὸς ἀνήρ)—for by awful (δεινός) we generally mean something bad—is one of many implicit jibes Socrates directs at Protagoras in the dialogue. I have largely followed R. E. Allen's translation of the *Protagoras* (Plato 1996), but I have altered that translation when necessary.

16. See Goldberg 1983.

17. For a detailed and persuasive argument that Socrates is represented in the *Clouds* as an esoteric philosopher, see Berg 1998. See also Strauss 1966 and Vander Waerdt 1994.

18. As Socrates' invocation of Homer in his initial description of the Sophists makes clear, Callias's home also represents Hades, and the dialectical contest between the young and clever Socrates and the old and grave Protagoras suggests Aristophanes' representation, in the *Frogs,* of the contest between the new poetry of Euripides and the old poetry of Aeschylus. However, Socrates' interchange with the eunuch at the door to Callias's home bears marked similarities to Dikaiopolis's exchange with a slave at the door to Euripides' home in the *Archanians.* If this is correct, it seems that Plato is posing the question, is it Protagoras or Socrates who best represents the "old poetry"? Socrates' identification with Prometheus at the end of the dialogue suggests that Socrates believes that it is he, rather than Protagoras.

describes the scene presented by the mixed company of foreigners and Athenians assembled at Callias's house to hear Protagoras speak. Socrates says that Protagoras had drawn his listeners "from every city through which he had passed, enchanting them with his voice like Orpheus, while they, enchanted, follow wherever the voice may lead" (315a–b). Socrates even refers to the assembled listeners as choral dancers in Protagoras's chorus (ἐν τῷ χορῷ. τοῦτον τὸν χορὸν, 315b2–3), and describes them as breaking into two groups and turning circles in opposite directions, in unconscious mimicry of the strophe and antistrophe of the tragic chorus.[19]

Protagoras's choice of the Prometheus story as the vehicle for his own not-quite-tragic poetry is significant. In Aeschylus's version of the story, Prometheus is represented as the savior of humanity from the tyranny of Zeus, who would have destroyed human beings were it not for Prometheus's theft of fire. Moreover, Zeus is not merely "tyrannical" in Aeschylus's account, he is quite literally described as a tyrant, one who has newly usurped the throne of heaven and rules through "Force" and "Might." As the chorus says, "There are new rulers in heaven, and Zeus governs with lawless customs; that which was mighty before he now brings to nothing."[20] Prometheus saves the human race by stealing from the gods the secret of fire and wisdom in the arts, and is punished by Zeus for his transgression. In Protagoras's version, however, Prometheus's gift of wisdom in the arts is not sufficient to save human beings.[21] This requires the now benevolent intervention of Zeus, who sends reverence and justice in order to allow human beings to live together. On one level, Protagoras does not seem to identify himself with Prometheus, who provides human beings with skill in such banausic arts as calculation and astronomy. Protagoras considers instruction in such arts beneath him (318e). Instead, the Sophist casts his lot with Zeus and considers himself a teacher of political virtue. At least this is how Protagoras presents his teaching publicly. However, there is another sense in which he is like Prometheus, and like Aeschylus (or whoever we think wrote *Prometheus Bound*).[22] Protagoras seems to have a "secret teaching" one aspect of which involves divulging the secret of the gods. This "secret" is one that, in a certain sense, is made quite manifest in *Prometheus Bound:* Zeus is a tyrant. What this means in Protagoras's case is that the gods are merely an artifact of the tyranny of human *nomos*—precisely that teaching which, according to the

---

19. Socrates is particularly impressed by the fact that in their well-behaved (εὐλαβῶς) revolutions they never stand in Protagoras's way, so that despite all the commotion, Protagoras always remains in front.

20. *Prometheus Bound,* in Aeschylus 1922, 150–51.

21. For a detailed discussion of the differences between Protagoras's version of the Prometheus story and the mythological and poetic tradition he is drawing upon, see Ferrarin 2000, 295–301.

22. See Griffith 1977.

Athenian Stranger, everyone thinks the Sophists go around teaching to people.

That Socrates, at least, considers this one aspect of the esoteric content of Protagoras's teaching is indicated by his invocation of Odysseus's journey to the underworld in his description of the assembled Sophists.[23] Directly after Socrates describes Protagoras amidst the chorus of listeners, he says, "'After him I observed,' as Homer says, Hippias of Ellis" (315b). The quotation is from *Odyssey* 11.601, where Odysseus makes out in the darkness of the underworld the shade of Heracles, and in Odysseus's narrative the figure who would correspond to Protagoras, that is, the figure whom Odysseus sees right before he sees Heracles, is Sisyphus rolling his stone up the hill. While Homer does not say what crime Sisyphus was guilty of, other sources indicate that, like Prometheus, he was punished for revealing a secret of Zeus.[24] Moreover, *Sisyphus* was the title of a satyr drama attributed to the tyrant Critias (who is also present among Protagoras's admirers), a lengthy fragment of which has been preserved. Critias's fragment appears to mirror aspects Protagoras's mythic account of human creation, but Critias chooses to make explicit what Protagoras chooses to leave implicit and esoteric. Critias writes:

> There was a time when human life was without order, bestial, and subject to force, when there was neither reward for the good nor chastisement for the bad. And then, it seems to me, human beings established laws as chastisers, so that justice would be tyrant of all alike and would have hubris as its slave, and if anyone did wrong they would be punished.
>
> Then, since the laws prevented men from openly committing acts of violence, they still did so in secret. So at that time, it seems to me, some wise and clever man invented [ἐξευρεῖν] for mortals the fear of gods, so that bad men would fear when they did or said or thought something bad in secret. For that reason he introduced the divine.[25]

Protagoras presents an account of law, punishment, and the role of the gods which is similar in certain respects to Critias's. His presentation, however, is

---

23. See note 18 above.

24. Apollodorus *Bibl.* 1.9.3. "But Sisyphus is punished in Hades by rolling a stone with his hands and head in the effort to heave it over the top; but push it as he will, it rebounds backward. This punishment he endures for the sake of Aegina, daughter of Asopus; for when Zeus had secretly carried her off, Sisyphus is said to have betrayed the secret to Asopus, who was looking for her." Frazer writes in his note to the passage, "Pausanius (ii. 5. 1) and the Scholiast on Homer (*Iliad*, i. 180) agree with Apollodorus as to the crime which incurred this punishment. Hyginus assigns impiety as the cause of his sufferings (*Fab.* 60)." Apollodorus 1921, 1:78n3; see Morgan 2000, 104.

25. DK 88B25.

esoteric, because he believes that his own sophistic activity undertakes the same task of forming human beings as the city, the laws, and the myths of the poets. Thus, as we will see, Protagoras considers himself engaged in a dangerous contest with "those with power in the cities" over the souls of human beings.

6.2 Athenian and Stranger (310a–320c)

As Martha Nussbaum has argued, the manifest dramatic theme of the *Protagoras* is "a competition for a soul" between Socrates and Protagoras, specifically the soul of the young Athenian aristocrat Hippocrates, who asks Socrates to accompany him to the house of Callias and plead his case to Protagoras.[26] However, Nussbaum does not note the significance of the background against which this competition plays itself out. This is a background of implicit antagonism between citizen and foreigner that runs throughout the dialogue, and in the dialogue Socrates seems to present himself as in league with Athens against the influence of a potentially dangerous foreigner. Socrates' narration of the dialogue begins with Hippocrates coming to his home in the early morning desperate for his help. Hippocrates desires to become the student of the great Sophist Protagoras, despite never having seen him or heard him speak, and he wants Socrates to intervene for him and speak on his behalf. It seems that the praises of others have been enough to convince him that it would be worth all his wealth, and indeed, the wealth of his friends, to study with Protagoras. Therefore, Socrates chides Hippocrates for being so recklessly willing to entrust his soul "to this foreigner who has just arrived" without having consulted his friends and relatives as he would in the case of a physician whom he did not know (313a).

After they have arrived at Callias's house, Socrates approaches Protagoras amidst the assembled chorus of citizens and foreigners and says that he and Hippocrates have come to talk to him. When Protagoras asks if Socrates and Hippocrates would prefer to discuss with him alone or in front of the others, Socrates puts Protagoras on the spot. He says that while it makes no difference to Socrates where they discuss, Protagoras should decide for himself when he has heard why they have come. Hippocrates here, Socrates says, is a native countryman who desires to become distinguished in our city, and he thinks the best way to do that is to become your pupil. It is now up to you, Protagoras, he says, to decide whether you "think it necessary" (οἴει δεῖν, 316c3) to discuss in private. Now, we must recognize that after this introduction it would look

---

26. Nussbaum 1986, 93.

rather suspicious if Protagoras were to announce to everyone that he thought it necessary to converse with Hippocrates behind closed doors. Socrates' "thoughtfulness" is, in fact, a challenge to the stranger Protagoras. Moreover, this move is not lost on Protagoras, who takes up the theme of the antagonism between native citizens and foreign Sophists in his first speech (316c–317c).

Protagoras graciously thanks Socrates for being so thoughtful (προμηθῇ) in letting him decide whether to answer their questions privately or in public. The reason such consideration is appropriate, he says, is that when a foreigner enters great cities and persuades the best of their young men to forsake their companions and associate with him alone, he must take precautions, because this activity creates jealousy, enmity, and intrigues. Sophistry is an ancient art, says Protagoras, and those men of ancient times who practiced it hid it behind veils, disguising it as the various arts. Homer and the poets, Orpheus and the founders of religious sects, Iccus and the physical trainers, Agathocles and the teachers of music all were, in fact, Sophists; but each disguised (προκαλύπτεσθαι) himself, and they used the arts they practiced as a cloak (πρόσχημα) or screen (παραπέτασμα) to hide the fact that they were Sophists. Protagoras says he does not agree with this practice, however, because he does not believe these Sophists achieved what they wished to achieve. They did not escape the notice of those with power in the affairs of the cities (τῶν ἀνθρώπων τοὺς δυναμένους ἐν ταῖς πόλεσι πράττειν). It is these men who discovered the secret sophistry behind the veil of the various arts; the many, so to speak, perceive nothing (οὐδὲν αἰσθάνονται) and merely chant whatever the others pronounce. Protagoras says that he considers it great folly to try to run away and get caught in the act, so he considers it a better precaution (εὐλάβεια) to admit rather than deny that he is a Sophist. As a result of this (ὥστε), he says, it would be more graceful for him to speak in the presence of everyone.

Protagoras's claims are, to say the least, strange. He says that the ancient Sophists tried, and failed, to hide themselves from the leading men in the city by using the *technai* as cloaks or outer coverings. This leads one to ask: outer coverings for what? The founders of the various "professions" of music, gymnastic, and the like have only this in common, it seems, that they are founders of a discipline and a way of life that is carried on in their name, and according to the paradigm they created (cf. *Resp.* 600a–b). If the great Sophist Homer used "poetry," merely as a *disguise* and the great Sophist Herodicus used "medicine" as a *disguise,* then, it seems, their greatness cannot primarily have consisted in their mastery of their respective arts—Homer's greatness cannot, it seems, consist primarily in creating well-wrought poems nor Herodicus's in giving health to bodies. These must be seen as, at best, vehicles for their true greatness: sophistry, which Protagoras defines as the "education of men." (This, of course, is the very point that Socrates presses. Educate men? Yes, but educate them in what?) This leads us back to Protagoras's original statement about the stranger who comes to town and persuades the best young men of the city to forsake their companions and associate with him alone. Why, we can ask at this point, must they forsake all their other associations? What do the leading men of the city see that is lost upon the many? Protagoras's conception of the "education of men," a conception wherein the manifest content of that education is thoroughly accidental to the activity of educating, seems to consist primarily in the transmission of the authority of the teacher. In this context it important to remember that Protagoras does not claim that he is more *honest* than those earlier Sophists; he merely says that he has hit upon a superior stratagem to running away. Nor does Protagoras claim to have resolved the tension between the authority of the Sophist and the authority of the city. He claims merely to have devised a better safeguard, that of proclaiming himself to be a Sophist. He seems to be saying, in other words, that his strategy is to hide in plain sight—to present an appearance in which the claims of the city and the authority of the Sophist *seem* not to be in tension. This explains why he first offered Socrates and Hippocrates the option of conversing alone but, when asked in public, found it better to converse in front of everyone. This does not mean, however, that he chooses to speak *to* everyone in the same way. Or so I will argue.

6.3 Teaching the Political Art (318a–320b)

When pressed by Socrates to give some at least putative content to the instruction he offers, Protagoras claims to make his students better by instructing them in good council in their own affairs and making them most capable in the affairs of the city. Socrates then asks if Protagoras means that he is a teacher of the art of politics and intends to make his students good citizens. Protagoras claims that this is precisely his intent. Socrates, however, expresses doubt whether Protagoras really has such a technique. The reason for his doubt, he claims, is that neither he nor the Athenians in general believe the art of politics to be teachable. Socrates adduces as evidence for this the fact that, while the Athenian assembly will listen only to acknowledged experts if they are undertaking a technical task such as building a wall, it is quite different when they have to deliberate about the maintenance of the city; about political matters per se, they listen to any citizen. Unlike the first case, where the Athenians require some evidence of expertise before they will allow someone to advise the city, in political matters no one ever asks to see credentials entitling someone to speak. This must be, Socrates concludes, because the Athenians believe that trades such as carpentry and the like can be taught, but do not believe that one can teach political excellence. Further proof of this is that in private life the best and wisest of Athenian citizens, men like Pericles, do not seem to be able to pass this excellence along to others. Nor do they pass their children on to someone else to be educated in these matters. Therefore, Socrates asks Protagoras to display (ἐπιδεῖξαι) to them all that virtue can be taught (319a–320b).

Before we turn to the epideictic myth Protagoras offers in response to Socrates' challenge, we should recognize something odd about the grounds upon which Socrates argues that the Athenians deny the art of politics can be taught. His two arguments are these:

1. The Athenians do not inquire about someone's education when deliberating about political matters in the Assembly.
2. In private life the best and wisest of Athenian citizens neither teach political excellence themselves nor do they hand their children over to an expert teacher of political virtue.

What both of these examples have in common is the way that they seem to abstract from the possibility of self-interest motivating political activity in general, and political education in particular. The first example is the more striking in this regard. Socrates' objection abstracts from the democrat's vested interest in denying expert knowledge in politics, as well as democratic skepticism about the altruism of such experts. He pretends not to notice that an admission by the demos that one can be an expert in political matters would be an argument in favor of a change from democracy to a technocratic oligarchy. If the democracy did not let any citizen speak, whether "rich or poor, well-born or common," it would no longer *be* a democracy, but some other form of government. In the second example, Socrates abstracts from the interest a father has in supervising the education of his children, seeing to it that they are not taught to believe things which he does not believe or even things which might run counter to his interest. (Consider, for example, the patricidal teaching of Euthyphro, that self-proclaimed expert in religious matters.) It also abstracts from the possibility that at least some of those fathers who most distinguish themselves in the affairs of the city, whether consciously or unconsciously, do not want to make their sons their equals in political affairs. This seems to be the implicit accusation Lysimachus and Melisias direct toward their fathers in the opening scene of the *Laches* (179b–d). In general, Socrates speaks as if there were no tension between private interest and public affairs and self-interest did not play a significant role in the political and ethical education fathers impart to their sons. With these examples, Socrates paves the way for Protagoras's myth about human creation and his later quasi-mythic account of human education, which depend in part on these same abstractions.

6.4 Husteron Proteron (320c–324d)

In response to Socrates' request for a demonstration, Protagoras asks his audience whether he should tell a story (μῦθον), as one older to those younger, or go through an argument. When his audience responds that he should do whichever he chooses, he chooses to recount a myth of human creation. Protagoras presents this myth as an argument for the claim that everyone teaches political excellence and that he is merely a little better at this common task than others. However, I will argue that the myth can be interpreted quite differently, and that Protagoras intends for his brightest students to interpret it this way. This should not, perhaps, be all that surprising, despite the fact that the myth is presented merely as a graceful way of making an argument. Protagoras makes clear in his challenge to Socrates later in the dialogue that he believes the interpretation of poetry in service of argument is the most important part of education. Moreover, the idea of an esoteric literary presentation of a deeper sophistic teaching is emblematic of Protagoras's hide-in-plain-sight stratagem for avoiding the enmity of those who have power in the cities. Consonant with such a strategy, Protagoras's myth is constructed like a good piece of detective fiction; all the clues for its interpretation are lying right on the surface. In particular, Protagoras makes repeated use of one particular literary device that, so to speak, provides the key to unlock the riddle of his literary creation.

This literary device could be called *husteron proteron,* that is, "the latter is the former." Throughout Protagoras's myth, and even beyond the point where the myth seems to end, there is a perturbation of the manifest temporal order of events. Things happen in the narrative before it seems they could possibly happen. Aspects of the creation story are described in terms that seem not to make any sense, because the meaning of those terms would seem to depend on things that have not yet been created. And it is by asking what meaning those terms possibly could have in absence of these later elements that we come to see the implicit meaning of Protagoras's creation myth. As we will see, the reversed temporality helps to indicate that what Plotinus later claims about myths in general is also true of Protagoras's myth; "myths present as separate in time things which actually coexist but differ in rank-order or powers."[27] The reversal in the temporal order is foregrounded and symbolized by the fact that, of the brothers Prometheus and Epimetheus, whose names means "forethought" and "afterthought," respectively, it is "afterthought" who acts and "forethought" who reviews the work that "afterthought" has done. Protagoras begins his myth, appropriately, "Once upon a time."

Once upon a time, Protagoras says, there were gods but no mortal kinds (γένη). When the allotted time came for the creation of mortals, the gods molded them "from earth and fire" and charged Epimetheus and Prometheus with distributing powers (δυνάμεις) to each. After having persuaded Prometheus to let him be the one to distribute, Epimetheus dealt the powers in the following order. First, he distributed strength to some, speed to others, bodily armor to some, winged flight to others, distributing capacities equally among them. The reason he distributed in this way, Protagoras says, is that he wanted to ensure that no kind was extinguished, and therefore provided them with "ways to avoid destroying one another" (ἀλληλοφθοριῶν διαφυγάς, 321a3). Second, he distributed protection from the seasons "sent from Zeus": thick hides and fur, hoofs for some and claws for others. Lastly, he provided food for each type of animal, so that some would eat grass, some, the fruit of trees, and to some animals he gave other creatures to devour.

Before turning to Protagoras's account of the creation of human beings, let us reflect on Epimetheus's work so far. At first, the gods are said to mold the various forms (τύποι), and Prometheus and Epimetheus are charged with distributing "the capacities proper to each" (δυνάμεις ἑκάστοις ὡς πρέπει, 320d5–6). However, here we must ask, what could the formative work of the gods have involved? The various types of creatures are brought into existence lacking any distinguishing capacities whatsoever.[28] They exist, as it were, merely as a system of differences; each type is itself only by not being any of the others. Next, when Epimetheus begins to distribute the various capacities, his first care is to equip them with means of avoiding destroying one another. Here we must ask, why is this Epimetheus's first task? Why must he take this step before providing animals with protection from the elements, or even the food that they live on? Prior to any compelling external necessity such as competition for limited shelter from the elements, prior to any inner need such as hunger which could drive one type of animal to kill and devour another, care must be taken to

27. See *Enn.* 3.5.9, 5.1.6–7. Ferrarin cites Plotinus's claim but rejects this hermeneutic principle as applying to Protagoras' mythic presentation of human creation (200, 305n48). I will argue that it is precisely this hermeneutic principle that allows us to see Protagoras as presenting a fully articulated and philosophically defensible antinaturalist theoretical position.

28. Cf. Nussbaum 1986, 100–101.

prevent mutual slaughter. In Protagoras's story it seems that the primary defining characteristic of each living thing is how it engages in the struggle to the death, and the primary ground for living beings as such is strife. This is the picture of "nature" Protagoras offers as the background against which we must understand the distinctive character of human beings.

Next, Protagoras relates how, due to his lack of wisdom, Epimetheus exhausted the determinate capacities for attack and defense, shelter, and finding nourishment on the "unreasoning animals" (τὰ ἄλογα), leaving nothing for human beings. This is what defines human being as such: human beings differ from the rest of created mortal beings in that they lack any positive, determinate capacities. All of the other animals are given *dunameis* which constitute their determinate characters—their "natures" in one sense of the term.[29] Significantly, prior to human attainment of *technê*, Protagoras refers to the other animals as *ta aloga*, those without reason or speech, despite the fact that it is only through the acquisition of *technê* that human beings come to name things and speak (φωνὴν καὶ ὀνόματα). In Protagoras's myth, human being is, quite literally, the "unfinished animal," a being whose nature is precisely *to lack* any determinate "nature."[30] It is this lack of any determinate capacities that necessitates and, it seems, makes possible their acquisition of the arts and the power of artifice. This is the reason that the beasts are called *ta aloga*; the fact that they have positive, determinate capacities means that they cannot and will not acquire the art of language. This is also the reason that human beings not only can acquire language, they can and will acquire culture. Unlike the other animals, human beings are essentially unformed and hence are receptive to the forming influence of laws and customs.

This much of Protagoras's story presents, as it were, his metaphysics. At its base is a profound antirealism about natural kinds. The "natural" world prior to or outside of the world of living things has no determinate character. It exists merely as a system of differences. The organic world which arises out of

---

29. Consonant with the broad antinaturalism I have attributed to him, Protagoras uses φύσις (one occurrence at 320e2) and its cognates (αὐτοφυής at 321a7) sparingly in his creation myth, speaking instead of types (τύποι), kinds (γένη), and powers (δύναμεις). Of course, each of these latter terms can, in certain contexts, be rough equivalents for one or another meaning of φύσις. What marks Protagoras's use of these terms from the outset as antinaturalist is the fact that, rather than presenting a distinctive capacity as the *expression* of particular determinate kind, he presents the various kinds as wholly determined by the powers associated with them, and these powers themselves as determined by their opposition to other powers or capacities. This is characteristic of his use of αὐτοφυής, where a secondary function of a devised capacity is said to be "innate" to the possessor of that capacity. (Contrast this with Critias's use of αὐτοφυής to mean "self-caused" or "self-begotten" in DK 88B19.) The full scope of Protagoras's antinaturalism, moreover, can only be seen retrospectively, once we have seen Protagoras's account of human beings as image-making and image-using creatures. On the significance of the one occurrence of φύσις at 320e, see §6.5.

30. See Ferrarin 2000, 289.

this featureless cosmos is primarily characterized by struggle. More fundamental to living things than desire for nutrition or even survival is an antagonism with other kinds of living things. Moreover, it is through their struggle to the death with one another that the various species acquire their determinate capacities. Separate from all other creatures are human beings, whose sole defining feature is the lack of any natural food, shelter, or means of protection. Despite their unique lack of determinate capacities for attack and defense, human beings still share with all other animals a fundamental directedness toward struggle. Unlike the other animals, however, which are divided according to determinate kinds and struggle with creatures different in kind from them, the indeterminacy of human "kind" leads humans to struggle as much with their own "kind" as they do with any other. As we will see in a moment, even though they are being destroyed by the other animals, they cannot band together for their own protection without destroying one another. Protagoras's man is *nothing* by nature, least of all a political animal.[31] This fact becomes the basis for Protagoras's anthropology, the account of which begins with Prometheus's gift.

As Protagoras recounts the pivotal event of his entire narrative, Prometheus's theft of fire and wisdom in the arts, he indicates its significance through a perturbation of the manifest temporal order so extreme that even the surface of his narrative doesn't seem to make sense. In what would seem to be the limit case of temporal reversal, Protagoras recounts the theft of fire as if it follows upon *itself.* He says first (starting at 321c) that, fearing for the preservation of human beings, Prometheus stole from Hephaestus and Athena "wisdom in the arts together with fire" and gave them to human beings. Thus human beings acquired "wisdom for the means of life" (περὶ τὸν βίον σοφίαν, 321d), but still lacked the political art, which belonged to Zeus. Protagoras next says, "Prometheus was no longer [οὐκέτι] able to go into the Acropolis, the dwelling place of Zeus, and the guards of Zeus were terrifying, but he secretly entered the building shared by Athena and Hephaestus . . . and stole the fiery art of Hephaestus and the other art belonging to Athena and gave them to human beings" (321d–e). Because of his theft, Prometheus was not able to enter the home of Zeus, so he crept into the home of Hephaestus and Athena and committed his theft!

31. Note, in this regard, the absence of any mention of procreation apart from the comment that Epimetheus gave to weaker animals the capacity to breed in larger numbers, to avoid the destruction of the species. Cf. Nussbaum 1986, 102. Nussbaum argues that the *aporiai* in Protagoras's myth indicate that it is an example of what Vlastos calls "simple irony"; i.e., that it is meant to mean precisely the opposite of what it seems to mean. Thus, on her account, Protagoras contends that man is most of all a political animal. However, Nussbaum does not recognize how systematically Protagoras uses the literary device I have called *husteron proteron,* and most of the *aporiai* of the myth go unaccounted for on her reading.

Once human beings had acquired wisdom in the arts and fire—"for by no means could they acquire and use them without fire" (321d)—the first thing Protagoras says they did was erect altars to the gods. "Man was the only animal that acknowledged [ἐνόμισεν] the gods, because of his kinship to the god, and he undertook to set up altars and images of gods" (322a). It was *after* this, Protagoras says, that men invented speech and names by their art. One can only wonder which nameless gods (in the plural) these speechless men erected altars to.

Protagoras's next presentation of an apparent diachronic sequence between events which must be considered synchronic is more subtle than these last two. After the invention of speech, Protagoras says, human beings invented houses and clothing and beds and shoes and agriculture. But they lived scattered and were destroyed by wild beasts "because they did not yet have the art of politics, a part [μέρος] of which is the art of war." Lacking the political art, when they tried to establish cities they committed injustice and destroyed one another, and once again disbanded. So Zeus decided to send Hermes to bring justice (δίκη) and reverence (αἰδώς) to human beings. Hermes then asked Zeus how these should be distributed. "Do I distribute them as the arts have been distributed? They have been distributed thus: one man with the medical art suffices for many private men [ἰδιώταις], and so with the other craftsmen. Am I to put justice and reverence among men in the same way too, or distribute to all?" (233c). Zeus responds that justice and reverence must be distributed to all, and says that it will be his law (νόμον) that whoever is without reverence and justice must die as a disease of the city. We will turn to the details of this distribution in a moment, but first we must ask: How could there have been altars and images of the gods if there was no reverence among men?[32] And how could there have been a distinction between professional artisans and "private men" (ἰδιώταις) before there were cities? The very notion of a "private man" seems to depend for its meaning upon a contrast with "public man"; that is, someone active in the public life of the city. As Hermes' way of phrasing his question makes clear, the man possessing the medical art practices that art in a community, where one man's knowledge of the art suffices for many. Even the most rudimentary form of professionalism in the arts cannot exist without some form of established communal life. It would seem, therefore, that Zeus's

32. "As a result of this fundamental association with *timê*, *aidôs* and *sebas* are very close, and can be used almost interchangeably, both when conveying the acknowledgement of the *timê* of mortals and gods in general and in those particular relationships to which *timê* is essential. Thus in supplication both *aidôs* and *sebas* can indicate the response (*a*) to the altar in which the *timê* of the gods is invested, and (*b*) to the suppliants themselves, and (*c*) to the god who guarantees the ritual" (Cairns 1993, 209). Cairns cites Aeschylus, *Libation Bearers* 106–8, where the chorus leader claims to feel *aidôs* for Agamemnon's tomb as she would for an altar. See also Pindar *Ol.* 7.43–47, where *aidôs,* here said to be the daughter of Prometheus, is associated with the mythic first construction of a public altar.

gift does not so much consist of reverence, which must have been in existence for there to be altar and of gods, nor the possibility of living in communities, for those must have existed for there to be "professional" and "private" men. Zeus's "gift," instead, seems to be the law that says that he who is without justice and reverence must die. That is, the gift of Zeus is capital punishment.

We now can see the outlines of Protagoras's anthropology. As was the case with his metaphysics, the apparent temporal order betokens not a temporal priority, but rather a priority in rank-order or power. Earlier elements in Protagoras's narrative are those aspects of the human that are considered more fundamental, and the most fundamental capacity of human beings is the making of images. This image-making capacity is even more fundamental to human beings than speech; it seems to be concomitant with their status as the animal that lacks a determinate "nature." Human beings as such do not relate immediately to the natural world, but relate to their world as mediated through their representation of that world, and it is this representational capacity that is what is most essential about human speech. Protagoras says that human beings recognized the gods because of their kinship (συγγένειαν) to the gods, and their share in a divine lot (θείας μετέσχε μοίρας). But human beings are not "kin" to the gods in any traditional sense of kinship; they are kin to the gods solely through their possession of the arts and fire.[33] We can recognize why these possessions entitle human beings to the claim of divine kinship once we recall that the gods are said to form all the kinds (γένη) of living beings out of earth and fire. Image-making, giving form to formless matter, is the divine activity par excellence. Human beings are not divine insofar as they are made in the image of god; they are divine insofar as they make images of gods. By making images, human beings are reenacting the very process by which they and the other animals were formed.

The reenactment of the creation in human image-making points toward an essential duality in the representational capacity of human beings. Human beings are "kin" or "of the same kind" (συγγένειαν) as the gods because they share with the gods the making of "kinds" (γένη). In the case of human beings these *genê* are physical and linguistic representations of the class character of individuals; images and names through which human beings relate to and give form to their world. Significantly, in Protagoras's story the external manifestation of this human representational capacity comes before perception according to those representations. Human beings are said to make images of gods before they have names for the gods of which they have made images. This indicates that it is the external representation of the class character of individuals that Protagoras conceives as more fundamental, that is, representation and language

---

33. See Plato 1996, 182n9.

are essentially public on his account. Consider, in this context, Protagoras's claim that man erected altars because he "recognized" or "acknowledged" (ἐνόμισεν) the gods. The word Protagoras uses is a form of the verb νομίζω, the basic meanings of which are "to hold as a custom" and "to share a common language." The representations through which human beings comport themselves toward their world and toward one another are essentially held in common. Thus, human beings, as image-making and image-using creatures, are themselves formed by the very representational capacity with which they give form to their world.

Protagoras's story intimates, however, that human beings do not share the power to form human beings equally. We can see this by reflecting on the "gifts" that Zeus distributes, and the implicit opposition in Protagoras's speech between the political art, on the one hand, and political virtue, on the other. As we have seen, Zeus's gift consists neither in the capacity for reverence nor the capacity to live in communities, both of which must already have been in existence. Instead, his gift is the law, backed by the threat of deadly force, commanding that *all* must partake of justice and reverence or die. It is this law that expresses the essence of the "political art" kept in the citadel of Zeus, and Zeus is never said to distribute the political art to all. Recall that Protagoras claims that the art of war is a part of the political art. Whatever the art of war is, it surely comprises more or other elements than reverence and justice. Indeed, it seems that essential to the art of war is the capacity to demand reverence and exact justice, or at least whatever the person possessing the art of war wants to call justice. For there to be cities, it seems, some few must partake of the political art, an art which seems to comprehend the making of laws which are backed by the threat of violence and presented to the people as the will of Zeus. The many, on the other hand, must partake of the political virtues of reverence and justice; they must revere these laws and fear the "just" punishment that enforces them.

One might object at this point that since the law of Zeus commands that *all* must partake of justice and reverence, that this would collapse the distinction between the many and the few that I am claiming is essential to Protagoras's teaching. This objection would be well taken if all partook in justice and reverence in the same way. However, in his interpretation of his myth, Protagoras makes clear that this is not the case. Protagoras claims to have shown through his mythic account of human creation the reason why everyone is allowed to advise the Assembly concerning political virtue, because all must partake in this if there is to be a city.[34] He then offers Socrates "another sign of this." In the case

---

34. This is already somewhat different than "Zeus's" claim, which is that the city cannot exist if only a "few" (ὀλίγοι) partake in justice and reverence, implying that, for a city to exist, it is necessary, at least, that the "many" partake in them.

of a skill like flute-playing, Protagoras says, if someone claims to be a good flute player and is not, people rebuke him and think that he is mad. Protagoras's next statement is so striking that I will quote it in full. He says, "But in justice and the rest of political virtue, even if they know someone is unjust, yet still, if he himself tells the truth about himself in front of many people, honesty, which they elsewhere count as temperance they here count as madness; they say that everyone ought to claim to be just whether they are or not, or that anyone who doesn't pretend [προσποιούμενον] to be just is mad. Because they think that everyone without exception must necessarily partake of it somehow or other, or not exist among men" (323b). Protagoras makes quite clear that there are two very different ways of partaking in political virtue and justice: one can be just, or one can *pretend* to be just.[35] We have good reason to doubt that Protagoras is instructing students such as Critias in the former of these two ways of partaking in justice.

At this point, Protagoras claims to have shown why it is that the Athenian demos accepts advice from everyone on questions concerning political virtue, but he has yet to show that they believe that it is a product of study, as opposed to nature and chance. He does so by describing how and why human beings punish one another for wrongdoing. In order to understand this aspect of Protagoras's demonstration, we must recognize his last use of his favored literary device. At the end of his description of what motivates human beings to punish one another—a full two Stephanus pages after he has ceased talking about Zeus and Hermes and Prometheus—he says, "I will no longer speak to you in myth but in argument" (324d). Thus, Protagoras makes clear that his entire description of human punishment is a myth.[36] Given what he says about the subject, this is not surprising. The entire force of Protagoras's "myth" of human punishment comes from its extremity. The picture of the rationality and benevolence of human punishment that he offers is so overdrawn that no sensible democratic partisan would believe it, much less the "well-born" member of Protagoras's audience. Protagoras paints the majority of human beings as so well intentioned that anyone with the slightest oligarchic leaning could hardly help but picture the bloodthirsty mob that Protagoras seems to deny has ever existed or will ever exist.

Protagoras claims that no one is ever angry over the badness that he believes comes to people by nature or by chance (φύσει ἤ τύχῃ), and never reproves or instructs or chastises people who are bad in this way in order to change them, but instead pities them. As a sign of this, he notes that no one punishes the ugly, the small, or the weak with the idea of changing them. We must note, however,

---

35. See Strauss 1953, 117.
36. Cf. Szlezák 1993, 96; and Kerferd 1953.

that this does not mean that no one ever punishes the ugly, the small, or the weak *without* the idea of changing them, nor does it mean that no one ever punishes the beautiful, the great, or the powerful *with* the idea of changing them. In regard to the general claim, consider Protagoras's example of the man who publicly claims that he is unjust. According to what Protagoras has said, such a man would be thought to be mad, and therefore bad by nature or chance. Nonetheless, since he is unable to partake of justice and reverence, the law of Zeus has proclaimed that he must die as a disease to the city.

Protagoras claims that no one punishes merely because he thinks someone has done something wrong, for to do so would be to exact unreasoning vengeance like a wild animal. Everyone who punishes, whether in public or in private, punishes only looking toward the future, to ensure that neither the wrongdoer nor anyone who sees him being punished will do wrong again. As Socrates' own Athenians are "not least" among those who punish, Protagoras says, they must believe virtue can be taught. I do not want to belabor what I believe is an obvious point—that almost no one, least of all Protagoras or Socrates, could believe that people have not, do not, and will not continue to punish perceived wrongdoers, looking to extract retribution for the wrong that has been done. So I hope that one example will suffice. In Thucydides' *History,* he represents the Athenian demagogue Cleon, whom Thucydides calls "the most violent man in Athens," defending the punishment that the Assembly had decided upon for the city of Mitylene (death for the entire adult male population, slavery for the rest) as most just. He claims to be amazed at those who have questioned this decision, and reopens the issue of how to punish the Mitylenians. He believes that it is a mistake to try to decide how to punish an offender when the edge of the offended party's anger has been blunted; "for where vengeance follows most closely upon the wrong, it best equals it and most amply requites it."[37]

It is precisely the fear of such men as Cleon that Protagoras is using in this portion of his speech.[38] By framing his eulogy of the noble intentions motivating all human punishment in such extreme terms, Protagoras intends for his audience, or certain members of his audience, to arrive at the opposite conclusions. Consider, in particular, his claim that no one punishes looking to a past wrong, because to do so would be to exact vengeance like a wild animal. This claim is striking in two ways. First, it equates what many people would consider just retribution with brutal vengeance. Second, it characterizes this vengeance as less than human, despite the fact that vengeance as such seems to

---

37. Thuc. 3.38; Richard Crawley's translation, revised by T. E. Wick (Thucydides 1982, 173).

38. Significantly, Cleon fills his demagoguery with accusations of the sophistry of his opponents and accusations of secret machinations away from the eyes of the assembly. See Thuc. 3.36–40, 4.21–22.

be a particularly human trait. By excluding the possibility that a human being could have the opinion that bad men *ought* to be punished for what they have done, *regardless* of what happens in the future, Protagoras demotes many human beings to the status of something less than human.

6.5 Nature, Education, and Political Virtue (324c–328c)

As I have indicated, it is only after presenting this fantastic portrait of corrective justice that Protagoras declares that he will no longer speak in myth, but in argument, and begins by reflecting on the kind of thing that political virtue is "itself by nature" (αὐτοῦ πεφυκότος, 325b2). Consonant with the shift to argument, the form this reflection takes is, in effect, one extraordinarily long conditional sentence, and all that is needed to understand Protagoras's argument here is a bit of rigor in parsing out precisely what this conditional entails.[39] Protagoras first asks Socrates to consider whether or not there is some one thing in which all must partake for there to be a city. If, he says, there is such a thing, and if that one thing is justice and temperance and holiness, in short, those qualities which Protagoras together calls a man's virtue, and if one must partake of this if one wishes to know or do anything else; if we should instruct and chastise those who do not partake in it until they have been improved, and exile or put to death those who do not respond to rehabilitative punishment—*if*, he says, virtue itself is like this by nature, and good men have instructed their children in everything else, but not in a matter where a penalty of exile or death awaits them, *then*, Protagoras concludes, we must consider good men to be quite surprising (θαυμασίως) indeed. It is sufficient to note, at this point, first, that the myth presented above in no way suggests that one must partake of justice if one is to know or do anything else, and second, all that Protagoras's conditional implies is that if we are to accept these claims about virtue and education, we must also accept the claim that the good (οἱ ἀγαθοί) should be objects of wonder.

Protagoras then proceeds to give a starkly "realist" description of the conventional education in "political virtue" citizens do, in fact, impart to their children, an education which is frankly coercive, violently formative, and stultifying in its conformity. Starting in childhood, Protagoras says, students are shown "in every word and deed" of their parents and tutors "that this is just, that unjust, this beautiful, that ugly, do this, don't do that." If a child obeys, good; if not, his

---

39. Consider, in this context, Protagoras's emphasis on unearthing logical contradiction in the interpretation of Simonides' poem, and his (ultimately wrongheaded) attempt to instruct Socrates in the rules of implication. See R. E. Allen's analysis in Plato 1996, 119–24.

benefactors "correct and straighten him out like a warped piece of wood, with threats and blows" (325c–d). Next, children are sent to teachers who are supposed to care, and do care, more about the orderly behavior of their students than they do about instructing them in "letters and the lyre." Students who are just beginning to understand the written word are made to sit and learn by heart the "poems of good poets," which contain "admonitions and narratives and songs praising good men of old," so that the child will zealously imitate these paradigms and desire to be like them. He will also have instruction in music, and his teachers will seek to instill in him temperance (σωφροσύνη), by teaching them the poems of good lyric poets, accompanied by the lyre, "to compel the rhythms and modes to dwell in the souls of the children, so that they become more gentle." Finally, after students have been released from their teachers, "the city also compels them to learn its laws and live according to them as according to a pattern or example." The reason the city does this, Protagoras claims, is to ensure that "they do not act on their own as they like" (μὴ αὐτοὶ ἐφ᾽ αὑτῶν εἰκῇ πράττωσιν, 326d1). This "education" starts from a citizen's earliest childhood, Protagoras says, and continues as long as he lives.

After this remarkable survey of the disciplinary practices that go by the name of education in the city, Protagoras completes his speech by explaining why it is that good fathers do not pass along the same level of excellence to their sons. Another pair of conditional clauses, which I will emphasize in the following quotation, marks the transition to this final piece of Protagoras's demonstration. Protagoras says, "Why is it, then, that many paltry sons are born to good fathers? Learn this as well. For, it is no wonder, *if indeed I spoke the truth in what I said before,* namely, that no one must be a private man [ἰδιωτεύειν] in this matter of virtue if there is to be a city. For, *if what I now say is the case*—and it is of all things most the case—consider any other practice or learning you choose" (326e–327a). "If indeed I spoke the truth in what I said before," but, as we have seen, Protagoras did not speak the truth in what he said before, and even if the story he told *had* been true, it did not imply that no one must be "a private man," that is, unpracticed in virtue, for there to be a city. Nor does Protagoras assert here that what he said before was true. In contrast, Protagoras does assert that what he will now say is, of all things, most true.

What is it that Protagoras says is "of all things" most true? That the reason worthless sons are born to excellent fathers is that different individuals are, by *nature,* more or less suited to training in different arts. The "son who happened to have come to be with the most natural aptitude for flute-playing" (ἔτυχεν ὁ ὑὸς εὐφυέστατος γενόμενος εἰς αὔλησιν) will become renowned if given the right education, while the one without natural aptitude (ἀφυής) will remain without distinction. And this sort of natural aptitude, according to Protagoras, does not seem to run in families. If everyone were instructed in flute-playing from an early age, the sons of good flute players would be no more likely to become good flute players than the sons of poor flute players, Protagoras says. We can now see that, if Protagoras's mythic account of human punishment was implicitly antidemocratic, his account of natural aptitude is explicitly anti-aristocratic, if what we mean by "aristocratic" is "of noble birth." Protagoras claims to be superior to the rest of human beings in assisting anyone (τινα) in becoming noble and good (καλὸν καὶ ἀγαθὸν γενέσθαι). That is, he can help anyone of sufficient natural ability become an aristocrat (καλὸς κἀγαθὸς). With this coda to his speech, Protagoras seems to be making an appeal for a kind of "natural aristocracy" to step forward and study from him, and be transformed into models of political virtue. However, we have ample reason to doubt that this education in political virtue is the highest form of education that Protagoras has to offer, and ample reason to doubt whether this kind of "natural aptitude" is, in Protagoras's view, a particularly admirable quality.

We are now in a better position to understand the status of nature in the various levels of Protagoras's account, and we can begin by returning to the one explicit use of the term *phusis* in Protagoras's myth. When describing Epimetheus's distribution of capacities for attack and defense among the various created mortal kinds, Protagoras says that while Epimetheus gave armor to some, to others "he gave unarmed nature, devising for them some different power for their salvation " (τοῖς δ᾽ ἄοπλον διδοὺς φύσιν ἄλλην τιν᾽ αὐτοῖς ἐμηχανᾶτο δύναμιν εἰς σωτηρίαν, 320ei–2). Nature is appealed to in the myth, therefore, to denote an absence of any positive capacity for defense, and the necessity of being determined from outside. Between this first reference to unarmed nature and Protagoras's reference to what I have called "natural aptitude," "nature" is invoked three times. It is used once at 323c5, when Protagoras argues that the Athenians deny that virtue comes either by nature or that it arises "spontaneously" (αὐτόματος), a word whose original meaning was "acting of one's own will, of oneself."[40] It is used twice more at 323d, paired both times with τύχη, when Protagoras asserts that people do not punish people for those ills that they believe come from nature or chance. And it is fairly clear that in this context φύσει τε καὶ τύχῃ functions as a hendiadys for "by things beyond one's control."[41] To be in a "state of nature" means, then, for Protagoras, to be subject to determination from without, and to be "naturally apt" in regard to political *virtue* is to be particularly receptive to the forming power of the political *art.*

---

40. See αὐτόματος in Liddell and Scott 1940.

41. Compare Polus's opposition between the significance of τέχνη and τύχη in human life (*Grg.* 448c5–7).

We can now also differentiate the different levels of Protagoras's rhetoric, and the different audiences to which he is addressing himself. On the most superficial level, Protagoras's account gives the appearance of supporting the democratic regime of Athens, and he seeks to assuage the fears the Athenian demos might have regarding expert teachers of the political art. However, one need not read very deeply into Protagoras's account to see an implicit criticism of the compelled conformity to the dominant culture he attributes to conventional civic education. Indeed, the very notion of a "private" and "liberal" education, which Socrates and Hippocrates agreed was the education that Hippocrates sought from Protagoras (312b4), stands in manifest contradiction to Protagoras's apparent denial that one can be a private man with regard to virtue. To one type of student, then, Protagoras seems to be offering freedom from total subjection to the laws of the city. These students, it seems, will be taught to "partake" of justice and reverence by learning how to pretend to be conventionally just and reverent, and at least have the opportunity, denied to their fellow citizens, of "doing as they like." However, the core of Protagoras's teaching will be the political art, an art that includes the art of war. The students who receive this deeper level of instruction will learn the art of legislation, which includes the art of making that legislation seem divinely sanctioned, and backing that legislation by the threat of violence. They will learn how to become "those with power in the cities," and, as we have seen, what it means to have power in the cities is to give form to the formless masses. However, at the deepest level, even these students will be, essentially, instruments of the creative activity of the Sophists; as in Protagoras's creation myth, the *dunameis* of those with power in the cities are bestowed upon them by the "titanic" cultural artist. We can now recognize the significance of Protagoras's initial way of phrasing the opposition between the Sophists, those with power in the cities, and the many. Recall that when speaking about the ancient Sophists who sought to hide their sophistry from those with power in the cities, Protagoras said they did not have to hide from the many, because the many, so to speak, "perceive nothing [οὐδὲν αἰσθάνονται] and merely chant whatever those others pronounce." From anyone else but Protagoras, this might only be a bit of snobbery thrown in without much thought. However, Protagoras is the author of the dictum "a human being is the measure of all things," which Socrates interprets as the claim "knowledge is nothing other than perception" (ἐπιστήμη οὐκ ἄλλο τί ἐστιν ἢ αἴσθησις; *Tht.* 160d5–6). The many, according to Protagoras, are the measure of nothing, they perceive nothing on their own. Instead, their "perception" of the world is formed for them by the poets, the laws, and wise men like Protagoras, and enforced and maintained by those with power in the cities. The many merely echo in chorus whatever these others have pronounced.

I cannot pursue here Socrates' response to and critique of Protagoras's account of the art of sophistry in the *Protagoras* itself. For now I will only note that throughout his argument with the Sophist, Socrates plays upon the tensions between Protagoras's exoteric teaching and his esoteric teaching. As we have noted, Socrates' interpretation of Simonides begins with the claim that Sparta and Crete are cities populated by esoteric philosophers. In addition, Socrates describes Simonides' poem in its entirety as a covert assault on the sayings of Pittacus, and claims that, according to Simonides, when good men have some reason to believe their parents or fatherland have acted unjustly, they do not reproach them openly, but conceal their anger and compel themselves to love and praise their own. Finally, Socrates forces Protagoras to identify with and defend an argument attributed to "the many" equating the good with pleasure, and does this despite Protagoras's evident distaste for defending this argument and his claim that the many "just say whatever happens to come to them."

Throughout his encounter with Protagoras, Socrates does not allow the Sophist to assume the tragic grandeur that he would so clearly like to appropriate. Like Aristophanes in the *Frogs,* Socrates in his narration places the would-be tragic poet Protagoras in a comic frame. He brings Protagoras down to the level of those human beings from whom he would like distance himself. Nowhere in Plato's dialogues is Socrates' dialogic manner more aptly described by Nietzsche's lines from *Beyond Good and Evil:*

> In the time of Socrates, among men of fatigued instincts, among the conservatives of ancient Athens who let themselves go—"toward happiness," as they said; toward pleasure as they acted—and who all the while still mouthed the ancient pompous words to which their lives no longer gave them any right, *irony* may have been required for greatness of soul, that Socratic sarcastic assurance of the old physician and plebian who cut ruthlessly into his own flesh, as he did into the flesh and heart of the "noble," with a look that said clearly enough: "Don't dissemble in front of me! Here—we are equal."[42]

However, as this quotation indicates, Socrates' dialogic treatment of Protagoras's esotericism seems to exhibit its own tension between exoteric and esoteric elements. Nietzsche describes Socrates' "sarcastic assurance," which said: "Don't dissemble in front of me!" as an artifact of Socrates' *irony,* that is, of Socrates' own *dissembling.* Moreover, in our own account of Socrates' conversation with Protagoras, Socrates is seen defeating Protagoras's would-be tragic poetry by his

42. Nietzsche 1966, aphorism 212.

own would-be comic poetry. To quote Nietzsche from *Twilight of the Idols*, "But I return to the problem of Socrates."

6.6 Socrates, Sophists, and the Image of Man

We have now seen Socrates' public encounters with three representatives of "sophistic," and through our analysis of these encounters we have developed the outlines of the radical theory of human creative and interpretive activity which is associated with the activity of the Sophists in Plato's dialogues. According to this theory, the most basic truth about human beings is their alienation from nature. Unlike the other animals, which belong to determinate kinds with determinate powers and capacities, human beings are essentially unfinished and indeterminate. Human beings do not relate immediately to "that which is" or nature; rather, human beings relate to their world through their representations of that world. The most fundamental human capacity is the capacity to make images or representations—communal human artifacts through which human beings create a shared world of meaning, and through which they create their own identities as human subjects. However, human beings do not share in this creative activity equally—indeed, most human beings contribute little if anything to this "shared" world. Most human beings exist primarily as the reflections of the creative activity of others; they are the human "matter" that takes the stamp impressed upon them by the laws, the poets, and the wise.

According to this sophistic theory, to rise above the "material" status of the average human subject, one must, first, recognize the chasm separating the human from the "natural" world and the essential role human creative activity plays in the forming of human beings—and this much, as we have seen, Gorgias recognizes. Secondly, and this is where Protagoras comes in, one must recognize that human beings are not blank slates, but are constituted by, as it were, a history of interpretations. Therefore, if one is to take on the "divine" task of forming human beings according to one's own will, one must engage in an interpretive appropriation of the tradition. One must take the myths that define a culture and, to paraphrase Nietzsche, force them to serve a new god.

This view of sophistic represents, as it were, the opposite extreme from the conventional image we have of Socratic philosophy. But here we must ask, how well grounded is this image, and how well do we understand the opposition between Socrates and his sophistic opponents. We can begin to pursue this question by noting that in those dialogues in which Socrates is represented in public debate (rather than private conversation) with a renowned Sophist— book 1 of the *Republic,* the *Gorgias,* and the *Protagoras*—Plato seems to go out of his way to cast doubt on various superficial ways one might distinguish Socrates' activity from that of his sophistic opponents. First, despite Socrates' disavowal of the "macrological" excesses of Polus and Protagoras, in both the *Gorgias* and the *Protagoras* Socrates gives speeches much longer than those of any of his interlocutors, a point to which Callicles draws particular attention (*Gorgias* 519c). Second, despite Socrates' frequent claims, in these dialogues and elsewhere, to be interested in examining only those beliefs his interlocutors sincerely hold,[43] in each of the dialogues we have been examining Socrates continues an argument long after one of his interlocutors has claimed that he is no longer answering in earnest. In the *Protagoras,* Socrates more or less completes his final "dialogue" with Protagoras in conversation with himself (360d6–e5). Third, each of these dialogues presents Socrates as involved in something of a competition with his interlocutor or interlocutors, and in each Socrates comes under the accusation of arguing out of a desire for public acclaim. He is called a lover of honor by Thrasymachus, a lover of contention and even a demagogue by Callicles, and Protagoras's final words to Socrates prophecy that Socrates will become renowned for his wisdom. Finally, while it is true that, unlike the Sophists, Socrates does not profess to teach anything, this would seem of little significance for the question of whether Socrates is a Sophist in Protagoras's sense of the term. For it is undeniable that more than any of his contemporaries— arguably more than any figure in the Western secular tradition—Socrates inspired those who came after him to seek to live their lives consciously following the example he set.[44] As Xenophon says in the *Memorabilia,* "He made [his associates] desire virtue and provided them with hope that, if they attended to themselves, they would become noble and good [καλοὺς κἀγαθοὺς]. And though he never at any time professed to be a teacher of this, by being manifestly so himself [i.e., noble and good], he made his associates hope that by imitating [μιμουμένους] him they would become of this sort" (1.2.2–3).[45]

Of greater significance, however, for our understanding of the relation between Socratic philosophy and sophistic is the *poetic* character of Socrates' dialogic activity. Like Plato's Protagoras, Plato's Socrates is represented as a figure who continually appropriates the poetic, religious, and philosophic tradition and transforms that tradition to serve his philosophic, pedagogical, and rhetorical ends. He is a fashioner of myths of the afterlife; someone who can, as Phaedrus says, easily make up Egyptian tales, or stories from anywhere he wishes (*Phdr.* 275b); he is, as Adeimantus suggests, more than a fair hand at speaking in

43. These claims are made most explicitly in these very dialogues. See *Resp.* 349a; *Prt.* 331c–d; *Grg.* 458a–b. See also *Euthphr.* 9d; *Cri.* 49c–d.

44. See Nehamas 1998.

45. My translation follows that of Amy L. Bonnette (Xenophon 1994).

images (*Resp.* 487e). Indeed, the central books of the *Republic,* where Socrates presents what seem to be the core metaphysical doctrines of the work, are dominated by the *images* of the sun, the line, and the cave. Moreover, as I have argued in §3.5 above, even when Socrates is engaged in step-by-step argumentation with an interlocutor, his therapeutic activity often requires that he speak the imagistic language of his interlocutor's illusions. He shows himself able, and willing, to use the poetic and imagistic power of language to persuade—that is, alter the conscious commitments—of at least some of his interlocutors, and he does so in such a way that few of his interlocutors are aware of the nature of the persuasion he has effected in them. Finally, there is ample evidence in the dialogues to ascribe to Socrates' thought a dichotomy between human beings insofar as they are individuals and human beings insofar as they are members of "the crowd" similar to the one we saw at work in Gorgias's thought.[46]

In addition to these aspects of Socrates' own dialogic activity, the relevant similarities between the account of sophistic activity we have developed and Socrates' presentation of the lawgivers and the philosopher-rulers in the *Republic* are even more striking. The first concern of Socrates and his interlocutors when they undertake to found their city in speech is a radical revision of the poetic representation of the gods and heroes. The founding of the city itself is said to be impossible without the aid of a "well-born falsehood" of the autochthony of the citizens, a falsehood which is, in part, a revision of Hesiod's account of the origins of human beings. The eugenics program undertaken by the philosopher-rulers is said to be impossible without "a throng of lies and deceptions for the benefit of the ruled" (*Resp.* 459c–d).[47] Finally, as we have seen above, Socrates claims that to do their work well, the rulers must take the city and the dispositions of human beings "as though they were a tablet . . . which, in the first place, they must wipe clean." Looking to what is just, beautiful, and temperate by nature, they are then said to "produce the image of a man, taking hints from exactly the phenomenon in human beings which Homer too called god-like and the image of god" (501b).

Of course, it is precisely the fact that the philosopher-rulers are said to look toward the natures of the just, the beautiful, and the temperate, rather than their own creative activity, that most obviously differentiates them from the Sophists; unlike the Sophists and unlike Socrates, they have ascended out of the cave and seen the *idea* of the good itself. This difference, of course, would seem to make *all* the difference. And it would, if the philosopher-ruler were something other

46. See *Ap.* 24d–25b; *Grg.* 471e–472d, 473e–474b, 475e–476a, 482b–c; *Resp.* 492a–494b; *Symp.* 175d–e, 194b–d.

47. For an excellent general account of the role of lying in the political program of the *Republic,* see Page 1991.

than he is. What he is, however, is the "image of a human being," an image crafted by Socrates, who has not himself made the imagined ascent to the *idea* of the good. Indeed, insofar as the philosopher-ruler corresponds to the "calculating" part of the soul in the city-soul analogy, the philosopher-ruler is like the human-formed part of the "image of the soul in speech" (Εἰκόνα . . . τῆς ψυχῆς λόγῳ) that Socrates molds in book 9. As part of the broader image of the soul that is the city in speech, the philosopher-ruler is an image of a human being *within* an image of a human being (588b–589a). While this image draws upon various elements in the traditional representation of both philosopher and ruler, it is without a doubt a radical transformation of those elements; Socrates, in his narration of the *Republic,* has molded something quite new.

This aspect of Socrates' account is intimated by the telling contrast between Socrates' description of the images Glaucon presents of the just man and unjust man in book 2 and Glaucon's description of Socrates' image of the philosopher-ruler, particularly when these two description are seen in the light of Socrates' image of the cave. In his "reconstruction" of Thrasymachus's argument, Glaucon recounts how, for the sake of their inquiry, the just man must be stripped of everything except justice, while the unjust man must be assumed to be "like a clever craftsman" who is always able to accomplish his unjust designs. Only when each "has come to the very limit" of justice and injustice, Glaucon says, can they be judged as to which of the two is happier. Socrates responds to this claim by commenting on how "vigorously" Glaucon "scours clean" (ἐκκαθαίρεις) each of the two men "just like statues for judgment" (ὥσπερ ἀνδριάντα εἰς τὴν κρίσιν, 361d). Glaucon makes a very similar pronouncement when Socrates has completed his account of the education of the philosopher-rulers in book 7, with, however, a crucial difference. After Socrates claims that the city will make public memorials and sacrifices to them as "daimons, if the Pythia is in accord; if not, as to happy and divine men," Glaucon responds to this apparent elevation of the philosopher-rulers to the status of divinities by saying, "Just like a sculptor [ἀνδριαντοποιὸς], Socrates . . . you have produced ruling men who are entirely noble" (παγκάλους, 540c). The difference between Glaucon's imaginative work and Socrates' seems to be this: Glaucon takes representations of justice and injustice that are already present in his culture and presents them in a purified form; he takes statues in the cave that have been crafted by other hands and cleans them up so that their shadows can be perceived more clearly. Socrates, on the contrary, is said to be a sculptor of the image of a man, an image that will cast a shadow unlike any seen before on the walls of this particular cave. After Socrates' work, it seems, the shadows of justice will be forever altered.

With this account of Socrates' image-making activity we have begun to uncover the lineaments of the Platonic version of what Nietzsche calls the "problem of Socrates." I believe that a comprehensive account of Plato's under-standing of the scope and limits of this problem would require a comprehensive account of Plato's representation of Socrates in the dialogues. To say the very least, this is an undertaking that stands outside the scope of the present work. Instead, in the remaining chapters I will attempt to sketch the outlines of a Platonic response to this "problem" by looking to those elements of Plato's pre-sentation of Socratic philosophy which militate against the view of Socratic "poetic" activity gestured toward here. At the same time, I will show how Socrates' implicit response to the challenge of Protagoras's account of human representational capacity will allow us to deepen our understanding both of Socrates' characteristic philosophic practice and of his account of human psy-chology. I will begin by arguing, in the following chapter, that the similarities between the image of the philosopher-ruler Socrates presents in the *Republic* and Protagoras's view of the Sophist are intentional artifacts of what I will call the "philosophic orientation" of the *Republic*. Socrates' presentation of the "city in speech" and the philosopher-rulers depends, I suggest, upon the hypothesis of a radical divide between the world as defined by human discursive activity, on the one hand, and the intelligible and divine realm, on the other. I will argue at the same time that Socrates indicates that this hypothesis is inherently limited and cannot account for what is most essential to Socratic philosophy.

7

Tyrannical Eros and the Philosophic Orientation of the *Republic*

In chapters 2, 3, and 4, I argued that in book 1 of the *Republic* Socrates presents an image of the historical context for his dialectical political activity. I have also suggested that this historically located dialectical political activity is identical to the activity Socrates describes in the *Gorgias* as his "true political art." Adding our analysis of Socrates' encounters with Gorgias and Protagoras to our reading of book 1, we can briefly summarize the resulting image of the historical context for Socrates' political activity as follows. In this historical period, despite the fact that the poetic and religious tradition was no longer experienced by most human beings as a living source of ethical norms, that tradition still exercised tremendous influence as a source of political authority. This fact—that a religious tradition that was in some sense ethically moribund nonetheless remained politically authoritative—had a dual significance for the self-conscious appropriation of ethical values for members of that culture. First, it led to a broad tendency to locate the sources of ethical value wholly within the sphere of human social and political activity. It led human beings to view, with varying degrees of self-consciousness, the norms governing the social and political world as self-enclosed and self-sufficient, independent of anything outside the self-determining actions of human individuals or communities. Second, it inspired some individuals to conceive of the poetic and religious tradition as nothing other than the blank authority it had become in the lives of many. These individuals saw that the traditional stories were profoundly formative of human beings and that the poets recognized their work as culturally formative, and reasoned that this was what poetry essentially was: the "divine" activity of the forming of human souls. These men also saw the human political world as self-enclosed and self-sufficient; however, they saw this self-sufficiency as reflective of their own self-sufficiency as "divine" artists. They conceived of themselves as positing those values that others found in the social and political world.

These two consequences of the decadence of the poetic and religious tradition can be characterized as two profoundly different perspectives on a shared metaphysical hypothesis, a hypothesis of *doxastic immanence* which sees the human ethical, emotional, and political world as essentially an artifact of autonomous human creative activity. In this chapter, I will argue that in the *Republic* Plato sets out to explore this hypothesis and demonstrate its limitations. I argue that Socrates' account of his "city in speech" is predicated on the assumption of a radical divide between the world of everyday human experience and the divine and intelligible realm. Furthermore, I will show that it is this hypothesis that determines Socrates' characterization of eros as a tyrant in this dialogue, a characterization to which we now turn.

Near the end of book 9, Socrates says to Adeimantus that the way in which the "tyrant-makers" manage to defeat the relatives of the nascent tyrant in the battle over the young man's soul is by contriving "to make in him some eros, a sort of great winged drone, to be the leader of the idle desires." This "leader of the soul," Socrates claims, "takes madness as its bodyguard and is stung wild, and if it detects in the man any opinions or desires deemed good and which still feel some shame, it kills them and pushes them out of him until it purges the soul of moderation and fills it with foreign madness." Adeimantus responds to this account of eros and madness with the claim that Socrates' description of the genesis of the tyrant is most perfect (παντελῶς). Socrates then asks, "Is it because of this that love has been from old called a tyrant?" (572e–573b).

Socrates' description of the role of eros in the genesis of the tyrant contains the fiercest criticism of eros in Plato's dialogues. And the strange coupling of an implanted (ἐμποιῶν) eros and an imported (ἐπακτός) madness cannot help but call to mind the very different association of eros and madness we find in the *Phaedrus.* Moreover, the assessment of eros as a tyrant is in marked contrast to Socrates' claim in the *Phaedrus* that eros is "a god, or something divine" (242e). Indeed, the *Republic,* the *Symposium,* and the *Phaedrus* not only contain, in general, strikingly different representations of eros, they also contain directly contradictory assessments of eros's supposed divinity, with each of these assessments seemingly endorsed by Socrates in the context of the various dialogues.[1] Traditional interpretations of these divergent assessments of eros have, for the most part, either gestured toward the more or less "ascetic" moods created by the different subject matters of the various dialogues or suggested that each dialogue presents us with a different stage in Plato's developing assessment of the role of eros in human life.[2] In contrast to these interpretations, I suggest

---

1. In the *Symposium,* Diotima tells Socrates that Eros is "a great daimon" (δαίμων μέγας) and as such is "between god and mortal" (μεταξύ ἐστι θεοῦ τε καὶ θνητοῦ) (202e).
2. See especially Nussbaum 1986, chaps. 6 and 7; Price 1989, 55, 85; Santos 1988, 64; Cornford 1971.

that Plato's intention in presenting these different accounts of eros is both more systematic and more programmatic.[3]

Whatever else we can say about Plato's conception of philosophic eros, it seems clear that it deals with the way in which we are led from our everyday experience of the world toward those things which "most truly are," and hence with the relation between opinion and knowledge. I suggest that the different representations of eros in the *Republic*, the *Phaedrus*, and the *Symposium* correspond to three different philosophic orientations or hypotheses concerning the relation between human discursive activity and the intelligible realm (by "human discursive activity" I mean to comprehend both discursive rationality and poetic activity). These three orientations are: (1) human discursive activity is considered relatively autonomous and conceived as radically separate from the intelligible realm, which is the orientation I associate with the *Republic;* (2) human discursive activity is considered directly dependent upon and revelatory of the intelligible realm, which is the orientation I associate with the *Phaedrus;* and (3) human discursive activity is indirectly revelatory of the intelligible realm, which can only be apprehended *through* human discursive activity but is not directly apprehended *in* that activity, which orientation I associate with the *Symposium.* I do not mean to suggest by this claim that each of these dialogues contains no reference to the perspectives represented by the other two dialogues. Instead, I believe that each dialogue gestures toward limitations of its given orientation. Moreover, although I believe that Plato viewed these three hypotheses as the most significant alternatives regarding the relation between human discursive activity and the intelligible, I do not believe that Plato viewed them as equally valid. Hence, after exploring the opposition between the "immanent" perspective of the *Republic* and the "transcendent" perspective of *Phaedrus,* and indicating how a recognition of this opposition can shed interpretive light on the *Republic* in particular, I will conclude by offering some brief reflections on the *Symposium* intended to suggest reasons for believing that the view of human discursive activity and its relation to the divine presented in that dialogue is closest to Plato's own views on the matter. However, I will devote the majority of this chapter to making plausible the most controversial aspect of my thesis, that the *Republic* presents us with a hypothesis

3. The interpretation I offer of eros in the *Republic* is broadly consistent with Leo Strauss's claim that the depiction of eros in the *Republic* is the artifact of "a deliberate abstraction from *eros*" in that dialogue (1978, 111). On my divergence from Strauss's interpretation, however, see note 7 below. Cf. Rosen 1965. Rosen claims that in the *Republic* "Plato camouflages Eros, or bends it to political use" (469), in effect arguing that *thumos* is a mask for eros. Contrary to Rosen's interpretation, and consistent with Strauss's claim, I contend that the "politicized" eros of the *Republic* is a mask for *thumos*. See also Rosen 2005, 21–25. Closer to the reading I offer here is Ludwig 2007, which also offers a nuanced account of the deployment of eros in Socrates' dialogic engagement with Glaucon.

of what I will call "doxastic immanence," wherein the world disclosed by our everyday discursive activity is conceived of as radically separate from the realm of the intelligible and the divine.

Before turning to the details of the transition between opinion and knowledge in these different accounts, I will first indicate the ways in which the difference between the "tyrannical" eros of the *Republic* and the "divine" eros of the *Phaedrus* points us toward systematic differences between the two dialogues concerning the connection or lack of connection between the everyday world of our experience and the intelligible and divine realm. I will show these systematic differences between these two dialogues with reference to a number of issues. First, I will discuss the character and assessment of madness. Second, I will examine the representation of the gods in each and its relation to their divergent accounts of poetic activity. Third, I will present, briefly and schematically, differences between the two dialogues in their representation of the Forms, their description of philosophic method, and their account of the sources of human character.

7.1 "What Is Madness?"

At *Memorabilia* 1.1.16 Xenophon differentiates Socrates from those who speculate on "the whole of nature" by listing those "human things" about which Socrates was "always conversing." He writes: "He was always speaking about the human things, considering what is pious, what is impious; what is beautiful, what is ugly; what is just, what is unjust; what is sanity [σωφροσύνη], what is madness; what is courage, what is cowardice; what is a city, what is a citizen; what is rule of human beings, what is a ruler of human beings." Xenophon's inclusion of the opposition between "sanity" and "madness" among (indeed, central among) those questions about which Socrates habitually conversed presents a problem for what has become a relatively standard account of the Socratic elenctic method and its relation to "Socratic intellectualism." This is an account most centrally associated with Gregory Vlastos and his students, but endorsed in one form or another by such disparate commentators as Terence Irwin, Jonathan Lear, and C. D. C. Reeve, among others. Speaking about the "intellectualist theory of desire" he finds in the "Socratic dialogues," Terry Penner writes: "According to this theory, all desires are rational desires, in that they always automatically adjust to the agent's beliefs about what is the best means to the ultimate end. . . . Rational desires adjust to the agents' beliefs. In fact, on this view the *only* way to influence my conduct is to change my opinion about what is best."[4] Clearly, this

---

4. Penner 1992, 121.

"intellectualist" understanding, not only of "rational desires" but of persuasion and education, is deeply at odds with the understanding which informs the account of the musical education of the guardians put forth by the Socrates of the *Republic*. For this very reason many commentators consider the intricate psychological reflections of the *Republic* to signal the decisive break between Socratic and Platonic views of the soul. Writing about the *Republic*, Jonathan Lear presents the case in this way:

> Socrates, as he comes to us in the earlier dialogues, did not have a psychology. Knowledge, for Socrates, was sufficient for virtue. Bad acts could only be committed out of ignorance and thus *akrasia* was impossible. Although a person might have conflicting beliefs, and thus there might be conflict within the psyche, there was no room for relations of the psyche with itself. Overcoming conflict was a matter of eliciting and expelling false belief. There was, therefore, no conceptual need for an account of psychological structure.
>
> It is in meditating on the failure of the Socratic project that psychology is born.[5]

This notion of the Socratic project and of Socrates' elenctic activity, however, is difficult to reconcile with Xenophon's claim that the question "what is madness" (τί μανία) was central to Socrates' concerns.[6] If, as Xenophon suggests, Socrates considered the question of madness to be as significant and puzzling as he considered the other human questions Xenophon enumerates, it seems extremely unlikely that he could have been guilty of the relatively simple-minded understanding of the process of overcoming all varieties of false belief that has often been attributed to him. For, whatever madness is, in whatever way it could be assimilated to error, it is surely different, at some level, from simply having the wrong account of the road to Larissa.

I believe that madness, and in particular the distinction between divine madness and human madness adduced by Socrates in the *Phaedrus,* is of central significance to our understanding of Socratic philosophy and Socratic elenctic method even, or especially, in those dialogues which seem to lack any reference

---

5. Lear 1994, 139.

6. Obviously, an appeal to Xenophon's presentation of Socratic philosophy cannot be considered in itself determinative for our judgments about any particular aspect of Plato's presentation of Socratic philosophy. However, many commentators who wish to separate "Socratic" from "Platonic" elements in Plato's portrait of Socrates appeal to Xenophon, and they do so whether, like Gregory Vlastos, they consider Xenophon simply to be recounting his own experiences with the historic Socrates, or whether, like Charles Kahn, they consider Xenophon to be responding to aspects of Plato's literary portrait of Socrates. See Vlastos 1991 and Kahn 1996.

to divine forms of madness. The *Republic* is one such dialogue, and by comparing Socrates' treatment of madness there to his account of it in the *Phaedrus* and other dialogues we can begin to see the outlines of the immanent hypothesis I have claimed characterizes the *Republic*.

As we have seen, madness first arises in the *Republic* in Socrates' conversation with Cephalus, and I suggested in my analysis of that conversation that with the introduction of madness, Socrates already frames the question of justice in terms which could only be adequately resolved by the introduction of philosopher-rulers and the ascent out of the cave. For, as Socrates makes clear, from the perspective of a degenerate regime it is the philosopher, the just man, and the just action which will appear insane. I have already noted in this context Glaucon's claim that for a person who is able to do injustice to "set down a compact with anyone not to do injustice and not to suffer it," such a person would have to be mad (359b). In addition, consider Socrates' statement at the beginning of the *Sophist* that it is not much easier to discern the class of true philosophers than that of the gods. Thanks to the ignorance of the rest of humankind, he says, the true philosophers can appear "disguised in all sorts of ways" (παντοῖοι φαντα ζόμενοι); they can appear as statesmen, or as Sophists, or sometimes "they may give people the impression that they are altogether mad" (τοτὲ δ᾽ ἔστιν οἷς δόξαν παράσχοιντ᾽ ἂν ὡς παντάπασιν ἔχοντες μανικῶς, *Soph.* 216c–d).

Now let us put Socrates' challenge to Cephalus in the broader context of madness as it is treated in the dialogues as a whole. A friend has given you a weapon to hold while she is away from town, and when she returns and demands back her weapons, she is, it seems to you, not *herself* anymore. In fact, she seems quite mad. It may be reasonable—or at least prudent (in our sense of that term)—not to return these things to this person. However, it also seems that one could only *know* that one was acting justly in refusing to return the weapons if one *knew* that she had become, as we would say, mentally ill. But what if she had become inspired by a god? Or become a true philosopher?

These, however, are not possibilities that arise in the context of the *Republic,* where madness is unequivocally presented as a bad thing. This is due to the fact that the goods that are associated with madness elsewhere in Plato's dialogues— prophecy, divine and poetic inspiration, even recollection—are, at least on the surface, *systematically excluded* from the *Republic,* as I hope to show. The valorization of madness in the *Phaedrus* depends on countenancing the possibility that within our everyday experience of the world there are moments that are decisively informed by something that transcends that experience. Central among these moments in the account of the *Phaedrus* is our perception of someone as beautiful and the experience of falling in love. Love in the *Phaedrus* is a divine madness, which reminds us of that time, before we were embodied, when we followed in the train of a god and caught some glimpse of the beings beyond heaven. It is my contention that this kind of transcendence is absent from the "city in speech" that Socrates, Glaucon, and Adeimantus found, if not entirely so from the dialogue in which they found it.

According to the account Socrates gives in the *Republic,* there are only two routes of access to the intelligible and divine realm: first, through the educational program of the philosopher-rulers and the ascent out of the cave, and second (in the myth of Er) through the report of an experience of life after death. At one level we can see this aspect of Socrates' account as an exemplification of the problem divine madness poses for the possibility of a wholly just rule, already alluded to in Socrates' counterexample to Cephalus. If divine madness in its poetic, erotic, or philosophic guises were to be countenanced in the "city in speech," it would bring with it the possibility of threats to the legitimacy of the philosopher-kings' attempt at imaging the intelligible and divine realm in the world of becoming. Insofar as the character of such "this-worldly" instantiation is *ex hypothesi* partial and imperfect, as long as there remained the possibility of access to the divine realm by figures other than the philosopher-rulers, there could be potentially legitimate alternative visions of how to best imitate the divine. The only way to ensure that in any conflict between the rulers and the ruled in Kallipolis, justice is on the side of the rulers, access to the divine and intelligible must be, in some sense, controlled.

However, at an even more fundamental level, I believe that the exclusion of divine madness and divine eros can be ascribed to what I have called the philosophical orientation of the *Republic.* Much of the *Republic* is concerned with presenting an account of the social and cultural forces which lead to the development of the character of both individuals and constitutions. I will try to show that this account is part of a larger attempt to work through a hypothesis of doxastic immanence, which contends that the world of our everyday experience is constituted by, and through, human discursive activity. The *Republic* contains, I believe, the most complete working through of this hypothesis we are given in Plato's dialogues, and the most complete assessment of the limitations of that hypothesis. It is for this reason that divine inspiration, poetic and prophetic madness, indeed the gods in general, are excluded from the *Republic* to the degree possible.[7]

7. By characterizing the "tyrannical" or immanent philosophic orientation of the *Republic* as more fundamental than the problem of a wholly just rule in determining the exclusion of divine eros and divine madness from the "city in speech," I mean to distinguish the reading I am offering here from Leo Strauss's reading as presented in his essay on the *Republic* in Strauss 1978—or at least one plausible interpretation of that essay. At least initially, Strauss seems to present the "deliberate abstraction from *eros*" which he claims

7.2 Poetry and the Image of God

In the *Phaedrus* Socrates distinguishes between four parts (μέρη) of divine madness, allotting each part to the inspiration of a god: prophetic madness to Apollo,
the mysteries to Dionysus, poetic madness to the muses, and love to Eros and
Aphrodite. And in three of the four kinds of madness (the rights of purification
are excepted) Socrates explicitly denigrates the power of merely human art and
sanity in comparison to divine madness. Of the poets in particular Socrates says,
"the man who arrives at the doors of poetry without madness from the muses
persuaded that art is sufficient to make him a poet, imperfect [or incomplete],
both he and his poetry are eclipsed, that of the sane by that of the mad" (245a).
The inspiration of the muses is not only praised in the *Phaedrus;* it is also
enacted in play or earnest by Socrates himself, who begins his first speech with
an elaborate invocation of the muses. And while Socrates' second speech begins
without an invocation to the muses, it ends with a direct address to the god Eros.
Even more significantly, Socrates' Stesichorean ode contains a mythic account of
the Olympian gods as they travel to the summit of heaven.

Now compare the *Phaedrus*'s account of poetry to that given in *Republic*
books 2 and 3, where poetry is discussed entirely as an art of imitation, a discussion from which the notion of divine inspiration is entirely absent. The
absence of any account of divine inspiration in the *Republic* conflicts not only
with the *Phaedrus,* but also with most treatments of poetry in Plato's dialogues.
It is, in fact, something of a Socratic cliché to say that the poets compose their
poems through divine inspiration and not by means of wisdom.[8] Moreover,
the absence of the muses from the account of books 2 and 3 is gestured toward
at various points in the dialogue. When Socrates is introducing the distinction

---

characterizes the *Republic* as following from the political concerns of the dialogue, and in particular, following from the requirements of Socrates' attempt to realize perfect justice in the "city in speech." On this
view, once Socrates has embarked on the question of whether the just or the unjust life is superior, this
very question leads to a consideration of the conditions under which justice might be perfectly realized.
The abstraction from eros, on this view, is a consequence of the attempt to perfectly realize justice. Therefore, on Strauss's presentation, it is the positing of justice as the highest virtue that leads to the presentation of eros as a tyrant. (A particular clear presentation of this view can be found in Hyland 1995, 150–51.
On the interpretation I offer here, it is less the case that the *Republic* abstracts from ἔρως than that ἔρως
as represented in the *Republic* abstracts from the divine. And, in contradistinction to the above presentation of Strauss's view, I believe that it is on the basis of this hypothesis that justice is posited as the highest
virtue. That is, if the "tyrannical" hypothesis were true, if the world of human thought and experience
were constituted by autonomous human discursive activity and human desires were not essentially
directed toward that which transcends their experience, then it would seem that the legislating activity of
the philosopher-ruler would represent the perfection of human possibilities. Or, to put the point another
way, according to Plato's Socrates, if human beings did not have some intuitive access to the intelligible
and divine, the highest political possibilities would be the highest human possibilities simply.

8. See *Ap.* 22c, *Phdr.* 241e, 249d, 253a, *Ion* 533e, 535c.

between simple narration and imitation in his discussion of the poet's manner of speaking, Adeimantus is at a loss to understand what Socrates means. To make matters clearer, Socrates chooses as an example what he calls "the first things of the *Iliad*" (τῆς Ἰλιάδος τὰ πρῶτα) "in which the poet tells of Chryses' entreating Agamemnon to release his daughter, and Agamemnon's anger, and Chryses' prayer to the god against the Achaeans when he failed." Socrates claims that before Homer represents Chryses as speaking, "the poet himself speaks and does not try to turn our thought elsewhere as though someone other than he were speaking" (393a). This claim, however, is false. Socrates has left out of his account Homer's invocation to the muse, an invocation in which he calls upon the *goddess* to sing of Achilles' rage and how it was that "the will of Zeus was accomplished since that time when first [τὰ πρῶτα] there stood in division of conflict Atreus' son the lord of men and brilliant Achilleus" (*Il.* 1.4–6, Lattimore trans.).[9] In his invocation, Homer does precisely that which Socrates claims he does not do: he directs our thoughts away from himself as author and toward the goddess whom he represents as the true source of his inspired poetry.

An even more obvious sign that something has been left out of the account of poetry occurs at 389d, where Socrates quotes Homer, as usual vastly out of context, when he is telling Adeimantus that the guardians will let no private man tell a lie in their city. He claims that the ruler will punish anyone in the city found lying, "among those who are craftsmen, whether prophet or healer of illness or worker in wood" (389d). The quotation is taken from the *Odyssey,* book 17. Eumaeus is the speaker, and he is defending his having brought a beggar, Odysseus in disguise, to Odysseus's halls. He complains that no one will accept a beggar or anyone else from a foreign land *unless* he is a craftsman, doctor, carpenter, or (and this is what Socrates leaves out) a θέσπιν ἀοιδόν, a singer filled with the words of the god.[10]

The clearest indication of Socrates' conscious exclusion of divinely inspired poetry, however, comes at the end of his discussion with Adeimantus of the art of imitation in book 3. There Socrates claims that if a man "who is able by wisdom to become every sort of thing and to imitate all things" should arrive in the city in speech, they would "revere him as one sacred and holy and pleasing." But, saying that it is not ordained (θέμις) for such a man to come to be in their city, they would send him out to another city, anointed with myrrh and crowned with garlands (398a–b). In this remarkable passage, the poet is first honored like a statue of a deity, and then expelled from the city like a sacred scapegoat.[11] The

---

9. See Griswold 1981, 150.
10. *Od.* 17.383–5. Cf. Bloom's note to *Resp.* 390a–b (Plato 1991).
11. See Ferrari's note to the passage (Plato 2000).

divinity of the poet is appealed to, in Socrates' account, only at the moment when he is sent beyond the limits of the city. I believe that we can see a similar gesture at 545d–e, where, in direct contradiction to Socrates' claims in book 3, Homer's invocation of the muse is allowed to reappear only with the dissolution of the best city and the degeneration into timocracy. Indeed, it is the muses now who tell us how "faction first attacked" (πρῶτον στάσις ἔμπεσε).[12]

Both more revolutionary and more significant for the argument of the *Republic,* however, are Socrates' earlier restrictions in book 2 on how the gods may be represented in poetry, or rather, how they may not be represented. Socrates argues that "however the god happens to be, so must he always be described" (οἷος τυγχάνει ὁ θεὸς ὤν, ἀεὶ δήπου ἀποδοτέον, *Resp.* 379a). Since, however, the god is wholly simple and unchanging, it seems that he cannot be represented at all. We can see this in two ways. First, as the argument about the lovers of sights and sounds at the end of book 5 makes clear, the objects of poetry are entirely in the realm of becoming. Therefore, it seems that there can be no strictly poetic representation of the god as he truly is. Second, to borrow an argument from the *Theaetetus,* if the god is wholly simple and pure, he is like an element that does not enter into any combination, a letter that forms no part of any syllable, and, as such, remains wholly unspeakable and unknowable (*Tht.* 201e–203c).[13]

Socrates continues his argument by asking Adeimantus whether the gods, though themselves incapable of transformation, "make it seem to us that they appear [φαίνεσθαι] in every way, deceiving and beguiling us?" To this question Adeimantus answers, "Perhaps"—and it is easy to see why. Defenders of god's simplicity who nonetheless consider it impious to exclude any possibility of god's communication with human beings have often argued in precisely this fashion. Socrates claims, however, that the god would never want to lie, either in speech or in deed, by presenting a phantasm. His argument is as follows:

1. A lie is only useful against enemies or, like a preventative drug for so-called friends, when, from madness or folly, they attempt to do something bad.
2. The god is not afraid of enemies
3. None of the foolish or the mad is a friend of the god.

Therefore, the god never lies.

---

12. The passage is taken by Adam, Bloom, and Ferrari to be a reference to *Iliad* 16.112, but Shorey takes the reference to be *Iliad* 1.6., i.e., Homer's first invocation of the muse quoted above. In truth, Socrates seems to be combining the two invocations. See notes to the passage in, respectively, Plato 1963, 1991, 2000, and 1969–70.

13. It seems significant in this context to note that Socrates claims to have heard the doctrine that the elements are unknowable in a dream.

The argument concludes: "The god, then, is entirely simple and true in deed and in speech, and neither changes himself nor deceives others, by phantasms, speeches, or the sending of signs—either in waking or in dreams" (382e). This argument is strange in many ways. It undermines the oracle at Delphi, from whom the city is to receive its most sovereign musical practices. It makes a liar of Socrates with his daimonic sign, and his dream messages of the *Phaedo,* the *Apology,* and the *Crito.* Strangest of all, in denying the god access to the medicinal lie, the same kind of lie the rulers will use later, it either doesn't consider the idea that every human being is foolish when compared to the god, or it accepts this possibility but denies that the gods are friends to any human.[14] I believe it is difficult to overestimate the significance of the fact that in the *Republic* the ruler and lawgiver can and must lie for the good of the city, but the god is forbidden to lie for the sake of any human being.

7.3 Immanence and Transcendence

Before turning to the *Republic*'s account of the transition from opinion to knowledge in books 6 and 7, I would like to simply present what I see as the most significant remaining contrasts between the picture of transcendence we are offered in the *Phaedrus* and the picture of immanence we are offered in the *Republic.*

In the *Phaedrus,* differences in human character (τρόπος) are said to be the result of the different gods each of us followed before we fell to earth and became embodied. As opposed to the account of the *Republic,* such differences in human character are not directly equated with better and worse kinds of life. Instead, there are nine kinds of life, determined by how recent and comprehensive was our glimpse of the beings beyond the heavens, and eleven kinds of human character, corresponding to the eleven Olympian deities who made the ascent to the summit of heaven (*Phdr.* 246e–248e, 252c–253c).

In the *Republic,* differences in human character are said to be the result of a combination of natural aptitude, education, and the formative familial and sociocultural experiences an individual encounters. In Socrates' description of the decline of the regimes, these first two largely drop out of the picture. Thus, on the account of the *Republic,* the character of human beings who do not happen to live in Kallipolis is largely socially and culturally determined.

In the *Phaedrus*'s account of the procedure of collection and division, collection is described as a "seeing together" (συνορῶντα), and the process of division

14. Cf. *Resp.* 352b.

aims at "being able to cut it up again according to its natural joints," the process being likened to anatomical analysis of an organism (265d–266b). The virtues are classed among "the beings beyond heaven" and are said to be recollected. The gods stand on the vault of heaven and contemplate the beings. Education to philosophy is described as "leading the beloved to the likeness of the god."

In the *Republic,* the "upward path" of dialectic uses hypotheses as "starting points" and "impelling forces" (ἐπιβάσεις τε καὶ ὁρμάς), while the downward path is likened to geometry and related arts (511b–d). "Seeing together" (σύνοψις) refers, in the *Republic,* not to the unification of many disparate perceptions under one form, but rather to the integration of the disparate mathematical studies (μαθήματα) undertaken by guardians in order to demonstrate the kinship of these studies to one another and to what is (537c). The forms of the virtues are found through the construction of a city in speech, and the subsequent analysis of that construction, a process that has been likened to geometrical analysis. The most extensive treatment of the forms is in book 10, where they are forms of artificial objects, the form of table and bed. At no point in the education of the guardians do they study organisms or natural bodies. Insofar as we are made privy to it, the distinctly philosophical education of the guardians in books 6 and 7 is devoted to the mathematical sciences severed from their appearances in the natural world.

These differences between the two dialogues are summarized in table 1, below.

7.4 Opinion and Knowledge

At the end of book 5 of the *Republic,* Socrates separates the lovers of seeing (οἱ φιλοθεάμονες) and the lovers of hearing (οἱ φιλήκοοι) from philosophers by making a radical distinction between opinion and knowledge, a distinction which, I will argue, carries over into the analogies of the sun and the cave in books 6 and 7 and which has profound implications for the account of the transition between opinion and knowledge given there. Socrates makes the following distinction between different capacities (δυνάμεις): "With a capacity I consider only this, what it is set over and what it accomplishes, and this is how it is I call each of the capacities a capacity—that which is set over the same thing and accomplishes the same thing, I call the same capacity, and that set over something else and accomplishing something else, I call a different capacity" (477c–d). In this context, Socrates gives sight and hearing as examples of what he means by capacities. "We will say that capacities are a certain class of beings by which we are capable of what we are capable, and also everything else is capable of whatever it is capable. I say, for instance, that sight and hearing are

Table 1   The *Republic* and the *Phaedrus* on immanence and transcendence

	Republic	*Phaedrus*
Eros	Eros as tyrant	Eros as god
Madness	Human madness	Human and divine madness
Poetry	All poets are imitators	The best poets are divinely inspired.
The gods	"The god is entirely simple and true in deed and in speech, and neither changes himself nor deceives others by phantasms, speeches, or the sending of signs either waking or dreaming."	The four types of divine madness are each attributed to the inspiration of a god. Socrates' second speech describes the ascent of the gods to the summit of heaven.
Human character	A combination of natural aptitude, education, and sociocultural influences. The lawgiver "wipes clean" the city and the dispositions of human beings.	Some aspects of character seem to be innate. In Socrates' second speech we are said to derive our character from the god in whose train we followed.
Philosophy	Mathematical education	Recollection and wonder
The ascent	Compulsion	Awe and desire
Dialectic	Up and down from hypotheses. The upward path uses hypotheses as "starting points" and "impelling forces" (ἐπιβάσεις τε καὶ ὁρμάς), while the downward path is likened to geometry and related arts.	Method of collection and division. Collection is described as a "seeing together" (συνορῶντα), while the proper method of division is likened to anatomical analysis of an organism.
Forms	The forms of the virtues are found through a process of construction and subsequent analysis of that construction. The most extended discussion of the forms (in book 10) deals with the Forms of human artifacts (the bed and table) and treats the forms themselves as divine artifacts.	Insofar as the forms as objects of contemplation are discussed (they are not referred to as εἴδη), they are such things as knowledge, justice, wisdom, and beauty. The gods do not make these "beings beyond heaven"; the gods contemplate them.

capacities—if you understand the form of which I want to speak" (477c). The examples of sight and hearing are significant because of the radical heterogeneity of their objects. As Socrates argues in the *Theaetetus,* we cannot perceive color, the proper object of sight, through the capacity of hearing, nor can we perceive sound, the proper object of hearing, through the capacity of sight. Indeed, Socrates uses the examples of sight and hearing in the *Theaetetus* to persuade his young interlocutor that, in general, it is impossible to perceive through one capacity what one perceives through another.[15]

15. *Tht.* 184c–185c.

In the *Theaetetus,* the impossibility of perceiving through one perceptive capacity the objects proper to another perceptive capacity is contrasted to our ability to *think* (διανοεῖσθαι) about both objects. In the *Republic,* however, Glaucon affirms that the same radical heterogeneity seen in the case of the objects of disparate perceptive capacities applies to the objects of opinion and knowledge. After it is established that opinion and knowledge are different powers, and Socrates and Glaucon have agreed that each naturally is directed toward or set over different things (ἐφ' ἑτέρῳ), Socrates asks Glaucon whether opinion opines the same thing that knowledge knows, and whether the knowable will be the same as the opinable. Or, Socrates asks, is this impossible? To this Glaucon responds that on the basis of what has been said before, it is impossible.

The definition of opinion as a power or capacity is, I believe, the crucial move which sets up everything that follows. The question we must ask is: What does it mean to conceive of opinion as a distinct capacity? Why not think of opinion, instead, as a relative incapacity when compared with knowledge? This seems to be the route taken in the *Meno,* where the difference between having true opinion and having knowledge seems to depend on whether or not one is able to give an account of one's true opinions. Thus, true belief is marked off from knowledge by the fact that the possessor of true opinion *lacks* a specific capacity that the possessor of knowledge has, the capacity to give an account. I even think that Plato (and/or his Socrates) is gesturing toward this alternative account of opinion with a bit of wordplay. When Socrates asks Glaucon whether opinion could opine the same things that knowledge knows or whether that is impossible, the words translated as "Or, is this impossible?" are ἢ ἀδύνατον. I think there is a pun on ἀδύνατον here gesturing toward τὸ ἀδύνατον, that is, powerlessness or lack of capacity.

By conceiving of opinion and knowledge as separate capacities, set over different things and accomplishing different things, Socrates and Glaucon have taken a crucial step toward conceiving the world disclosed in our everyday discourse about the world as radically separate from the world as conceived outside of that discourse. If opinion and knowledge are not set over the same things—forms or class characters or objects or events or states of affairs in the world—it is hard to see how it is at all possible to move from one to the other. Opinion and knowledge come to seem like separate and freestanding realms, each governed by their own distinct capacities and populated by wholly distinct kinds of objects. This impression is reinforced once we note the specific way in which Glaucon describes opinion as a capacity. When asked by Socrates whether opinion is a capacity or some "other kind" (ἄλλο εἶδος), Glaucon asserts that opinion is the capacity "with which we are able to opine" (ᾧ γὰρ δοξάζειν δυνάμεθα, 477e2). Here again, a salient contrast with the *Theaetetus* is instructive. In the *Theaetetus,* Socrates and Theaetetus explicitly reject the notion that perceptive capacities are capacities "with which" (ᾧ) we perceive; rather, they are capacities "through which" (δι' οὗ) we perceive what we perceive. To contend otherwise, Socrates says, would be to suggest that that various disparate perceptions were merely "sitting in us" (ἐν ἡμῖν . . . ἐγκάθηνται) as if in some wooden horse, and that there were not some one single form or soul toward which all these strive (*Tht.* 184d). If Socrates' claims in the *Theaetetus* are correct, then this would imply that to conceive opinion as the capacity "with which" we opine is to conceive of it as somehow separate, not only from knowledge, but from the soul of the human being who opines. This, at least, seems to be the consequence that Socrates draws when he frames the contrast between the objects of knowledge and the objects of opinion as a contrast between what "knowledge knows" (ἐπιστήμη γιγνώσκει) and what "opinion . . . opines" (δόξα . . . δοξάζειν, 478a).

I have suggested that the *Republic* is a working out of the hypothesis that everyday human discursive activity is relatively autonomous and radically separate from the intelligible realm. I believe that the conception introduced in book 5 of opinion as an independent capacity that has its own proper objects is a crucial aspect of this hypothesis—indeed, I believe some such account is a necessary aspect of any theory that wants to present human language and thought as autonomous. Coherence theories of truth and/or knowledge provide familiar examples of this kind of theory, and indeed, some interpreters of the central books of the *Republic* have argued that Plato is explicating there an essentially "coherentist" account of knowledge.[16] However, I believe a more illuminating comparison can be drawn between the *Republic* and Kant's account of the autonomy of human discursive activity; not least of Kant's virtues for this purpose is that he lifts his terminology right out of the *Republic.* According to Kant's transcendental idealism, we can consider all objects in the world either as *phenomena,* insofar as they can be objects of possible experience for us, or as *noumena,* insofar as they can be thought abstracted from the conditions of possible experience. The "noumenal" or intelligible character of an object is merely this abstraction from the conditions under which it can be an appearance for us. As Kant writes in *The Critique of Pure Reason:* "But this something, thus conceived, is only the transcendental object; and by that is meant something = x, of which we know, and with the present constitution of our understanding can know, nothing whatsoever." Despite Kant's claim, however, that we cannot know "things in themselves," Kant argues that we can know, and know *a priori,* the transcendental conditions that make our experience possible.

---

16. See, especially, Fine 1978 and 1990. For a brief but persuasive critique of coherence accounts of Plato's epistemology in the *Republic,* see Gonzalez 1998, 229–30.

In what follows, I will begin to sketch out a reading of the sun, the cave, and the mathematical education of the guardians that is Kantian in two respects.[17] First, I will argue that the analogy of the cave gives us an account wherein the phenomena of our everyday world of experience are radically separate from the intelligible realm. Second, I will argue that the mathematical education of the philosopher-rulers in book 7 begins with a hypothesis that implicitly denies any direct access to the intelligible realm and attempts, instead, to delineate the logical conditions under which any phenomenal experience of the world can be apprehended.

7.5 Cave and Sun[18]

We are all familiar with the basic situation—the prisoners chained from child-hood, the wall, the human beings carrying artifacts, the shadows, the fire, and above and behind it all the opening of the cave. As I have by now made clear, I want to emphasize what I see as the radical separation between the "visible" and "intelligible" worlds we are offered in this image. The first thing I would like to note is the fact that what the prisoners see before them are *shadows,* that is, gaps in the light created by the statues and artifacts dancing on the wall behind them. In the original analogy between the sun and the good, Socrates stressed the role of light as the yoke that binds together the sense of sight and the power of being seen. "Surely, when sight is in the eyes and the man pos-sessing them tries to make use of it, and color is present in what is to be seen, in the absence of a third class of thing whose nature is specifically directed to this very purpose, you know that the sight will see nothing and the color will be unseen" (507e). In contradistinction to the image of the sun/good, in which the light/truth discloses things seen/things known to the sight/intellect, in the image of the cave the prisoners see not an object in the light but rather an absence of light caused by an unseen object. The prisoners see no color, no object; indeed, in some sense what they see *is* a nothing, an artificial gap in an artificial light. This artificiality is the second point I would like to stress; the shadows are shadows of artifacts, all sorts of implements, we are told, and statues

17. Despite my appropriation of Kantian terminology, my interpretation differs in a number of obvious respects from the Neo-Kantian interpretation made famous by Paul Natorp in his *Platos Ideenlehre* (1994), the most obvious differences being my focus on the discontinuity between the accounts of human discur-sive activity given in the *Republic,* the *Phaedrus,* and the *Symposium,* and, of course, my claim that the *Republic* demonstrates *limitations* of the hypothesis of the radical autonomy of human discourse.

18. For reasons that will become apparent in my analysis of Socrates' critique of mimetic poetry in book 10 of the *Republic* in the next chapter, I will defer my discussion of the divided line until that chapter.

of men and animals. We are not told who made these artifacts nor how they made them. Yet the answers to these questions are of the utmost importance because, it seems, the only thing that connects these artifacts to the intelligible beings outside the cave is the mimetic capacity of whomever fashioned these statues. Unless we know that the sculptors have been out of the cave, have seen the intelligible realm, and have at least some "true" mimetic capacity (however that is to be conceived), there is no reason to think that these statues correspond in any way to the beings outside the cave. This problem is particularly troubling in a dialogue that casts mimesis in such an unfavorable light.

There is, of course, a great deal of controversy over who makes and who carries these statues. If we follow the suggestion of Protagoras, we should count among the sculptors the poets, lawgivers, and founders of cities, and, of course, wise men such as Protagoras and Socrates. However, considering the way in which Socrates describes the scene, it seems likely that among the shadows and echoes the prisoners perceive we should also include less conscious artifacts and artificers of culture. Indeed, insofar as the cave is said to be an image of "the effect of education and lack of education on our nature," and the fire seems to represent the power of human artifice therein,[19] I believe all of the artifacts of human culture and language are intended, including the concepts embedded in any natural language. This is consonant with the fact that the one natural thing the cave denizens could be said to perceive truly, albeit indirectly, is the voices of human beings echoing off the wall.

Turning now to Socrates' description of the journey up out of the cave, and returning for a moment to the theme of eros or its lack, I note that there is no mention at any point of that account of anything beckoning the prisoner to the world outside the cave. Instead the cave dweller has to be dragged every inch of the "steep upward path" and pulled out into the light of the sun. Nor is there any description of any awe or pleasure he experiences when he is becoming accustomed to the outside world. It is only when he recollects (ἀναμιμνῃσκόμενον, 516c4) his experiences in the cave and the pity he feels for those still below that he is said to consider himself happy for the change.

Once he finally becomes accustomed to the intelligible realm, our potential philosopher-ruler stares directly at the sun/good and "infers [συλλογίζοιτο] that this provides for the seasons and the years, and is the steward of all things in the visible place and is in a certain way [τρόπον τινὰ] the cause of all those

---

19. Recall the myth of the *Protagoras*, where the subject is also education and its lack. There Protagoras describes Prometheus's theft as "wisdom in the arts, along with fire," saying that "without fire there was no means for anyone to possess or use art itself." See §6.4 above.

things he and his companions had been seeing" (516b–c). The way in which the good is the cause of those things is left deliberately vague, and from Socrates' description it is hard to see what relation the knowledge he receives in the intelligible world could have to his former home. The things specifically mentioned outside the cave are all natural things: human beings, the heavens, the stars, the moon, and finally, the sun. The conclusions he draws about the "intelligible sun" are about how it is the source of the seasons and the years. He is not said to discern anything that could play the role of bridging the gap between the natural world outside the cave and the artifice-dominated world within it. He doesn't see anything that would seem to correspond to the "true city," nor, more significantly, is he said to catch a glimpse inside the human soul.[20] He sees neither the two horses and charioteer of the *Phaedrus* nor the hydra/lion/human composite of the *Republic*. According to the *Phaedrus,* unless a speaker knows both the truth of the things that are *and* the nature and variety of human souls, she will not be able to persuade anyone who doesn't already know the truth of the things that are. If this is correct even in part, then it remains mysterious how any of what is seen outside the cave will help the philosopher-ruler in his contest with the perpetual cave dweller over the phenomena inside the cave, phenomena which are, as Socrates says, "the shadows of artificial things."

7.6 The Presentiment of the Good and Mathematical Education

I have been arguing that the *Republic* presents a vision of the world based on the hypothesis of a radical separation between the world of human discursive activity and the intelligible and divine realm, between the world inside the cave and the world outside the cave. This hypothesis, which I have described as a hypothesis of doxastic immanence, precludes any direct intuition of the world outside of our ways of speaking and thinking about the world from within the world of our experience. This does not mean that we have no apprehension *that* there is a world outside of the world constituted by our discursive activity; rather, we are presented with just such an apprehension in Socrates' discussion of the presentiment every soul has about the good. However, as we will see, this presentiment is not a direct intuition of what lies beyond our customary ways of thinking and speaking of the world. It does not specify a limit to the

20. Nor, indeed, is he said to see "true justice." At 520c, when Socrates imagines himself and Glaucon speaking to the philosopher-king who has been raised in the city-in-speech, he speaks not of "true justice" but rather of "the truth about the fair, just, and good things." See also 517d–e, where Socrates comes very close to equating the just with the statues rather than with their originals. Cf. Adam's note to 517d29 (Plato 1963).

world of our experience; rather, it is presented as merely an inchoate sense that the world of our experience has limits.

Socrates claims that while many people would choose to do, have and enjoy the reputation for things that are opined to be just and beautiful even if they are not, things are quite different in regard to the good. Here people are not satisfied with mere opinions about the good but seek out what really *is* good, and this is what every soul pursues and for the sake of which it does everything it does. Every soul has, Socrates claims, "a presentiment that the good *is* something," but since the soul is unable to sufficiently grasp what this something is and cannot attain the kind of "stable trust" that it has about other things, it "loses whatever advantage it might have had in those others" (505d–e).[21] Thus, Socrates makes quite clear that this presentiment by itself offers us no guidance in our inquiry into the nature or character of the good. The best it can do is instill in us the conviction that there *is* some such good for us to direct our inquiries toward.[22]

This hypothesized lack of any direct intuition into the nature of the beings can, I believe, also account for the character of the educational program Socrates prescribes for the guardians in book 7. Starting at around 521d, Socrates and Glaucon consider what studies would have the power of turning the soul away from becoming and toward being, and their first step is to exclude the entire education of the guardians up to that point as "wholly engaged with coming into being and passing away" (521e). They put aside music, gymnastic, and the arts as all having, in the language of the image of the cave, the status of the shadows of artificial things. When Glaucon despairs of finding any study besides these, Socrates suggests that they take something that applies to them all, "that small matter of distinguishing the one, the two, and the three, I mean in sum [ἐν κεφαλαίῳ] number and calculation" (522c).

I would like to point out one salient feature of the way Socrates introduces the studies of number and calculation and then offers an interpretation of its significance. Throughout this passage Socrates puts a great deal of stress, first, on the universality, and second, on the absolute necessity, of number and calculation in all areas of human thinking. Socrates says that number and calculation are common to all kinds of art, thought, and knowledge; that they are something

---

21. *Rep.* 505d–e. The word I have translated as "presentiment" is ἀπομαντεύομαι, an apparent neologism coined, I suggest, to distinguish it from μαντεύομαι, which I will discuss in §7.7 below. That this "presentiment" is not presented as a direct intuition of the character of the world outside the cave is confirmed by the fact that its only other occurrence in the *Republic* is at 516d, where it is used to refer to the habit-based ability of the cave dwellers to predict the succession of appearances in the cave. See Bosanquet's characterization of this capacity as "induction" (1976, 236–37). Compare *Soph.* 250c.

22. Thus, returning to the analogy I have been drawing to Kant's transcendental idealism, the presentiment of the good has roughly the same status in the central books of the *Republic* as the "refutation of Idealism" has in the first *Critique*.

necessary for everyone to learn from the first; that every kind of art and knowledge is compelled to participate in them. Most significantly for my reading, when Socrates asks Glaucon whether the study of calculation and number is a necessary study for a warrior, Glaucon responds, "Most of all, if he's going have any understanding whatsoever of how to order the troops, or rather, if he is even going to be a human being" (522e).

What I want to suggest is that number and calculation are being presented as necessary or logical conditions for the possibility of any human thinking, conditions which have objective status even in the cave. These are conditions that must apply to our perception of the world regardless of whether or not the shadows we see in the world of our everyday experience correspond to any objects in the world outside the cave. Thus, whether or not there is any reality which corresponds to our concept "finger," and whether or not we are mistaken in the particular predicates we unify under that concept, the very fact that we can perceive them as a unity depends upon there being some unity that is not given to us in sense perception. I suggest that we should understand all of the mathematical studies prescribed for the guardians in book 7 as explicating necessary conditions for the possibility of experience, and that these necessary conditions include not only number, calculation, and proportion, but also space—in the study of solid geometry—and time—in the study of astronomy abstracted from the actual motion of the heavens. Time is the only content that I, at least, can give to a study of those movements in which the "really fast" (τὸ ὂν τάχος) and the "really slow" (ἡ οὖσα βραδυτὴς) are moved in relation to one another and move in turn those thing which are "in them" (τὰ ἐνόντα, 529d).

This "conditions of the possibility of experience" reading of the mathematical education of the guardians can only go so far. It cannot give us any clear sense of the dialectical studies the guardians are to take up after they have been fully trained in mathematics. But, of course, the *Republic* gives us no clear sense of the content of those studies either, and it is my contention that in Plato's view the philosophical orientation of the *Republic* cannot give any content to those studies. This, indeed, appears to be Socrates' own conclusion when he looks back and reflects on everything he has talked about prior to the introduction of dialectics: "All of the other arts are turned toward human opinions and desires, or to generation and composition, or to the tending of everything that is grown or put together. And for those remaining, which we said did grasp something of what is—geometry and the things following it—we see that they dream about what is but are unable [ἀδύνατον] to see it itself in waking as long as they leave unmoved the hypotheses they use and are incapable of giving an account of them [μὴ δυνάμεναι λόγον διδόναι αὐτῶν]" (533b–c). He completes this summary with what seems to be a direct statement of the problem we have been following throughout, the problem of the radical heterogeneity of human discursive activity and intelligible realm as it is presented in the *Republic*. He says, "For, when the beginning is what one doesn't know, and the end and what is in between is woven from what one doesn't know, what contrivance could ever turn this sort of agreement into knowledge?" (533c).

7.7 Philosophic Madness

I have been arguing that the *Republic* is a working through of a philosophical hypothesis of doxastic immanence that conceives of human discourse as relatively autonomous and radically separate from the intelligible realm. I have also suggested that this hypothesis is inherently limited, that it leaves out aspects of human experience that Plato considered central to an adequate account of the philosophic life.[23] That *something* is left out of the central books of the *Republic* and that something is lacking in the approach taken there is signaled from the very moment Socrates introduces the *idea* of the good into the discussion. Socrates says at 506d–e, "Blessed men, what the good itself is, let us let it go for now, for my current opinions about the good appear to me to be more than our present impulse can attain." And at 509c we have this exchange between Glaucon and Socrates:

> "Don't in any case stop," he said, "Not at least until you've gone through the likeness with the sun, if you leave out anything.
> "But I am leaving out much," I said.
> "Don't," he said, "leave out even a bit."
> "I believe I will." I said, "Probably, a lot. But nonetheless, at least insofar as it is possible in the present case, I won't willingly leave anything out."

As I have suggested above, I think the crucial move that compels Socrates to leave something out "in the present case" is the identification of opinion and knowledge as different capacities dependent upon or set over different things. The question now is, what is it that Socrates is leaving out.

The answer to this question leads us back to the issues of eros and madness. Madness, I suggest, is what is left out of the philosophic education of the guardians in book 7, specifically its philosophic variety, which Alcibiades calls in the *Symposium* "the Bacchic frenzy and madness" of Socratic philosophy. In

---

23. Compare Socrates' claim that the man who has received the right kind of musical education will "have the keenest sense for what has been left out and what isn't a fine product of craft and what isn't a fine product of nature" (401d–e).

my discussion of divine madness in the *Phaedrus,* I referred to the idea that there are moments in our experience that seem to be informed by something that transcends that experience. Put in another way, it is an experience of something which seems at once wholly strange and somehow recognizably our own. This experience Plato and Aristotle seem to have referred to as the experience of wonder, and both Plato and Aristotle seem to have thought that philosophy begins in wonder. In the *Theaetetus,* for example, Socrates claims "this feeling of wonder very much belongs to the philosopher, for there is no other beginning to philosophy than this" (*Tht.* 155d).

But, again, wonder is systematically excluded from Socrates' account of the good, the sun, the line, the cave, and the philosophic education of the guardians. There are only six occurrences of a form of the words θαῦμα, θαυμάζω, and θαυμαστός between the introduction of the likeness between the sun and the good at 506d and Socrates and Glaucon's agreement that "the treatment of the studies is complete" at 535a. Five of these appear in phrases that explicitly *exclude* wonder, phrases like "do not be surprised at x" or "is it any wonder that y." The one remaining appearance is at 514b. In a phrase used to describe the wall behind the prisoners upon which the human beings carry the artifacts which cast the shadows on the back of the cave, the wall is said to be "just like the screen that wonder workers [τοῖς θαυματοποιοῖς] set in front of people and over which they show their marvels [τὰ θαύματα]." This is the only instance of the noun form of wonder in book 7.[24] Here it refers to a conjurer's trick, and it is used to describe the architecture behind the illusions of the cave. I think we can see a similar gesture at 516c, where the one appearance of "recollection" is used to refer to the memory the philosopher outside the cave has of his former prison home.

I have suggested earlier that the goods associated with madness elsewhere in Plato's dialogues are systematically excluded from the surface of Plato's *Republic.* One form of divine madness, however, though not entertained as an explicit theme in the dialogue, is very much on display throughout. This form is the distinctly Socratic variant of divination or prophecy (ἡ μαντικὴ τέχνη). Fully one-third of the occurrences of μαντεύομαι in Plato's dialogues, eleven out of thirty-three, are in the *Republic,* and eight of those eleven surround the account of the good and the education of the guardians, with two occurrences at 506a, one at 523e, one at 531d, and four at 538a–b. In each case the meaning is the same. Socrates is prophesying what effect a particular kind of experience is going to have on a particular kind of person, what good or harm will come to him from that experience and what can be expected of him in the future. That is, Socrates' divinations always have to do with thinking about what kinds of

---

24. The only other occurrence in the *Republic* is in the phrase "it's no wonder" at 498d7.

education are appropriate for which kinds of souls. This is precisely the kind of thinking that has been on display throughout the *Republic*, from the founding of the true city, throughout the musical and gymnastic education of the guardians, the decline of the regimes, and down to the critique of poetry in book 10. This is also precisely the kind of thinking that is absent from the mathematical education of the guardians and the ascent out of the cave, a thinking concerned with those human things about which, according to Xenophon, Socrates was always conversing. To put it in something of a formula, what is missing in the philosophical education of the guardians is the reflection on divine and human madness in Socratic philosophy.

7.8 Divine Eros and Rhetoric in the *Phaedrus*

Before turning to the *Symposium,* I would like to venture a couple of brief suggestions about the way in which the transcendent orientation of the *Phaedrus* abstracts from Socratic philosophy in ways complementary to the *Republic,* consonant with its setting outside the city walls in a place dedicated to pastoral deities. As I have suggested, I believe that the "divine" eros of the *Phaedrus* corresponds to the hypothesis that human discursive activity is directly dependent on and revelatory of the divine and intelligible realm. In it there seems to be little distinction drawn between Socrates' "second sailing" and a direct inquiry into the beings. This can help to account for Socrates' apparently "pre-Socratic" speculations about the nature of the self-moving soul.[25] The orientation of the *Phaedrus* also suggests a resolution to the problem posed by the apparent disunity of the two halves of the dialogue. As many commentators have noted, while eros is the dominant theme of the dialogue up to 257b, from that point forward the discussion of eros seems to be entirely supplanted by an inquiry into the nature of rhetoric and writing.[26] I suggest that the account of a science of rhetoric given in the latter part of the dialogue depends upon the account of "divine" eros presented in the former part. A number of features of the argument of the *Phaedrus,* in particular the notion of a direct and natural correspondence between "forms" of soul and "forms" of rhetoric (271d), the implication that the principle of "logographic necessity" could give to a written speech the organic unity of a living being (263b–c), and Socrates' claim that when one employs the dialectical art one can sow speeches like living seeds in the soul of the listener

25. See Plato 1995, 29n63.
26. See ibid., xxvi–xxix.

(276e–277a), all seem to rely on radically discounting the artificiality which dominates the account of human discursive activity given in the *Republic*.[27]

The transcendent orientation of the *Phaedrus* can also help to explain the extraordinary claims about philosophy made in Socrates' second speech. The philosophic lovers, followers in the heavenly procession of Zeus, are said to seek out a soul "that is something of a Zeus itself" and hence look for "a philosophic and commanding nature." In their quest to make their beloved like their god, they "seek in themselves the nature of their god" and "find a way because they have been compelled to look upon the god" (*Phdr.* 252e–3a). Earlier in the speech the thought (διάνοια) of the philosopher is said to be winged. This is due to the fact that memory, as far as it is capable, always keeps the thought of the philosopher close to the beings—the same beings which make the gods divine because *they* are close to them.[28] To say the least, these claims seem quite distant from that "human wisdom" which recognizes it is, in truth, worth little or nothing with respect to wisdom.

7.9 Daimonic Eros

Alongside the "tyrannical" hypothesis of the *Republic* and the "divine" hypothesis of the *Phaedrus* there is, I have suggested, a third, "daimonic" hypothesis which I have associated with the *Symposium*. This hypothesis contends that, insofar as the intelligible world can be apprehended, it can only be apprehended through human discursive activity but is not directly revealed within that activity. Of the three hypotheses, it is the one most didactically presented and, I believe, the most difficult to understand. That Socrates presents the education in erotic matters he received from Diotima as containing some such view of the relation between human discursive activity and the divine and intelligible realm is relatively clear. Her account of the ladder of ascent begins with the love of one beautiful body and the production of beautiful speeches and ascends to "a certain single philosophical science," but it is pointedly not for the sake of this philosophical science that the ascent is made. Rather, the initiate who has been

---

27. Consider, also, Socrates' representation of the art of rhetoric and the "arguments approaching to testify against her" as interlocutors (260d–e), his characterization of written and spoken discourse as brothers (276a), his claim that Lysias is "present" through his written words (παρόντος δὲ καὶ Λυσίου, 228e1), and his request that Phaedrus read Lysias's speech so that "I may hear the man himself" (Λέγε, ἵνα ἀκούσω αὐτοῦ ἐκείνου, 263e). These last two should be contrasted with Lysias's appearance in the *Republic* among the mute personae.

28. Διὸ δὴ δικαίως μόνη πτεροῦται ἡ τοῦ φιλοσόφου διάνοια· πρὸς γὰρ ἐκείνοις ἀεί ἐστιν μνήμῃ κατὰ δύναμιν, πρὸς οἷσπερ θεὸς ὢν θεῖός ἐστι (*Phdr.* 249c).

correctly educated in erotics and has viewed the beautiful things in the right way
will suddenly get a glimpse of "something wonderfully beautiful in its nature,"
for the sake of which all his previous efforts were undertaken. This is something
not to be found in any body, nor in any speech or knowledge. Indeed, it is not to
be found *in* anything else, "not in an animal, or in earth, or in heaven," but is
said to "by itself with itself always being of a single form" (*Symp.* 211b).

How we are to understand the scope and limits of the daimonic hypothesis,
and what sense we can give to the claim that philosophic discourse is a necessary
propaideutic to this wondrous vision which seems to stand so entirely outside
that discourse—these are, to say the least, more difficult questions, ones that I
will defer to the final chapter of this study. For now, I will merely indicate a way
in which one aspect of Socrates' speech, Diotima's description of the daimon
Eros himself, suggests that this daimonic hypothesis discloses something essential about Socrates' discursive activity as it is presented to us in Plato's dialogues.

The *Symposium* is set in the home of the tragic poet Agathon, at a party cele-
brating his first victory at the Lenea, one of the two great Athenian dramatic
festivals in honor of the god Dionysus. The occasion for speeches on the theme
of eros is provided by Eryximachus, who recounts Phaedrus's complaint that
neither the poets nor the Sophists have ever made a fitting eulogy to the god
Eros. The various encomia to Eros offered by Agathon's guests are intended to
make up for this lack. Thus, the proper relation between human speech and
the divine provides, in some sense, the organizing theme of the dialogue.[29] If
we view the six speeches concerning eros from this perspective, we can divide them
into two groups. The first three speakers, Phaedrus, Pausanias, and Eryximachus,
center their respective accounts of eros around the authority of a particular kind of
existing human discursive activity: Phaedrus is primarily concerned with myth,
Pausanias with laws and customs, and Eryximachus with science or craft. The
second group of speakers, on the other hand, is made up of individuals famous
for producing distinctive kinds of discourse: the comic poet Aristophanes, the
tragic poet Agathon, and Socrates—who, according to Alcibiades, makes speeches
of a kind wholly unlike those of any other human being, past or present.

It is this Socratic variety of discourse that seems to be at issue in Diotima's
description of the birth and nature of the daimon Eros. He is the offspring of
Poros and Penia, that is, resource and poverty—though he is, by her account,

---

29. The contrast between their divergent dramatic contexts can suggest another way of formulating
the distinction between the tyrannical, daimonic, and divine hypotheses as presented in the three dialogues under consideration, a way which makes more explicit the intimate relation between Plato's conception of human discursive activity and the polis. If the *Republic* presents the attempted self-perfection of
the city, and the *Phaedrus* begins at the boundary of the city, the *Symposium*—like the Lenea and the City
Dionysia—shows the city pointing beyond itself to the divine.

closer in nature to his impoverished mother than his resourceful father. He is neither wholly wise nor wholly ignorant, which is to say he is wise to the degree that he knows he is ignorant. He is a seeker after wisdom, a philosopher. Having the nature of his mother, he is not tender and beautiful, but tough, dusty, shoeless, and homeless; by virtue of his father, he is an awesome hunter of the beautiful and the good, and a skilled druggist, wizard, and Sophist. Clearly this barefoot, daimonic philosopher is meant, at some level, to call to mind Socrates himself; it seems to be an idealized portrait of Socratic philosophy, one which abstracts from what is merely human or contingent about Socrates the individual. Consider, in particular, Diotima's characterization of Eros as "homeless" (ἄοικος). Socrates may be, as Alcibiades suggests, somehow essentially "strange" (ἄτοπος), but he is not a stranger (ξένος); he is an Athenian who, apart from that rare walk outside the city walls, leaves Athens only to fulfill his civic duty in military service.[30] Despite its mythic frame, however, this account of daimonic eros discloses something essential about Socrates as he is represented in Plato's dialogues, a duality that seems to correspond to the dual lineage of the daimon Eros. Like Eros, Socrates is characterized by a seemingly limitless capacity for generating discourses while in conversation with others, a peculiar resourcefulness which seems to be connected with his ability to "divine" what kinds of education are appropriate for different kinds of human souls. It is in these pedagogic contexts that Socrates makes the strongest claims about his discursive practice, professing to a kind of technical knowledge which he variously characterizes as knowledge of erotics,[31] the practice of the one true political art,[32] or his participation in the art of maieutics.[33] It is also in these contexts that we see Socrates associated with the drugs and wizardry Diotima attributes to the resourcefulness of the daimon Eros.[34] However, like daimonic Eros, Socrates seems to be even more fundamentally characterized by a kind of poverty or lack, and it is his recognition of that lack that seems to be his central defining characteristic. As he claims in the *Apology*, Socrates differs from most human beings in his awareness that he lacks understanding of the greatest and most important matters, and this claim seems to imply both that he can recognize when he lacks understanding and that he has a sense for what kinds of understanding fail to qualify as understanding the greatest and most important matters.[35] This ability to recognize his

30. See *Ap.* 29d–31b, 35b, *Cri.* 50a–54e, *Chrm.* 153d, *Meno* 70e–1b; compare *Ti.* 19d–e. On the resemblance between Plato's depiction of Socrates and Diotima's portrait of Eros, see Osborne 1994, 93–101.
31. *Symp.* 177d–e, *Chrm.* 155c–e, *Lysis* 206a.
32. *Grg.* 521d.
33. *Tht.* 149a–51d.
34. *Resp.* 608a, *Phd.* 77e–8a, *Tht.* 149d, *Chrm.* 155c, 156d–7d, *Meno* 80b.
35. *Ap.* 21b–23b.

lack of understanding seems to include a sense for which questions are prior and which questions are posterior in the order of a given inquiry. Socrates is skilled at seeing when something necessary has been left out of an account, something without which a given avenue of inquiry seems to come to an end. In short, he recognizes that he is at a loss (ἀπορέω), and, as Meno suggests, he makes others at a loss when he speaks to them.

Socrates continually asserts, and perhaps overstates,[36] his own sterility and incapacity for giving birth to beautiful discourses that he would call his own. Like the daimon Eros, he continually believes himself to be in need, he philosophizes throughout his life, but his sense of the insufficiency of his understanding of the intelligible and divine makes it such that he never attains anything like the one philosophic science of Diotima's higher mysteries. He is always more in lack than resource with respect to the divine, and it is this poverty, rather than his lack of monetary resources, that I believe Socrates is gesturing to when he characterizes himself in the *Apology* as "in *infinite* poverty through service to the god."[37]

One final difference between the *Republic,* the *Phaedrus,* and the *Symposium* will help to summarize the interpretive strategy I have been pursuing. This is the divergence between the roles Socrates' "daimonic sign" plays in each dialogue. If, following most scholars, we bracket the *Theages* as questionably Platonic, the fullest description of Socrates' *daimonion* occurs at *Apology* 31c–d. There Socrates claims that a certain daimonic sign has appeared to him from childhood, which when it comes always turns him away from something he is about to do, but never urges him forward. As we might now expect, this spiritual voice has a special prominence in the *Phaedrus.* While Socrates refers in the *Apology* to numerous occasions in the past when the *daimonion* came to him to dissuade him from a course of action, only in the *Phaedrus* does it come to Socrates, as he claims, in the course of the dialogue itself. When it does so, moreover, it is a little more voluble than his description of it in the *Apology* would seem to allow. It not only dissuades him from what he is about to do, but demands he make atonement for an offense against the god.[38] In the *Republic,* on the other hand, Socrates' daimonic sign is silent. It is gestured toward only to be dismissed as something "not worthy of speech" (οὐκ ἄξιον λέγειν) for the enigmatic reason that "it may have come to pass, perhaps, to some one other, or no one before" (*Resp.* 496c).

By contrast to both these accounts, in the *Symposium* Socrates himself is identified with the daimonic. This can indicate a respect in which Plato intended his own discursive activity to have a "daimonic," mediating role. As Julius Moravcsik

36. Compare *Tht.* 150c–d with 149c.
37. *Ap.* 23c (emphasis added).
38. *Phdr.* 242b–c. Compare Rowe's translation (Plato 1986, 164–65).

has argued, Plato's poetic representation of Socrates in the dialogues is meant to play a particular role in a reader's philosophic education.[39] As Socrates presented an idealized portrait of Socratic philosophy in his account of his dialogue with Diotima, Plato presents an idealized portrait of Socrates in the dialogues, and the beautified Socrates of the *Symposium* seems to gesture toward this Platonic idealization.[40] Plato is suggesting, I believe, that our reflections on the good must centrally involve reflections concerning what a good human being is like. This activity is necessarily an imaginative, poetic activity; we think about the good by imagining to ourselves what a good human being would do in a particular situation, or to think about what we ourselves would do if we were that good human being. Socrates as he is presented in the dialogues is a mediating figure whose poetic representation is meant to aid us in our reflections about the beautiful and the good. However, as the *Symposium* shows, such idealizations are inherently problematic. There is, with all such poetic representations, a danger that we will become stuck on the beauty of the image and become lovers of philosophy rather than lovers of wisdom—lovers of Socrates rather than lovers of the good that Socrates points us toward. Alcibiades, who thinks he has seen "mind" *inside* Socrates' "most divine" speeches and glimpsed *inside* Socrates himself to find statues "divine and golden and entirely beautiful," shows that this was by no means a danger that Socrates was simply able to overcome.

The above-sketched account of the duality of daimonic eros and the corresponding duality in Plato's presentation of Socrates raises a series of questions about how we are to understand the relation between these two aspects of Socrates' dialogic activity. It raises questions about how we are to understand the relation between theory and practice, between cognition and imagination, and between metaphysics and ethics in Socratic philosophy. It also raises questions about how we are to relate the individualized psychological reflections that I have argued inform Socrates' engagements with his interlocutors to Plato's investigation of different metaphysical orientations or hypotheses. Finally, we need to understand more clearly the relation between the duality of Socrates' dialogic activity and the dichotomy between the scientific knowledge and ethical psychology we saw at work in Thrasymachus's and Gorgias's conceptions of the rhetorical art. These are the questions I take up in the final three chapters of this study.

39. See Moravcsik 1992, 108–15.
40. See §6.2. Cf. *Symp.* 174a with *Letter II* 314c.

8

Imitation and Experience

In the previous chapter, I argued that Plato sets out to explore and demonstrate the limitations of a hypothesis of doxastic immanence which envisages the world of our everyday experience—the human ethical, emotional, and political world—as essentially an artifact of human representational activity. This hypothesis, I have argued, is most evidently manifested in Socrates' image of the cave. According to that image, the meaning that most human beings find *within* the world of their experience has been put into that world by human discursive representation. Or to put the point another way, according to the image of the cave, what most people *mean* is determined by the authoritative pronouncements of some other person or persons who *know*. Inside the cave of political opinion, whatever intelligibility there is in everyday human discursive activity is wholly dependent upon a prior authoritative discursive activity—the philosophic and legislative activity of the philosopher-kings. This authoritative discourse, in turn, is not articulated through a reflection upon or a refinement or transformation of everyday discursive notions of the true, the beautiful, and the good—it is not, in this sense, "dialectical" or "Socratic." Instead, the intelligibility of the legislative activity of the philosopher-ruler depends upon a wholesale turning away from the objects and experiences of everyday life to focus on mathematical studies severed from their appearances in the natural world and see in them the logical structure of the phenomenal world. On this view, if it were not for the intercession of the mathematically trained philosopher-kings into the benighted world of the cave, there would be little reason to consider the cave dwellers' experience of their world to be intelligible in any sense. In any case, this is an intelligibility which the cave dwellers themselves experience only through the authoritative pronouncements of the philosopher-rulers; the world of their experience remains a world populated by the shadows of artificial things.

In the following chapter, I will argue that Socrates' explicit critique of mimetic poetry in book 10 extends the *Republic*'s demonstration of the limits of the hypothesis of doxastic immanence. The "ancient quarrel" that Socrates announces and engages in his book 10 discussion of mimetic poetry, I contend, has less to do with Socrates' (or Plato's) judgment concerning the beauty or wisdom of Homer's literary production than with an assessment of the limitations of a particular

Sophistic theoretical conception of poetry associated with Gorgias and Protagoras: a radical constructivism which posits a kind of creative "poetic" activity as ultimately responsible for the character of the human social world. Socrates' immediate opponent here is not tragic poetry per se but rather the theoretical position which takes spontaneous human discursive productivity as the highest theoretical activity.[1] Pursuing this line of interpretation, I will defend Socrates' claim in *Republic* X to be, as he says, a friend of Homer (595b).[2] At the same time, I will explore in greater detail how Socrates' implicit and explicit appropriation of Homer's poetry allows us to better understand the relation between the "poetic" character of Socrates' dialogic practice in the dialogues and his understanding of the human soul.

What most obviously unites Socrates' depiction of the legislative activity of the philosopher-rulers with his book 10 critique of *mimêsis* is an underlying assumption that some authoritative cultural representation could be wholly determinative for the social and political world, and could provide a determinate horizon for human ethical and political action. In Socrates' critique of *mimêsis,* this assumption appears in the guise of a conception of mimetic representation as a wholly determinate *reproduction.* This is a conception of a mimetic representation that requires no interpretation on the part of its audience, and one that requires no broader horizon of intelligibility within which it must be understood. It is in this context, I suggest, that we should approach the distinction Socrates draws in his critique between *graphic* or pictorial imitation, on the one hand, and *poetic* imitation, on the other. Through a careful reading of Socrates' critique, we will see how the opposition between the *graphic* and the *poetic* relates to and depends upon the central Platonic opposition between the *visible* and the *intelligible.* Ultimately this will help us see that the very aspects of *mimêsis* that make it politically or ethically questionable point to an essential connection between mimetic poetry and Socrates' philosophic practice. I will argue that, rather than viewing mimetic poetry as something that determines

---

1. One sign of this can be discerned in the fact that Plato never undertakes to represent Socrates in conversation with the greatest of the tragic poets. In retrospect, this is a remarkable lacuna in the line of illustrious fourth- and fifth-century Greeks with whom Socrates converses. As we have seen, Socrates speaks with the most famous Sophists of his era. He is also represented as in dialogue with two of the most renowned pre-Socratic philosophers and indisputably the greatest of comic poets. However, instead of Sophocles or Euripides, the tragic poet with whom Socrates speaks is Agathon, a figure whom Socrates explicitly associates with the influence of Gorgias. Dialogues with Sophocles and Euripides would certainly have been chronologically possible—Sophocles was younger than Parmenides and Euripides younger than Protagoras—and of course, Plato does not limit himself to the chronologically possible.

2. One measure of Plato's respect for Homer is the fact that, given the myriad of explicit and implicit allusions to and frequent quotations and interpretively significant misquotations of the *Iliad* and the *Odyssey* in the dialogues, a familiarity with Homer is a precondition for reading Plato well. Thus, Plato ensures that as long as there is an audience for the dialogues, so too will there be an audience for Homer's poetry.

the world of our experience, Socrates views mimetic poetry, in the best case, as helping us to become philosophically mindful of that experience.

8.1 Homer's Army

In the *Theaetetus,* Socrates offers a theoretical genealogy of Theaetetus's first attempt at a definition of knowledge, a genealogy that is significant for our understanding of the critique of Homeric poetry presented in book 10 of the *Republic.* It is significant not only for the specific line of descent Socrates gives for Theaetetus's claim that "knowledge is perception," but also for the strong sense in which it is a genealogy, that is, a narrative of generation and descent. Socrates famously begins his examination of Theaetetus's conception of knowledge by citing his own parentage as a basis of his authority. He tells Theaetetus that just as his mother had been a midwife tending to women as they gave birth to "bodily" offspring, he is a midwife who tends to the souls of young men as they give birth to offspring of soul. Despite the notoriety of Socrates' metaphors of pregnancy and midwifery, very few commentators note the central role given in the deployment of these metaphors to the subject of intellectual paternity.[3] However, Socrates makes quite clear that his maieutic art concerns not only the progress of an intellectual pregnancy and the viability of an intellectual offspring, but also the question of who "fathered" the account (*Tht.* 149d–150b). That is, Socrates implies that an important part of his role as midwife to Theaetetus is finding out who got the young man pregnant in the first place. And just as Socrates' first question about Theaetetus in the dialogue is "who is his father?" (144b), his first step in examining the fruit of Theaetetus's philosophical labor is determining Protagoras as its progenitor.

This is, however, merely the first step in Socrates' description of the theoretical lineage of Theaetetus's account of knowledge. Socrates suggests that Theaetetus's conception of knowledge is a descendant of Protagoras's claim that "human being is the measure of all things," but he contends that the *homo mensura* thesis is itself a descendant of an earlier argument, an argument asserting that "nothing is one, itself by itself, nor can one correctly ascribe any quality to anything whenever." Behind this argument in turn, he finds a line of influence that stretches all the way back to Homer. "Nothing ever is, but always becomes [or 'is born']. Concerning this let there be gathered in succession all the wise except

---

3. Klein 1965, Benardete in Plato 1984, and Derrida 1981 are notable exceptions. David Sedley's recent book-length interpretation of the *Theaetetus,* for example, which focuses on the metaphor of midwifery, makes no mention of the subject of intellectual paternity (2005).

Parmenides—Protagoras, Heraclitus, and Empedocles, and the utmost of the poets in both kinds of poetry, Epicharmus in comedy, and in tragedy, Homer, saying 'Oceanus genesis of the gods and Tethys their mother.' Everything, he has said, is the offspring of flux and movement" (152e). What is most noteworthy about this passage in the current context is the fact that Socrates does not merely identify Homer as the earliest source for the doctrine of ceaseless genesis, he also implies that Homer's position as the terminal point in a line of theoretical succession confers on him the role of ultimate and enduring authority. The theorists who follow Homer in denying that the world has any determinate character in itself are characterized by Socrates as soldiers in an "army" (στρατόπεδον) which has Homer as its "military leader" (στρατηγός) and, he implies, Protagoras as its most recent champion.

Even apart from the specific thesis Socrates attributes to Homer in this passage, the genealogical interpretive gesture itself is significant. In his critique of Theaetetus's appropriation of Protagoras, Socrates engages in a style of allegorical interpretation of Homer associated with the Sophists.[4] By grouping together all of the wise except Parmenides in a line which runs from Homer to Protagoras, Socrates also mirrors Protagoras's explicit claim in the *Protagoras* that from Homer on, all the distinguished practitioners of the arts were really Sophists in disguise. Moreover, the equation of historical authorship of a theoretical perspective with authority over those individuals who accept or affirm that theoretical perspective mirrors Protagoras's and Gorgias's implicit accounts of poetic and sophistic persuasion. It seems, therefore, that in his examination of Theaetetus's claim "knowledge is perception," Socrates is adopting for the sake of the argument a Protagorean perspective on authorship and authority, and that it is on this basis that he characterizes Homer as a general leading an army of theorists who deny any stable reality to the world. This Protagorean Homer, I suggest, is also the object of Socrates' critique in book 10, where Socrates takes as his opponent not Homer in his role as storyteller or myth-maker (μυθολόγος), but Homer understood as "first teacher and leader [πρῶτος διδάσκαλός τε καὶ ἡγεμὼν] of all these fine tragic ones" (595b10-c2).[5]

Socrates claims, at the beginning of book 10, to be resuming a critique of mimetic poetry he began in books 2 and 3. However, the problematic character of this putative "return" to the subject is one of the few points most commentators can agree upon concerning the passage. Indeed, any attentive reader can see the difficulty of reconciling much of the manifest content of the first half

---

4. See, in particular, 153c–d.
5. Both διδάσκαλος (teacher) and ἡγεμών (leader) can be translated as "chorus leader" in the appropriate context.

of book 10 with the rest of the *Republic,* much less with Socrates' views expressed in other dialogues. Few other passages seem to call more straightforwardly for an ironic reading. Indeed, I will suggest that, at least in the first instance, what the passage calls for is a straightforwardly ironic reading. That is, both Socrates' unnamed auditors, and we as readers, are meant to see that the arguments against mimetic poetry offered in book 10, at least insofar as it is presented as a critique of Homer, are almost wholly off the mark. It is by seeing how and why this critique misses its apparent target that we can come to appreciate its true aims. On the one hand, Socrates' arguments extend the *Republic*'s depiction of the hypothesis of doxastic immanence to the point of an open caricature of that hypothesis. On the other hand, the limitations in his critique of mimetic poetry begin to sketch out in negative an alternative understanding of Homeric poetry and its significance for Socrates' dialectical practice.

8.2 Socrates' Contest (595a–603c)

Socrates begins his investigation of *mimêsis* in book 10 by asking Glaucon whether they should proceed in their "customary method" (τῆς εἰωθυίας μεθόδου) by positing one particular form (εἶδος) for each "many" to which the same name is applied. It seems, however, that a doctrine of the forms which asserts a one-to-one correspondence between names and forms is only "customary" in the sense that it takes custom or linguistic practice as determinative of the forms themselves. The sovereignty of the customary in this account is further suggested by the examples of "couch" and "table" which Socrates chooses as paradigmatic *eidê*. On the one hand, the classes "tables" and "couches" seem to be fairly obviously conventionally determined. As concepts, "couch" and "table" seem to be best understood along the lines suggested by the prototype theory of concepts; the various objects one calls couches would seem to share no more than what Wittgenstein called a "family resemblance."[6] On the other hand, couches and tables are precisely those objects whose use "as is conventional" (ἅπερ νομίζεται) Glaucon demands in order to differentiate the nascent city in speech from a city of pigs. Thus, the "form" the various craftsmen look to in fashioning the many tables and couches seems, in the first instance, to be determined by the use of the words "table" and "couch" in some more or less determinate discursive community. The question at issue thus becomes (as it will in the second half of Socrates' critique[7]), what

---

6. For the prototype theory of concepts, see Rosch 1975. For Wittgenstein's analysis of the members of a class kind bearing no more than "family resemblance" to one another, see Wittgenstein 1974, 73–75.

7. 602c–d.

determines linguistic use? One possible and initially plausible answer to this question is the poet himself. It is this possibility that Socrates is apparently determined to combat.

As Charles Griswold has argued, the naïve essentialism that characterizes this version of the "one over many" argument must be seen as an artifact of Socrates' ad hominem appropriation of the perspective against which he argues.[8] Contrary to Griswold's interpretation, however, I do not believe that we should simply identify this perspective with "the poet's conception of the whole." Rather, as I have suggested, the view Socrates opposes and implicitly appropriates here is a particular sophistic view of poetry as wholly responsible for the determinant character of the human social world.[9] On this view, the poet-Sophist in fashioning "an image of a human being" gives form to the human communities whose linguistic usage provides the "original" that the several craftsmen copy in making individual tables and couches. However, as discussed in §6.6, the role of the philosopher-king within the city in speech differs from the role of the poet-Sophist in a crucial respect the philosopher-king is said to fashion his image of a human being looking to "the just, beautiful, and moderate by nature, and all such things" (501b3).

Even if we were to accept this putative difference between the poet-Sophist and the philosopher-ruler, it remains the case that each adopts a similar role with respect to the members of the political or discursive community. As I have argued above, both Protagoras's conception of sophistry and Socrates' articulation of the city in speech present the world as it is experienced by most human beings as the product of human discursive activity. The radical dependence of the intelligibility of common experience on a prior authoritative discursive productivity is symbolized in the present context by the claim that the *eidê* themselves are artifacts of a divine craftsman. In his first of two tripartite schemes placing the imitator at third remove from what he imitates, Socrates distinguishes between three kinds of couches (τρισὶν εἴδεσι κλινῶν): the one the painter paints; the one the carpenter produces; and the one couch that *is* in nature, which is said to be produced by a god. This mysterious artisan god is distinguished from the mere imitator by being the original "begetter" (φυτουργός) who engenders the couch in nature. However, this divine creator appears to be entirely unlike the demiurge of the *Timaeus,* who in his generosity desires that all things be as like to himself as possible.[10] Instead, the artisan god's motivation

---

8. Griswold 1981, 146.
9. The identification between the mimetic poet and the Sophist is all but explicitly asserted by Glaucon, who responds to Socrates' postulation of a craftsman who can make all things on the earth, in heaven, and in Hades by saying, "That's an entirely wonderful Sophist you speak of" (596d1).
10. *Ti.* 29e.

looks more like that of Gorgias's "rhetorical man." The god creates from a desire to distinguish himself from the mere manual artisan; he "wants to be a real maker of the couch that really *is* and not a certain couch maker of a certain couch."[11] The god asserts his own reality through his creative activity. The distinction between the poet-imitator and the artisan-god is a distinction in authenticity, authority, and generation; the poet is worse than the god precisely because his creation is derivative. Indeed, the imitator himself is presented as a product of the artisan-god's "begetting"; he is "the third generation from nature." In so far as he is derivative and inauthentic he also lacks authority; "he is naturally third from the king and the truth."

It has been suggested by C. D. C. Reeve that the king-as-divine-craftsman of 597e should be identified with the philosopher-king of the city in speech.[12] This identification becomes persuasive once we recall what Socrates says about the philosopher "who keeps company with the divine and becomes orderly and divine to the extent possible for human being." If he is compelled by some necessity "to practice putting what he sees there into the dispositions of human beings, instead of moulding himself alone [μὴ μόνον ἑαυτὸν πλάττειν]" he will not prove "to be a bad craftsman [δημιουργὸν] of moderation, justice, and demotic virtue all together [συμπάσης τῆς δημοτικῆς ἀρετῆς]" (500d).[13] On the interpretation we are pursuing here, it is in fashioning the image of a human being that both Socrates' philosopher-ruler and Protagoras's poet-Sophist give form to human discursive communities. Moreover, in giving form to discursive communities they determine linguistic use within those communities, not by stipulating the meaning of terms but by dictating the "forms of life" upon which linguistic use depends. On this view, the various *eidê* are not crafted individually. Instead, as in Socrates' description of the philosopher-ruler as craftsman of demotic virtue, they are fashioned "all at once" (σύμπας) in fashioning the image of a human being.[14]

---

11. See Benardete 1989b, 216–17. In the *Timaeus*, the demiurge's creation is unique for the sake of that creation, "in order that it may be like the all-perfect living being in its uniqueness" (31b1).

12. See Reeve 1988, 81–94. Reeve stresses, moreover, "that the description that introduces the discussion of poets and philosophers fits both poet-imitators and philosopher-kings" (89). Of course, the conclusions that Reeve draws from this identification are decidedly different from those I am pursuing here. In particular, even though he suggests that Plato is "showing just how difficult it is to distinguish [poet-imitators] from philosophers," nothing in his analysis indicates that he takes this difficulty as itself philosophically significant.

13. It is important to note here that, just as in our reading of the ascent out of the cave, what the philosopher sees seems different in kind from what he "puts into" the dispositions of human beings. In the one case, he looks to "the just, beautiful, and moderate by nature"; in the other, he is a craftsman of the vulgar analogues to these virtues.

14. This can help resolve the apparent inconsistency between Socrates' first definition of μίμησις as likening *oneself to* another (Οὐκοῦν τό γε ὁμοιοῦν ἑαυτὸν ἄλλῳ ἢ κατὰ φωνὴν ἢ κατὰ σχῆμα μιμεῖσθαί

This interpretation can help explain an otherwise mysterious transition in Socrates' account, the jarring transition from a criticism of the painter's imitation of the *couch* to his criticism of the painter's imitation of a *couch-maker*.[15] Socrates initially takes the painter as his favored example of the imitative artist, and agrees with Glaucon that a painter attempts to imitate the works of the craftsman rather than "the thing itself in nature" (598a). He argues that because the painter reproduces the couch only as it appears from one particular vantage point, such an imitation is "far from the truth" (598b). He illustrates this claim, however, by looking to the painter's imitation of the carpenter who makes the couch, rather than the imitation of the couch itself. Moreover, it is only once Socrates moves to the example of the imitation of the craftsman that he explicitly criticizes the imitator for lacking knowledge of that which he imitates. The painter, Socrates says, will paint a shoemaker, a carpenter, and the other craftsmen even though he does not understand their respective arts. Nonetheless, if he is a "good painter" he could deceive children and foolish human beings into the belief that he has portrayed "a carpenter in truth," at least if the painting were shown at a distance (589b–c).

The transition in the argument from the imitation of craft-objects to the imitation of craftsmen coincides with the transition from the painter as imitator to a critique of "tragedy and its leader [τὸν ἡγεμόνα], Homer" (598d). In particular, Socrates turns to the question of whether there is any evidence that Homer had expert knowledge of the arts possessed by the characters he mimetically represents. Socrates concludes that, on the basis of the evidence, Homer "does not grasp the truth" (τῆς δὲ ἀληθείας οὐχ ἅπτεσθαι) of the things he imitates and can present only "images of excellence" (εἰδώλων ἀρετῆς, 600e5–6). If we were to take Socrates' assessment of that evidence at face value, however, we would have to consider it an egregious example of arguing in bad faith.[16]

ἔστιν ἐκεῖνον ᾧ ἄν τις ὁμοιοῖ, 393c5–6), and his eventual treatment of the mimetic artist as a "maker of all things" (ὃς πάντα ποιεῖ, 596c2). See Belfiore 1984.

15. Janaway takes the transition as part of a move from a consideration of *mimēsis* in general to the specific case of poetic imitation. However, not only does this conflict with Socrates' contention that the shift to a focus on poetic imitation begins at 603c, but Janaway provides no argumentative motivation for Plato to conceal the fact that such a shift has occurred. Instead, he concurs with Halliwell's judgment that the shift to the imitation of the craftsman is "a blatantly rhetorical means of preparing the ground for (Plato's) main argument." See Janaway 1995, 133–34, and Halliwell, in Plato 1988, 120.

16. Among the points taken against Homer are: (1) that if Homer had knowledge of the things he imitates, he would be more serious about "deeds" than imitations; (2) that no city was well governed or war well fought due to his ruling or advice; (3) that there is no record of particular improvements he made in arts or practices; (4) that there is no record of Homer having been "in private a leader in education" (ἰδίᾳ τισὶν ἡγεμὼν παιδείας), or evidence that a Homeric way of life was passed down to his successors; and (5) that if Homer (or Hesiod) had been able to help human beings toward virtue, he would have been attended wherever he went or compelled to stay at home. The first point begs the question concerning the

Indeed, throughout the passage Socrates looks like a dogmatic partisan of the explicit legislative activity of the philosopher-ruler over against the implicit, "unacknowledged" legislative activity of the poets.[17] One of the central questions posed by Plato's presentation of "the problem of Socrates" is whether Socrates' antagonism toward Protagorean sophistry is merely the agonism of a poetic rival in a contest over who will inherit or appropriate the "divine" task of cultural formation from Homer and the tragic poets. On the surface, Socrates' polemic against Homer seems to offer ample evidence to answer this question affirmatively. We are, however, given every reason to look beyond the surface of Socrates' polemic. This is not only because of the weakness of this polemic as a critique of Homer's poetry, but also because of its strength as a·critique of Socrates' poetic activity in the *Republic*.

Each of the criticisms Socrates levels against the cognitive authority underlying the mimetic artist's imitation of the craftsman can be deployed with greater force against the work of Socrates, Glaucon, and Adeimantus in founding the city in speech. Throughout the argument Socrates and his interlocutors assume authoritative knowledge about the natures appropriate for a variety of craftsmen, real or imagined. The construction of the city begins with Socrates and Adeimantus's institution of the principle "one human being, one job" as appropriate to the disparate natural talents of disparate craftsman. Moreover, the tripartite structure of the city is determined by the problem of finding a nature suitable to the task of guarding the city. Finally, the argument culminates in Socrates' depiction of the kind of philosophic education appropriate to the philosopher-rulers. But in none of these cases do we have reason to believe that Socrates (much less Glaucon or Adeimantus) possesses knowledge of these craftsmen's respective arts. More generally, we can say that the depiction of craftsmen in the service of serious ends is characteristic of Socrates' art, rather than that of Zeuxis, Aeschylus, or Homer. As Alcibiades tells us in the *Symposium*, it is Socrates, rather than either the painters or tragic poets, who is famed for talking about "cobblers, smiths, and tanners"; and unlike the work of the comic poets, Socrates' banausic-seeming speeches are, according to Alcibiades, the only really

---

worth of poetic practice. The fifth point begs the question concerning the educational value of the poetic work. The remaining three points all depend upon artificially limiting the scope of Homer's achievement in a way directly contradicted at various points in Socrates' argument. He is not a considered a *private* leader in education, but rather is called by Socrates "the first leader and teacher of all these fine tragic things," and one who is praised as the poet who "educated Greece." He is not credited with some particular improvement in the art of poetry but rather is, as Socrates says, "the most poetic and first of the tragic poets." Finally, as we have seen, even if no particular military campaign was well fought due to his advice and governance, he is nonetheless characterized by Socrates in the *Theaetetus* as a commanding and largely victorious general in the theoretical war over the nature of the whole.

17. Cf. Adam's note to 599e (Plato 1963).

serious speeches there are. Socrates' speeches are the ones most filled with images of excellence (πλεῖστα ἀγάλματ' ἀρετῆς, *Symp.* 222a).

When viewed in this context, Socrates' description of the painter's imitation of the craftsman, an imitation which can deceive the ignorant when shown at a distance, seems designed to call our attention to the possibility that Socrates' own depiction of craftsmen in the city in speech may be equally deceptive. Recall that Socrates originally introduces the analogy between city and soul as a means of overcoming the difficulty of discerning justice in the soul, a difficulty he compares to dim-sighted people being ordered to read little letters at a great distance. In such a case, Socrates says, if "someone had the thought that the same letters are somewhere else also, but bigger and in a bigger place, I suppose it would look like a godsend to be able to consider the little ones after having read these first, if, of course, they do happen to be the same" (368c–d). But, as should be obvious, if they do *not* just happen to be the same, the process is almost guaranteed to mislead.[18] If Socrates' accounts of the three classes in the city were held to the standard he applies to the mimetic artist's representations of carpenters, shoemakers, and smiths, we would have to conclude that he too lacks authoritative knowledge of their respective arts. In the case of the manual artisans, Socrates famously disavows the kind of technical knowledge he attributes to them. In the case of the philosopher-ruler, to assume that Socrates had knowledge of the requisite art would require that Socrates had himself made the hypothesized ascent out of the cave. And to assume this would require that we forget that the philosopher-ruler is himself a Socratic artifact, an "image of a human being" inside the broader "image of a human being" that is the city in speech.

If, however, we review the conversation as it has developed to this point, we will see that Socrates goes to extraordinary lengths to remind his auditors of this fact. Socrates calls attention to the poetic and rhetorical character of his confrontation with Homer from the very beginning of book 10, and the means he uses to do so are themselves poetic and rhetorical. Consider, in this context, the curious and dramatic way he introduces Homer as the object of his criticism. "'It must be said [ῥητέον],' I said. 'And yet, a certain friendship for Homer, and shame before him, which has possessed me since childhood, prevents me from speaking [λέγειν]. For he seems to have been the first leader and teacher of all these fine tragic things. Still and all, a man must not be honored before the truth, but as I say, it must be said [λέγω, ῥητέον]'" (595b9–c3). Here Socrates

---

18. The connection to the book 2 discussion is further emphasized by Socrates' comparison at 596a between Glaucon and "those with duller vision," and his reminder at 602c that "the same magnitude surely doesn't look equal to our sight from near and from far."

brackets a claim that shame prevents him from speaking (λέγειν) on one side with an assertion that "it must be spoken" and on the other with an assertion that he has *said* "it must be spoken."[19] The tension between Socrates' denial that he can speak and his reiterated assertion that he must speak should forcefully remind us of Socrates' role as narrator of the *Republic*. Even more significant in this context, as we will see, is the extremely unflattering depiction Socrates gives of himself in the opening pages of book 10, an ironic self-portrayal that will help us see the ironic character of Socrates' account of mimesis as a whole.

8.3 Irony and Self-Imitation

I have suggested above that Socrates' critique of mimetic poetry is ironic. Its ultimate aim, I contend, is to show us the role that *mimêsis* plays in the philosophic contemplation of our experience. To see how this is so, however, we have to begin with our own experience of reading this very passage; we have to begin with our experience of reading Socrates' attack on poetry in book 10. And here I will take the liberty of assuming I can speak for many readers by suggesting that our first experience is one of extreme annoyance at Socrates. To put it bluntly, Socrates comes off here as a bit of jerk. Earlier in the *Republic,* when Socrates took up the question of what sort of poetry to allow in the city in speech, however questionable some of his claims about poetry may have been, *at the very least* he showed an awareness of the complex role that poetic imitation plays in our ethical education. Now, when he returns to the subject in book 10 any such caution and sensitivity he may have shown previously seem utterly absent. Looking back, Socrates now claims to see that he, Glaucon, and Adeimantus were "quite entirely right" in the way they founded the city in speech, particularly in their decision to not admit any part of poetry at all that is imitative. Now, what makes this assertion of certainty particularly odd, and particularly frustrating, is the fact that Socrates' earlier discussion of poetry did nothing like this; instead, it placed limits on the scope and kind of imitation that should be allowed in the city in speech. This dogmatic opening flourish on Socrates' part sets the tone for much of the argument that immediately follows. In stark contrast to the solemnity and caution that mark the closing passages of book 9, Socrates appears in book 10 to adopt the pose of a kind of professional Platonic philosopher, a doctrinal "friend of the ideas" in firm possession of a

19. Compare *Apology* 22b, where Socrates' claim that he is ashamed of speaking the truth in denunciation of the poets is immediately followed by an assertion that "nonetheless, it must be spoken" (ῥητέον). Moreover, the dramatic character of Socrates' pronouncement gives it the character of a ῥῆσις, a speech in a dramatic work. Compare 605d1.

truth that "must be spoken" regarding poetry's dangers. The truth about mimetic poetry must be told, Socrates knows it, and he will tell it—to Glaucon and to us.

Perhaps the most telling comment Socrates makes in this context is when he tells Glaucon that he should "listen, or rather, answer questions " (ἄκουε δή, μᾶλλον δὲ ἀποκρίνου). With this apparent slip, Socrates strongly suggests that the "dialogue" that he and Glaucon are engaged in is a kind of didactic pretense. That is, the way Socrates proceeds here seems to have more in common with the "Socratic method" as practiced in an American law school than any even minimally shared inquiry between interlocutors. Given what we see of Glaucon's character throughout the rest of the dialogue, it is not all that surprising that he is put off by the shift in Socrates' tone and approach.[20] And the situation is not improved when Socrates tells him that he really should help, since, after all, sometimes people with dimmer vision see things before those with sharper vision. In fact, Glaucon basically refuses to play along at this point. He says that with Socrates present he wouldn't be eager to say something even if it *should* occur to him, so Socrates should do the looking himself. When Socrates *does* proceed, as we have seen, he asks Glaucon whether they should follow their "customary method" by positing one particular form for each and every "many" to which the same name is applied. However, on the basis of what we see elsewhere in Plato, this is not Socrates' "customary method"—it is, in fact, the most questionable account of the forms we ever see in the dialogues. And in any case, it is far from clear that Socrates *has* a "customary method" or that there *could be* anything like a "customary method" for an inquiry into the forms.

To summarize, then, the character we see in the opening passages of book 10—a character that comes off as smug, careless, and dogmatic—looks less like Socrates than someone doing a bad imitation of Socrates. Now, there is nothing strange about a bad imitation of Socrates as such; the history of Western culture is littered with bad imitations of Socrates. What *is* odd in this case, however, is that the person doing the bad imitation is Socrates himself. What I want to suggest is that, by beginning his critique of mimetic poetry in this way, Socrates draws our attention to the fact that, in recounting yesterday's conversation in the Piraeus, he has been performing an extended piece of self-imitation. He reminds us that the *Republic* in its entirety is presented as a piece of Socratic imitation, both in the sense that in narrating the *Republic* Socrates gets to play all the parts, and in the sense the biggest part he plays is a version of himself. He makes this fact manifest in part through a kind of self-caricature. It is precisely because the self-portrait that Socrates offers is distorted that we as readers become reminded of the fact that he is portraying himself. This shows us

20. See Ludwig 2007, 222–30, and chap. 10, below.

something about the logic of imitation, namely, that it is only an imperfect imitation that manifests itself *as* an imitation, a point we will return to below. For the moment, we should note that by obliquely drawing our attention to the fact that his critique of mimetic poetry is itself a piece of mimetic poetry, Socrates shows us something about poetic representation that is at odds with what he explicitly says about it. Moreover, what he shows us is that poetry can show us something at odds with what it explicitly says. Or, to put the point another way, Socrates' ironic critique of mimetic poetry exhibits mimetic poetry's capacity for *irony*, an aspect of poetic representation that is as central to ancient tragedy and comedy as it is spectacularly missing from Socrates' explicit critique.

Now, what I want to suggest is that the two themes we have seen made dramatically manifest in the opening pages of book 10—the theme of irony and the theme of self-imitation—are essential to understanding Socrates' complex and ironic argument. Socrates' attack on *mimêsis* has two major parts: the first focuses on graphic or visible imitation; the second focuses on nonvisible or poetic imitation. In what follows, I will argue that, contrary to how it may appear, the distinction Socrates draws between visible and poetic imitation is not ultimately a distinction between different *kinds* of imitation at all. It is rather a distinction between different ways of conceiving what imitation is and how it works. I will argue that when Socrates talks about *visible* imitation, he is talking about a way of understanding imitation that assimilates *mimêsis* to something like a direct copy of the world of perception. When Socrates talks about *poetic* imitation, to the contrary, he is talking about a way of understanding imitation that takes imitation as necessarily open to the possibility of irony; that is, the possibility of an interpretation that radically contradicts what appears to be the manifest meaning of some utterance or representation.

In a context where Socrates is apparently advocating the elimination of all *mimêsis* from the city in speech, Socrates' manifest self-imitation suggests, at the very least, that he believes some aspect of *mimêsis* will resist the attempt to eradicate it from political life. This much is consonant with the Sophists' (and the Athenian Stranger's) conception of legislative activity as implicitly dramatic or mimetic, and mimetic poetry as implicitly legislative.[21] Socrates' ironic self-representation, however, also suggests that the function of *mimêsis* in human ethical and political activity is more complex than can be accounted for in Protagoras's account of the poet-Sophist giving form to tractable human "natures." Socrates' self-conscious self-representation reminds us that even in performing

---

21. In the *Laws* (817a–c), the Athenian Stranger explicitly describes the activity of the lawgiver as rivaling the work of the tragic poets. The laws of the city are described as a poetic imitation of the fairest and best life, and the lawgivers as authors of the truest tragedy.

a cultural role crafted by the poet or the legislator, it is the individual who must *enact* that role, and this involves a level, however minimal, of self-conscious interpretive activity on the part of each individual. Furthermore, the ironic character of Socrates' self-imitation points to the gap between any cultural role and the individual's interpretative appropriation of it; it makes manifests the indeterminate relation between the performance of a cultural role and the meaning of that performance.[22]

I have argued in previous chapters that recognition of this indeterminacy is essential to both Socrates' conception of human agency and the description of his "method of hypothesis" he offers in the *Phaedo*.[23] More specifically, I have argued that Socrates understands agency to be inseparable from self-ascription of agency on the part of the agent, and any self-ascription of agency to be relative to what he calls a "hypothesis" concerning who we are and what is best for us. It is the failure to recognize the necessary role of this interpretive self-ascription that is the crucial error Socrates diagnoses in both Polemarchus's implicit belief that justice arises in individuals as an immediate expression of their immersion in political culture, and Gorgias's explicit belief in the self-evidence of his persuasive mastery of his students. In both cases, there is an underlying assumption that some authoritative cultural representation could be wholly determinative for the social and political world that provides the horizon for human action. In the present context, this assumption appears in the guise of a conception of mimetic representation as complete or self-sufficient, a sophistic conception of a wholly determinate mimetic *reproduction* requiring no interpretation that is passively received by its audience.

It is in this context of *interpretively indeterminate* versus *wholly determinate* imitation, I suggest, that we should approach Socrates' final account of the specific character of *poetic* as opposed to *graphic* imitation. After having moved freely between discussions of painting and poetry throughout his critique, Socrates suddenly becomes scrupulous about the distinction between imitation that is seen and imitation that is heard, and turns to the question of whether the critique of imitation as "a base thing having intercourse with the base producing base offspring" applies only to "that which relates to sight or also that which relates to hearing, which we call poetry" (603b10). While he and Glaucon answer this question affirmatively, the description Socrates offers of "the part of thought which has intercourse with poetry's imitation" suggests a far-reaching opposition between the graphic and the poetic. As we will see, it points to the

22. One might consider in this context the relation between Socrates' manifest religious orthopraxy and the accusation of heterodoxy.
23. See §§3.3–3.5 and §5.4.

contrast between the sophistic account of a wholly determinate mimetic reproduction and an account in which the indeterminacy of mimetic representation
is essential to poetic imitation. Indeed, Socrates' final critique suggests that
what defines poetic imitation as such is an imitation of the very indeterminacy
that characterizes human agency.

8.4 Imitation and the Visible

Recall that Socrates first introduces the mimetic artist in his book 10 critique
of *mimêsis* in the form of an analogy to a supposed craftsman of the visible
world, an artist who becomes a "maker of all things" by holding a mirror up to
everything that is (596c–e). What makes this analogy especially curious, of course,
is the fact that Socrates doesn't only speak of mirroring inanimate objects, plants,
and animals, but also of mirroring heaven, the gods, and everything in Hades.
He thus presents the mimetic artist as someone who imitates everything, even
the "unseen," solely through the reproduction of the visibly manifest.[24] The
work of the graphic imitator is said to be deficient in truth and being because,
in reproducing this visible aspect, it is limited to only one view of the thing it tries
to imitate. The painter makes something essentially incomplete and dependent;
he reproduces not *the* couch or even *a* couch, but a couch only as it appears from
a particular perspective (598a–b). Despite the limited character of his perspectival
grasp of the appearing object as it appears, the mimetic artist can still have the
power to deceive us. But he only has this power over us due to an aspect of our
nature that can allow us to be deceived (602c4–5), which Socrates first articulates
in terms of the correspondingly perspectival character of our vision. It is only
insofar as we are the sort of beings for which the same thing can appear to our
vision as large or small, straight or bent, convex or concave, depending on the
context of viewing that the graphic imitator has power over us (602c7–11).

   At 602d1–3, Socrates sums up his critique of the graphic imitator in a passage densely allusive to the image of the cave, and to the hypothesis of doxastic
immanence that governs that image. Socrates claims that "shadow-painting" (ἡ
σκιαγραφία), "wonder-working" (ἡ θαυματοποιία), and "all such contrivances"
(αἱ ἄλλαι πολλαὶ τοιαῦται μηχαναί) work on this "affection of our nature"
(ἡμῶν τῷ παθήματι τῆς φύσεως), "leaving out nothing of witchcraft" (γοητείας

---

24. Socrates' suggestion that the imitative artist "mirrors" the gods and Hades is often taken as a sign
of the ironic character of this passage. However, it can also be taken as an indication of the Protagorean
background to Socrates' initial account of artistic representation. Recall that on Protagoras's account the
gods exist in and through the medium of public representation. On Hades as the "unseen," see *Phd.* 80d;
cf. *Cra.* 403a–b.

οὐδὲν ἀπολείπει). This is the same verb, ἀπολείπω, that Socrates uses in book 7 to indicate that aspect of his likeness between the sun and the good he will have to leave out of his account.[25] Socrates here implies that a mimetic representation that did not leave anything out would have the "divine" power that Gorgias attributes to *logos* in the "Encomium to Helen."[26] The ensuing discussion will show, however, that this conception of a perfect or total mimetic representation depends upon the hypothesis of a radical separation between the visible world of our experience and the intelligible, and consigns our perception of mimetic representation wholly to the realm of the visible.

Socrates suggests that we have only one defense against the deceptive power of the mimetic artist, and that defense is the *trust* we place in the science of measurement. Because of the threat posed by the imitative artist, we must allow ourselves to be ruled by measurement and calculation, which Socrates calls the work of the "calculating" aspect of the soul. When this aspect of the soul measures something and determines that it is great rather than small, or convex rather than concave, it is sometimes the case that the contradictory appearance remains present to us at the same time. What this shows, Socrates says, is that there is a division in our soul between the best part of our soul, the part which *trusts* measurement and calculation (τὸ μέτρῳ γε καὶ λογισμῷ πιστεῦον, 603a4), and a base part of our soul which contradicts them.[27] Indeed, Socrates claims here that *anytime* we are confronted with contradictory appearances it is an indication of a division between better and worse aspects of the soul.

It is these claims about contradictory appearances that show most clearly that there is something amiss in Socrates' account of graphic or visible imitation. To see how this is so, however, we need to compare what Socrates says here to his book 7 description of the mathematical education of the philosopher-rulers. There the same aspect of our nature that has Socrates so worried in book 10, the susceptibility of our souls to contradictory perceptions, looks to be essential to the possibility of philosophy. Indeed, Socrates suggests that it is our very susceptibility to contradictory perceptions which provides the occasion for awakening our intellect (νοῦς), the best part of our souls. He distinguishes between two kinds of perceptions, one kind that seems adequately judged by perception on its own and one kind that does not, and includes among the latter kind the perception of relatives such as large and small. In the case of

---

25. See §7.7.

26. Compare *Grg.* 403e6 and *Symp.* 203d8. See Halliwell, in Plato 1988, 128; Janaway 1995, 142–43.

27. The claim that contradictory opinions indicate a division in the soul appears to be an illegitimate extension of the original formulation of the principle of opposites. In any case, if contradictory opinions were sufficient to indicate distinct parts of the soul, the soul would not be tripartite but, as the present passage suggests, an indefinite multiplicity. On the former point, see Murphy 1951, 241, and Nehamas 1999, 265.

relative judgments, perception alone is said to be manifestly inadequate, insofar as the very same object is seen as both large and small depending upon the context of comparison. Because these "strike perception as the same time as their opposites" (523d), the soul summons the intellect to the activity of inquiry (παρακαλοῦντα τὴν νόησιν εἰς ἐπίσκεψιν, 523b1). The intellect distinguishes the large and small, seeing each as one and separate, where vision alone saw these opposites mixed up together. It is on the basis of this experience, Socrates asserts, that we are first drawn to ask what large and small are, and it is for this reason that we call one kind of apprehension visible and another intelligible. He then goes on to identify "number and the one" as preeminent among those aspects of perception that can summon the intellect and lead us to contemplate what is.

Now, in stark contrast to what Socrates says about contradictory perceptions in book 7, his discussion of the deceptive power of *mimêsis* makes no mention of the possibility of contrary perceptions summoning intellect, in fact, he doesn't mention intellection (νόησις) at all. Nor does Socrates say anything in book 10 about contradictory appearances providing a basis for questioning the adequacy of our trust (πίστις) in measurement and calculation. The absence of *noêsis* from the discussion[28] paired with the identification of that which is best in our soul not with intellection, or even thought (διάνοια), but with *that which trusts* measure and calculation provides us with an indication of what is lacking in Socrates' account of *mimêsis* to this point. The entire discussion has been restricted to what he calls in his image of the divided line "the class that is seen" (τό τε τοῦ ὁρωμένου γένους, 509d). That is, in order to understand Socrates' treatment of "visible" *mimesis,* we must see it as governed by "the visible" portion of the divided line, the section comprising imagination and trust.

What Socrates here calls "the visible," I suggest, should be understood as mode of experience, and a cognitive attitude toward our experience intrinsic to that experience. This is an attitude that takes the mere presence to perception of an appropriate object as sufficient explanation for the apprehension of what that object is. The visible, in this sense, is analogous to what Husserl will later call "the natural attitude"; it is characterized by a naïve acceptance of, or trust in, the mind-transcendent reality of its objects as such objects are given to perception. From within the context of the "visible" so understood, contradictory

---

28. There are no instances of a form of νόησις in book 10. If we exclude διάνοια and διανοέω, Socrates' words for thought as opposed to intellection, there are only four occurrences of words formed from νοέω between 595a1, where Socrates considers (ἐννοῶ) the correctness of their previous discussion of poetry, and his final positing of the mimetic poet as the "antistrophe" of the painter at 605a6–c4. The first two (συννοῶ at 595c9 and συννοήσω at 595c10) are in phrases denying knowledge "of what *mimêsis* wants to be"; the third is in Socrates' claim that no one is "like-minded" (ὁμονοητικῶς, 603c10) with respect to actions; the fourth is in his claim that mimetic poetry gratifies the "mindless" (ἀνοήτῳ, 605b8) aspect of the soul. The one instance of νοέω (615c1) in book 10 occurs in the cosmology of the myth of Er.

perceptions are taken, not as an indication of the limitations of unaided perception, but rather as more or less local aberrations against a background faith in the adequacy of perception.[29] The apparent *inadequacy* of any given perception is judged as such not in comparison with an intellectual inquiry into the meaning of contradictory concepts, but rather in comparison with an idealized perceptual experience which overcomes the internal and external causes of perceptual error. Similarly, when Socrates talks about visible *imitation,* he is referring to a corresponding view of mimetic representation. This is a view that takes the mere presence of a mimetic representation to its audience as sufficient to explain the apprehension of that representation. Moreover, the adequacy or inadequacy of mimetic representation is judged with respect to the ideal of a *complete* representation of a perceptual object.

As Heidegger saw, much in Socrates' description of the philosopher-rulers' apprehension of the forms assimilates eidetic "seeing" to the intellectual counterpart of this mode of perception.[30] Moreover, his description of their legislative activity proceeds on the assumption of the corresponding view of *mimêsis.* In the image of the cave, the philosopher-ruler is represented as seeking a direct acquaintance knowledge of the forms, and as reproducing this knowledge by fashioning a "paradigm" in his soul. Moreover, it is to the paradigm in his own soul that the philosopher-ruler looks to in legislative activity, "looking off, just as painters do, to what is truest" (ὥσπερ γραφῆς εἰς τὸ ἀληθέστατον ἀποβλέποντες, 484c). The adequacy of the guardian as legislator depends upon the clarity and precision of his inward-directed vision. According to Heidegger's interpretation, this is the pivotal moment in the history of the transformation in the essence of truth, from ἀλήθεια as "unhiddenness" to "ὀρθότης, the correctness of apprehending and asserting."[31] It is a consequence of conceiving our comportment toward beings "always and everywhere as a matter of the ἰδεῖν of the ἰδέα, the seeing the 'visible form,'" and has as its corollary a subjectification of truth.[32] Heidegger's account, however, neglects the tension between

---

29. "'The' world is always there as an actuality; here and there it is at most 'otherwise' than I supposed; this or that is, so to speak, to be struck *out of it* and given such titles as 'illusion,' and 'hallucination,' and the like" (Husserl 1983, 57).

30. See Heidegger 1998.

31. Ibid., 176

32. "With this transformation of the essence of truth there takes place at the same time a change of the locus of truth. As unhiddenness, truth is still a fundamental trait of beings themselves. But as the correctness of the 'gaze,' it becomes a characteristic of human comportment toward beings" (ibid.). Obviously, the interpretation I am offering differs in attributing the view Heidegger is confronting not with Socrates himself, but with the tyrannical hypothesis he is setting out in the *Republic* to show the limitations of. Moreover, even within the context of that hypothesis, I have suggested, following Nietzsche, that it is a subjectifying turn that compels the reconception of truth in term of correctness, a subjectifying turn that is itself a consequence of the "decadence" of the poetic and religious tradition.

the metaphor of visible apprehension which dominates the cave analogy and Socrates' account of contradictory perception awakening the intellect. Moreover, he fails to follow out two crucial implications of the analogy between the sun as the source of light disclosing things seen to sight and the good as the source of truth disclosing things known to the intellect. First, the analogy between light and truth implies that intellection is in some sense perspectival without for that reason being "merely" subjective. Second, Socrates' description of truth as a "yoke" binding the good and the intellect implies that the "locus of truth" is neither "the things themselves" nor "the human comportment toward beings," but in the beings disclosing and as disclosed by an individual's orientation to the good.[33] These two aspects of Socrates' account of the intelligible, the perspectival character of our apprehension of the truth and the understanding of such apprehension in terms of our orientation to the good, are also absent from Socrates' account of graphic or visible imitation. They are, however, essential to his account of nonvisible, poetic imitation as a representation of human agency.

8.5 Poetic Imitation and Human Action

Anticipating Aristotle's description of tragedy in the *Poetics,* Socrates maintains that poetic imitation is an imitation of human action.[34] More specifically, as we will see, his account implies that poetic imitation is an imitation of human agency and the beliefs and emotive states concomitant with the self-ascription of agency. Poetic imitation, Socrates says, "imitates human beings doing [πράτ-τοντας] forced or voluntary actions [πράξεις], and as a result of the action [ἐκ τοῦ πράττειν] believing themselves to have done [πεπραγέναι] well or poorly, and in all of this grieving or rejoicing." In terms of this description of poetic imitation, we can see that what most crucially distinguishes human action as the proper object of poetic imitation from the craft objects that the painter was said to imitate is the fact that human action is, in Socrates' terms, essentially *invisible.* This is perhaps most clearly seen in the case of the central distinction between forced and voluntary actions, the distinction upon which all the other distinctions depend. All the other conflicts in the soul—over whether we have fared well or poorly, are pleased or pained—take for granted that what is in question is the consequences of our action. But the question of whether an action is *voluntary* or *involuntary* is inseparable from identifying an action *as*

33. Francisco Gonzalez (2009) argues that the failure to adequately confront the significance of our orientation to the good is characteristic of Heidegger's interpretation of Plato. For the contrary view, see Crowell 2001.

34. See Adam's note to 603c (Plato 1963).

an action—to see something as an action involves taking some event in the world as something we *choose,* in some sense, to bring about. And for Socrates, at least, the question of what makes a voluntary action voluntary—the question of what makes or could make an individual human being *responsible* for his or her actions—is not a question that can be adequately posed at the level of distinctions that can be drawn at the level of visible manifestation.[35] In the terms Socrates uses in the *Phaedo,* to confuse human intentional action with the visible or bodily is to confuse that which "in actuality" is responsible for something with that without which that which *is* responsible could never *be* responsible; it is to confuse a condition of human agency with agency itself.[36]

As Socrates continues, he makes clear that the very aspects of *mimêsis* that were central to his critique of the graphic imitation of tables and chairs essentially characterize the very things that poetic imitation strives to imitate. That is, it turns out that it is not only the poetic *imitation* of action, but action and deliberation *themselves* that are perspectival and incomplete. Socrates says that, just as our vision can give rise to "contrary opinions . . . at the same time about the same things," so, too, a human being is always at war with himself "with regard to actions" (ἐν ταῖς πράξεσι). However, in contrast to what he says about the case of sight, Socrates never claims that our contradictory opinions about freedom or compulsion, faring well or faring poorly, grief or joy are caused by the divergent, potentially deceptive, conditions under which the selfsame object is viewed. Instead, he says that "in all of these things" (ἐν ἅπασι)—in all of our cognitive and emotive states concerning action—a human being is not "of one mind" (ὁμονοητικῶς). What Socrates *never* suggests is that in the case of human action we ever come into contact with an unambiguous nonperspectival original against which one or another of our contradictory perceptions can be measured and found wanting. Nor does he suggest that in representing this conflict in the soul tragic poetry misrepresents the character of human action. Instead, he focuses his critique entirely on the ethical and political effects of tragic poetry; poetic imitation, Socrates says, weakens our resistance to grief and thereby reduces our capacity to deliberate when confronted with misfortune. However, as we will see, his depiction of this process of deliberation not only reinforces the suggestion that the perspectival character of poetic imitation discloses a corresponding perspectival character in human action, it suggests why this is so, by depicting practical deliberation itself as mimetic in character.

35. Even within the context of ancient tragedy itself, the question of whether and in what sense the actions of an Oedipus or an Ajax are voluntary or involuntary is not a question for which a determinate answer is made manifest within the drama. See Davis 1988. See also Bernard Williams's discussion of the *Ajax* (1993) and §8.5 below.

36. See §3.1.

Now let us consider in this context Socrates' vivid and dramatic description of a decent man (ἀνήρ . . . ἐπιεικὴς) confronted with the loss of a son or something else "of which he makes much" (περὶ πλείστου ποιεῖται). The decent man, Socrates claims, will be more able to withstand overwhelming grief when he is "visible to those like himself" (ὁρᾶται ὑπὸ τῶν ὁμοίων) than when abandoned (μονωθεὶς) to himself in some deserted place.[37] When alone "himself by himself" (αὐτὸς καθ᾽ αὑτὸν), he will say things he would be ashamed to have heard by others and do many things (πολλὰ δὲ ποιήσει) he would not choose to have anyone see (ἃ οὐκ ἂν δέξαιτό τινα ἰδεῖν δρῶντα). What exhorts him to resist is argument and the law (λογὸς καί νόμος).[38] "The experience itself" (αὐτὸ τὸ πάθος), however, draws him toward the pain.[39] The law, presumably, says (λέγει που ὁ νόμος) that it is best to keep as quiet as possible in misfortunes and not be vexed because the good and the bad in such things are not manifest, nor will taking it hard get you ahead, nor are any of the human things worthy of great seriousness, and because being in pain impedes the coming to be of deliberation about what has come to pass. The best part of the soul, Socrates says, is ready to be persuaded by calculation, and to follow in whatever direction the law leads it.[40] But the part which turns toward recollection of the *pathos* (τὸ δὲ πρὸς τὰς ἀναμνήσεις τε τοῦ πάθους) is called irrational, idle, and a friend of cowardice. Socrates identifies this irrational aspect of soul as "the irascible" (τὸ ἀγανακτητικόν), and claims not only that this aspect of soul is most easily imitated, but also that it is to this part of the soul that poetic imitation is directed.[41] The imitative poet, Socrates concludes, awakens and nourishes the unthinking part of the soul, and implants a "bad constitution [κακὴν πολιτείαν] in the soul of each private man by making phantoms that are very far removed from the truth."

This account of the conflict in the soul of the decent man between grief and restraint presents political life in starkly dramatic terms, a point that is underscored by the way Socrates plays on the semantic ambiguity of the words *poieô* and *dran* throughout the passage. The actions of the suffering individual are presented as a kind of public performance of a script that can be written either

37. 603e–604a.
38. Note that λογὸς καί νόμος is treated here as a hendiadys, with Socrates using the singular ἐστίν.
39. The translation of πάθος as "experience" (with Halliwell) rather than "suffering" (as Bloom translates) is warranted, in the first instance, because the πάθος in question seems to be that which has happened to the man, his "having as his lot some stroke of fortune such as the loss of a son," rather than any "bare feeling" (Shorey) that arises as a consequence of that misfortune. The bare feeling or suffering is the pain (λύπη) that the "*pathos* itself" draws the man towards. Compare Gould 1990, 32n3.
40. 604b–c.
41. The identification of the *irrational* with the *irascible,* and the claim that imitative poetry is directed toward this irascible aspect of soul, points to the significance of τὸ θυμοειδής in the account of poetry.

by the lawgiver or by the dramatic poet. This is made explicit in Socrates' final remarks concerning the constitution implanted in the soul of the suffering individual, but is implicit in the analysis as a whole. Consider Socrates' first question to Glaucon, concerning how a grieving father might act when alone in some deserted place, and how he might act when observed by "those like himself." As plausible as the claim is that a "serious man" might be more likely to restrain his impulse to grief in public, we must ask how this claim is relevant in a critique of mimetic poetry. If the conflict in the soul is to be understood simply as a result of the competing influences of argument and custom, on the one side, and the *pathos* itself, on the other, the question of whether the suffering individual is "visible" to others or not would appear to be a complete non sequitur. Nothing in the dictates of custom (604b9–c3) makes any reference to the public display of grief; the focus is solely on overcoming grief so that one is able to deliberate about what has happened, and follow the course that reason chooses.[42] It is only if we consider practical deliberation itself to involve reference to an *imagined* public performance of grief that the visibility or invisibility of the sufferer would have any relevance to the argument.

That the argument must have recourse to such an imagined public performance is indicated by the fact that reason or argument (ὁ λόγος) is presented in the passage as not only inseparable from, but essentially dependent upon law or custom (ὁ νόμος). This is most evident in the fact that after Socrates says that "reason and custom" exhorts the suffering individual to resist, it is custom alone that prescribes for him what is finest (κάλλιστον) and worthy of great seriousness (ἄξιον ὂν μεγάλης σπουδῆς). But it is also apparent in the fact that on Socrates' account, regardless of whatever misfortune may have occurred, deliberation and argument always suggest the very course that custom has already dictated, the course of overcoming grief. It is *custom* that asserts that being in pain impedes the coming to be of deliberation about what has come to pass, but the only argument that "*argument*" presents for resisting grief is the imaginative evocation of customary attitudes. Neither Socrates, nor his "reason" or "deliberation," presents any *reasons* why the aspect of soul that turns toward "recollection of the experience" is called irrational, lazy, and cowardly.[43] The argument, insofar as there is one, consists in the comparison between this aspect of soul and a child who when struck cries out and holds on to the place

42. Ferrari notes that on Socrates' account of the grieving man "shame attaches not to the feeling itself but to its expression." This helps to clarify the fact that what is at issue here is the imaginative evocation of customary attitudes rather than any argument meant to show the irrationality or viciousness of grief. See Ferrari 1989, 138.

43. Contrast *Meno* 86b–c, where Socrates contends that believing that we have a *duty to inquire* makes us better (βελτίους), braver (ἀνδρικώτεροι), and less idle (ἧττον ἀργοι).

that hurts. This mode of imaginative ad hominem is not, moreover, accidental; it is made necessary by two facets of Socrates' account of mimetic poetry to this point. These are: (1) the implicit denial of the possibility that the contradictory perceptions inherent in the reflection of human action can lead to an awakening of the intellect, and (2) the absence in the case of human action of any perceptible original to which calculation can apply objective standards of measurement. Without access to an unambiguous original, and denied the intellective resources to view contradictory perceptions as an occasion for further reflection, any conflict between custom and experience seemingly must result either in bowing to the authority of custom or to ethical paralysis. Moreover, the only argument that custom can offer under these conditions is the imaginative or dramatic expression of the customary itself. The claim that "the good and the bad in such things is not plain" issues not in an exhortation toward further inquiry through recollection of the experience, but rather is invoked as a reason to *avoid* such recollection and hence such inquiry. Finally, the trust in counting and measurement Socrates had previously attributed to the best part of the soul is here replaced by a willingness *to be persuaded* by law or custom.

I have suggested that Socrates' question concerning whether the suffering individual is seen by others points to the role that an imagined public performance plays in his account of practical deliberation. More specifically, I want to suggest that in the absence of any perceptible original to be measured, counted, or weighed, the individual confronting profound misfortune "measures" himself against an image of his actions as he imagines those actions would be seen by others, an imagined community of those "like himself."[44] Practical deliberation appears on this view to be doubly mimetic; the individual chooses to act in one way or another by *imagining* himself acting in that way, and judges those actions with reference to an *imagined* community that embodies the dictates of custom. It is through this implicit identification with this imaginary political community that the dictates of custom acquire their persuasive force. That is, it is insofar as we identify ourselves as the selves we would prefer to be when visible to a community of those "like ourselves" that we are willing to be persuaded by custom.[45]

The role played by implicit role-playing in this account of deliberation becomes even clearer when Socrates turns to what he calls "the greatest accusation against poetry," the charge that it "suffices to harm even the decent, except for some rare few." Socrates says that even the best of us are pleased when we

---

44. Compare Aristotle's famous claim that the fear tragedy evokes for the human being who passes from good to bad fortune must be "fear for one like ourselves" (φόβος δὲ περὶ τον ὅμοιον, *Poet.* 1453a6).
45. See Ferrari 1989, 138.

hear Homer or some other tragic poet imitating the lamentations of a hero in mourning, and we praise as a good poet the one who is best at making us suffer along with the tragic hero. However, in the case of "some grief of our own" (οἰκεῖόν τινι ἡμῶν κῆδος), Socrates claims, we "we preen ourselves upon the opposite, on our ability to remain quiet and persevere, taking *this* [way of acting] to be manly and the other, which we praised before, to be womanly" (ἐπὶ τῷ ἐναντίῳ καλλωπιζόμεθα, ἂν δυνώμεθα ἡσυχίαν ἄγειν καὶ καρτερεῖν, ὡς τοῦτο μὲν ἀνδρὸς ὄν, ἐκεῖνο δὲ γυναικός, ὃ τότε ἐπῃνοῦμεν, 605d8-e1). The first thing we should notice about this passage is Socrates' claim that our praise for the poet who makes us suffer along with his hero is, *eo ipso,* praise for the lamentation of the hero the poet depicts.[46] In eliding the distinction between our praise for the mimetic poet who imitates an action, and the action the poet imitates, Socrates suggests an intimate connection between action and poetic imitation, a connection also suggested by his account of the pride taken in acting in a way contrary to that evinced by the poet and/or tragic hero. The word translated above as "we preen ourselves" is *kallôpizometha.* Its literal meaning is "to beautify oneself," usually with the connotation of cosmetic embellishment.[47] Metaphorically, it can mean simply to take pride in something about oneself, but in the vast majority of its uses in Plato, it has the clear connotation of a false pretense, of "putting on a show."[48] Significantly, its only other use in the *Republic* is in Socrates' description of the attitude of the unjust man who, due "to inexperience with what is beautiful [ἀπειροκαλίας], is persuaded to preen himself [καλλωπίζεσθαι]" because he is clever enough to be unjust and escape punishment.[49]

As Stephen Halliwell notes, Socrates' use of *kallôpizesthai* suggests that in denying our desire to mourn we are covering something over. However, what we seem to be covering over is not merely the strength of that desire, as Halliwell suggests, but also our ignorance concerning whether we should succumb to that desire, and more generally, our ignorance of how we should respond when confronted with profound misfortune. In our suffering, we seek to deny not only our grief, but the full implication of the advice offered by custom, that "the good and bad in such things are not clear." We cover over our ignorance by turning toward an enactment of customary roles—in this case wholly conventional

46. Halliwell notes "a crucial ambiguity in the argument" between "praise of the poet on artistic grounds" and "approving of the behaviour portrayed in his poetry." See his note to 605e4 in Plato 1988.

47. See Xenophon *Mem.* 2.1.21.

48. See Halliwell, in Plato 1988, 145–46.

49. See *Resp.* 3.405b, *Cra.* 409C, *Prt.* 317C, 333d, *Phdr.* 236d, *Tht.* 195D, *Cri.* 52c. Compare *Lege.* 762e. This is also the word Socrates uses to describe how he has made himself beautiful for Agathon's party in the *Symposium* at 174A.

conceptions of masculine and feminine attitudes toward mourning. By claiming that in the case of "a grief of our own" we make a show of our ability to restrain our desire to mourn, Socrates implies that, insofar as we self-consciously identify an experience as "our own," we act as we believe we are *supposed* to act. We allow ourselves to be persuaded by custom, and in so doing we attempt to turn away from "the experience itself."

Socrates continues his argument by asking Glaucon whether it is fine to praise and enjoy seeing a man whom we would be ashamed to be, rather than being disgusted by it. When Glaucon responds that this doesn't seem reasonable, Socrates counters that it is, if seen in the right way. It is precisely because in *our own* misfortunes (ἐν ταῖς οἰκείαις συμφοραῖς) the part of us that wants to grieve has been forcibly restrained that we enjoy the poet's representation of a grieving hero. When we look at (or contemplate) the experience of another (ἀλλότρια πάθη θεωροῦν), there is nothing shameful *for us* in praising and pitying an *other* man (ἄλλος ἀνὴρ) who claims to be good and who is grieving. But, Socrates says, few are able to reckon that enjoying that which belongs to another necessarily affects that which is our own: the pitying part, made strong feeding on the former, is not easily held back in one's own experiences (literally, "in the experiences of the self," ἐν τοῖς αὐτοῦ πάθεσι). Now, it is in this context that we can begin to see both what is most ethically problematic and what is most philosophically significant about mimetic poetry on Socrates' account. For that account suggests that the power of mimetic poetry lies in the fact that under its influence we allow ourselves to experience the mourning that custom forbids in the case of *our own* (οἰκεῖος) suffering by seeing that mourning and that suffering as *belonging to another* (ἀλλότριος). By "experiencing along with" the suffering tragic hero, we circumvent our self-conscious identification with the dictates of custom. And in so doing, we allow ourselves to participate in that part of our experience that we denied when we imagined that experience as visible to others like ourselves. These are the most pointed ironies of Socrates' critique of mimetic poetry. It is precisely when we are viewing tragic drama that we cease to view ourselves as performers in what the Athenian Stranger calls the "truest tragedy" of political life, and it is when we look away from that which we consider "our own" (οἰκεῖος) and toward the contemplation of the suffering of the tragic hero that we can come to contemplate and recollect what we ourselves have experienced.

Poetry is ethically or politically questionable, on this account, insofar as the recollection of what we have experienced draws us away from our self-conscious identification with customary ethical or political norms. But, of course, this would only be a reasonable argument against mimetic poetry if we were assured that in any conflict between experience and our prior commitments to ethical or political norms, choosing to affirm these normative commitments was a choice for the best. However, as we have seen, our ignorance of "the good and bad in such things" is explicitly affirmed by custom in this very context. If we had reason to question the adequacy of our customary ethical and political beliefs, then the disavowal of the recollection of experience would be ethically irresponsible. And even were it not ethically irresponsible, it would seem, in any case, to be unphilosophic. As I have argued in the previous chapter, it is only if we reject the possibility that our everyday experience of the world could be informed by an intelligibility that goes beyond what we can articulate of that intelligibility would we assume that experience has nothing to teach us beyond what law or custom tells us. Moreover, in this instance, we have very good reasons to think that *Socrates* would question the adequacy of what custom asserts.

Insofar as the pity directed toward the suffering of a grieving tragic hero is presented as deriving from our own desire to mourn, it seems to be in some sense pity for ourselves, a point that is reinforced by Socrates' claim that it is "the pitying part" (τὸ ἐλεινὸν) that is not easily held down in our own experiences. If this is correct, then the essence of "the greatest accusation" against poetry is that it allows us to mourn for ourselves where custom forbids it. This points us toward the crucial underlying assumption of Socrates' entire account of mourning, not only in book 10, but in the *Republic* as a whole. Throughout the discussion of the suffering of the decent man, Socrates never so much as considers the question of whether or not this man's life might no longer be worth living for him. His argument simply assumes that this man's deliberation must direct him toward the end of "correcting and restoring what has fallen and is ill" (604d1–2). It has been common for readers of Plato from Nietzsche onward, however much trouble they have with this assumption, to consider it unproblematic as an aspect *of Socrates' self-representation* in the *Republic*.[50] However, we have every reason to question this assumption, both on its own terms and as representing Socrates' views. In the *Crito,* for example, Socrates apparently maintains that if our bodies, much less our souls, have become sufficiently corrupted, then life is no longer worth living for us (*Cri.* 47d–48a). While we know that Socrates claimed that the unexamined life is not worth living for a human being (*Ap.* 38a), Plato presents us with no evidence that Socrates ever claimed that examined life as such is worth living. And, in a famously difficult textual passage in the *Phaedo,* Socrates suggests at the very least that it would be surprising if life were always preferable to death (62a). Why then, we must ask,

---

50. Charles Griswold characterizes Socrates' attitude as a rejection of the "tragic vision of life" (2005, n17).

does Socrates' argument against mimetic poetry proceed as if this question—the question of whether life is always preferable to death for a human being— could not, or should not, be asked?

What cannot be at issue here is any claim that human lives are always worth preserving. For this is shown by Socrates' account of a "statesmanlike Asclepius" who chooses to treat only those human beings who can be "advantageous" (λυσιτελῆ, 407e) to the city and themselves in book 3. Instead, Socrates' rejection of mourning seems to depend upon the assumption that a decision regarding the value of one's life is not to be left up to the individual, but rather should be left in the hands of the lawgivers, and by extension, the political community as the embodiment of their legislative pronouncements. It is a particularly troubling ramification of the hypothesis of doxastic immanence that governs the *Republic,* a hypothesis that denies to any but the philosopher-ruler any relation to the good other than that provided through the mediation of human discursive representation. Mimetic poetry, we have seen, is suspect because, in drawing a human being toward the recollection of what he has experienced, it can put into question his self-conscious identification with customary ethical or political norms. To this we can now add the claim that mourning is suspect insofar as it leads one to ask whether that which he has *taken to be good* is or remains good for him. In the extreme case, the question may be whether life is still worth living for him. But, in less extreme cases, it would seem that the question could be precisely the Socratic question of whether *this* life, the life he has been leading, has been good, and whether the choices he has made are choices for the best.

Looking back on Socrates' account, we can see that this possibility, that the experience of suffering can in some cases lead to reflection upon the good toward which we direct our actions, has already been gestured toward by the peculiar way Socrates presents custom's prima facie argument against grieving. Recall that, on Socrates' account, custom advises that it is finest to be as quiet as possible in misfortunes and not be vexed by them, because "being in pain impedes the coming to be of that which we need most quickly to be at hand in cases such as these . . . the deliberation about what has come to pass." Now, of all the claims in Socrates' extended argument against mimetic poetry, this, I think, is the one we are most likely to take as reasonable, perhaps even obvious; it has the look of commonsense. However, the surface plausibility of the argument quickly dissolves upon further scrutiny. The reason the argument *seems* plausible is that we are likely to take it as if what custom had asserted were that being in pain impedes the *process* of deliberation about *what we are to do*. However, that is not what custom says. It says, instead, something that would be false were it not ultimately nonsensical, that being in pain impedes the *coming to be* (γιγνόμενον) of deliberation about what *has come to pass* (τὸ γεγονὸς). First, while it may be obvious that being in pain can be an impediment to the *process* of deliberation about how we are to achieve some end, it would seem equally obvious that suffering can be the cause or occasion for the "coming to be" (γιγνόμενον) of such deliberation. We do not, for the most part, deliberate about how to proceed when it seems to us we are "faring well" in our practical engagements. It is only when we encounter some manifest impediment to the smooth functioning of the everyday that we have any reason to step back, as it were, from those practical engagements. And suffering, we might say, is the most manifest of impediments. Moreover, while reflection upon the experience of suffering doesn't seem to be much help with narrowly instrumental reasoning about how we are to achieve some end, the case looks quite different when we are asking such questions as: Is my life a good one? Is what I have been *taking* as the good *really* good for me? In this case, it seems essential not only to be able to realize *that* we have suffered, but also to reflect on *what* we have suffered.

The kind of deliberation that reflection upon our suffering makes possible, therefore, is deliberation about the *ends* for the sake of which we act, rather than the *means* we use to attain those ends. It involves reflection upon the good for human beings as such, and not only how we are to achieve the ends that have been set for us. This is not, however, the kind of deliberation that law or custom countenances, for the obvious reason that what law or custom means in this context is precisely our unreflective imaginative commitment to ethical or political norms. Deliberation means, for law or custom, solely a reflection on the means by which the individual can "habituate the soul as quickly as possible to healing and restoring that which has fallen and is sick."[51] Socrates, however, implicitly indicates the illegitimacy of custom's notion of a deliberation that is wholly restricted to the instrumental, by having custom exhort the individual to deliberate about "what has happened" (τὸ γεγονὸς). For, according to Aristotle at least, "what has happened" is precisely the thing about which we do not deliberate (βουλεύομεν). We deliberate about that which is in our power and can be done, about what is possible, not what is necessary. For this reason, Aristotle says, no one deliberates about the past (τὸ δὲ γεγονὸς), because it cannot be otherwise. "Nothing that is past is an object of choice, e.g., no one chooses to have sacked Troy; for no one deliberates about the past, but about what is future and contingent, while what is past is not capable of not having taken place."[52] By having custom advise the suffering individual to deliberate about the past, Socrates indicates that a deliberation that turns away

---

51. It is worth noting the law's interest in doing this all as quickly (τάχιστα) as possible.

52. *Eth. Nic.* 1139B9–11. This seems exactly the sort of insight that tragic poetry as an imitation of human action helps us to see, as Aristotle himself shows by following this claim with quote from Agathon about how even a god cannot alter the past.

from questions about ends, about the good for human beings as such, is deliberation in name only.[53]

If this is right, it would seem that the recollection of our experience, even or especially in profound misfortune, could provide the occasion for the most significant of philosophic questions. And it is only if we deny human beings any way of recollecting the experience of profound misfortune without becoming captive to their memory, as helpless before it as a child holding on to the place that hurts, that we would categorically deny the philosophic significance of such recollection. What I would now like to suggest is that Socrates' account of tragic poetry implies that this is precisely what it can provide, a way of remembering our experiences without suffering from that very reminiscence. Tragic poetry may address itself to that in us which "leads us to lamentation" (πρὸς τοὺς ὀδυρμοὺς ἄγον), but nothing in Socrates' account suggests that it must issue in such lamentation. While he says that we surrender ourselves to the imitation and sympathetically follow the experience of the tragic hero, he does not say that we weep in response, but rather that we "earnestly praise" the poet for putting us in this state. Nowhere does Socrates speak of tears shed by the audience of tragic poetry. Instead, Socrates speaks of the part in us which "hungered for tears and sufficient lamentation and satisfaction" receiving from the poets "satisfaction and *enjoyment*."[54] When we view tragic poetry, we enjoy contemplating the experience of another; and enjoying the experience of another, Socrates says, necessarily carries over into the experience of the self. But just as that in us which hungers for lamentation is satisfied by something other than lamentation, the "pitying part" which is nurtured by tragic poetry need not express itself in self-pity. If, as Socrates suggests, the "pitying part" is that in us which can "experience along with" (συμπάσχω) the

53. This way of conceiving deliberation conflicts with Aristotle's claim in book 3 of the *Nicomachean Ethics* that deliberation (βουλεύεσθαι) is not a thinking about ends, it is a thinking about the means to an end. It is, he says, in this respect like the calculative thinking involved in the analysis of a figure in geometry. We take the end result as given, and try to reason toward that end. Later in the *Ethics*, however, Aristotle, too, shows that there is a problem with this circumscribed way of thinking about deliberation when he turns, in book 6, to the question of deliberative excellence. In this context he claims that practical wisdom (φρόνησις) is most exemplified by someone who can deliberate about "what sorts of thing conduce to the good life in general." This is shown, he says, by the fact that we attribute practical wisdom to someone who reasons well with a view to some good end which is not the object of any art. Deliberation, it turns out, must involve more than mere calculation; it involves "understanding" (σύνεσις) which is to be identified neither with opinion nor with knowledge. It is in the sphere of judgment what practical wisdom is in the sphere of choice and action.

54. Nor, I think, do we have reason to assume that Socrates' failure to mention any tears or lamentation on the part of the audience shows an insensitivity to tragic poetry. When we are confronted with the suffering of Oedipus, for example, I do not think that most of us are moved to tears, but rather something more ambiguous and multivalent. Consider in this context the chorus' description of its own attitude toward Oedipus' tragedy at *Oedipus Rex* 1303–1306.

tragic hero, it may, instead, express itself in philosophic contemplation of our own experiences, as I will now argue.

8.6 Knowledge, Ignorance, and Imitation

In the previous section, I suggested that Socrates' final critique of mimetic poetry points us toward the possibility that mimetic poetry can have a specifically philosophic import. In this section we will try to become clearer on precisely in what sense mimetic poetry can be philosophic. On the reading I have offered, mimetic poetry enables us to view that which we have experienced as if it were the experience of another, a dramatic character with whom we share an experience we do not self-consciously identify as our own. By circumventing our self-conscious identification with a particular ethical or political role, our mimetic participation in the suffering of the tragic hero can provide a context in which we can direct our attention to aspects of experience that we deny in our everyday engagements, particularly in those cases where experience conflicts with that which we tell ourselves about how we should act and what we should feel. Thus, in the most obvious case, if some experience were to reveal a desire or belief that we would be ashamed to admit in ourselves because it conflicts with our self-understanding, poetry could allow us to recollect that experience as we sympathetically share in the experience of the tragic hero. However, if this were all there were to it, we might think that we should assign to mimetic poetry only a comparatively narrow and negative role in philosophic reflection. Mimetic poetry, we might think, can help us guard against parochialism in our attitudes toward the kinds of experience that play a part in our ethical deliberation, without contributing positively to that reflection. While I do not want to downplay the importance of this aspect of philosophic reflection, I believe that *mimêsis* has a substantially larger role to play in Socratic philosophy. Socrates' ironic critique of mimetic poetry can help us to understand both Socrates' dialogic method and his conception of contemplation as such.

It is the latter of these two claims I will focus on first, and I will begin by extending the analogy offered above between from Socratic philosophy and Husserlian phenomenology. I have suggested that Socrates' conception of *pistis* or "trust" is a mode of experience analogous to what Husserl calls "the natural attitude." To be more precise, Husserl's conception of the natural attitude involves aspects of both the *pathêma* Socrates refers to as *pistis* and the *pathêma* he refers to as *dianoia* or discursive thought. On Husserl's account, the natural attitude comprises both the givenness of the natural or spatiotemporal world and our scientific or technical reflection on the natural world as so given.

Quoting Husserl, "To cognize 'the' world more comprehensively, more reliably, more perfectly in every respect than naïve experiential cognizance can, to solve all the problems of scientific cognition which offer themselves within the realm of the world, that is the aim of the *sciences belonging to the natural attitude*."[55] In terms of the image of the divided line that Socrates offers at the end of book 6, these "sciences belonging to the natural attitude" would come within the province of the mode of experience he calls *dianoia* insofar as *dianoetic* reflection takes as its object the visible objects which populate the domain of trust, that is, "the animals around us, and everything that grows, and the whole class of artifacts." Geometry in its practical application as the science of measurement, which works to correct our natural susceptibility to visual illusion, would be an example of this kind of *dianoetic* reflection.

The "pure" science of geometry itself, however, while it proceeds as if in abstraction from the visible objects, remains on Socrates' account fundamentally tied to the domain of trust. Significantly for our argument, Socrates contends that "the men who work in geometry, calculation, and the like" take visible objects (literally "visible forms," τοῖς ὁρωμένοις εἴδεσι) and use them "as images" (ὡς εἰκόσιν) of intelligible, mathematical objects.

> Don't you also know that they use visible forms besides and make their arguments about them, not thinking about them but about those others that they are like? They make the argument for the sake of the square itself and the diagonal itself, not for the sake of the diagonal they draw, and likewise the rest. These things themselves that they mold and draw, of which there are shadows in images and water, they now use as images, seeking to see those things themselves that one can see in no other way than with thought. (510b–c)

By proceeding this way, the geometers exhibit the same attitude with regard to these "images" of mathematical realities that the science of measurement evinces with regard to visible illusion. Just as the science of measurement takes as its goal an idealized perceptual experience which overcomes the contingent causes of perceptual error, geometry takes the object of its investigation to be an idealized form of the mathematical character of the visible object, the "square in itself" or "the diagonal in itself."

The problem with the practice of the geometers, however, is not *that* they take visible objects as images of the intelligible, but rather how they understand that imaging relation. Crucial to Socrates' depiction of *dianoetic* calculation in

---

55. Husserl 1983, I, §30.

his image of the divided line is the same misunderstanding of the "imaging" relation we have seen him make manifest in his account of "visible" imitation in book 10. The geometers, Socrates tells us, "make hypotheses" (ποιησάμενοι ὑποθέσεις) of the elements of geometrical analysis—the odd and even, the three forms of angles—treating them as known and not worthy of further account. They then reason from these hypotheses as premises to mathematical objects as their conclusions. However, despite the "poetic" activity involved in their making of hypotheses, they treat visible objects as images in the restricted sense given to "image" in the lower subsection of the visible portion of the divided line, which Socrates calls *eikasia* or "imagination"—as reflections or shadows of mathematical objects distinguished from their imitations only by their clarity.[56] However, in so doing, geometry "and related disciplines" can at best re-present in a purified form the assumptions (ὑποθέσεις) embedded within a particular way of experiencing "the visible." They do not reflect on these assumptions as *assumptions,* but merely reason from these assumptions taken as premises to a conclusion. For this reason, Socrates says, "a soul is unable to step out above the hypotheses [οὐ δυναμένην τῶν ὑποθέσεων ἀνωτέρω ἐκβαίνειν], since it uses as images those very things of which images are made by things below." Moreover, this is said to be characteristic of *dianoia* as such; it is a mode of experience in which a soul, "using as images the things that were previously imitated, is compelled to investigate on the basis of hypotheses and makes its way not to a beginning (ἐπ᾽ ἀρχὴν) but to a conclusion (ἐπὶ τελευτήν).

In contrast to *dianoia,* Socrates characterizes *noêsis* as "that which argument itself grasps by the power of dialectic, making the assumptions not principles but really assumptions—that is, starting points and impelling forces—in order to reach what is free from assumptions, the principle of the whole." Once having attained this, argument is said to proceed to a conclusion without making any use of anything perceived. Using forms alone it goes "through forms to forms, ending in forms as well." Now, given the arguments of the previous chapter, I believe that we have reasons to doubt whether Socrates indeed believed it was possible for a human inquirer to "grasp" (ἅπτω) such a principle free from any assumption. But even were we to assume that Socrates believed in the possibility of a dialectic that proceeded from forms to forms "making no use in any way of anything perceptible" (αἰσθητῷ παντάπασιν οὐδενὶ προσχρώμενος), it is

56. Compare Wittgenstein's comments on the comparison between the experience of seeing one aspect of an ambiguous figure (that is, seeing the duck-rabbit as a duck or a rabbit) and having an "inner picture" of one or another aspect: "The concept of the 'inner picture' is misleading, for this concept uses the '*outer* picture' as a model; and yet the uses of the words for these concepts are no more like one another than the uses of 'numeral' and 'number'. (And if one chose to call numbers 'ideal numerals', one might produce a similar confusion)" (1958, 196).

by no means clear that he could tell us anything about it. Moreover, it is clear that Socratic philosophy as it is presented to us in Plato's dialogues is characterized by *aporia* and wonder rather than dialectical mastery of the forms; it is not characterized by knowledge of the greatest and most important matters, but rather by Socrates' awareness that he lacks understanding of these very things. Nonetheless, Socrates' dialogic practice has at least this much in common with the dialectical practice of the philosopher-rulers: as a "method of hypothesis" it involves seeing hypotheses *as* hypotheses, and at least to this degree "stepping out above the hypotheses." Socrates' dialogic examination of lives, I have argued, is an investigation of "the truth of the beings" in the "images" provided by the words and action of the individuals whose lives he examines. I have also suggested in that the locus of this truth is neither "the things themselves" nor "the human comportment toward beings," but in the beings disclosing and as disclosed by an individual's orientation to the good.[57] These individual or collective orientations to the good are the assumptions or hypotheses that are the subject of Socrates' philosophic inquiries.

In our readings of Socrates' conversations in book 1, we have already seen how Socrates' elenctic practice involves confronting and unearthing his interlocutor's imaginative orientation to the good. What we have yet to see is *how* he is able to do this. That is, in the terms of the foregoing discussion, we have yet to see how Socrates is able to see the hypotheses that structure these individuals' experience of the world as what he calls "hypotheses in reality" (τῷ ὄντι ὑποθέσεις), as objects of *noetic* contemplation rather than *dianoetic* calculation. It is here that we will begin to see the crucial theoretical significance of mimetic poetry for Socratic philosophy. And it is also here that the analogy to Husserlian phenomenology can be of help, in the first instance, by allowing us to clarify the problem. Husserl, who self-consciously took Socrates and Plato as his predecessors in articulating the task of philosophy, identified that task with a kind of purified contemplation of our experience of the world. Essential to engaging in the theoretical activity of philosophy is *disengaging* from a naïve acceptance of the assumptions embedded in the "natural attitude." This disengagement Husserl calls the "transcendental *epochê*," which he describes as a "putting out of action" the "general positing which characterizes the natural attitude." Through transcendental *epochê* we "bracket" our prereflective certainty in a given, mind-transcendent world of "natural," that is, spatiotemporal, objects. That is, we bracket the implicit claim made in the natural attitude positing a mind-independent "real world' as the ultimate foundation of the objects toward which we direct

---

57. I will return to this issue in chapter 10 below.

our attention.[58] Crucially, the *epochê* is not to be understood as a denial of, or even doubt concerning the reality of the world so conceived. It is not any kind of negative judgment regarding the validity of claims about matters of fact; it is instead a refusal to assert the validity of those claims. In this regard, it looks like the "suspension of judgment" practiced by the ancient skeptics, from whom Husserl has appropriated the term *epochê*.[59] Husserl contends that through the transcendental *epochê* we allow to emerge the autonomy of the first-person standpoint in which we can direct our attention to objects of our conscious perception as those objects actually appear to us. That is, in Husserl's terms, we can see the objects of our conscious perception as those objects are "in themselves."

I will now argue that we can ascribe to mimetic poetry as presented in Socrates' ironic critique a theoretical role parallel to Husserl's transcendental *epochê*. Mimetic poetry, I suggest, in providing us a way of viewing our experience without conceiving that experience as "our own" enables us to view it as it is "in itself" (αὐτὸ τὸ πάθος).[60] Through encountering that which we have experienced as the experience of another, we can direct our attention to that which we have experienced without asking whether or not that experience corresponds to that which we believe ourselves to know, or tell ourselves we *should* know, about "our" world. When we view dramatic poetry, however, we do not explicitly doubt or deny the truth of these beliefs. Nor do we try to examine our experiences as if they could be understood *as those experiences* in the abstract, apart from any implicit claims inherent in those experiences about that for the sake of which one acts. Rather, in viewing or reading dramatic poetry we *suspend* our belief and disbelief, and we do so through our sympathetic engagement with the experience of the tragic hero. This suspension of belief, I will argue, is not only essential to the dramatic effect of tragic poetry, it is also essential to taking experience itself as a subject for contemplation.

58. "Denying acceptance to all the sciences given us beforehand, treating them as, for us, inadmissible prejudices, is not enough. Their universal basis, the experienced world, must also be deprived of its naïve acceptance" (Husserl 1973, 58).

59. In ancient skepticism, *epochê* or suspension of judgment was to be achieved through a certain philosophic practice of opposing appearances to appearances and arguments to arguments. In this it differs from Husserl's conception, which takes *epochê* to "belong to the realm of our perfect freedom."

60. This distinction I am drawing depends upon the possibility of distinguishing between our experience, on the one hand, and the experience *of* that experience as "our own," on the other hand. If this distinction is a coherent one, this indicates different ways of conceiving the significance of the "first person" in a "first-person standpoint." In reference to the phenomenological tradition, it raises the question of the degree to which what is identified as the first-person standpoint necessarily entails either (a) an indefeasible, noncriterial authority governing referential uses of the first-person singular pronoun, or (a) a "mineness" which is constitutive of that experience. On these questions, see Crowell 2001 and Zahavi 2006.

As we have seen, the first mention of experience as a possible subject for contemplation is when it is seen as the experience of another, when that experience is "foreign" (ἀλλότρια) to us. We can make sense of this claim, first as a feature of imitation as such, and second, as a feature of tragic imitation in particular, by following back the implications of *allotrios* from its more metaphorical to its more literal senses. In the first instance, the association between contemplation and an experience of our own as foreign can be understood as gesturing toward a conception of the *alienation* of the familiar as central to the theoretical enterprise. Our everyday experience of the world first becomes an object toward which we direct our attention when the pervasive familiarity of that experience is somehow disrupted, when what had been taken as obvious appears strange.[61] As Socrates' favored word *atopos* reminds us, a central way in which the familiar can become strange is by a displacement of context; we see something as if for the first time when we see it somewhere it doesn't "belong," when it is "out of place." Successful imitation—dramatic, poetic, or graphic—provides a particular form of such a displacement of context, one in which aspects of the thing imitated which allow us to identify it *as that very thing* are reproduced in a novel setting.[62] Moreover, in the foreign context provided by imitation, we not only see something *as* something, we can confront the experience of "seeing as." We notice aspects that characterize our perception of some object, and this allows us to understand the object in the light of that characteristic aspect.[63] This understanding, according to Aristotle, is the reason we derive pleasure from imitation even when we are looking at something painful: "as we contemplate, we learn and infer what each is, i.e., 'that *this* is that.'"[64]

As the quotation from Aristotle suggests, however, this much can be said about the cognitive or theoretical significance of imitation as such. To see the particular theoretical significance of mimetic poetry as an imitation of human action, we need to return to the claim that human agency essentially involves conflicts in the soul between contradictory opinions about the freedom or compulsion with which we act, and whether, as a result of our action, we have done well or done poorly, experienced joy or sorrow. If, as Socrates claims, these contradictory opinions are intrinsic to human agency as such, contemplating

---

61. Husserl describes this disruption in terms of the disappointment (*Enttäuschung*), Heidegger in terms of breaks in the referential whole within which circumspection operates.

62. Consider the most mundane instance, the dramatic imitations of an impressionist. When someone does a good impression of George Bush or Bill Clinton, for example, we can, by seeing familiar verbal or physical mannerisms somewhere new, look at those aspects of a familiar personality framed for our inspection.

63. Compare Wittgenstein 1958, 193, "I contemplate a face, and then suddenly notice its likeness to another. I see that it has not changed; and yet I see it differently. I call this experience 'noticing an aspect.'"

64. *Poet.* 1448b5–20.

the experience of agency as it is in itself would necessarily involve confronting aspects of an object of our perception that, like our perceptions of unity and plurality in visible objects, "goes over into a contradictory perception at the same time" (ἐκβαίνει εἰς ἐναντίαν αἴσθησιν ἅμα, 523b–c). To take the central example Socrates offers, that of the forced or voluntary character of human action, the suggestion would be something like this: every instance of human action involves our taking some perceptual object, ourselves, to be both unfree and free, both a subject of compulsion and a spontaneous cause of our actions. As a subject of compulsion, we take some state of affairs outside ourselves to be that which is responsible for what we experience; as a spontaneous cause, we take ourselves and our choice of what seems best to be responsible. Indeed, we would not act—we could not desire to act—if we did not take ourselves to be subject to the necessity that is denied by our taking and bearing the responsibility for our actions. As Aristotle's account of voluntary and involuntary action implies, we could only truly take ourselves as responsible for our actions if we could take ourselves to be responsible for our own character, if we could see ourselves as, in some sense, self-caused (*Eth. Nic.* 3.1114b19).

On Socrates' account of the distinction between the visible and the intelligible, it is contradictory perceptions of this kind that lead to an awakening of the intellect. Our perceptions of the freedom or lack of freedom in human action, like our perceptions of unity and plurality in any perceptible object, raise the kinds of questions that cannot be addressed by perception alone. When we view the experience of agency as it is in itself, the contradictions that are an ineliminable part of our perception of a human being as an agent can bring us to ask such questions as what freedom and compulsion themselves are. It is obvious that questions of this kind are precisely those that are raised in the great works of Attic tragic poetry. If, as Plato and Aristotle contend, ancient tragedy is an "imitation of an action," it seems to be so primarily as the imitation of a human being confronting the problem of action, the problem of a taking or bearing responsibility for who one is and why one acts.[65] Oedipus's tragedy, for example, seems to be the tragedy of a finite human being who confronts, on the one hand, the impossibility of being wholly self-caused, and, on the other, the impossibility of finally knowing who one is and what one has done in a world in which one is not responsible for one's own coming to be.[66]

Through Oedipus's tragedy, I suggest, we can come to experience as "in another" the contradictions inherent in our own experience of human agency,

---

65. The author who has done the most to defend the idea that the problem of action is central to both ancient tragedy and Aristotle's account of tragedy is Michael Davis. See Davis 1999 and 1988.

66. See Benardete 1964.

contradictions that, as Oedipus himself shows, cannot become apparent to us in so far as we ourselves are in action. Moreover, we do so through our recognition of contradictions in Oedipus's *character* that show the tragic limitations of what *he* takes to be good. We come to see certain hypotheses as open to question through recognizing the tragic consequences of Oedipus's *failure* to question them. The tragedy is meaningful to us, however, to the degree that we can sympathetically participate in Oedipus's sufferings because his limitations are, in some sense, our own.

Mimetic poetry, I suggest, allows us to put into question the implicit hypotheses concerning the good through which we understand not only our own practical engagements, but ultimately the world of our experience, and it does so by allowing us to see those experiences as "belonging to another." Moreover, it is only through the "alienation" of these hypotheses in some sense, only insofar as we put these hypotheses "out of action," that we can come to take them as objects of possible theoretical inquiry. Insofar as we act, we take our hypotheses concerning the good not as hypotheses or assumptions, but as premises or principles which constitute our actions as actions. As we have seen, we can only act insofar as we *take* ourselves to be acting toward some end, and it is only on the basis of a hypothesis concerning the good considered as a premise or principle that we can so take ourselves. Conversely, by attending to the ways that our self-ascription of agency "goes over into a contradictory perception" (ἐκβαίνει εἰς ἐναντίαν αἴσθησιν), we may be able "to step out above the hypotheses" (ὑποθέσεων ἀνωτέρω ἐκβαίνειν). That is, rather than simply experiencing the world on the basis of a particular hypothesis concerning the good, we may be able to perceive *what it is to be* that hypothesis. We may be able to take our hypotheses as objects of *noetic* contemplation rather than *dianoetic* calculation.

The foregoing arguments do not, of course, imply that mimetic poetry is the only route to such contemplation. What I do want to suggest, however, is that the model provided by this account of the philosophic significance of mimetic poetry is crucial to helping us understand Socrates' theoretical activity. Socrates' inquiries into the truth of the beings, I will argue, are inseparable from the kind of alienation of one's own experience one encounters in mimetic poetry. They centrally involve recognizing in another one's own contradictory hypotheses concerning the good. However, to understand why this is so, we will need to better understand the relation between the "poetic" character of Socrates' dialogic practice in the dialogues and his understanding of the human soul. To this end, in the following chapter we will explore in greater detail Socrates' implicit and explicit appropriation of Homer's poetry, and in particular, his frequent invocation of the character of Odysseus in the context of the *Republic*. This examination of the character of Odysseus will not only help orient our inquiry into Socratic *mimêsis*, it will help us see more clearly why Socrates takes seeing beyond "one's own" to be both essential to philosophy and essentially problematic.

9

Poetry, Psychology, and τὸ θυμοειδές

In the previous chapter, I argued for an interpretation of Socrates' critique of mimetic poetry in book 10 that stressed the relation between mimetic poetry and philosophy. In this chapter, we will extend our inquiry into the philosophic significance of *mimêsis*. I will argue that central to Socrates' philosophic activity as represented in Plato's dialogues is a kind of *mimetic* activity through which Socrates makes manifest in his arguments an image of his interlocutors' incomplete or incoherent orientations to the good. At the same time, I will show in greater detail how Plato's engagement with and critique of the immanent philosophic orientation informs the explicit philosophic and political program Socrates enunciates in the *Republic*. In particular, I will argue that two of the aspects of the *Republic* that have received the most critical attention in recent years, the city-soul analogy and the critique of poetry, are parts of a larger account of the human soul as constitutively *mimetic,* an account which presents ethical development as dependent on the process by which an individual internalizes and identifies with different kinds of lives, life-projects, and modes of social justification. In this context, I will show how Socrates' introduction of the *thumoeidic* or "spirited" aspect of the soul in the city-soul analogy deepens and problematizes this conception of ethical internalization. It is also in this context that we will be able to see how Socrates' treatment of *to thumoeides* ties together many of the seemingly disparate argumentative threads and philosophic questions we have been following in our reading of the *Republic*. In previous chapters we have seen how the argument of the *Republic* raises questions concerning (1) the relation between the goods central to a way of life and the self-conscious appropriation and justification of that way of living, (2) the relation between cognitive capacities and acquired dispositions in human motivation and action, and (3) the role of poetic representation and rhetorical persuasion in giving form to individual and collective human identities. In this chapter, I will argue that these questions can all be seen as questions about *to thumoeides*.

This is to ascribe a more fundamental and pervasive role to *to thumoeides* in the argument of the *Republic* than do most commentators, even given the wealth of recent work dealing with the city-soul analogy in general and *to thumoeides* in particular. This is due to the fact that I do not consider *to thumoeides* to be, as it were, merely one piece of the interpretive puzzle of the *Republic;* instead, I believe that Socrates' presentation of *to thumoeides* is Plato's primary means of making imaginatively concrete the central problematic of the dialogue. To anticipate the argument of the following chapter, in Socrates' account of *to thumoeides* in the *Republic* we can find a similar constellation of concepts to those familiar to us from post-Kantian philosophical analyses of the will, particularly the disparate inquiries into a conception of the will as providing the horizon for the human experience of the world which we associate with Schopenhauer, Nietzsche, and Heidegger. Perhaps unsurprisingly, Nietzsche's inquiries into the will in his mature works will be the most immediately significant for my argument. We will find parallels in Socrates' presentation of *to thumoeides* to many of the central themes Nietzsche explores in his account of the will: his conception of the soul as a hierarchy of drives; his investigation into "bad conscience" and the internalization of instinct as constitutive of human interiority; his account of the divergence between moral types, and his conception of representation, interpretation, and the creation of value.

On Angela Hobbs's characterization, "the essence of the human *thumos* is the need to believe that one counts for something, and . . . central to this need will be a tendency to form an ideal image of oneself in accordance with one's conception of the fine and noble."[1] Socrates' presentation of *to thumoeides,* I suggest, is an extended meditation on this human striving to "be someone," how it structures our ethical and political experience, and how it enables or impedes our cognitive access to an intelligible reality outside the boundaries of those things we already call our own. This meditation takes the form, however, of an elaborate *reductio* of those theoretical positions that take human individual or collective self-determination as sufficient to explain the intelligible character of the world as it is given in human experience.

These are far-reaching claims, and for reasons that will become clear presently, I believe they are best approached via a reconsideration of Socrates' engagement with Homeric poetry in general, and the character of Odysseus in particular. Socrates' articulation of *to thumoeides* as an aspect of the soul distinct from calculation crucially depends upon his invocation of a passage in the *Odyssey* in which Odysseus recounts his struggle with his *thumos.* As other commentators have noted, however, the passage he cites is decidedly more complex and of greater interest that Socrates' initial gloss on it makes it appear. I will argue that when seen in the broader context of the *Odyssey* as a whole, Odysseus's account helps point the way to the understanding of *to thumoeides* indicated above. Furthermore, I will argue that Odysseus's character as revealed in that account will also

1. Hobbs 2000, 30.

provide us guidance in our investigation of Socrates' character as revealed in the dialogues, and the role of *mimêsis* in Socrates' characteristic activity. We can best begin examining all these issues, however, by turning briefly to the *Lesser Hippias,* a dialogue which takes Odysseus's character as its explicit theme, and Socrates' character as its implicit theme.[2]

9.1 The Character of Odysseus

As the *Lesser Hippias* begins, the Sophist Hippias has just completed a rhetorical display (ἐπίδειξις) in which he said "all sorts of things about Homer and the other poets" (*Hp. mi.* 363c). In that display, Hippias made a distinction between Odysseus and Achilles that inspires Socrates to question Hippias further. Socrates indicates the popular preference for Achilles in men of Cephalus's generation by saying to Eudicus, the third speaker in the dialogue, "your father used to say that the *Iliad* is a finer [κάλλιον] poem than the *Odyssey,* to the extent that Achilles is a better man than Odysseus" (363b). Later in the dialogue Socrates claims that he himself believes that both Achilles and Odysseus "are extremely good, and it is hard to decide which of the two is better" (370e), but for now Socrates wants to know which Hippias himself considers the better man.

Asked by Socrates to repeat what he had said about Achilles and Odysseus, Hippias gives a reply that is difficult to translate. Hippias says that Homer made Achilles best (ἄριστον) of the men who went to Troy, Nestor wisest (σοφώτατον), and Odysseus "πολυτροπώτατον," a word that R. E. Allen, H. N. Fowler, and Nicholas D. Smith all translate as "wiliest." However, whether this translation is appropriate is, in a sense, the subject of the dialogue.

Polutropos, literally "much turned" or "of many turnings,"[3] is a relatively rare word in pre-Socratic Greek. Its first and most famous use is in the opening line of the *Odyssey*—"Tell me, Muse, of that *polutropos* man"—where it stands in for the name of the hero of the poem, a name that the poet conspicuously holds back from mentioning for the first twenty lines.[4] It occurs one other time in

---

2. The brief interpretation of the *Lesser Hippias* offered below first appeared in my 2001 doctoral dissertation. For two recent articles that offer more extensive defenses of similar interpretations of the *Lesser Hippias,* see Lampert 2002 and Lévystone 2005.

3. The LSJ derives the word from πολύς (much, many) and τρέπω (to turn)—hence "much-traveled" or "much-wandering," though it is also translated as "of many ways" or "much-devising," i.e., roughly synonymous with πολύμητις (of many counsels), another of Odysseus's epithets. On the history and significance of the term, see Pucci 1987, 16–17, 49, 127–28; Dawe 1993, 87n4.

4. "The absence of a name here is likely to have been so startling to the expectations created by traditional practice that, but for the first word in the poem, *andra,* we would be programmed to take *polutropon* as a proper name" (Peradotto 1990, 114).

the *Odyssey*, as an epithet for Odysseus, and twice in the Homeric Hymns as an epithet for Hermes. The majority of other occurrences of *polutropos* before the dramatic date of the *Lesser Hippias* are in medical and scientific contexts.[5] The significance of its first recorded use, along with its scarcity in literary or philosophic texts, suggests that, in practice, the word was roughly synonymous with our "Odyssean." This would explain Socrates' surprised reaction to Hippias's apparent introduction into the language of the superlative form in the phrase "πολυτροπώτατον δὲʼ Ὀδυσσέα," since Hippias would seem to be saying that Odysseus was, of all the men who went to Troy, most like Odysseus. "When you said that he made Achilles best and Nestor wisest, I thought I understood what you meant, but when you said he makes Odysseus most *polutropos,* there, to tell you the truth, I don't at all know what you mean. But tell me—perhaps here I may understand better. Did Homer not make Achilles *polutropos?*" (*Hp. mi.* 364e). As Hippias has provided no more and no less context for *polutropos* than for *aristos* or *sophos,* it seems unlikely that Socrates is balking at what he sees as an inconsistent or incoherent use of this word. Instead, it seems that Hippias and Socrates are taking the first recorded use as definitive, and their sense of the valence of the word is determined by their sense of the man whose epithet it is. For now, I will translate *polutropos,* somewhat clumsily, as "manifold" to preserve the contrast with *haplous* (simple) upon which Hippias's argument depends.

Hippias rejects Socrates' suggestion that Homer makes Achilles "manifold," and to demonstrate his position he half quotes, half paraphrases Achilles speaking to Odysseus in the embassy scene in book 9 of the *Iliad*. "Zeus-born son of Laertes, much-devising Odysseus, I must speak out the word without refraining, as I shall act and think will be accomplished. For hateful to me as the gates of Hades is he who hides in his heart [κεύθῃ ἐνὶ φρεσίν] one thing and says another. But I shall speak that which shall be accomplished." "In these lines," Hippias continues, "he makes clear the character [τὸν τρόπον] of each of these men, that Achilles is true and simple [ἀληθής τε καὶ ἁπλοῦς] and Odysseus manifold and false [πολύτροπός τε καὶ ψευδής], for he makes Achilles say these things to Odysseus" (*Hp. mi.* 365a–b). Now, we can take Hippias's interpretation

---

5. See Diogenes of Apollonia, DK 64 B5. A use of πολύτροπος contemporaneous with the *Lesser Hippias* which is particularly relevant here is the second of two occurrences in Thucydides, where he is describing the collapse of civic virtue brought about by political instability and the spread of civil war. On the internecine struggles between democratic and oligarchic factions in the various cities, Thucydides writes that "simplicity, in which nobility greatly participated [τὸ εὔηθες, οὗ τὸ γενναῖον πλεῖστον μετέχει], was laughed at and disappeared," and the cities were divided into opposing camps in which there was no trust. In these struggles, Thucydides writes, "the paltrier understandings prevailed" because they chose to strike first, fearing that they would be beaten in debate and surprised by their more their "more versatile" (πολυτρόπου) opponents. Thus, Thucydides seems to indicate in this one use both of the aspects of πολύτροπος we find in the *Lesser Hippias:* intelligence and the *appearance* of untrustworthiness. See also Herodotus *Hist.* 2.121.

of this passage in either of two ways. If we take Hippias to be explicating the literal significance of Achilles' words, then he is clearly wide of the mark. The man whom Achilles hates "as the gates of Hades" is Agamemnon, of whom Achilles says "he has taken the prize from my hands and tricked me" (δ' ἐπεὶ ἐκ χειρῶν γέρας εἵλετο καί μ' ἀπάτησε, *Il.* 9.344); he wants Odysseus to proclaim openly to all what Achilles has told him, lest Agamemnon "hope to deceive some other of the Danaans, as he is ever clothed in shamelessness" (εἴ τινά που Δαναῶν ἔτι ἔλπεται ἐξαπατήσειν / αἰὲν ἀναιδείην ἐπιειμένος, *Il.* 9.371–72).[6] Furthermore, Achilles has proclaimed that the embassy, with Odysseus at its head, comprises "my dearest friends in all the Achaean armies" and "the men I love most" (9.200–204). However, if we allow Hippias to be making a subtler point here (and bracketing for the moment his description of Odysseus as false), he is surely on to something. Achilles' speech is in direct response to a speech in which Odysseus describes the impending rout of the Greek forces at the hands of Hector, details the many gifts Agamemnon has offered to Achilles in recompense for his affront, and reminds Achilles of the glory he will win if he kills Hector in battle. Achilles replies in his speech to each of Odysseus's overtures, but the contrast between the two speeches is stark. Here is how James Redfield describes it: "Where Odysseus' speech was organized and pointed, Achilles' speech comes through with blunt, obsessive power. He leaves each topic only to return to it, as though his mind were prowling in the close circle of his rage. Odysseus's speech was composed with a careful view to his ends; Achilles begins with a claim to simple truth, and he explodes with the raw truth of his mental condition. It is as if he were talking to himself."[7] Redfield's contrast between this eruption of "the raw truth" of Achilles' mental condition and Odysseus's careful rhetoric makes plain the basis for Hippias's preference. Achilles' speech appears to give us unmediated access to the movements of his soul. Of course, Redfield sees, as Hippias does not, that Achilles' direct expression of his bitterness of heart is terrifying. It is of a piece with his absolute rejection of the embassy, a sign that he has begun to loose himself from any direct concern for how his words or actions appear to others. As his speech pitches back and forth between Agamemnon's outrage against him, the fate that his mother has foretold him, and the death that comes to all, he reveals the unknowing rightness of Agamemnon's words, the only words Odysseus suppresses as he recounts the gifts Agamemnon offers:

6. Indeed, ἐχθρός appears in the *Iliad* on only two other occasions (9.378 and 16.77). In both instances, Achilles speaks and Agamemnon is the object of his hatred.

7. Redfield 1994, 7.

All this
I would give to him if he will end his anger.
Let him be mastered; Hades, implacable and unmastered,
Is therefore of all gods hated most by mortals.

(*Il.* 9.157–59)

Achilles senses what the remainder of the poem will show, that his real quarrel is not with Agamemnon but with this implacable god; he speaks as if to himself because these men and their embassy are, in the end, of little consequence to this struggle.

Achilles does not "hide anything in his heart" in this scene not because, as Hippias suggests, he is openhearted (*Hp. mi.* 371e) but because, as Patroclus says, he is without pity (*Il.* 16.33). Nonetheless, Hippias is surely right to see irony in Achilles directing these words to Odysseus, who, despite the pity he feels for his weeping wife, "hides his tears" (δάκρυα κεῦθεν) so thoroughly that his eyes remain unmoved, as if they were made or horn or iron (*Od.* 19.211–12). Hippias's concern, however, is not just with Odysseus's mastery of his emotions but with the form this mastery takes. Recall that when Hippias describes the contrast between Achilles as simple (ἁπλοῦς) and Odysseus as manifold (πολύτροπος), he says that Homer "makes clear the character [τὸν τρόπον] of each of these men."[8]

What Hippias is objecting to is not only Odysseus's ability to hide his own character, but also his mimetic capacity to take on the characters of other men and to offer complex tales of their travels and sufferings as if they were his own. Nonetheless, despite Odysseus's many characters and many stratagems, Hippias is wrong to suggest that as Odysseus is manifold he is also *panourgos*—"a doer of all things." Instead, Odysseus's manifold deceptions are all of a kind. Wanderers like himself, each persona Odysseus adopts is a human being of humbler origins and less magnificent gifts than his; Odysseus's dissembling is always a denial or deferral of his famous name and exalted station. Isolated from the social and political world in which this name corresponds to ties of friendship and kinship, Odysseus adopts masks of obscurity, with each successive mask bringing him closer to reclaiming his name and position in the social world.[9] And despite an

8. Based on the evidence of Antisthenes' "Ajax" and "Odysseus" speeches, Hippias's ethical interpretation of *polutropos* as "often changing one's character" had been suggested by other sophistic detractors of Odysseus in the late fifth century. However, as Eustathius noted, τρόπος does not mean ἦθος in Homeric Greek. See Stanford 1954, 99, 260–61n28.

9. His first character is, literally, "nobody" (οὔτις) in his account of his stratagem against the Cyclops. Once he has returned to Ithaca he adopts the following characters in succession. To Athena he is a nameless

apparent fondness for telling tales more elaborate than may be absolutely necessary, Odysseus always plays his roles for either of two reasons:[10] to protect himself or his companions from harm, or to test or make trial of (πειρητίζω, πειράζω, γεύσεσθαι) those to whom he speaks.[11]

9.2 Exteriority and Interiority

Achilles and Odysseus are profoundly complementary characters, and their complementarity can be expressed in terms of their divergent responses both to the social and political world and to the human experience of the self in its relation to the social and political world. As their names, derived from words signifying grief (ἄχος) and wrath (ὀδύσσομαι), suggest, their stories revolve around emotions which can be characterized as at once social, ethical, and self-conscious: shame and vengeance, loyalty and betrayal, pity and friendship. In the context of the *Republic,* as we will see, they represent different answers to what I have identified in §2.9 as the problem of heteronomy. In radically opposed ways, both heroes strive to stand outside their social world as given to them, both succeed to a degree, and both are reconciled—again in profoundly different ways—to a social world altered in significance or substance by their struggles. Following the account given in the *Lesser Hippias,* we can describe Achilles and Odysseus in their relation to the social and political world as occupying opposite extremes on a spectrum of relative *exteriority* and *interiority.* The characterization of Achilles as a paradigm of exteriority is relatively uncontroversial; it is consonant with a by now familiar (if increasingly challenged) picture of the Homeric hero and Homeric social psychology. Here is how Redfield, following Herman Fränkel, summarizes this view:

> Homeric man, being objective, has no innerness. He expresses himself completely in words and acts, and is thus completely known to his fellows.

---

fugitive who claims no lineage, who fled from Crete having killed King Idomeneus's son and who says only that he has heard of Ithaca. To Eumaios, again nameless, he is now a bastard son of a wealthy Cretan named Castor Hylakides. He went with Idomeneus to Troy and served there under Odysseus, who showed him a kindness. To Penelope he becomes a prince, Aithon, Idomeneus's younger brother, who himself played host to Odysseus in Crete as Odysseus sailed toward Troy.

10. Thus, according to Aristotle, Odysseus is not false, because "a false man is one who is easy with and deliberately chooses those sorts of accounts, not for some other reason but for their own sake. . . . Because of this the account in the *Hippias* that the same man is true and false is misleading" (*Metaph.* 51025a2–8).

11. Cf. *Od.* 1.3: "Many were they whose cities he saw and whose minds he came to know" (πολλῶν δ᾽ ἀνθρώπων ἴδεν ἄστεα καὶ νόον ἔγνω).

He has no hidden depths or secret motives; he says and does what he is. Such a man is not an enclosed identity; he is rather a kind of open field of forces. He is open to others—to the words of other men and to the intervention of the gods. There is no clear line for him between *ego* and *alter;* he can recognize his own thoughts and wishes as having been implanted in him by another. Similarly, when he is in doubt, parts of himself become alien to himself; he argues with himself until he takes charge of himself and sees his way to action.[12]

Redfield suggests that this description applies better to Achilles, "the perfection of the character type," than to any other figure. I would suggest that insofar as Achilles represents a kind of perfection, he diverges in crucial ways from this description. Achilles, as "by far the best of the Achaeans," resists this openness to being governed by the wishes and opinions of others.[13] He resists, however, not by limiting his outwardness, but by radicalizing it; the *Iliad* becomes, after the failed embassy, a narrative of Achilles' *externalization* of his individual struggle between long-lived obscurity and immortal *kleos* won at the cost of an early death. After Achilles withdraws from battle and prays for the defeat of the Greeks at Hector's hands, the framing story of the battle between the Achaeans and the Trojans recedes, and the characters begin acting out Achilles' personal drama: Patroclus donning Achilles' deathless armor and with it his mortal visage (16.278–84); Hector slaying Patroclus and taking on, with Achilles helmet, his own appointed death (16.799–801, 16.201–8) and deathless *kleos* (22.300–305); and finally, Achilles in armor and shield crafted by Hephaestus killing Hector in Achilles' armor and so consummating his fate. Achilles' externalization of the conflict in his soul, I believe, can explain why the shield given to him by Hephaestus seems to represent the power of the poet conceived as a world-creating force, and why Achilles is, as Redfield says, "the only character in the *Iliad* who is himself a poet."[14] In his attempt to master his fate, Achilles, in effect, remakes the world of the *Iliad* in his own image. Homer indicates the limits of Achilles' externalization, and, by implication, this way of conceiving the poetic art, by the fact that what reconciliation Achilles achieves with the social world he has renounced comes about by a moment of identification

---

12. Redfield 1994, 21.

13. Redfield himself suggests as much when he says that for the majority of the poem after Achilles' speech "the other characters in the poem find him baffling and speak to him in protest and incomprehension" and when he says that Phoenix, Odysseus and Apollo "all say that Achilles is not behaving as human beings behave" (7). See also his description of Achilles' "clarity of vision," which makes him "badly placed at a deliberative assembly" (13).

between Achilles and Priam, the only moment in the *Iliad* where Achilles sees himself "in another" and likens another's suffering to his own (24.507–51).

Again, however controversial the interpretation of Achilles' *externalization* I have offered, the broader claim about Achilles' *exteriority* is, as I have said, relatively uncontroversial. This is not the case, however, with my claim that Odysseus represents a kind of interiority, which has been disputed both by authors who consider the absence of a fully developed notion of inwardness indicative of the primitive character of Homeric conceptions of self, action, and ethical reasoning[15] and by authors who, on the contrary, believe that such an absence demonstrates the superiority of Homeric representations of ethical life to modern representations, particular those that these latter authors associate with (a) the Cartesian concept of the self and (b) the Kantian conception of moral reasoning. It is these latter accounts that will most concern us here, not least because I am deeply unpersuaded by the kind of account of archaic and classical Greek ethical views which Bernard Williams characterized as "progressivist." My treatment of this issue will focus on *Odyssey* 20.9–25, a passage of crucial import in the *Republic* and one that has been much discussed. However, before turning to that passage we will look at two passages from the *Iliad* which bear on the issue of Odysseus's exteriority, one which has received a great deal of attention in recent treatments of this issue and one which has, to the best of my knowledge, received none in this context.

In the first passage, Odysseus, left alone in the front lines of battle and facing superior numbers, is deliberating whether to stand his ground or retreat.

> And troubled, he spoke then to his own great-hearted spirit: "Ah me, what will become of me? It will be a great evil if I run, fearing their multitude. But it will be more terrible if I am caught here alone; and Cronus' son drove to flight the rest of the Danaans. But why does my spirit debate this with me? I know that it is cowards who leave the fight, but whoever is best in battle must stand his ground strongly, whether he be struck or strikes down another. (*Il.* 11.403–10, adapted from Lattimore trans.)

14. Ibid., 221.

15. In the former camp we find, most famously, Bruno Snell's account of Homeric man as having no concept of an integrated, reflexively conscious self and therefore lacking that distinction between what is internal and what is external to oneself upon which, according to Snell, any genuinely personal decision-making depends. Other influential authors who, while rejecting or modifying the most extreme aspects of Snell's account, particularly his contention that Homeric man lacked even an integrated sense of body, agree with Snell's contention that the lack of inwardness in Homeric characters indicates a deficiency in Homeric ethical psychology include Adkins (1970) and Dodds (1951).

Bruno Snell, in *The Discovery of Mind,* uses this passage as an example of Odysseus's heteronomy; on Snell's account, Odysseus does not make a genuinely personal ethical decision in this passage, but merely "reminds himself that he is an aristocrat and thereby resolves his doubts how he should conduct himself in a critical situation."[16] However, as Christopher Gill has observed, Snell's argument depends on his assumption that the key evaluative terms in Odysseus's mono-logue are entirely class-based and, furthermore, that "in Homer one's class or status carries unequivocal ethical implications."[17] In explicit response to Snell, Gill examines this passage alongside three other deliberative monologues from the *Iliad,* Menelaus's at 17.90–105, Agenor's at 21.552–70, and Hector's at 22.98–130. Gill begins with Odysseus's monologue because, he says, "it provides the clearest illustration of the relationship between Homeric and Greek philosophical ethical thinking," and he argues, I believe correctly, that far from being an example of a mechanical response to a wholly determinate status-based code of conduct, Odysseus's monologue is remarkably consistent with Aristotle's account of practical reasoning.[18] However, Gill's account gives us ample reason for doubting that Odysseus is our best choice for a generalized portrait of the ethical delib-eration of Homeric heroes. First, Gill notes that, uniquely among those he examines, Odysseus's monologue lacks any explicit reference to the considerations of shame or honor thought to be central to Homeric ethics. Gill also observes that Aristotle uses another of the deliberative monologues he examines, Hector's, as an example not of courage in the full sense in which a fine thing is done for its own sake, but of "civic" courage which "is due to shame and the desire for something fine (namely, honor) and avoidance of criticism, which is disgraceful" (*Eth. Nic.* 1116a28–29).[19]

Odysseus's role in the second passage is quite brief but, if anything, more remarkable than the monologue discussed above. The setting is the beginning of a rout spurred on by a sign from Zeus, a flash of lightning which "stunned [the Achaeans] and pale terror took them all" (8.77). All of them flee toward the ships except Nestor, whose horse has been struck down by an arrow and upon whom Hector is closing fast.

And now the old man would have lost his life, there had not
Diomedes of the great war cry sharply perceived him.
He cried out in a terrible voice to rally Odysseus:

---

16. Snell 1960, 159. Also cited in Gill 1995, 39.
17. Gill 1995, 69.
18. Ibid., 69–74.
19. Ibid., 74. Cf. *Eth. Nic.* 1116a17–23 with *Resp.* 429a–430c.

"Son of Laertes and seed of Zeus, resourceful Odysseus,
where are you running, turning your back in battle like a coward?
Do not let them strike the spear in your back as you run for it,
but stay, so that we can beat back this fierce man from the ancient."
    He spoke, but long-suffering great Odysseus gave no attention [οὐδ᾽
ἐσάκουσε πολύτλας δῖος Ὀδυσσεύς]
as he swept by on his way to the hollow ships of the Achaians. (8.90–98,
Lattimore trans.)

One might think this a strange passage to look to for Homer's depiction of
Odysseus as exceptional, but it is absolutely unique in the *Iliad*. Both Trojan and
Greek warriors frequently upbraid one another for the appearance of cowardice,
and in every instance but this one the warrior who is accosted responds in
some way, whether with anger (as Odysseus himself does to a challenge from
Agamemnon at 4.349–55) or with some form of explanation or rationalization
(the latter is characteristic of Paris; e.g., 3.58–75). In most cases these responses
include some account of the hero's lineage and famous deeds.[20] Nowhere else
does a character in the *Iliad* simply "pay no heed" (οὐδ᾽ ἐσάκουσε) to an accusation of cowardice;[21] Odysseus, after he has seen the sign from Zeus that the
battle has turned against the Achaeans (8.137–44), does not pause to justify his
actions to Diomedes, nor does the poet pause to explain them to his audience.
Whatever Odysseus's ultimate reasons are for rejecting Diomedes' entreaty, he
keeps them to himself.

    I begin with these passages from the *Iliad* to make clear that the interiority
I am ascribing to Odysseus is not, as some authors have claimed,[22] an artifact
of an intellectual and ethical progress which transpired in the years between

20. There is one other partial exception to this rule in the *Iliad*, but it is one that only serves to under-
score the singularity of Odysseus's reaction. It occurs when Diomedes is "overawed by the majesty" of
Agamemnon's rebuke, and in this case Kapaneus, who is standing with Diomedes, immediately makes
good on the omission and answers Agamemnon for both Diomedes and himself. Moreover, Diomedes'
response to Kapaneus is to reprove him in turn for answering back to Agamemnon, "shepherd of the people"
(4.401–18).

21. This has troubled some translators (e.g., A. T. Murray and, more recently, Robert Fagles) enough to
translate the key phrase as "Odysseus heard him not," but this is clearly a mistranslation for a number of
reasons. According to the LSJ, εἰσακούω, "to hearken or give ear to one," does not acquire the secondary
meaning of simply "to hear" until Sophocles. Furthermore, when Homer wants to say that someone has
failed to hear something, he uses two other words for two different senses of "to hear": ἀκούω when someone has failed "to hear tell of" a report or proclamation because the news has not yet reached him, and ἀΐω
when someone fails "to perceive by ear" a sound (as, e.g., *Il.* 23.429–30). Lastly, the explanation that
Odysseus simply missed the words which Diomedes "of the great war cry . . . cried out in a terrible voice"
suggests a kind of representational realism which is utterly alien to Homer's poetry.

22. See Snell 1964.

the composition of the *Iliad* and that of the *Odyssey*. Although the character of Odysseus is obviously developed at greater length in the *Odyssey*, and wherever we stand on the question of Homeric authorship, this aspect of Odysseus's character is quite consistent between the two epics, and already in the *Iliad* we are given evidence that Odysseus occupies a unique position in relation to the ethical norms of the world of the Homeric poems. Odysseus stands in marked contrast to the other Homeric heroes in the degree to which he manifests a reflective distance from his social and political world. More significantly, Odysseus manifests a reflective distance from *himself* as socially constituted. In terms of the argument of the *Republic*, as we will see, Odysseus manifests a capacity to reflect upon and distance himself from what Socrates presents as the *thumoeidic* aspect of soul. It is understanding this latter issue, of course, that is my primary goal here, and the primary reason for my interest in Odysseus's character as portrayed in the Homeric poems is the light it helps to shed on Socrates' character as manifested in Plato's dialogues. A number of recent commentators have stressed the significance of the numerous literary references in Plato's dialogues to Homer's portrayal of Odysseus for our understanding of Plato's depiction of Socrates.[23] In line with these commentators, I believe that by looking at Odysseus's struggle with his *thumos* in *Odyssey* 20, and the context in which this struggle is invoked in the *Republic,* we can begin to sketch out an account of Socrates' own interiority and the implications of this interiority for Socrates' dialogic practice.

9.3 Odysseus's Doglike *Thumos*

If there is any passage in Homer to which Plato directs our attention, it is *Odyssey* 20.17–18. Socrates quotes it twice in the *Republic* and once in the *Phaedo*. It first makes its appearance in the *Republic* as Socrates' prize example of the kind of poetry, "speeches and deeds of endurance by famous men," that must be seen and heard in the city that he, Glaucon, and Adeimantus are founding (*Resp.* 390d). But it is its second occurrence in the *Republic* which, when compared to its use in the *Phaedo,* demands that we examine the passage more closely. While in each instance Socrates invokes the passage in order to help demonstrate a claim that is crucial for the arguments of the respective dialogues, the claim the passage is said to support in the *Republic* is not only different from but seems to contradict the claim it is said to support in the *Phaedo:* at *Republic* 441b–c

---

23. In addition to Lampert 2002 and Lévystone 2005, see Howland 1993; Hobbs 2000, 193–97 and 239–40; and O'Connor 2007.

Socrates uses the passage as an example of a conflict between two parts of the soul and, hence, evidence for the distinction between the spirited and calculative aspects of the soul; at *Phaedo* 94d–e he uses it as an example of a conflict between the soul and the affects of the body (τῶν τοῦ σώματος παθημάτων), and hence for a divide between soul and body.

First, we should remind ourselves of a couple of passages in the *Republic* that provide the context for the one we will be examining. *Thumos* enters the argument of the *Republic* as a characteristic of dogs before it is said to be a characteristic of human beings. Inquiring into what kind of nature makes one fit for the guarding of a city, Socrates uses the nature of a "well-bred pup" (γενναίου σκύλακος) as a guide: dogs must be swift and strong, with sharp senses, and, most of all, they must be spirited (θυμοειδής). However, as soon as "irresistible and unconquerable spirit" is introduced, it presents a problem. With such natures, Socrates asks Glaucon, how "will they not be savage to one another and to the rest of the citizens?" The puzzle is how to find a disposition (ἦθος) at once gentle (πρᾶος) and great-spirited (μεγαλόθυμος), for, Socrates says, "they must be gentle to their own and cruel to their enemies." Once again this puzzle is solved by looking to the "disposition by nature" of dogs, who are gentle to those they are accustomed to and familiar with and the opposite with the opposite. This next step that Socrates takes in praise of canines, however, indicates a deeper problem; in fact, it is one way of formulating the central problem of the *Republic*. Socrates, noting something "worthy of wonder" (ἄξιον θαυμάσαι) about dogs, claims that they have something in common with philosophers, by this curious chain of reasoning: (1) When dogs see someone they don't know, they are angry with him, even though they never had a bad experience with him, and when they see someone they know, they greet him warmly, even if they have had no good experience with him; (2) hence, dogs distinguish friendly from hostile in terms of having learned and being ignorant; (3) hence, dogs are lovers of learning; (4) but loving learning is the same as loving wisdom; (5) therefore, dogs are like philosophers (374e–376c).

Now, this is clearly a joke, but it is a joke with serious implications for our reading of the *Republic*. It should motivate us to look back at the entire passage and question the various moves and identifications Socrates has made along the way. It should raise questions about the relation between disposition (ἦθος) and nature (φύσις), about the relation between familiarity (γνώρισις) and knowledge (γνῶσις), and about the relation between love of learning (φιλομάθεια) and love of wisdom (φιλοσοφία). It should, moreover, alert us to the difference between (1) the nature here ascribed to the guardians, (2) the nature of the "true philosopher" described in book 6, and (3) the character of Socrates: the guardians love what is familiar to them and hate what is unfamiliar; the true philosopher, who "has his understanding turned toward the things that *are*[,] has no leisure to look down towards the affairs of human beings" (*Resp.* 500b–c); Socrates wonders about the paradoxical nature of dogs. Moreover, this joke intimates the characteristic dangers of the doglike *thumoeidic* soul—confusing what is one's own with what is best and mistaking second nature for first.[24]

Leaving aside both the doglike physical characteristics Socrates attributes to the guardians (404a, 422d) and the fact that they will be bred like dogs (416a, 451d, 459a), and focusing only on the way Socrates uses this metaphor to describe the souls of the guardians, we can discern two ultimately interrelated traits, one ascribed to *thumos* as such, the other ascribed to the *thumoeidic* guardians. First, *thumos* is "irresistible and unconquerable" (ἄμαχόν τε καὶ ἀνίκητον) when it is roused against someone. As he makes clear at 440c–d, Socrates is not making the indefensible claim that the adequately spirited guardian will always be victorious is battle. Instead, he is making a claim about *thumos* as a psychic principle. *Thumos* is, in the first instance, directed outward toward conquest and victory. While the human being in whom *thumos* is roused can be killed, *thumos as a principle* cannot by overcome by what it deems external or foreign to itself; it can only "be called in by the speech within [that human being] like a dog by a herdsman" (440d). Second, the guardians "must guard and hunt together like dogs, and insofar as possible have everything in every way in common" (466d). They identify themselves entirely with those they call their own, achieving to as great a degree as possible a "community of pleasure and pain" (462b). This imaginative, and often flatly counterfactual, identification beyond the individual body and with the body politic gives a first indication of a point I will return to below, the central role imagination plays in Plato's account of the *thumoeidic* soul. For now, we can see the extreme fallibility Socrates attributes to this imaginative division between enemy and friend by a comment he makes about those who engage in the "illiberal" practice of plundering corpses of fallen enemies, whom he compares to "dogs who are harsh with the stones thrown at them but don't touch the one who is throwing them" (469d–e).[25] With these passages in mind, we can now turn to Socrates' invocation of *Odyssey* 20.17–18 at *Republic* 441b.

---

24. Compare Ferrari's very similar account in Ferrari 2007b, 184–88. Unlike the interpretation I have been pursuing here, Ferrari's interpretation takes the presentation of "the ideally just soul" in books 5–7 to resolve the problem of *to thumoeides*. In particular, he argues that "when a man identifies himself with the goals of reason . . . the inner and outer man match and . . . natural integrity can be achieved" (196).

25. To these passages from the *Republic* we can add two from the *Odyssey* which show dogs being savage to Odysseus as supposed enemy and gentle to him as a recognized friend. At 14.29–38 Odysseus, on his return to Ithaca, narrowly escapes being mauled by Eumaios's "howling dogs" (κύνες ὑλακόμωροι), who have never seen him before; at 17.290–327, Odysseus's aged and "patient-hearted" (ταλασίφρονος) dog Argos dies after immediately recognizing and greeting Odysseus despite his disguise, without a sign, without a test, something no human character in the *Odyssey* is able to do.

The broader context is, as I have said, Socrates' attempt to demonstrate, in conversation with Glaucon, that *to thumoeides* is distinct from both calculation and desire. He has putatively distinguished desire from anger, and hence from *to thumoeides,* by the example of Leontius's anger at his own desire to look at the corpses of executed criminals (439e–440a), and turns to the question of whether spirit is also distinct from the calculating part. The quotation occurs less than a Stephanus page after the passage noted above where Socrates explicates the sense in which *thumos* is "unconquerable." What I did not allude to there is the significant fact that the situation Socrates is describing is one in which someone considers himself to be suffering unjustly. The passage in full reads, "And what about when a man believes he's being done injustice? Doesn't his spirit in this case boil and become harsh and form an alliance for battle with what seems just; and, even if it suffers in hunger, cold and everything of the sort, doesn't it stand firm and not cease from its noble efforts before it has succeeded, or death intervenes, or before it becomes gentle, having been called in by the speech within him like a dog by a herdsman?" (*Resp.* 440c–d). Taking this as evidence that "in the faction of the soul it [i.e., spirit] sets its arms on the side of the calculating part," Socrates asks whether spirit is merely a "particular form" of calculation, or, as there are three classes in the city, is there "in the soul too this third, the spirited, by nature an auxiliary to the calculating part" (441a). Glaucon adduces in support of this claim the example of children, who are spirited straight from birth but acquire calculation "quite late," if at all, to which Socrates adds the example of beasts. We can note in passing that neither of these examples tends to support the contention that spirit is by nature allied with calculation. Perhaps for this reason, Socrates deems these examples insufficient, and cites in addition this "testimony of Homer."

"He smote his breast and reproached his heart with word."
    Here, you see, Homer clearly presents that which has calculated about better and worse and rebukes that which is irrationally spirited as though it were a different part. (441b–c)

If we turn to the passage in the *Odyssey,* from which these words are quoted, we will be given reasons to doubt the clarity of Homer's demonstration of the distinctness of calculation and spirit.[26] In its place we will be given clues to another

---

26. Again, compare Ferrari 2007b. Ferrari contends that the example of Odysseus's struggle with his *thumos* differentiates the conflicting aspects of the soul on instrumental rather than moral grounds. The example, therefore, "is not well gauged to convince us that the two parts are fundamentally rather than superficially distinct—for their goals are not distinct" (172).

way of conceiving the distinction between mind and spirit. We will see the most striking example of what I have called Odysseus's interiority, and we can begin to articulate how Odysseus's interiority provides a pattern for the role that Socrates' interiority plays in the *Republic*.

Odysseus, still disguised as a beggar, is preparing for sleep in the forecourt of his home and is "devising for the suitors bad things in his spirit" when the women who have slept with the suitors walk by him, laughing and greeting one another. Seeing them, Odysseus is angered and struggles with himself. I quote the passage in full.

> But the spirit [θυμὸς] was stirred in his chest
> and he argued much in his mind and spirit [κατὰ φρένα καὶ κατὰ θυμόν],
> whether he should rush amidst them and kill each of them,
> or suffer them to lie with the insolent suitors
> for the last time; and his heart howled within him.
> And as a bitch stands over her helpless pups
> howling at a man she does not know and yearns to fight,
> so the heart within him howled, indignant [ἀγαιομένου] at their evil deeds.
> But striking his chest, he reproached his heart with a word
> "Endure, heart. You have endured things more doglike [κύντερον] than this.
> On that day when the implacable Cyclops devoured
> my strong companions, but you endured until intelligence
> lead you out from the cave [μῆτις ἐξάγαγ' ἐξ ἄντροιο] though you
> thought you would die there."
> So he spoke, addressing the dear heart in his chest; and the
> heart in great obedience endured and stood fast
> in perseverance.
>
> (*Od.* 20.9–30)

We can begin our analysis of this passage by noting that it is an elaboration of and a reflection on "troubled, he spoke to his great-hearted spirit," the standard form of deliberative self-address in Homer. Whenever a character in the *Iliad* (and in most cases in the *Odyssey*) is presented as *talking to himself* in a moment of decision, this character is always said to speak to his *thumos*. Furthermore, as we saw above in Odysseus's deliberative monologue from *Iliad* 11, after he has addressed his *thumos* a character will sometimes ask, "but why does my spirit debate this with me?"[27] Thus, in Homeric deliberative self-address, *thumos* seems

---

27. See Engel 1997, 71–72.

to stand in for the self-regarding self, the self as it appears in our self-conscious reflections upon our motivation and action, a point which will be of crucial significance for our understanding of *to thumoeides* in the *Republic*. Unlike other instances of deliberative self-address in Homer, when Odysseus addresses his heart here, he does not offer arguments for and against a particular course of action. Instead, Odysseus addresses his heart as a superior to an inferior; he rebukes (ἠνίπαπε) his heart, as he rebuked (ἠνίπαπε) Thersites at *Iliad* 2.245, and he commands his heart to endure. Moreover, he does not offer his heart reasons why it should endure in this case. Rather, he reminds his heart of what it has suffered and how its obedient endurance has saved it in the past. This, too, is unique in Homer, that the heart is said to be obedient, a point that is emphasized in the passage with the pleonastic "endured and stood fast in perseverance" (μένε τετληυῖα νωλεμέως). As in *Republic* 374e–376c, Odysseus's *thumos* is compared to a dog "angered at a man she does not know," and it is this anger that Odysseus is responding to with his rebuke; he is, in effect, calling his heart to heel.

9.4 *Thumos* and Self-Consciousness

At first glance this example of "self-mastery" seems quite appropriate to the parallel between city and soul around which the *Republic* is structured. As Socrates glosses the passage, "Homer clearly presents that which has calculated [τὸ ἀναλογισάμενον] about better and worse as reproving [ἐπιπλῆττον] that which is irrationally [ἀλογίστως] spirited as though it were a different part," which seems consonant with the idea that the calculative part rules and the spirited part obeys (441e). However, on closer inspection, the passage indicates a cleavage between city and soul, and a problem for Socrates' demonstration of the division between calculation and spirit. This is due to the fact that both in the passage itself and in Socrates' gloss on it, "that which has calculated" does not offer reasons to spirit but instead emotively and rhetorically asserts its *authority* over "unreasoning" spirit, in effect putting spirit in its place. Such a blank assertion of authority makes sense in a strictly political context, where no matter how coolly rational one imagines a ruler to be, one can also imagine that ruler choosing to adopt emotive rhetoric when speaking to those over whom she rules. It makes little if any sense, however, in the context of the "rule" calculation exerts over spirit. Socrates' invocation of Odysseus's struggle with his *thumos* raises the very question which, it is commonplace to suppose, the introduction of the *thumoeidic* soul in the *Republic* is intended to solve: how does calculation acquire emotive force? It would seem to be the case that either (1) calculation would have to already be emotive for it to coax or threaten irrational spirit to obey its commands, or (2) spirit would have to already be rational for it to accept calculation's reasons for obedience.

The difficulty alluded to here is, I suggest, an intentional artifact of the city-soul analogy, insofar as that analogy implies something like a calculative-self asserting its mastery over a spirited-self. The social-political relations between the parts of the soul seem to demand, as T. H. Irwin has argued,[28] a degree of self-awareness present in each part. Unlike Irwin, however, I believe that this fact serves as Plato's way of posing a problem rather than offering a solution to one. In the first instance, this is the problem of implicitly social or political character of the self-regarding or self-conscious self. One way of stating this problem is that insofar as the three parts of the soul each are subject to social and political determination each appears not as a distinct part but rather as three modifications of the *thumoeidic* or "honor-loving" soul. This is most clearly suggested by Socrates' account of the decline of the regimes in books 8 and 9. Consider in this context the central role that societal recognition and questions of shame and honor play in each transition between father and son in the decline of character types, and Socrates' claim at 551a that in every regime type "what is honored is practiced and what is without honor is neglected." Consider, in particular, Socrates' description of the ascent of the appetitive part to the "throne of the soul" in the transition from dishonored timocratic father to oligarchic son.

> And the son, my friend, seeing and suffering this and having lost his substance, is frightened, I suppose, and thrusts love of honor and spiritedness headlong out of the throne of his soul; and humbled by poverty, he turns greedily to money-making; and bit by bit saving and working, he collects money. Don't you suppose that such a man now puts the desiring and money-loving part on the throne, and makes it the great king within himself, girding it with tiaras, collars, and Persian swords. . . .
>
> And, I suppose, he makes the calculating and spirited parts sit by it on the ground . . . and be slaves. (553b–d)

Here, in the passage that is supposed to signal the transition from a soul type dominated by honor to one dominated by pleasure, that very transition is

---

28. Irwin 1995, 214–22. This is an aspect of the broader controversy in the literature concerning whether or not Socrates' account of the parts of the soul requires the supposition of subpersonal agents or "homunculi" within the soul. For references, see most recently Gerson 2004, 107n17; and Bobonich 1994, 3n4.

imaginatively represented in terms of public honor and dishonor: the desiring principle is crowned and decorated, and the honor-loving aspect of the soul is forced into abject obeisance. As I have tried to stress in my analysis of Socrates' encounters with Cephalus, Polemarchus, and Thrasymachus in book 1, the problem of the political character of the self-conscious appropriation of a way of life and a justification for that way of life dominates Socrates' dialogic encounters throughout the *Republic*. In this broad sense, the problem of *to thumoeides* is the problem of the social and political aspect of any self-conscious appropriation of a conception of worth or value, and in this sense the problem of *to thumoeides* is already very much on display in Socrates' conversations in book 1. At a deeper level, however, the question raised by Socrates' account of the *thumoeidic* aspect of soul is the question of the self-conscious self or soul in its unity or disunity. Reflecting on previous chapters, we can see this question intimated in two inter-related ways. The first concerns the unity or disunity of the self or soul insofar as it is understood as both cognitive and affective;[29] the second concerns whether, and in what sense, we can attribute self-identity to the soul.[30] We will return to the question of soul's self-identity or non-self-identity in the penultimate section of this chapter in the context of Plato's account of human openness to that which transcends the self or soul. But to understand Plato's account of our openness to that which transcends the self or soul, we must see more clearly his portrait of that which needs to be transcended. This, I will argue, is the function of Socrates' account of *to thumoeides* in the *Republic*. It is his way of making imaginatively concrete a mistaken conception the political character of the human soul. While this mistaken conception is closely allied in Socrates' presentation to the sophistic theories of human creative activity associated with Gorgias and Protagoras, Socrates' invocation of Odysseus's struggle with his *thumos* indicates that they have merely refined and made explicit a misconception of the soul that is intrinsic to political life, and intrinsic to human soul insofar as it strives to be a self and manifest an identity.

---

29. The opposition between cognitive and conative aspects of the soul was implicit both in the separation between "ethos" and "worldview" we saw in Socrates' encounter with Cephalus and in the conflict between virtues conceived as dispositions and virtues conceived as cognitive capacities we saw as central to Socrates *elenchus* of Polemarchus's view of political action. It became thematic in Thrasymachus's dichotomy between the art or science of rhetorical persuasion and the ethical-psychological matter of that art, a dichotomy we saw elaborated and refined in Protagoras's opposition between the form-giving power of poetic representation and the passive receptivity he chooses to call "political virtue."

30. The question of the soul's self-identity is raised most forcefully by the apparent indeterminacy attributed by Gorgias and Protagoras to human "material" existence prior to the work of the Sophist or poet or legislator; but it is also suggested, in a quite different sense, by the portrait of Socrates as the embodiment of "daimonic" eros.

9.5 To Thumo-eides

As Seth Benardete has observed, the name Socrates gives to the aspect of soul concerned with honor is strange. While in Homeric usage *thumos* had a semantic range that allows it to be translated in various contexts by such disparate English words as "soul," "life," "desire," "will," and "mind," by the time Plato composed the *Republic,* Xenophon could write in clarification of the term that *thumos* is in horses precisely what anger (ὀργή) is in human beings; as Glaucon's comment at 441a suggests, *thumos* seems to have lost the intimate connection with deliberation we find in Homer and had come to mean something like "brute" assertiveness or aggression.[31] As if to compensate for this loss of a cognitive component to the concept of *thumos,* Socrates apparently coins the term *to thumoeides.*

To thumoeides is formed in a different way from the principal terms for the other parts of the soul. *To logistikon* (the calculative) and *to epithumêtikon* (the appetitive) are simply substantive uses of the adjectives *logistikos* and *epithumêtikos,* the strict parallel for "the spirited" should be *to thumikon,* and there is no grammatical reason for avoiding this formulation.[32] However, Socrates chooses to call the spirited aspect of soul *to thumoeides,* and not only does the addition of the suffix -ειδής seem unnecessary, but it is difficult to understand what this neologism should mean. Elsewhere in Plato this suffix means "with the form of" or "like," but it is far from obvious what it could mean to say that some aspect of the soul was "*thumos*-like" or "had the form of *thumos.*"[33] If, however, we focus on the etymological relationship between -*eidês* and *eidos,* we seem to be asked to view *to thumoeides* as running together or combining the notion of brute assertiveness with the notion of perceived shape of form. On this view, Socrates' choice of the term *to thumoeides* would gesture toward a fundamental duality in the soul as both *thumic* and *eidetic;* it is yet another question whether we are to understand this duality primarily in terms of an opposition between "will" and "representation," or primarily in terms of an opposition between conation and cognition.

That it is the former possibility we should first pursue is suggested when we look to Socrates' one use in the *Republic* of *theoeidês* (godlike), the most common

---

31. See Benardete 1989b, 55; and Koziak 1999.

32. See Aristotle *De an.* 432a25, 433b4.

33. This sense is evident in, e.g., Timaeus's repeated claims that the heavens have the form of a sphere (σφαιροειδής) or Socrates' claim in the *Cratylus* that Pan's lower half is goatlike (τραγοειδής). It is, of course, less clear exactly what Socrates means when he famously claims at 509a that vision and light are "'sun-like" and knowledge and truth are "good-like" (ἀγαθοειδής). Indeed, this lack of clarity is explicitly thematized in that passage as belonging to the attempt to offer an image or likeness of that which is "beyond being."

word with the suffix -eidês in Greek poetry or prose, indeed the only relatively common word with this morphology outside of medical texts or pre-Socratic cosmology. The passage in question is Socrates' description at 501b of the philosopher-rulers as artists working in the medium of human souls, artists who "make in human beings the image of a human being, basing their judgment on that which Homer also called, when it came to be in human beings, the likeness and the image of god [θεοειδές τε καὶ θεοείκελον]."[34] Taking this use of theoeidês as our context, the -eidês in to thumoeides seems meant to draw attention to the significance of "likeness" and "form" in Socrates' account of the thumoeidic soul. As we will see, Socrates presents to thumoeides as that aspect of soul through which human beings mimetically give form to themselves and others, and through which they are formed. Moreover, his account of to thumoeides presents it as embodying the same problematic duality between "material" and "formal" elements we have seen at work in the sophistic conception of rhetorical persuasion.

When he first discusses the formative power of "music," Socrates treats the soul as an indefinite quasi-material medium which is given shape by the process of education (377a–b). As Jonathan Lear notes, the Republic presents the soul of a young human being as if it were "a plastic resin, able to receive the impress of cultural influences before it sets into definite shape,"[35] and on Socrates' account, it is the thumoeidic soul which provides the key to this process of cultural formation. Indeed, a large part of Socrates' discussion of thumos focuses on how to produce the proper "consistency" in the plastic material of the soul, so that it best receives and preserves the impress made upon it by the laws of the city. When considering the question of the appropriate balance between music and gymnastic in the education of the guardians, Socrates claims that the souls of those who focus exclusively on gymnastic exhibit "savageness and hardness" (ἀγριότητός τε καὶ σκληρότητος), while those who focus exclusively on music exhibit "softness and tameness" (μαλακίας τε καὶ ἡμερότητος, 410d). He likens the correct training of the spirited part of the soul to the "tightening" of the strings of a musical instrument; if correctly tightened, it produces someone with courage, but if tightened too much, it produces someone "hard and difficult" (σκληρόν τε καὶ χαλεπὸν, 410d). He compares the effect of music on the spirited part of the soul to the softening of iron for forging, making something soft and useful from something "useless and hard." Too much music is to be avoided, however, because it "melts and liquefies" a guardian's spirit, making him

---

34. See §6.7, above.
35. Lear 1994, 140.

spiritless and a "feeble warrior" (411a–b). Finally, Socrates describes the virtue proper to the guardians, "political courage," as a "preserving of the opinion produced by law through education about what—and what sort of thing—is terrible" (429c–d). In this context, Socrates describes the proper education as like the preparation of a piece of cloth so that it will receive and preserve the color given to by a dyer, and explicitly likens the "right and lawful opinion about what is terrible" to a colorfast dye (430a–b).

This "materialist" description of the educational power of poetry and the character of *thumoeides* is not the dominant feature of Socrates' account, however. The greater part of Socrates' account of poetry focuses on the representational content of that poetry—what kinds of stories about gods, heroes, and human beings should be permitted in the city in speech—and, no less than the materialist description, Socrates' account of representational content seems to concern the *thumoeidic* aspect of soul. The critique and revision of the poetic representation of heroes undertaken in book 3, in particular, focuses on the question whether the poets provide politically salutary models for imitative emulation, and both the virtues aimed at and psychological processes at work in character formation are described in *thumoeidic* terms: courage and honor, righteous indignation and shame. These emotions and virtues, like the ideational content of *thumoeides* itself, seem principally constituted by an individual's self-conception and his implicit understanding of his relation to the social and political world. Insofar as imitative poetry is presented in the *Republic* as primarily influencing what is considered honorable or shameful, what is to be feared and what is not to be feared, imitative poetry concerns the emotional and representational content Socrates associates with *to thumoeides*. Moreover, as we have seen in the context of the critique of mimetic poetry in book 10, Socrates claims that "the irascible" (τὸ ἀγανακτητικόν) aspect of soul is both that aspect of soul which is most easily imitated, and the part of the soul to which poetic imitation is directed.

Given this apparent bifurcation between the material and representational in Socrates' account of the musical education of the guardians and the *thumoeidic* soul, we must ask what relation there is between the two. I suggest that our discussion of Protagoras's account of human representational capacity, when viewed in the context of Socrates' encounters with Gorgias and Thrasymachus, provides us with the tools to understand this relation. *To thumoeides*, I suggest, is Socrates' imaginative articulation of the hypothesis that underlies both Protagoras's conception of human creative activity and Socrates' conception of the legislative activity of the philosopher-rulers. *To thumoeides* represents what the soul would have to be like if the hypothesis of doxastic immanence that governs the explicit argument of the *Republic* were held to be true; it is the soul conceived as an indefinite duality of "will" and "representation." That is, Socrates' presentation of *to thumoeides* is Plato's analogue to the thought experiment Nietzsche describes in aphorism 36 of his *Beyond Good and Evil,* the aphorism in which Nietzsche asks his readers to suppose that "we could not get down, or up, to any other 'reality' besides the reality of our drives." This is a conception of the soul in which the distinction between "form" and "matter" is understood as a distinction between that which *forms* and that which is *given form* by another. It is allied with a conception of "education" in which there is no ultimate distinction between *teaching* and *persuasion.*

Consider in this context the fact that in each of Socrates' conversations with these three representatives of sophistic, the rhetorical displays of the Sophist are metaphorically described in the same quasi-material terms we have seen at work in Socrates' description of musical education. In the *Republic,* Thrasymachus's rhetorical tirade is likened to "a great shower of speech" poured in the ears of his audience (344d), and Thrasymachus threatens to "stuff" Socrates' soul with his argument (345b). Similarly, in the *Gorgias,* Socrates and Callicles liken Gorgias's rhetorical display (ἐπίδειξις) to a feast (*Gorg.* 447a). However, it is the occurrence of this metaphor in the *Protagoras* that is most striking. In his warning to Hippocrates about the danger of going to study under a Sophist, Socrates describes their teachings as "wares upon which the soul is fed" (*Protag.* 313c). Socrates claims that the great danger of going to one of these merchants of learning is that, while other kinds of foodstuffs can be taken home in a separate container and examined by an expert before they are ingested, one cannot do this with learning. "On the contrary, having paid the price, you necessarily take what is learned into your very soul, and depart either benefited or harmed" (314b).

Consider how strange it seems for Socrates to present learning as the passive acquisition of a quasi-material teaching. Do we think that Socrates ever considered himself harmed by a "learning," or that he thought of himself as a passive recipient of "learning" which he did not know whether it was bad for him or good for him? On the contrary, I believe that it is clear that the conception of "knowledge" Socrates is invoking here is the one seen at work in Gorgias's and Protagoras's accounts of "education," which amounts to nothing more than authoritative persuasion. It is, moreover, not difficult to see that this kind of authoritative persuasion dominates Socrates' account of the relations between the philosopher-rulers and the guardian-auxiliaries. The most obvious manifestation of this is the necessity of lies in both the education of the guardians and the rule exercised over them by the philosopher-rulers. However, it can also be seen in the radical disjunction between the distinctly philosophic education of the philosopher-rulers and the musical education of the guardian-auxiliaries discussed in chapter 7. If the mathematical and dialectical education the philosopher-rulers receive is a necessary precondition for their own understanding of the goodness and justice of the legislation they enact, it seems that the guardian-auxiliaries cannot understand the goodness and justice of that legislation except as it is dependent on their assumption of the goodness and justice of the philosopher-ruler.

As I argued in §2.3 above, the *Republic* presents character development as dependent on the process by which an individual internalizes and identifies with a variety of different kinds of lives, life-projects, and modes of social justification. And, as we have seen in our analysis of Socrates' account of the democratic soul (§2.4), Socrates presents this process as an internalization of image-like representations of paradigmatic human lives. The full significance of the fact can only be recognized, however, once we see that this claim extends to the role of *reason* in the development of human character. That is, Socrates seems to limit the role that reason plays in the education of everyone except the philosopher-ruler to the internalization of the *image of reason* as authoritative. Within Socrates' city in speech, this image of reason is the internalized representation of the philosopher-ruler in the souls of the guardian auxiliaries and the craftsmen, outside of the city in speech this image of reason is the internalized representation of the philosophic individual.

Consider, in this context, Socrates' account of the genesis of the timocratic man at the beginning of the decline of regimes. He describes a young man of a "good father who lives in a city that is not under a good regime," a man who is not serious about money or public honors. The young man's mother complains that the reason for his father's failure to engage seriously in public affairs is that he lacks courage. This complaint is echoed by the domestic servants of the household, who see that the father does not prosecute those who owe him money or have committed "some other injustice" against him. They "urge the son to punish all such men when he becomes a man, and thus to be more of a man than his father." Furthermore, when the son goes out into the city, he hears similar charges levied against "those in the city who mind their own business," who are called "simpletons and held in small account." The young man's development into a timocratic individual is then explained as the outcome of a tug-of-war in his soul between two influences: on the one hand, he hears these complaints and charges levied against his father by his mother, the household servants, and many in the city; on the other hand, he hears his father's arguments and sees his practices first-hand. Socrates says, "His father waters the calculating part of his soul, and causes it to grow; the others, the desiring and spirited parts. Because he doesn't have a bad man's nature, but has kept bad company with others, drawn by both of these

influences, he came to the middle, and turned over the rule in himself to the middle part, the part that loves victory and is spirited; he became a haughty-minded
man who loves honor" (550a–b).

What is most striking about this account is the fact that both the influence of
the young man's father on the calculative aspect of his soul and the influence of
everyone else on the spirited and appetitive parts are described in precisely the
same quasi-material terms. Each "waters" a part of the soul and each "draws" the
young man in one direction or another. Moreover, the spatial metaphor wherein
the three aspects of soul are described as relatively "higher" or "lower" seems to
be taken quite literally in this account. The competing "influences" drawing the
young man toward the calculative, the spirited and appetitive aspects of soul, are
treated as if they were physical vector forces, whose resolution leaves the young
man in the "middle." Hence he turns over the rule in himself to the "middle"
aspect of soul and becomes a lover of honor. Socrates does not suggest that the
young man *comprehends* the truth of any of his father's arguments, and thus
understands why his mother's complaints should not be taken at face value.
Indeed, nowhere in this story—nor, for that matter, in any of the genetic accounts
Socrates offers in the decline of the regimes—does Socrates suggest that the young
person exercises any judgment concerning the various sociocultural influences
which are said to form his character.

Consonant with the interpretation I have offered of the immanent philosophic orientation of the *Republic,* Socrates seems to describe the representation
of reason in the lives of most human beings as representationally *opaque.* That
is, the representation of reason in the lives of those who are not philosophers
does not inherently point beyond itself to a good which it can only imperfectly
instantiate. Instead, it functions as a motivational and intellective terminus.
The arguments and practices of the "good man" who is father to the timocratic
son, for example, are not taken by his son to gesture toward some good beyond
those arguments and practices, and which those arguments and practices only
imperfectly instantiate. Instead, the son internalizes an imaginative representation
of his father, and it is that internalized representation *itself* which embodies the
motivational force of reason in the young man's life. This internalized representation of the father figure, however, is not said to point beyond itself. It does not
lead the son to reflect upon the reasons why his father should be considered
good. Like Gorgias's self-conception as the "good" which guides the actions of
his students, the "idea of the good" in this young man's soul is simply the internalized representation of his father *as* good. Consider the fact that Socrates'
description of the good father—like his description of the *idea* of the good itself
in books 7 and 8—gives no positive content to the good to which the father

aspires or embodies. He is said to "water the calculative part" of the young man's soul, but we are given no positive sense of what makes his actions or arguments good, either in themselves or for the young man. Instead, he is described wholly negatively, in terms of those things that he does *not* honor, desire, or take seriously. He is said to flee the honors, ruling offices, and lawsuits which dominate the public life of the less-than-good regime of which he is a citizen (549c). He is said to be not very serious about money and to neither honor nor dishonor his wife very much (549d). Most significantly, Socrates does not represent the father as engaged in philosophic activity. He is not said to turn his mind toward the things that *are;* rather, he is perceived to have his mind always turned toward *himself* (ἑαυτῷ μὲν τὸν νοῦν προσέχοντα ἀει, 549d).

It is most of all his apparent self-sufficiency, that is, his *indifference* to the opinions of his fellow citizens, that seems to define the goodness of the good father. This indifference, in one form or another, dominates the description of the philosopher throughout the *Republic,* from Socrates' claim in book 1 that the "decent man," despising both money and honors, would choose to rule only to avoid the penalty of having to be ruled by a worse man (347a–e), through his account of the true philosopher who "has no leisure to look down toward the affairs of human beings" (500b–c), his description of philosopher-rulers as those "least eager to rule" (520d), and culminating with Glaucon's admission that, if what Socrates has said is true, the good man "won't be willing to mind the political things" (592a).[36] Moreover, we can recognize that such apparent self-sufficiency is central to the appeal Socrates has for many of the characters with whom he associates in the dialogues; Socrates appears to them to be a paradigm of self-mastery and self-sufficiency. In the *Symposium,* Apollodorus uses the same turn of phrase to describe Socrates in a moment of apparent philosophic reflection that Socrates uses above to describe the attitude of the father of the timocratic man. In this moment, Apollodorus says, Socrates was "turning his mind toward himself" (Σωκράτη ἑαυτῷ πως προσέχοντα τὸν νοῦν, *Symp.* 174d).[37] For Alcibiades in the same dialogue, Socrates is a divine model of temperance, whose divinity is best exemplified by the fact that he despises (καταφρονεῖ) whatever wealth, honors, or physical beauty a man may have, even that of the most beautiful and

---

36. The theme of self-sufficiency will be further elaborated in the following chapter in terms of Socrates' engagement with what I will term the "narcissistic" character of the ethical and psychological orientations of Glaucon and Adeimantus. See also Ferrari 2003, 11–34.

37. In contrast, Socrates has Diotima say that he should "try as much as possible to turn your mind toward *me*" (πειρῶ δέ μοι . . . τὸν νοῦν προσέχειν ὡς οἷόν τε μάλιστα, *Symp.* 210e) as she prepares to tell him about the "wonderful vision beautiful in its nature" that is that for the sake of which the lover of beauty toils.

honored Athenian of his time, Alcibiades himself. What these lovers of Socrates do not see, or do not understand, is the implication of Socrates' poetic association of himself with *daimonic* Eros. The *daimonic,* on Socrates' account, is nothing *in itself;* it is beautiful or good only insofar as it directs one toward that which is itself beautiful or good. What Socrates' followers take for divine self-sufficiency, Socrates himself presents as seeing beyond the self toward the divine and intelligible. Like Alcibiades, they do not heed Socrates' warning to "look closer, in case you are deceived and I am nothing" (ἄμεινον σκόπει, μή σε λανθάνω οὐδὲν ὤν, 219a) Indeed, as we will see in greater detail in the remainder of this chapter and the next, for Socrates the possibility of philosophy essentially involves seeing beyond the boundaries of the self, to a reality whose intelligibility is not conceived as constituted by and through our sense-making practices.

9.6 "But you endured until mêtis led you out of the cave . . ."

I have argued that Socrates' invocation of Odysseus rebuking his doglike heart points us toward the problem of *thumoeides* as the central problem of the *Republic.* I will now argue that returning the passage will indicate another reason for Socrates' profound interest in it. As I have suggested, Odysseus's struggle with his heart exemplifies his capacity to distance himself from his socially and politically determined self. The question is, of course, how Odysseus is able to achieve this distance. As we have seen, there are reasons to doubt the adequacy of Socrates' claim that what we see here is the calculative part of Odysseus's soul "ruling" over the spirited part. Instead, Odysseus's words imply that his capacity to stand apart from his *thumoeidic* self is predicated on his recognition of a kind of intelligence that is emphatically contrasted with the notion of the intellect as a kind of self, the same recognition which, I have suggested, is crucial to understanding Socrates dialogic practice.

Odysseus recalls to his heart his stratagem in the cave of the Cyclops, an episode which he recounts in his "story of Alcinous"[38] and which presents in mythic form the denial and deferral of name and station that epitomize Odysseus throughout the *Odyssey.* Essential to Odysseus's characterization of the Cyclops, as Aristotle saw, is their lack of any communal life and concomitant disregard for the most fundamental human sanctions. Odysseus's encounter with the Cyclops Polyphemos represents the most extreme isolation from the social and political world within which the name of Odysseus finds its meaning. His stratagem,

---

38. Cf. *Resp.* 614b.

famously, is to tell Polyphemos that his name is *Outis,* "nobody," so that when Odysseus and his companions succeed in blinding Polyphemos, and Polyphemos attempts to enlist the aid of other Cyclops by crying out, "Nobody is killing me by treachery and not by force," they take him to be babbling. Significantly, when Odysseus recalls this story, saying to his heart, "intelligence led you out from the cave," the word he uses for intelligence is *mêtis,* a punning reference to the relation between *mêtis* (intelligence), *mê-tis* (that no one, that nothing), and *outis* (nobody).[39] Outside of the social context in which his name carries authority, and thrust into an environment where who he is either lacks meaning or presents a positive danger, Odysseus survives by means of an intelligence that is not dependent on one particular social and political world, by a *mêtis* that is *outis.* This intelligence allows him both to take on other characters and to conform himself to different social worlds, and allows him to endure the indignity of his beggarly disguise until he can reclaim his place in his home and homeland; it binds together his three characteristic epithets: *polumêtis, polutropos,* and *polutlas.*

This preliminary sketch of what I have called Odysseus's interiority can, I suggest, help us understand Socrates' dialogic activity in a number of ways. First, it provides a context in which to understand what we might call the prudential aspect of Socratic irony, which Aristotle characterizes as a disavowal of "qualities that bring reputation."[40] Second, it can help us understand Socrates' strategic and pedagogical deployment in the dialogues of the *figure of Socrates*—a subject we have touched upon in our discussion of the *Symposium* in chapter 7. Third, and most significantly for our discussion of Socrates in the *Republic,* it suggests the crucial contrast between Socrates and the great majority of his interlocutors: Socrates' interlocutors, with a few possible exceptions, always display an intelligence that *is someone.* What Nietzsche claims to have discovered about every great philosopher previous to him is true of the characters to whom Socrates speaks in the dialogues: their thinking about the world is "a personal confession of its author and a kind of involuntary and unconscious memoir" (BGE 6). At the root of this "confession" and "memoir," Nietzsche claims, is a drive (*Trieb*) that "would only like too well to represent just *itself* as the ultimate purpose of existence and the legitimate *master* of all other drives." Plato's characters display, in their conversations with Socrates, a self-deceptive vision of the world distorted to carry the self-justifying meaning they project on to it. It is this self-deceptive, self-justifying vision of the world rather than any individual mistaken belief about the world that is the primary object of Socrates' elenctic activity.

---

39. See Goldhill 1991, 34–35; and Casevitz 1989, 55.
40. *Eth. Nic.* 1127b24–5.

9.7 The Lie in the Soul and Socratic Awareness of Ignorance

Near the end of Socrates' discussion with Adeimantus concerning the appropriate models the lawgivers will set down concerning imitative poetry in book
2, he introduces the notion of what he calls the "true lie" (ἀληθῶς ψεῦδος), a
pathema in the soul he distinguishes from a mere "lie in words." As opposed to
the true lie, Socrates says, "that in words [ἐν τοῖς λόγοις] is a kind of imitation
[μίμημά τι] of the experience in the soul, and an image [εἴδωλον] of it that
comes into being after it, and not quite an unadulterated lie" (382a–c). Insofar as
Socrates equates the true lie with ignorance (a claim to which we will return
below), it might seem advisable in this instance to translate the key term *pseudos*
as "falsehood" rather than "lie" in order to avoid the apparent attribution of
intentional deception to a state of ignorance, a state which might seem better
characterized as merely "an emptiness of the soul's condition" (585b) and not an
artifact of intentional activity of any kind.[41] However, Socrates is quite insistent
in choosing to characterize the true *pseudos* in terms of the self's relation to the
self. One lies truly, Socrates says, when one lies "to what is most sovereign in
himself about the most sovereign matters" (382a); to lie truly is "to lie and to have
lied to the soul about the things that are" (382b). Even that aspect of the passage
under examination which might seem to militate against the notion that the true
lie is to be understood as a kind of self-deception can be interpreted to support
that very claim. In the closest thing to a definition of the true lie offered in
the passage Socrates says that what "would most correctly called the true lie" is
ignorance in the soul of *tou epseusmenou*, a word that can be translated as either
"the one who is mistaken" or "the one who has been lied to." However, the form
of the participle is ambiguous between the middle and passive voice and could
be construed to mean something like "the one who lies with respect to himself."
Given the apparent lack of analogous uses of the verb ψεύδω in the literature,
we would be advised to resist this interpretation were it not for the fact that
Socrates explicitly claims not only that the lie in speech is an *imitation* of the lie
in the soul, but "comes into being after it" (ὕστερον γεγονὸς). If, as Socrates
claims, the lie in speech is both logically and temporally posterior to the lie in the
soul, it cannot be the case that it is the result of "having been lied to" by another.
Rather, as I have been suggesting, the "lie in the soul" is the imaginary representation of the self to the self which, in the context of the *Republic,* seems to be
constitutive of the social or political self as such.

Identifying the social or political self with falsehood in this way, however, does
not mean that the self is simply to be understood as an impediment to intellection.

41. I have discussed the problematic character of this characterization of ignorance in §7.10 above.

Instead, it appears to be what Stewart Umphrey has called an "enabling imped-iment." What Socrates says is true of the body in the *Phaedo* is also true of the self so conceived; it is not itself *aitios* but is that without which an *aition* could never be *aitios*; it is what we can call a "material condition" of our experience of the world. Like Aristotle's or Timaeus's conception of "matter," the self is not an independently intelligible "this." Indeed, considered in abstraction from the intelligible form (λογός) it receives, it can only be said to exist in a qualified sense. The self *is* and is intelligible, on this account, as an orientation to an intelligi-bility which transcends both the self and the beings as disclosed within that orientation. In the *Phaedo,* as we have seen, Socrates claims to contemplate the *truth* of the beings in words (ἐν τοῖς λόγοις) and deeds (ἐν τοῖς ἔργοις) under-stood as images (εἰκόνες); we can now understand that claim in relation to Socrates' description of the lie in words (ἐν τοῖς λόγοις) as an image (εἴδωλον) or imitation (μίμημα) of the lie in the soul in the following way. As we have seen in our discussion of the philosophic significance of mimetic poetry in the previous chapter, to take human arguments and actions as images is to see them as *meaningful* expressions of our ethical and psychological orientations to the world of our experience. As such, they are expressions of the limitations of our particular perspective that *as images* of that perspective involve refer-ence to an intelligibility that transcends that perspective. They involve not merely the *pathos* that is that particular perspective, but a perception of *what it is to be* that perspective.

One way of construing the Socratic response to the underlying hypothesis of much of modern philosophy—that we can only know what we are responsible for or make—would be to suggest that we could only know what we are respon-sible for or make if we already knew who we are in the most significant respect. And, if we know anything of Socrates, we know that he does not believe he knows who he is in the most significant respect. What can be difficult to understand in this context, however, is what makes Socrates' awareness of his own igno-rance different from the skepticism that, as I have tried to show, pervades the cultural environment in which he pursued his philosophic mission. Moreover, it can be difficult to understand both the sense in which Socrates' awareness of his ignorance is an active philosophizing, rather than a more or less dogmatic stance regarding the fallibility of human knowledge, and how it is a philosophic achievement. Our account of *to thumoeides* can suggest the beginnings of a response to these questions. Plato's Socrates believes, as Nietzsche does, that a human being's orientation to the world is inseparable from some narrative of self-justification, some account of the ways in which that human being's life is a life worth living. Moreover, Plato's Socrates agrees with Nietzsche that this narrative of self-justification is largely constituted by an implicit account of the individual's relation to the social and political world. Finally, Plato's Socrates seems to believe that each individual comprises more than one such narrative of self-justification, and that an inquiry into the self is a confrontation with an indefinite multiplicity of such narratives—hypotheses regarding the good that insofar as they are unrecognized as hypotheses are mistaken for the truth. These are, I suggest, the "true lies" in the soul that Socrates refers to in book 2.

Unlike the science of knowledge and lack of knowledge that Critias attempts to defend in the *Charmides* (166eff.), Socrates' awareness of his own ignorance, I suggest, is inseparable from his awareness of the problem of *to thumoeides,* and from his mimetic capacity for sharing in the experience of those with whom he converses. It is this that ultimately differentiates Socrates' philosophic activity from both the direct metaphysical speculation of his pre-Socratic predecessors and the theoretical and practical activity of his sophistic opponents. Socrates' inquiries with his various interlocutors reveal the connections between the different narratives individuals or communities tell themselves to justify a particular way of living and the commitments of these individuals or communities to what counts as *real* in their experience of the world. He uncovers the implicit imaginative relations between who it is these characters believe they should be, what they believe they can know, and what they take to be most real. So understood, Socrates' theoretical inquiries are inseparable from his dialogic encounters with others and his interrogation of their convictions. Unlike the philosophical activity of the philosopher-ruler, Socrates' philosophizing is not and cannot be separated from his political activity. It is inseparable from his awareness of the necessarily social and political character of our representational capacity. However, as I have argued in chapter 7, it is equally inseparable from his recognition of the limitations of the attempt to understand such representational capacity in abstraction from an intelligibility that informs and makes such representation possible.

9.8 Philosophic Image-Making

As we have seen, and as is now generally recognized, Socratic arguments are ad hominem in the specific sense that in conversation with others, Socrates will often implicitly adopt the perspective of his interlocutor. We have seen this aspect of Socrates' dialogic practice at work in his conversations with Glaucon (§§2.10–11), Polemarchus (§§3.2–5), and Thrasymachus (§4.4). Moreover, in our analysis of these conversations, and Socrates' conversations with Gorgias and Protagoras, we have seen that Socrates' role-playing, like Odysseus's, is often for the sake of testing those with whom he speaks. Moreover, as with Odysseus, there are good reasons for assuming that Socrates often adopts his roles for the sake of protecting himself or others. Indeed, Socrates' esotericism in the *Gorgias* and the *Protagoras* seems to be more for the sake of his audience, and even for the sake of his sophistic opponents, than for his own sake. To choose one example, while Socrates is willing to use the tensions between the esoteric and exoteric elements of Protagoras's speech in his dialogue with Protagoras, he does not choose to make explicit what Protagoras has left implicit. He leaves such work to people like Critias.

However, even if we accept this as a partial account of Socratic irony insofar as that irony pervades Socrates' conversations with his interlocutors, we must still account for the other aspects of Socrates' poetic activity. We must account, not only for Socrates' activity as a participant in dialogues, but also for his poetic activity as a maker of myths, as a fashioner of the "image of a man" in his account of the philosopher-rulers, and, finally, as the author of his own narration in dialogues such as the *Republic* and the *Protagoras*. We must ask: what distinguishes these aspects of Socrates' "true political art" from the image-making activity espoused by Protagoras? To begin to answer these question, I will turn once again to Achilles and Odysseus. I will suggest that not only can Achilles and Odysseus be seen occupying opposite extremes on a spectrum of relative exteriority and interiority in their respective relations to the social and political world, but they can also be seen as representing two different kinds of *poetic* response to that social and political world.

I have suggested that after the failure of Phoenix, Ajax, and Odysseus in their attempt to persuade Achilles to forsake his anger and return to battle, the *Iliad* becomes the narrative of Achilles' unconscious externalization of the conflict in his soul, and that this can explain both why Achilles is the only character in the *Iliad* who is represented as himself a poet, and why the shield given to him by Hephaestus seems to represent the power of poetry as, quite literally, world-creating. On the surface of Achilles' shield, Hephaestus is said to make the earth, the sky, the seas, the sun, and all the constellations in heaven. He makes two cities of mortal men, one displaying the inner workings of the city, in marriages, festivals, and civil proceedings, the other displaying the city at war with two forces of armed men. He represents the tilling of the fields, and their harvesting; domesticated and wild animals; even the gods Ares and Athena find their way into the vast tableau Hephaestus creates. In this way, Hephaestus's crafting of Achilles' shield parallels the sophistic imitator in book 10 who becomes a "maker of all things" by holding a mirror up to everything that is (596c–e).

I will now suggest that Hephaestus, the craftsman god, is invoked in the *Odyssey* is a similar way. As in the *Iliad*, Hephaestus's craft seems intended in the *Odyssey* to represent the power of poetry, and as was the case in the *Iliad*, this power is implicitly attributed to the hero of the poem. However, the character and power of Hephaestus's poetic craft as represented in the *Odyssey* is quite different from the world-creating power attributed to that craft in the *Iliad*. Hephaestus's craft is presented in the *Odyssey* as serving two distinct functions on two different levels, which correspond, I will argue, to the two different levels on which Odysseus's own poetic capacity operates. I will further suggest that these same two levels are at work in Socrates' "poetic" art.

In *Odyssey* book 8, shortly before Odysseus begins the narrative of his travels which will occupy the majority of the next four books, Alcinous summons the minstrel Demodocus to entertain the as yet unrecognized stranger Odysseus. Demodocus is said to sing of the love of Ares and Aphrodite, but, as soon becomes apparent, the bulk of his tale concerns not this love, but the revenge enacted against the lovers by the cuckolded Hephaestus. When Hephaestus hears the "heart-grieving tale" (θυμαλγέα μῦθον), he descends into his smithy and in his wrath against Ares forges a "snare" (δόλον) to capture the god of war. His snare is said to be made of bonds as fine as a spider's web, "so guilefully forged that not even the blessed gods could see them" (τά γ' οὔ κέ τις οὐδὲ ἴδοιτο, οὐδὲ θεῶν μακάρων· περὶ γὰρ δολόεντα τέτυκτο). Hephaestus arrays the invisible threads of his *dolos* all around the bed that he shares with Aphrodite, and pretends to leave for Lemnos. No sooner has he left than Ares and Aphrodite take to his bed and are trapped by Hephaestus's snare. Hephaestus then calls out to all the Olympian gods to come and see the spectacle of the ensnared lovers.

> Father Zeus, and all the gods who are forever
> come here and see a laughable and unseemly deed
> how, because I am lame, the daughter of Zeus, Aphrodite,
> shames me and loves annihilative Ares
> because he is beautiful and strong-footed
> where I was born misshapen.
>
> (*Od.* 8.306–12)

Thus, we can see that the art of Hephaestus, in Demodocus's story, has two distinct functions, and two levels upon which it operates. On one level, Hephaestus uses his delicate art to ensnare his enemy; on another level, his invisible *dolos* is the means whereby Ares' transgression is made visible.

These two levels of Hephaestus's art, I suggest, correspond to two distinct functions of Odysseus's poetic capacity as that capacity is made manifest in the *Odyssey*. This correspondence, however, is more easily seen in the case of Hephaestus's art of entrapment than it is with Hephaestus's art of display. In the context of the Homeric poems, the word Demodocus uses to describe the "snare" that Hephaestus sets for Ares, δόλος, is unmistakably linked to the figure of Odysseus. It is the word which Polyphemos uses when he says that "Nobody is killing me by treachery [δόλῳ]" (*Od.* 9.407); it is the word which Odysseus himself uses to describe his most famous stratagem, the Trojan horse (*Od.* 8.494); most significantly, it is frequently used when Odysseus seeks to "make trial" of those to whom he speaks. I suggest that the story of Hephaestus's entrapment of Ares is meant to correspond to this aspect of Odysseus's own poetic craft, his own ability to weave "snares" in speech that his "interlocutors" are unable to detect.

However, there is another level to Odysseus's poetic art very much on display in the *Odyssey*, which differs in form and intent from the invisible "snares" he sets in speech. As I have noted above, Demodocus's tale of Hephaestus, Ares, and Aphrodite occurs shortly before Odysseus's own narration of his travels, a fantastic tale which occupies the center of the *Odyssey* as a whole. This tale came to inspire a proverbial expression for a lengthy and outrageous fabrication, "a tale of Alcinous," which expression Socrates gestures toward in his introduction to the myth of Er. In book 11 of the *Odyssey*, Odysseus pauses in the midst of the most outrageous part of his tale, his account of his journey to the underworld and his interviews with the shades of the dead. In this pause, Alcinous, whose name means "strong of mind," pays Odysseus a most unusual compliment, and with this compliment indicates the difference between the two levels of Odysseus's poetic capacity. Alcinous says,

> Odysseus, looking at you we do not in any way consider you
> to be a cheat and a deceiver, such as many men
> scattered far and wide whom the black earth nourishes,
> devising lies which no one can in any way see.
> But you give a fine shape to words, and have a good mind within you
> and you have told your tale with knowledge as a minstrel.
>
> (*Od.* 11.363–69)

What is most striking about Alcinous's praise, of course, is that he does not simply claim that Odysseus has not been telling lies.[42] Instead, Alcinous praises Odysseus for not telling lies that no one can perceive; that is, Alcinous seems to be praising Odysseus for telling lies that can be perceived as such. Alcinous uses the very same words for "no one can see" that Demodocus used to describe

---

42. The LSJ construes Alcinous's "you give fine shape to words" (σοὶ δ᾽ ἔπι μὲν μορφὴ ἐπέων) to mean "to give the colour of truth to lies."

Hephaestus's snare: τις οὐδὲ ἴδοιτο. These are, moreover, the only two occurrences of this phrase in the *Odyssey* (indeed, the only two occurrences of this form of the verb ὁράω). What Alcinous seems to be suggesting is that, unlike Hephaestus's invisible trap, the lies Odysseus tells in his tale of Alcinous are meant to be seen and learned from by those who listen with understanding. That is, Alcinous recognizes Odysseus's story of his travels and trials as a poetic representation of what Odysseus has learned about human beings and the world. But to learn from it, one has to see the falseness of the tale and understand it in terms of that which isn't said.

This, too, has its analogue in Socrates' mimetic art, in the ways in which what he says needs to be understood in light of what has been *left out,* in the paradoxes of his images and the paralepses in his arguments. Unlike the sophistic conception of poetry, which looks toward a complete poetic representation as a form of creative mastery of the world, Socrates' mimetic productions are *intentionally* incomplete and self-contradictory images of what he has learned about human beings and the world. Like tragic poetry viewed as a means toward philosophic contemplation, they are imitations of the paradoxes inherent in human beings' practical engagement with the world of their experience. Unlike tragic poetry, however, Socrates' mimetic activity calls attention to its own self-contradictory character. Socrates' ad hominem arguments, that is, are *manifest* imitations of the "lies in the soul" he unearths in his interlocutors' distorted orientations to the good, and of which he sympathetically finds analogues in his own soul. They are evident in their incompleteness as images, and this is what makes them particularly apt as *philosophic* images.

This is an often overlooked implication of the cave as an image of our nature in its education and lack of education. On the account offered in the image of the cave, education is not placing sight into souls that were blind, but rather a turning of the soul away from what is less real toward what is more real (518d). If we are to conceive education in this way, the images that are most likely to educate are precisely those that are paradoxical, self-contradictory, or manifestly incomplete. These are the kind of imitations that manifest themselves as imitations. Moreover, as paradoxical or self-contradictory imitations, they are the kinds of imitations most likely to dissuade us from the error displayed in Socrates' account of "visible" imitation—the mistake of thinking that an imitation or image was of the same kind as that which it imitates and only distinguished from it by lacking the clarity and precision of the original. Socrates' images are intended to awake us from the dream of believing a likeness of something to be not a likeness but rather the thing itself to which it is like. They are meant to help us recognize that an image, like any discursive representation, is intelligible only with reference to something which transcends that representation. In this way, Socratic images, like the image of Socrates himself offered in the *Symposium,* manifest the *daimonic* character of mimetic representation. By showing us how poetic imitation is, or can be, something "in between wisdom and ignorance" (τι μεταξὺ σοφίας καὶ ἀμαθίας, *Symp.* 202a3), Socrates' imaginative representations of the human soul—in its limitations and its ability to recognize those limitation—enable us to distinguish between knowledge, ignorance, and imitation (ἐπιστήμην καὶ ἀνεπιστημοσύνην καὶ μίμησιν ἐξετάσαι, 598d5).

Psychology and Ontology

Socrates' dialogic examinations of his interlocutors, I have argued, uncover the implicit imaginative relations between who these characters believe they should be, what they believe they can know, and what they take to be most real. Or, to put the point in terms of contemporary philosophy, Socrates' conversations disclose the relations between (1) the ways characters in the dialogues apparently justify their own lives, that is, see the lives they are leading as *good* in the significant respect, (2) their implicit commitments to specific norms of epistemic justification, and (3) the ontological commitments that accompany these norms. In this chapter, I will try to demonstrate these claims in more concrete detail by focusing on Socrates' portrayal of his principal interlocutors in the *Republic,* Glaucon and Adeimantus. Moreover, in keeping with my practice throughout much of this work, I will do so by engaging the work of a contemporary philosophic critic of Plato, Bernard Williams, whose criticism of Plato's ethical thought and moral psychology can be seen as a descendant of Nietzsche's critique of "Plato's invention of the pure spirit and the good in itself."[1]

Guided by Williams's criticisms of Glaucon's restoration of Thrasymachus's argument for the superiority of the life of injustice, I will argue that Socrates presents Glaucon and Adeimantus as exemplifying complementary ethical, psychological, and ontological orientations. These differing orientations, I will argue, correspond in many respects to contemporary accounts of what have been called "shame morality" and "guilt morality." I will show then show how this understanding of Socrates' presentation of his two principal interlocutors in the *Republic* can help illuminate the argumentative structure of the dialogue as a whole. In addition, I will argue that by recognizing the character of Glaucon's and Adeimantus' orientations to the good, we can begin to see the relation between the account of *to thumoeides* I have offered above and the problem of justice as articulated in the *Republic.*

Williams's *Shame and Necessity* is one of the most profound reflections we have on the relation between ancient Greek and modern conceptions of ethical agency, responsibility, and deliberation. A central concern of Williams's book is

---

1. *Beyond Good and Evil,* preface, in Nietzsche 1966.

a revised account of the opposition between what has been called the "Greek culture of shame" and our own supposed "guilt culture." Responding to a tradition whose significant figures include Margaret Mead, Ruth Benedict, Bruno Snell, Arthur Adkins, and E. R. Dodds, Williams convincingly refutes the claim that archaic and classical Greek representations of ethical deliberation and action disclose a primitive conception of the ethical subject and a world view in which agents are motivated exclusively by the threat of external sanctions and public disapproval. Williams does not want to argue, however, that the distinction between an ancient Greek shame culture and our modern guilt culture is without explanatory import.[2] Instead, he claims that the ethical self-consciousness demonstrated in the ancient Greek poetic tradition was in significant ways superior to our own. Moreover, he maintains that the priority of what we would call shame, as opposed to what we would call guilt, in that ethical self-consciousness is, in fact, an important indication of its superiority. This is due, in part, to the fact that shame makes immediately manifest the ineliminable social dimension of our ethical experience. It allows us to see more clearly the role that an internalized "imagined other" plays in the formation of our ethical identities. The tendency to isolate guilt from shame, and to then prioritize guilt as a wholly autonomous, and hence genuinely moral, emotive response is, on Williams's account, part and parcel of an objectionable tendency in modern moral systems. This is the tendency to abstract illegitimately from the particular contingent goals, aspirations, and concrete human relationships that give content to our ethical worlds.

Williams, therefore, while disagreeing with progressivist accounts that seek to view archaic and classical Greece as the moral infancy of the West, nevertheless agrees that there is an important historical narrative to tell about the transition from what we can still call a Homeric shame culture to a modern Western guilt culture. And like many of those narratives, Williams's account views Plato as the most significant pre-Christian figure in effecting this transition. Williams takes an essentially Nietzschean view of what he calls the "ethicised psychology of the *Republic*" and of the relation between the detached, intellectual, "featureless moral self" he finds in Plato and the richer conception of moral agency he finds in Homer, Sophocles, and Thucydides.[3] In particular, Williams singles out the challenge to conventional morality that Glaucon presents in book 2 of the *Republic* as symptomatic of the abstract, proto-Kantian moral psychology he contends informs and deforms Plato's ethical thought.

I will suggest that Williams's critique of the overly abstract picture of moral agency he finds in book 2 of the *Republic* is very much on target. Indeed, I will

---

2. This position is defended in Cairns 1993.
3. Williams 1993, 43, 159–60.

suggest that the paradoxes attending Glaucon's demand for a defense of justice which entirely severs the being of justice from its social manifestations are even more severe than Williams suggests. However, unlike Williams, I will suggest that it is part of Plato's intention that we confront these paradoxes. What this reading will show, in the first instance, is that Plato is concerned with many of the same issues of ethical internalization that occupy Williams in *Shame and Necessity*. I will argue that a careful reading of Socrates' presentation of the characters of Glaucon and Adeimantus will show them as exemplars of two opposed ethical-psychological orientations and that these two modes correspond to a great degree to what Williams and other contemporary theorists have to say about shame moralities and guilt moralities. However, I will argue that, unlike either Williams or the "progressivist" theorists he is responding to, Plato is not concerned with showing the superiority of either of these ethical-psychological orientations to the other. Instead, I will try to show how the complementary skeptical challenges to conventional morality presented by Glaucon and Adeimantus are informed by their incipient self-conscious realization of their own moral responses to the world as tied to forms of ethical internalization. Problems in their respective defenses of the unjust life, however, reveal the inadequacies in their attempts to distance themselves skeptically from their socially mediated moral experience of the world. Ultimately, I contend, Plato wants us to see both (1) that processes of ethical internalization are necessary aspect of human moral development and (2) that these processes of ethical internalization are insufficient in themselves for understanding our orientation to the good.

10.1 Williams on Shame and Guilt

One of the most philosophically interesting aspects of *Shame and Necessity* is Williams's discussion of the differences between the phenomenal experiences of shame and guilt. While Williams stresses that the opposition between shame and guilt is not as clear-cut or absolute as the progressivist theorists he argues against claim, it is nonetheless important to recognize real psychological differences between them. In articulating these differences, I draw not only from Williams's discussion, but also from the psychoanalytic work of Freud, Heinz Kohut, and Piers and Singer, as well as Herbert Morris's illuminating discussion in his *On Guilt and Innocence*.[4] Shame, on these accounts, is centrally associated with the imagined experience of being seen, as Williams says, "inappropriately,

---

4. I have tried to summarize the central points of the accounts of Williams, Morris, and Piers and Singer in table 2 below.

by the wrong people, in the wrong condition."[5] More specifically, it involves imaginatively taking the position of an internalized observer of our actions and seeing ourselves as we imagine another could see us: as exposed, exploitable, weak, a potential object of ridicule, disdain, or disgust. It is, Gabriele Taylor has argued, an emotion of self-protection.[6] It is directly associated with nakedness, with sexuality, and with a division between public and private spheres. For Freud, famously, shame is a reaction-formation against the sexual instincts, which inhibits the experience of sexual thoughts and the behavior that would follow from those thoughts. Shame works against promiscuity and, centrally, incest.[7] And Heinz Kohut, in his work on narcissism, states that "shame . . . arises when the ego is unable to provide a proper discharge for the exhibitionist demands of the narcissistic self . . . it is therefore the ambitious, success-driven person with a poorly integrated grandiose self-concept and intense exhibitionistic-narcissistic tensions who is most prone to shame."[8]

Guilt, by contrast, has been traditionally connected with hearing rather than sight. We speak of the call of conscience, or the sound in ourselves of the voice of judgment. Whereas shame induces the desire to hide ourselves away, or, as Williams suggests, to disappear, guilt seems to leave us no place to hide. "With guilt," Williams writes, "I am more dominated by the thought that even if I disappeared, it would come with me."[9] In cultural-anthropological accounts of the distinction between shame cultures and guilt cultures, shame is said to be a response to the general social prohibitions and taboos of the community at large, while guilt is said to be a direct internalization of a parental figure who assumes the role of absolute interpreter and executor of the ethical demands of a culture. Guilt, in these accounts and in the psychoanalytic theories that inform them, is seen as the punishment enacted on the ego by the superego, a redirection of the aggressive impulses that would be aimed at the disciplining parent. This redirection is ultimately itself caused by the fear of parental punishment, or the loss of parental love.

To these preliminary remarks about the dichotomy between shame and guilt, we can, I believe, add the following considerations in terms of the opposition between *seeming* and *being,* so central to Glaucon and Adeimantus. In Morris's analysis, an act of an agent can work to overcome shame only insofar as it reveals that the agent is somehow *better* than the shameful act taken on its own would seem to indicate. If we are ashamed of a perceived failing in ourselves, we

5. Williams 1993, 78.
6. Taylor 1985, 81.
7. See especially "On Narcissism" (1914).
8. Kohut 1986, 71.
9. Williams 1993, 89.

want that feeling to be overwhelmed by contrary evidence. We want to fit the shameful episode into a narrative that makes our momentary weakness an aberration or at least a stage on our way to an eventual overcoming of that failure. If we feel ashamed about having done something stupid or awkward or selfish, our retrospective experience of that act can be altered in the light of subsequent experiences. Guilt looks different. It presents itself as something essentially revelatory. Whereas one shameful act can get weighed in with many glorious acts and be diluted and discounted, one guilty act can be experienced as the one truth that makes all the rest of one's apparent virtue look like a hypocritical charade. If both shame and guilt involve experiencing oneself as *bad,* it seems characteristic of guilt, rather than shame, to experience oneself as *false.*

10.2 Glaucon's Thought Experiment

The above account of shame and guilt remains very rough, particularly in its reference to the psychoanalytic literature on these emotions, which is voluminous. Much more could be said, inter alia, about the distinction between the superego and the ego ideal in shame and guilt reactions, and the divergence between Kleinian and Freudian accounts of the developmental role of guilt. Nonetheless, I believe that even with this provisional articulation of the shame/guilt dichotomy we have the materials in hand to recognize the ways that Glaucon's challenge to conventional morality is saturated with shame imagery and, moreover, that the inconsistencies of his account are the inconsistencies of a wholly shame-oriented conception of ethical life. Glaucon's restoration of Thrasymachus's argument for the superiority of the unjust life is shot through with paradoxes that spring from his desire to entirely control the conditions of his social appearance, while remaining nonetheless dependent upon those very social appearances for his sense of his own self-worth. In this respect at least, the position Glaucon adopts resembles the moment of consciousness that Hegel refers to as the Master in his account of the dialectic of Mastery and Servitude in *Phenomenology of Spirit.* As in Hegel's account of the existential attitude of Mastery, the deficiencies of Glaucon's position will ultimately revolve around paradoxes of dependence and independence in his attempt to ground and justify his ethical self-conception, but, consonant with his shame psychology, these paradoxes will express themselves in terms of visibility and invisibility, seeing and being seen.[10]

Glaucon proposes to Socrates that we will most clearly perceive that those who practice justice do so unwillingly, only from an incapacity to do injustice,

---

10. Compare the account I have offered in chapter 5 of Socrates' response to Gorgias's self-conception.

Table 2   Shame and guilt

Bernard Williams (1993)	
"The basic experience of shame is that of being seen, inappropriately, by the wrong people, in the wrong condition. It is straightforwardly connected with nakedness, particularly in sexual connections."	"[I]t has been suggested that guilt is rooted in hearing, the sound in oneself of the voice of judgment."
"Shame . . . is not just the desire to hide . . . but the desire to disappear."	"With guilt . . . I am more dominated by the thought that even if I disappeared, it would come with me."
What arouses shame is something (not necessarily an act or omission) that elicits contempt or derision from others.	What arouses guilt is an act or omission that elicits anger, resentment, or indignation in another.
Shame moves primarily from *what I have done* to *what I am.*	Guilt looks from *what I have done* to *what has happened to others.*
Internalized figure is "watcher" or "witness."	Internalized figure is "victim" or "enforcer."
Piers and Singer (1953)	
Shame is related to failure; it is felt over shortcomings.	Guilt is related to transgression; it is felt over wrongdoings.
Shame arises out of a tension between the ego and the ego-ideal.	Guilt arises out of a tension between the ego and the superego.
Shame occurs when a goal (presented by the ego ideal) is not being reached.	Guilt is generated whenever a boundary (set by the superego) is touched or transgressed.
Morris (1976)	
Shame is evaluated through comparison to a model identity.	Guilt involves a relation to a rule.
Shame morality is a *scale* morality.	Guilt morality is a *threshold* morality.
An act of ours can work to overcome shame only insofar as it reveals that the agent is somehow better than the shameful act seemed to indicate.	Guilt, not shame, calls for acts of reparation, or undergoing punishment.

if, in thought, we give to the just man and to the unjust man license to do whatever he wants, while we follow and watch where his desire will lead. We can note from the outset the voyeuristic vividness with which Glaucon imbues his thought experiment. We are not merely told to ask ourselves whether the just man would act unjustly if given the license to do so. Instead we are told to follow him and watch over him while he follows the path of his desires. If we do so, we are told that we will "catch the just man in the act, going the same way the unjust man out of a desire to get the better" (359c). The phrase just translated as "to catch in the act" is ἐπ᾽ αὐτοφώρῳ λαμβάνειν, and the key term *autophôros* means literally "self-detected." It is the word Ismene uses in the *Antigone* to describe Oedipus's discovery of his crimes, and the word Socrates uses in the *Apology* to describe his own attempt to catch himself in the act of being less wise than the various experts he interrogates.

The use of *autophôros* at this juncture lays bare a crucial feature of Glaucon's hypothetical examination of the just and unjust lives. When asked to engage in a thought experiment such as the one Glaucon suggests, we are not endeavoring to make explicit some essential connection between apparently disparate concepts, or to display a hidden paradox in some hypothesis in natural science. That is, we are not passengers on Einstein's train or looking after Schrödinger's cat. Instead, it is clear that Glaucon's hypothetical just man is an imaginative aid to an act of psychological *introspection:* to take up Glaucon's thought experiment is to put *ourselves* in the place of the just man given freedom to do whatever he wants, and to ask ourselves what *we* would do given that freedom. Of course, we are also explicitly putting ourselves in the place of the witness who follows and watches the just man doing unjust actions. Thus, Glaucon's thought experiment enacts the very psychic structure of shame. We take the place of the internalized observer of our own unjust inclinations and catch ourselves in the psychic act.

The next step in Glaucon's thought experiment involves the so-called ring of Gyges, and here the theatrical accoutrements of Glaucon's shame psychology become increasingly obtrusive. Glaucon tells the following story about an ancestor of Gyges the Lydian:

> They say he was a shepherd toiling in the service of the man who was then ruling Lydia. There came to pass a great thunderstorm and an earthquake; the earth cracked and a chasm opened at the place where he was pasturing. He saw it, wondered at it, and went down. He saw, along with other quite wonderful things about which they tell tales, a hollow bronze horse. It had windows; peeping in, he saw there was a corpse there that appeared to be too great to be human. It had nothing on except a gold ring on its hand; he slipped it off and went out. (359d, trans. altered)

Before we turn to the ring's magical powers, let us pause to notice the circumstances of its discovery. This rather feverish dream image involves, minimally, an investigation of things under the earth, a voyeuristic glimpse through a window at a giant naked corpse, and, ultimately, grave robbery. It is a vision both grandiose and transgressive, and indicates that an ability to overcome certain fundamental shame prohibitions *already* characterizes Glaucon's protagonist prior to his coming into possession of the power to conceal himself from the eyes of others. It is significant to recall in this context Socrates' later invocation of Leontius's struggle with his own wish to view the corpses at the foot of the public executioner as the primary example of anger directed at one's own shameful desires (439e7).

It is with the next stage of Glaucon's narrative, however, that we begin to see how Glaucon's shame orientation has lead to distortions in his ethical outlook and involves him in a series of paradoxes revolving around issues of seeing and being seen, the manifest and the immanifest. This ancestor of Gyges, Glaucon tells us, discovers that the ring he has taken has the power to turn its bearer invisible when the collet of the ring is turned "toward himself."[11] Perceiving this, Glaucon says, "he immediately contrived to be one of the messengers to the king. When he arrived, he committed adultery with the king's wife and, along with her, set upon the king and killed him. And so he took over the rule." Now consider for a moment what an odd demonstration this is of the power of a ring of invisibility. Not only does invisibility play no obvious role in this account of the usurpation of the throne of Lydia, but it seems that essential to our understanding Gyges' ancestors' success is some account of his being seen, indeed being seen in a favorable light. This should be obvious once we recognize that this story of the overthrow of the *king* of Lydia depends upon the successful seduction of the *queen* of Lydia. And it seems fair to suggest that a successful seduction depends, in some sense, on being seen.

That this is the inference we should draw from Glaucon's account of the ring of Gyges becomes more evident when we compare it with the story Plato most obviously meant his readers to compare it to: Herodotus's account of Gyges himself.[12] In Herodotus's version of the story, Gyges is the faithful and trusted servant of Candaules, the king of Lydia, a man who is so impressed by the beauty of his wife, and so vain, that he compels Gyges to hide in the royal chambers so that he might see her naked and come to know for himself that the queen is the most beautiful woman in the world. Unfortunately for the king, his wife sees Gyges as he attempts to slip out unnoticed, and in her shame and anger at the king gives Gyges an ultimatum. "You must either kill Candaules and take me and the kingdom of Lydia, or you yourself must now be killed, so you will not obey Candaules in all things in the future and see

---

11. As Michael Davis (2000) indicates, πρὸς ἑαυτόν is typically used as a spatial metaphor for a psychological "turning inwards." In Plato, this metaphor is invoked in contexts which stress the opposition between the privacy of an act of introspection or contemplation and the public status of the individual who is said to "turn toward himself." See, inter alia, *Resp.* 549d and *Symp.* 174d.

12. Compare Davis 2000. Davis notes how the comparison between Glaucon's account of the ancestor of Gyges and Herodotus's Gyges story points us toward what I have characterized as paradoxes of visibility and invisibility in Glaucon's account. He does not, however, connect these paradoxes to the specificity of Glaucon's psychological orientation or to the role such a psychological orientation plays in the argument of the *Republic* as a whole.

what you should not see. Either he that planned this must die, or you must, who have looked at me naked and did what ought not be done."[13] Gyges opts for tyranny and the queen over death. Now, the most obvious connection between Herodotus's story of Gyges and the interpretation I have been offering of Glaucon's thought experiment is the crucial role shame plays in both. However, we can also see that it is precisely due to the fact that the queen *sees* Gyges as *he sees her* naked that he is given the opportunity, or compelled by the necessity, of killing the king. As in Glaucon's account of Gyges' ancestor, the overthrow of the king depends, not on the ability to go *unseen,* but on the necessity of his being seen as a potential rival to the king's power.

What this all points to in Glaucon's case, what it reveals about Glaucon's character, is his paradoxical and fantastic demand for both (1) complete control of the social manifestation of action and (2) the ability to derive from the magnificence of these social manifestations something meaningful about his own self-worth. The tension between these two demands becomes increasingly evident as he continues his thought experiment by imagining the consequences of giving rings of invisibility to both the just and the unjust man. No one, he says, would remain just if he "had license to take what he wanted from the market without fear, and to go into houses and have intercourse with whomever he wanted, and to slay or release from bonds whomever he wanted, and to do other things as an equal to a god among humans." Quite apart from the fact that the desire to be "a god among humans" seems essentially related to being *recognized* as godlike, we can see that Glaucon's language discloses a desire not just to wield power, but to be loved for it. The phrase translated above as "have intercourse with whomever he wanted" is συγγίγνεσθαι ὅτῳ βούλοιτο, and the key term *suggignesthai* means literally "being with." Just like the English "to be with someone," it is an almost abashedly euphemistic term for sexual intercourse, and like its English equivalent, it is not used to describe a rape.[14] However, the most remarkable example of Glaucon's conceptual confusion comes in his final demonstration that all human beings are only unwillingly just. He says, "Indeed, all men [πᾶς ἀνὴρ] believe injustice is much more profitable for them as individuals than justice is. And what they believe is true, . . . since if someone were to attain this sort of license and were not at some time willing to do injustice and grab what belongs to others, he would seem to be [δόξειεν εἶναι] most pathetic and unintelligent to those who perceived it [τοῖς αἰσθανομένοις]" (360d). That is, Glaucon argues that the way that we can know that anyone, given the power to go *unperceived,* would

13. Herodotus *Hist.* 1.11.2–3.
14. Attic Greek, of course, had ample resources to describe acts of sexual violence. Compare the use of ὕβρεις at Aristotle *Rh.* 1375a35, or the use of ἁρπαγάς at *Resp.* 391d1.

commit injustice, is that if such a man were *perceived* to abstain from committing injustice, he would become an object of disdain.

Now we come to the portion of Glaucon's challenge to Socrates that Williams directly comments on and critiques in *Shame and Necessity:* the comparison between the "perfectly just" and "perfectly unjust" human lives. Williams argues that this comparison is part of Plato's attempt to demonstrate that "the moral self is indeed characterless," a claim that I am arguing against, but his critique points out the very problems with Glaucon's thought experiment that I believe Plato intends us to see.[15] "We are," as Williams notes, "to suppose the just man and the unjust man in isolation from any corresponding social appearances, abstracted from all the normal conventional forces that respectively encourage and discourage those dispositions,"[16] and his further comments clearly elucidate how questionable this supposed abstraction is.

> A great deal is assumed in the formulation of this thought experiment. When we are presented with it, we are simply told that this man *is* just and that he is misunderstood by a perverse or wicked world. This is something we are supposed to understand from outside the imagined situation. We are given the convictions of the just man himself, and those are taken to be both true and unshakable. But suppose we decline to stand outside and to assume the man's justice. . . . Then we should describe the situation in these terms: this is a man who thinks he is just, but is treated by everyone else as though he were not. [But] given this solitary description, there is nothing to show whether he is a solitary bearer of true justice or a deluded crank.[17]

These criticisms are, I believe, all well taken, but they do not go far enough in articulating the difficulties with Glaucon's hypothetical comparison. For, in detailing his comparison, Glaucon entirely separates all positive social manifestations of action from any underlying disposition to act, and creates two opposed caricatures. His unjust man becomes a figure of pure capacity, an omnipotent figure of Glaucon's narcissistic imagination, who, like a clever craftsman, is always able to correct for any incidental error he might make. He can speak persuasively when he wishes and is capable of using force when he must. He is courageous and strong. He rules in the city, marries whomever he chooses, wins the contests he engages in, and is able to help his friends and harm his

15. Williams 1993, 100.
16. Ibid., 98.
17. Ibid., 99.

enemies. His just man, on the contrary is stripped of any and all capacity to act; indeed, he is "stripped of everything but justice." "Doing no injustice, let him have the greatest reputation for injustice, so that his justice may be put to the test. . . . Let him go unchanged until death, seeming throughout his life to be unjust though he is just." Now, as Williams suggests, there seems to be nothing in this description that would allow us to give any positive content to the conviction of this putatively just man. More than that, it seems as if there would be no way for the just man *himself* to give any content to that conviction.

To see how this is the case, we must first recognize that what we are asked to imagine is an individual who has *never* appeared just to anyone other than himself. This is a point that Glaucon stresses. As we have seen, in his putative attempt to gain theoretical precision, Glaucon demands that his hypothetical just man "attain the very limit" of justice by being "stripped of everything but justice."[18] It is not one or several honors or gifts of which the just man is deprived. Instead, it is the appearance of justice *tout court* that is taken from him and transferred to the unjust individual, "throughout his life" (διὰ βίου), "unchanged until death." Now, let us really try to imagine what Glaucon asks Socrates to imagine. Imagine someone who has never been taken by another as just, someone who has never had the experience of someone telling him, "You did the right thing." Imagine someone who, for every promise he believes he has kept, is told that he has broken that promise; for every duty he believes he has done, is told that he has been faithless; for every confidence he believes he has kept, is told that he has betrayed it; and is told by every would-be friend he believes he has helped that he has been an agent of harm. What, we can ask, could this man's sense of justice consist in?

To imagine a human being isolated in this way from any possible intersubjective recognition of the justice of his actions is to imagine an individual stripped of the context in which justice claims could be meaningful for him.[19] And without a context in which claims about justice are meaningful to the individual, there would seem to be little reason for us as hypothetical observers to consider what he does to be just. For Socrates, as for Aristotle, ethical virtue cannot simply be a matter of performing actions that can be described as the right sort of action, but must also involve the agent acting for the right reasons. Now the question we can ask is: "Could someone whose putative justice was never ever recognized have the right reasons for acting justly?" or "Could such a person think of himself

---

18. Of course, Glaucon is misguided in defending his approach as argumentatively rigorous. On strictly logical grounds, his attempt to challenge the claim that justice is good both for itself and for its consequences is a perfect example of an *ignoratio elenchi*. For he sets out to prove that justice is not necessary for a good human life. Even were we to accept his arguments, however, all he could be said to have shown is that justice alone is insufficient.

19. See Hobbes, *Leviathan* 1.13.13.

as making justified claims on others and responding to the justified claims of others on him?" Think about the notion of fulfilling a promise. What makes us think we have fulfilled a promise to someone? More particularly, what makes us think we have fulfilled the letter of a promise but not its spirit?

Imagine a child who says certain words and does certain things with the still inchoate intention of engaging in the practice adults call "keeping a promise." Imagine, furthermore, that whenever he does so, he is always told that the action he subsequently performs is an example of breaking a promise. No matter how carefully he listens to the chastisement he receives, no matter how hard he tries to do better, his attempts are not only deemed unsuccessful, they are condemned as signs of his injustice. It seems that such a child would have to conclude (if we can imagine him as developing rational reflective capacities at all) that the words "to break a promise" don't actually *mean* anything—it is just a phrase that adults use as a prelude to acting unpleasantly. Such a child would, at best, become a kind of disenchanted outside observer of the "moral" practices of adults. He or she would be very much like the individual Socrates describes in the cave, for whom moral education consists in recognizing customary conjunctions in the procession of moral shadows. Unlike such an individual, however, this child would believe that the shadows are merely shadows; he or she would feel trapped in the cave of moral opinion without anywhere to turn.

Glaucon's thought experiment ends with a rather gruesome catalogue of the many tortures the just man will undergo, culminating in his crucifixion and ultimate apostasy. This just man will finally confess to himself in his dying moment that one shouldn't wish *to be,* but rather *to seem to be,* just. This final stroke should indicate to us the dual role that Glaucon's shame orientation plays in the production of his hypothetical. On the one hand, the paradoxes of seeing and being seen that riddle his imaginative construction arise from his desire to appear glorious in the eyes of others without subjecting himself to the threat of ridicule or rejection that the attempt to appear magnificent brings with it. On the other hand, Glaucon's thought experiment seems to be part of an attempt on his part to *use* shame to *overcome* shame—to convince himself that it is only his own shameful weakness that allows him to be so shamefully subject to the opinions of others. Consonant with this attempt, Glaucon seems to take a certain sadistic pleasure in the excessive tortures to which he subjects the putatively just man. For it is the just man, or people like him, people with the conviction of their own justice, who threaten to shame Glaucon, in reality or fantasy, for his hidden unjust desires.

Glaucon's contraposition of just and unjust men is, as Williams argues, illegitimately abstract. And while the phenomenally ungrounded conviction of his hypothetically just man does bear some resemblance to the noumenal purity of the Kantian good will, as Williams suggests, we can see that the motivating spirit of Glaucon's speech is less Kantian than Nietzschean. Glaucon's account, we might say, is an exercise in inverted Platonism. It is an attempt to imaginatively demonstrate something like Nietzsche's claim from the *Genealogy* that "There is no 'being' behind doing, effecting, becoming; 'the doer' is merely a fiction added to the deed—the deed is everything."[20] It will be left to Glaucon's brother, Adeimantus, to begin to fill in the other side of this picture.

10.3 The Voice of the Father

"Fathers say to their sons and exhort them, as do all who have care of anyone, that one must be just. However, they don't praise justice by itself but the good reputations that come from it" (362e5–363a2). So begins Adeimantus's extension and refinement of Glaucon's challenge to justice as conventionally understood. I have suggested that Adeimantus represents an alternative model of ethical internalization to Glaucon's shame orientation, one which corresponds in its structure to aspects of contemporary analyses of guilt morality and/or guilt psychology. The most obvious manifestation of this contrast is his emphasis on hearing, and in particular, the formative influence of explicit parental prohibitions on children's psychological makeup. Moreover, we can see that, just as Glaucon's thought experiment seems to be part of his attempt to use shame to overcome shame, Adeimantus's supplement to that thought experiment seems to be directed toward using feelings of guilt (or, put positively, feelings of responsibility for the welfare of others) to overcome feelings of guilt.

Adeimantus says that while fathers exhort their children to be just, they do so merely in terms of the rewards one attains for being just and the punishment one suffers for being unjust, both in this life and the next. On one level, this seems to be merely a restatement of Glaucon's fundamental assertion, that no one really loves justice; instead everyone loves success. However, on another level, we can take Adeimantus to be responding to a possible objection to Glaucon's challenge. One might say that even if we were to be given the license afforded by the ring of Gyges, and we could get away with any and all manner of unjust deeds, our happiness would still be less than secure. After all is said and done, one might object, "doing wrong" simply makes you *feel* guilty about past wrongs, and that if you commit injustice as a youth you will spend your old age haunted by fear of punishment in the other world. Like Cephalus in book 1, you will barely have time to say hello before you have to rush off to

---

20. *On the Genealogy of Morals* 1.13, in Nietzsche 1967c.

another sacrifice to make amends for past wrongs. The problem, therefore, is not merely avoiding the explicit condemnation of one's fellow citizens, but overcoming the feelings of guilt that would threaten the serene magnificence of Glaucon's unjust man.

Adeimantus, I suggest, can be seen as offering a possible solution to this problem of a guilty conscience. The key, he seems to be saying, is to see that you have internalized the voice of the father and the voices of the poets "who tell of an inexhaustible store of goods that they say gods give to the holy" (363a6–7) and who "bury the unholy and unjust in mud in Hades and compel them to carry water in a sieve" (363d4–7). However, he suggests, we can see that the very sources that speak of divine reward and punishment also claim that the gods can be bought off. They can be swayed and perverted by luxurious sacrifices to reward the unjust and punish the just. The gods (and, by implication, the fathers) don't really care about justice either; they, too, care only about rewards and punishments. In fact, this is really all there is to the feeling of guilt; the pangs of conscience are nothing more than a deeply internalized and largely unconscious fear of punishment. Once we recognize this fact, we can either choose to believe the narratives about the gods or not. If we don't believe that there are gods, we have no reason to refrain from injustice; if we do believe that the gods exist, so too should we believe that we can win their favor, whatever injustice we commit.

The differences between Glaucon's and Adeimantus's ethical orientations can best be seen by noting a series of telling contrasts in their respective accounts. First, we can note that while Glaucon begins by denying any essential difference in the motivational structure of the just and unjust individuals—on his account, the just man will do exactly what the unjust man does if he is given the license—Adeimantus seems to maintain throughout his speech a fundamental conviction in the difference between good and bad human beings. The problem with the gods of the poets, on Adeimantus's account, is precisely that they can be perverted to honor human beings whom they know are bad and punish ones they know to be good. Second, while the force of Glaucon's argument is simply to equate the happiness of the unjust individual with that individual's public success, Adeimantus views public success as an instrument for attaining certain private pleasures and protecting oneself from the attacks of a fundamentally unjust world. The significant question for Adeimantus is "will I 'with justice or with crooked deceits scale the higher wall' where I can fortify myself all around and live out my life?" (365b2–4). Third, where Glaucon says to Socrates that he wants to know what power justice and injustice gives to its possessor, Adeimantus wants to know what "each in itself *does to the man who has it* . . . that makes the one good and the other bad" (367e1–5, emphasis added). Finally, near the end of his speech, Adeimantus introduces something that looks very like the Freudian concept of the superego, an internalized figure that is the bearer of internalized parental prohibition and enforces those prohibitions on the developing ego. He imagines himself saying to all who have been responsible for the care and education of the young that if they had only defended justice in the right way "and persuaded us, from youth onwards, we would not keep watch over one another for fear injustice be done, but each would be his own best watchman, afraid that doing injustice he would dwell with the greatest evil" (367a1–4).

Adeimantus's speech, unlike his brother's, is less paradoxical than it is performatively self-undermining. That is, it is not so much his analysis of justice and injustice, but the context in which this analysis is presented, that reveals something profoundly problematic about his psychological orientation to the philosophic problem of justice. Adeimantus's speech evinces a profound disappointment with the figures in his world he has taken as authoritative. For an implicit subtext to his critique of the fathers' merely instrumental praise of justice is the suggestion that the only reason fathers care for sons at all is the material rewards they hope to receive or the material punishments they hope to avoid. But this disappointment does not lead Adeimantus simply to reject arguments from authority. Instead, he wants a new and better authority figure to replace the old deficient ones, and he tries to place Socrates in that role. He wants to hear Socrates, in particular, demonstrate that justice is the greatest of goods and injustice the greatest of evils that a soul can have in it, because Socrates has spent his whole life considering nothing but this.[21] He could endure other people praising justice for its rewards, but not Socrates. Unless, he says, Socrates were to order him to accept it (367d8).

10.4 The Transformation of Narcissism

What I hope to have demonstrated at this point is that, while Williams is right to suggest that the challenge to conventional justice presented by Glaucon and Adeimantus in book 2 displays an overly abstract and distorted conception of the role that social recognition plays in ethical life, this abstraction is not to be attributed to Plato, or to Plato's Socrates, but rather to Glaucon and Adeimantus themselves. Indeed, Socrates says quite clearly that, given the presuppositions of Glaucon's challenge in particular, it is impossible for him to defend justice. In fact, he says this twice, once at 362e and again at 368d. And Socrates never does answer the challenge in these terms. Instead, Socrates' response to Glaucon and

21. Compare 506b–d.

Adeimantus involves fundamentally altering the presuppositions of their complementary challenges by both appealing to and transforming aspects of their respective psychological orientations. The principal device he uses to accomplish this transformation is the analogy between the city and the soul.

It has been suggested by Jonathan Lear that the key to understanding Socrates' elaborate comparison between the structure of the city and the structure of the soul, particularly as developed in the interrelated portraits of souls and cities offered in books 8 and 9, is recognizing that the city-soul relation is more than simply an illuminating analogy.[22] Instead, Socrates' argument depends on the ways that the social structure of the city and the psychic structure of the soul mutually form and inform one another. As Lear writes: "If we examine Plato's tale of political decline, we see that the degeneration occurs through a dialectic of internalization of pathological cultural influences in individuals which provokes a generation in character-structure . . . which is in turn imposed on the polis, which thus acquires and provokes deeper pathology."[23] The reciprocal processes of, on the one hand, the individual's internalization of sociocultural structures and, on the other hand, the externalization onto the city, in legislation and artistic production, of an individual's psychic harmony or disharmony allow us ultimately to speak of both the *psychic* structure of the city and the *social* structure of the soul.[24]

This pre-Nietzschean, pre-Freudian theory of "the soul as subjective multiplicity" has some immediate consequences for our discussion. The soul, as Socrates presents it in the *Republic,* develops through a process of internalization that crucially involves a dialectic of social recognition.[25] Moreover, the account Socrates gives of intentional action centrally involves viewing the relations between different parts of the soul in social and political terms. Thus, we can see that, on this account, it is not possible to speak about the disposition or motivation toward

22. Lear 1992 and 1994. As shown by the arguments of the previous chapter, my understanding of the significance of externalization and internalization for Socrates' argument differs significantly from Lear's. See note 24, below.

23. Lear 1992, 202.

24. Lear argues that the processes of internalization and externalization can be understood as causal relations grounding a correspondence between individual character types and regime types in Socrates' account of the decline of the regimes in books 8 and 9. Ferrari (2003) argues against Lear that the details of that account do not support such a reading. In particular, he argues, correctly in my view, that the correspondence between regimes and character types depends upon both being characterized by the same virtues and vices, and this occurs in cases where the citizens of the regime in question are not themselves characterized by these traits. However, this criticism does not address the broader interpretation of externalization and internalization I have argued for above.

25. As we have seen in the previous chapter, Socrates' account of the decline of the regimes in books 8 and 9 focuses on the central role that societal recognition and questions of shame and honor play in each transition between father and son in the transition between character types.

just action without referring, at least implicitly, to some idealized social manifestation of those dispositions and motivations. Or, to put this point another way, if the image of justice-as-psychic-harmony that the *Republic* presents is one of an idealized political rule, we need not only to understand the soul if we want to understand politics, but to understand politics if we want to understand the soul.

This is the most obvious way that Socrates' city-soul analogy responds to Glaucon's contentless picture of the human motivation to be just. However, the city-soul analogy does more than this; it also provides Socrates with the means to engage and transform Glaucon's and Adeimantus's respective psychological orientations. As the title of his essay "Plato's Politics of Narcissism" indicates, Lear argues that the goal of the psychopolitical argument of the *Republic* is providing a model wherein members of a well-functioning polis achieve a certain level of what he calls "narcissistic contentment." Individual citizens participate in and identify with the healthy polis considered as a psychosocial unity, and thereby attain a measure of psychic self-sufficiency. In Lear's essay, the narcissistic completeness of the citizens of the city in speech is contrasted primarily with the psychic pathologies of the oligarchic and democratic soul-types described in book 8. I believe, however, that narcissism plays a larger and more complex role in the dialogue.

I have argued that Glaucon and Adeimantus exemplify two opposed ethical orientations, which I have associated with contemporary accounts of shame and guilt, respectively. From the perspective of psychoanalytic theory, we can also associate their *psychological* orientations with two aspects or stages of the narcissistic personality. These two forms of narcissism occur when the development from the "primary narcissism" to mature object-oriented love is somehow disrupted and the libidinal energies that should be directed to the object are reinvested in the self. To put this point in loose, nontechnical language, every child begins as an undifferentiated mass of self-love, and the progress toward adulthood should involve a recognition of others and a redirection of some of that self-love toward them. In the narcissist, this transformation of self-love is impaired, and the love that would be directed toward others gets reinvested in the ego in one of two ways. It becomes attached to either (1) what Heinz Kohut calls the *narcissistic self* or (2) an internalized idealized image of the parent, with whom the narcissist now identifies. I have already quoted a passage from Kohut above that should indicate the reasons we have for identifying Glaucon's shame orientation with the first of these two forms of narcissism.[26] On the other hand, Kohut's

---

26. Consider also Kohut's description of the ways in which narcissistic personalities remain "fixated on archaic grandiose self-configurations and/or archaic, overestimated, narcissistically cathected objects" in relation to Glaucon's Gyges story. See Kohut 1971, 3.

account of the narcissistic attachment to and identification with an idealized parental figure is a correspondingly fitting description of what I have called Adeimantus's guilt orientation. On Kohut's description, this form of narcissistic self-attachment is a result of the loss of the parent as the appropriate locus for object-oriented love. This object loss, he says, must be conceived broadly "ranging from the death of the parent . . . to the child's unavoidable disappointment in circumstantial aspects of the parental imago, or a parent's prohibition of unmodified instinctual demands."[27] So, on Kohut's account, the idealized self-identified parental image takes the place of the absent or disappointing parental figure.[28]

Herbert Marcuse identifies narcissism as an "egoistic withdrawal from reality," and it is fair to say that this accurately characterizes the common features of Glaucon's and Adeimantus's ethical orientations.[29] The *therapeutic* task placed before Socrates is, therefore, to draw his interlocutors out of their egoistic isolation. Socrates does this, in the first instance, by engaging their assistance in the construction of a hypothetical city and getting them to care about the welfare of its hypothetical denizens. And he does this in two ways. On the one hand, he draws on Glaucon's implicit identification with the guardians, the heroes, as it were, of this poetic construction. Thus, it is always in conversation with Glaucon that Socrates outlines the details of how the guardians will live, how they will go to war, the specific training they will receive, and the public memorials and sacrifices that will be dedicated to them. On the other hand, he draws on Adeimantus's identification with an idealized parental figure charged with the task of the education of the city as a whole. It is with Adeimantus that Socrates discusses the stories about the gods and heroes that will be appropriate to upbringing of children, and the question of whether it is philosophy, or rather the demos itself, that is responsible for the corruption of the youth.

The differences between Glaucon's and Adeimantus's orientations inform Socrates' dialogic engagement with them throughout the *Republic,* in ways I can only touch upon here. These differences are reflected not only in their views of social relations, but also in their views of nature, education, and philosophical inquiry. As we have seen in our discussion of Glaucon's initial presentation of the argument for the superiority of the unjust life, Glaucon wants to know what power justice and injustice give to their possessor. Unlike Adeimantus, he does not distinguish between the ways in which power could affect the soul to make "one bad and the other good." Consonant with this as the focus on his inquiries,

27. Kohut 1986, 65.
28. If we were to explore in greater depth the comparison between Glaucon's and Adeimantus's speeches in terms of psychoanalytic theory, another possible approach would be to look at Melanie Klein's opposition between what she calls the "paranoid schizoid position" and the "depressive position."
29. Compare Ferrari's discussion of Glaucon's and Adeimantus's "aristocratic quietism" (2003, 11–34).

Glaucon seems to conceive of nature in terms of more or less "brute" powers or capacities. The operative imaginative analogy in Glaucon's conception of nature seems to be to what we would call physical forces. The essential difference between human natures is thought of in terms of oppositions such as those between health and sickness, strength and weakness, forcefulness and tameness (see especially 374e–375d, 407d–408a, 410a). This conception of nature seems to be presupposed in Socrates' conversations with Glaucon about political education. It is in conversation with Glaucon, rather than Adeimantus, that Socrates describes the task of political education as analogous to tempering the quasimaterial substance of the soul. The correct education is thus agreed to be one that preserves the natural forcefulness of a "spirited" nature while making it "supple" enough that it can be made to conform to the common good (410d).

Glaucon, as we have seen, presents the unjust man as a figure of unlimited capacity and the just man as stripped of any and all capacity to act. Adeimantus, however, clearly distinguishes the various "capacities of mind, money, body, or family" one may possess from the "counterfeit façade" (εὐσχημοσύνης κιβδήλου) of conventional justice (366b). He maintains throughout his speech a fundamental conviction in the difference between being good and seeming good, and the question he poses is whether being good or seeming good is better for the individual. These views are reflected in Adeimantus's conception of nature as revealed in his dialogues with Socrates. Unlike Glaucon, Adeimantus conceives of nature in terms of *occult qualities,* essential properties that are distinct from their manifestations. In this case the operative metaphor seems to be that of a germinating seed that needs appropriate nurture to realize and manifest its true nature (see especially 491a–e). In conversation with Adeimantus, the difference between good and bad natures does not map onto the difference between strong and weak natures. Instead, strong natures are said to be those most in danger of corruption or perversion. If they do not receive the nurture appropriate to them, it is agreed, they will become exceptionally bad, not as an *expression* of their nature, but as a *perversion* of it (491d). Appropriately, it is in conversation with Adeimantus that Socrates proposes that human natures come in innumerable different varieties, and that a city is well governed if each nature is doing the work appropriate to it.

Differences in Glaucon's and Adeimantus's orientations also dictate differences in the ways that Socrates poetically engages the brothers in conversation. In fact, we can discern in Socrates' conversation with each of them a characteristic dialectical inversion of the imaginary structures that govern their respective orientations. In Adeimantus's case, it is the inversion of parent and child, or more generally, an inversion of a potentially threatening authority to a potentially defenseless object of concern. We can see this in the decline of the regimes, which proceeds from an account of the negative consequences of paternal neglect to an account of the apex of the tyrant's depravity coming when he raises his hands in violence against his mother and father. We can also see it in Socrates' response when Adeimantus suggests that philosophy might, after all, corrupt the youth. Socrates argues in three stages. In the first stage, he claims that the demos, envisioned as a noble ship owner, is misled by Sophists who wrest control of the ship of state from the natural philosopher as "true pilot" (488a–489a). In the second stage, youths are corrupted by the demos-as-great-Sophist and are drawn away from philosophy (492–93). In the third stage, philosophy, "abandoned by her relatives like an orphan," is defenseless against the overtures of her unworthy suitors (495e). Finally, it is in conversation with Adeimantus that Socrates presents the image of "true philosophers," in which the highest philosophic activity is presented as a quasi-sexual communion with the forms that engenders mind and truth (γεννήσας νοῦν καὶ ἀλήθειαν) as its offspring. In Glaucon's case, not surprisingly, the key imaginative movement is an inversion of the manifest and the immanifest, the seen and the unseen. For in the images that dominate the central books of the *Republic,* images presented in conversation to Glaucon and responsive to his demands, the idea of the good is imagined as the sun that illuminates the bright daylight realm of the intelligible, while the great actions and events of the political realm become a play of shadows.[30]

10.5 Narcissism, Tyrannical Eros, and the Turning of the Soul

I have argued that Socrates' narration of the *Republic* should be understood as the imaginative representation of a hypothesis of doxastic immanence wherein the world disclosed by our everyday discursive activity is conceived of as radically disjunct from any reality which transcends the world so conceived. It is this hypothesis, I have argued, that determines Socrates' characterization of eros as a tyrant in the dialogue. The *Republic* begins from a certain perspective on eros. This perspective, which I have called the "tyrannic" perspective, holds that human eros is not intrinsically directed to those things that "most truly are." Eros does not find itself directed toward the beautiful; rather, the beautiful is whatever eros finds itself directed toward.[31] Eros, on this view, is a polymorphous outward striving, something drive-like (ὁρμή) which seeks to assimilate all things to the self. As such, tyrannic eros in the *Republic* appears to be an instantiation or modification of *to thumoeides*. The narcissism that jointly characterizes Glaucon

30. For a further account of Socrates' dialogic engagement with Glaucon, see Ludwig 2007, 222–30.
31. See 474c–475c.

and Adeimantus is the psychological correlate of the metaphysical hypothesis of doxastic immanence that informs much of the manifest argument of the *Republic.* It has as its epistemic correlate the dichotomy between opinion and knowledge conceived of as radically heterogeneous capacities, and as its onto-logical correlate the divergent proper objects of opinion and knowledge so conceived.[32] In the broader context of the *Republic,* we have also seen how this hypothesis has as its *cultural* analogue the tendency to view the norms govern-ing the social and political world as largely independent of anything outside the self-determining actions of human individuals or communities.

I have argued that what distinguishes Socratic philosophy both from the theoretical views of his sophistic opponents and from most contemporary philosophy is a thesis concerning the interrelation between the ethical, the metaphysical, and the psychological. Socrates' investigations into what is most real are inseparable from his ethical and psychological inquiry into human opinions about what is, what is knowable, and what is valuable. So, too, his conception of education apparently depends upon the interrelation of these areas of human inquiry. Education, Socrates claims, is not placing knowledge into a soul that lacks it; it is a turning or conversion of "the whole soul" at once (518c8). It involves a transformation of his interlocutors' orientations rather than a refutation of one or many individual beliefs. In the case of Glaucon, in particular, the first stage in this transformation is Socrates' ultimate response to the young man's initial defense of the unjust life.

Recall that Glaucon, speaking on behalf of the many, says that doing injus-tice is good by nature and suffering injustice is bad by nature (358e3–4). As we noted in §4.2, he does not claim that there are some naturally good things—food, shelter, sexual partners—which exist only in limited supply, and that it is therefore sometimes necessary to harm others. He instead claims that it is *naturally* good to commit injustice (or to harm others). In fact, one of the most striking things about Glaucon's account is that while there is no justice in nature—according to what he says, the lawful and just only come to be after the social contract—there is injustice in nature.

Assuming that Glaucon is not simply a sadist, I believe that he has to be thinking something like this: it is natural for each person to desire to have all good things as his own. That is, desire is essentially and naturally limitless. Thus, to be thwarted in our desires—to have someone else take or possess something that we want—is to suffer at that person's hands. This suffering is worse when what the other person wants is our bodies or our lives. Prior to laws concerning property and assault and murder, prior to the social contact and

32. See §7.4.

established convention, there is only a fundamental conflict of desire. In a world where there are people who are naturally strong and others who are naturally weak, the largest group will be those in the middle, neither exceedingly weak nor outstandingly strong (359a5). For them it would be good if they could subjugate those weaker than they are, take their goods, and impose their will on them. But this good would be far outweighed by the evil they would suffer if they were subjugated by the naturally strongest. So it is in the interest of those who are not naturally strongest to make a contract to protect themselves from harm at the hands of the strongest, and to place severe restrictions on the natural struggle for domination. But for the naturally strongest, for the person or persons who would emerge victorious from this natural struggle and be able to fulfill all his desires, to limit himself in this way would be, Glaucon says, madness (359b3).

We can now begin to see the way in which Socrates' defense of justice in the *Republic* is related to this limitless self-conception implicit in Glaucon's argument, and to the problem of *to thumoeides* articulated in the previous chapter. Justice, on this account, involves setting boundaries between an individual's expression of "drives" and the drives of other individuals. Justice is, in some sense, about integrity, both in the sense of moral integrity and in the sense of what constitutes the identity conditions of individuals in social relations to one another. It is about "mine," "yours," "ours," and "theirs." Someone who had never been given reason to believe that some part of the world was his own, was proper to him, or belonged to him, and so on would not have any way of giving sense to any of those claims. And, as Glaucon and Adeimantus help show, one cannot have a sense of what is "one's own" without implicit reference to what "belongs to another." In Socrates' terms, without a sense of what "belongs to another," one cannot have a sense of what it is to "do one's own" (τὸ τὰ ἑαυτοῦ πράττειν); and some sense of what it is to "do one's own" is integral to what it is to have or be a self as such. In book 2, after the completion of the first city in speech, the city Socrates calls the "true city" (372e4) and Glaucon calls the "city of pigs" (372d3), Socrates asks Adeimantus where justice and injustice would be in this city. Adeimantus replies by saying: "I can't think . . . unless it is somewhere in some need these men have of one another" (372a1–2). One of the lessons of the *Republic* consists in broadening our understanding of the kinds of human needs that define our political selves.

Conclusion

An Image of the Soul in Speech

Let us shape an image of the soul in speech, so the one who says these things knows what it is he is saying.

—*Republic* 588b10–11

I have argued that central to Socrates' philosophic activity as represented in Plato's dialogues is a kind of mimetic activity. Socrates makes manifest in his arguments an image of his interlocutors' incomplete or incoherent orientations to the good. Moreover, I have suggested that Socrates' mimetic activity operates on at least three distinct levels within the dialogues.

First, I have argued that image-like representations of distortions in his interlocutors' orientations to the good are essential to Socrates' inquiry into the "truth of the beings." Socrates mimetically represents in his arguments the connections between the narratives individuals tell themselves to justify a particular way of living and the commitments of these individuals to broader claims about what is, what is knowable, and what is valuable. And it is through these mimetic representations that Socrates comes to recognize similar experiences in his own soul, similar tendencies to misunderstand himself and his world in relation to the good. In support of this contention, we note that in two of the three autobiographical narratives Socrates offers in the dialogues regarding how he came to pursue philosophy in the way that he does (*Symp.* 201d–212b, *Phd.* 96a–101b), he recounts his own experience of a particular philosophic confusion, and explicitly likens it to the confusion he diagnoses in his interlocutor.[1] It is in terms of this mimetic representation of the experience of another, and a sympathetic recognition of how that experience is his own, that I suggested we should understand Socrates' awareness of his own ignorance.

---

1. The exception is Socrates' account in the *Apology* of his attempt to refute the oracle proclaiming that no one was wiser than he. There he also draws attention to the experience he had in examining those reputed to be wise (21c) and the experience of the poets in lacking wisdom (21e). Furthermore, after he is condemned, he speaks about looking forward in the afterlife to comparing his experience (ἀντιπαραβάλλοντι τὰ ἐμαυτοῦ πάθη πρὸς τὰ ἐκείνων; 41b3–4) with that of various mythic heroes who had also been unjustly condemned. Cf. Zuckert 2004 and Benardete 1994, 69–71.

Second, I have argued that the mimetic representation of his interlocutors' orientation to the good is essential to Socrates' dialogic engagement with his interlocutors. More specifically, what I have called above the elenctic aspect of these encounters involve Socrates' use of mimetic representations as a means of diagnosing and manifesting aspects of his interlocutors' orientations to the world of their experience. As Pierre Hadot has argued, at key moments within his conversations with others, Socrates seems to switch roles with his interlocutors, taking upon himself whatever doubt or confusion they may be experiencing. On Hadot's interpretation, this is to be understood primarily as a form of encouragement wherein Socrates "assumes all the risks of the dialectical adventure."[2] I suggest that in mimetically representing his interlocutors' implicit beliefs, Socrates provides them the opportunity to recognize "in another," in Socrates, the limitations of their orientations. I have also tried to show how the mimetic character of Socrates' arguments is essential to what I have called the *apodeictic* intent of his arguments; that is, it is essential to Socrates' making manifest to the auditors of his dialogues or narrations the limitations in his interlocutors' orientations. It is under this rubric, I believe, that we should place much of the philosophic work that has been done in explicit or implicit confrontation with Socrates' arguments as they are presented in the dialogues. For if, as Whitehead famously suggests, the European philosophical tradition consists of a series of footnotes to Plato, these footnotes are often in the form of scholarly corrections to views that Plato himself did not espouse, but are errors Socrates mimetically represents in Plato's dialogues.

Third, I have argued that Socrates is willing to use poetic, even mythopoeic, means to transform and redirect aspects of his interlocutors' orientation to the world of their experience when they show themselves incapable of or resistant to a recognition of contradictions or distortions in those orientations. This I have called the "therapeutic" aspect of Socrates' *pragma*. In our inquiry into the "problem of Socrates," this aspect of Socrates' poetic activity provided the most forceful grounds for identifying Socratic philosophy with the account of creative activity espoused by Gorgias and Protagoras. I concluded one line of defense against this identification by arguing that the images Socrates constructs have a specific pedagogical intent. Socrates' imaginative constructs in argument are intentionally paradoxical, self-contradictory, or manifestly incomplete. As such, they are intended to help us recognize their dependence on an intelligibility that informs, but transcends, those images and arguments.

Ultimately more significant, however, in distinguishing Socrates' philosophic activity from that of his sophistic opponents is the interdependence exhibited in

2. Hadot 1995a, 149.

Socrates' inquiries between his self-inquiry, his examination of his interlocutors, and his inquiry into "the truth of the beings." For, as we have seen in Socrates' narration of his dialogue with Protagoras, the Sophist also deals in paradox. Essential to Protagoras's self-conscious self-presentation is a complex and apparently self-contradictory myth of human creation. Part of Protagoras's allure for his students seems to be the sense he conveys that there is something mysterious and awesome lurking behind the surface of his stories and arguments. And so there is, at least on Protagoras's account. What transcends Protagoras's images and arguments is the awesome figure of Protagoras himself and his "divine" mythopoeic creative activity. As we saw in the quotation from the *Phaedrus* with which this work began, however, Socrates does not believe that he knows himself well enough to know whether and in what sense he is divine. Until he completes his inquiry into himself, an inquiry that is inseparable from his dialogical encounters with others concerning their beliefs about what is, he will be unable to derive the satisfaction Protagoras and Gorgias find in their poetic creations. For, as opposed to their view of poetic activity as a manifestation of their good as creative artists, Socrates' mimetic activity is intrinsic to his always-unfinished inquiry into himself, what is, and the good.

Finally, there is a further dimension to Socrates' mimetic activity, a dimension that I have not made thematic but has informed my inquiry throughout. This is Socrates' presentation of himself, sometimes implicitly and at other times explicitly, as a paradigmatic human inquirer. We have seen in our discussion of Socrates' self-presentation in the *Symposium* how Socrates implicitly identifies himself with *daimonic* eros. More explicit is Socrates' presentation of himself as the god-appointed philosophic examiner of the Athenians in the *Apology*. In the *Apology*, at least, it seems that a large part of this self-presentation is intended to have a *culturally therapeutic* import, a point to which I will return below. First, however, I would like to focus on the way that Socrates' self-presentation as an ideal inquirer relates to the central thesis I have attributed to Plato's Socrates: the claim that human opinions about what is, what is knowable, and what is valuable are intrinsically interdependent.

As we have seen in our discussion of Glaucon and Adeimantus, Socrates presents to each of his two chief interlocutors in the *Republic* different images of the ideal inquirer. Moreover, the imaginative character of each of these ideal inquirers—the philosopher ruler in Glaucon's case, the "true philosopher" in Adeimantus's—is essentially related to each interlocutor's broader ethical and ontological commitments. More specifically, Socrates' portraits of the philosopher-ruler and the true philosopher seem designed to function as counter-exemplars to the ethical exemplars the brothers provide in their respective arguments for the superiority of the unjust life. Glaucon and Adeimantus each offer in their presentations of justice and injustice a portrait of what human excellence would look like if certain things were true. In Glaucon's case, his unjust man is meant to be a portrait of human excellence in a world where justice is an artifact of a contractarian conspiracy of the weak against the strong. For Adeimantus, the man who appropriates a counterfeit façade of justice is meant to be a portrait of human excellence in a world where the call of conscience is nothing more than an internalization of parental and cultural prohibitions. The portraits of the ideal philosopher Socrates presents to each brother are clearly designed to rhetorically refer to and contrast with these original ethical exemplars. Their significance, however, is more than merely rhetorical.

I have suggested that, in their book 2 defenses of injustice, Glaucon and Adeimantus present portraits of what human excellence would look like if the world were a certain way. Socrates' divergent portraits of the ideal philosopher are corresponding accounts of human beings who could know the truth in those worlds. That is, they are epistemic or cognitive exemplars intrinsic to the imaginative worlds constructed by Glaucon and Adeimantus. Glaucon, as we have seen, conceives of nature as a realm of forces that differ not in kind but in strength or magnitude. The corresponding philosophic ideal Socrates presents to him is the philosopher-ruler, a portrait of the human being who acquires mathematical knowledge of the causes underlying the phenomenal and natural world. Adeimantus conceives of nature in terms of the inner nature of a growing thing. The corresponding philosophic ideal Socrates presents to him is the true philosopher, whose reproductive coupling with the forms is the generative source of mind and truth. The force of Socrates' imaginative refutation of the brothers' portraits of human excellence consists in showing the disjunction between the ethical orientations of these ideal philosophers and the ethical exemplars proposed by Glaucon and Adeimantus. That is, he shows them that, even in the hypothetical worlds they have proposed, the human being who could know the truth *in that world* would *know better* than to act unjustly.

This aspect of his response to Glaucon and Adeimantus can help us see that Socrates' various portraits of the ideal human inquirer are not extrinsic to his dialogic examination of human lives. That is, they are not supplementary artifacts of his conviction that the best human life is a life of inquiry, but intrinsic to his examination of his interlocutors' orientations to the good. For Socrates, as we have seen, the questions "What ought I do?" and "What can I know?" are interdependent. For Socrates, claims about human excellence cannot be understood apart from a characteristic experience of the world and a characteristic interpretation of that experience. Questions about human excellence cannot be severed from questions about how we can know about human excellence. Nor, as Socrates' philosophic exemplars suggest, can questions about an interpretation of our experience be severed from questions about who we would have to be to interpret our experience well. That is, intrinsic to any interpretation of human experience is some *human ideal* of perfect interpreter, some vision of what sort of sensitivity, rigor, imagination, ambition, self-denial, generosity, etc. such an interpreter should ideally have. On this account, theoretical perspectives embody, consciously or, more often, unconsciously, an internalized ethical exemplar—a vision of some human type. Insofar as we hold to a particular theoretical perspective, we are holding that human type as an ideal.

Socrates, in Plato's dialogues, is presented as such an ideal. Indeed, Plato not only presents Socrates as a paradigmatic inquirer, he presents Socrates presenting *himself* as such a paradigm. In the *Apology*, Socrates interprets the assertion of the oracle at Delphi that no one is wiser than Socrates in the following way. "It is apparent that in saying 'Socrates' he is using my name, making of me a paradigm [παράδειγμα], as if to say, 'The one among you, human beings, is wisest who, like Socrates, is aware of being, in truth, worth nothing in relation to wisdom'" (23a7–b4). In Plato's dialogues, Socrates uses the name "Socrates" in the very same way, as a paradigm of a kind of human wisdom, as an epistemic and ethical ideal type. Plato and Plato's Socrates both deploy the character "Socrates" as an image of the soul in speech, an idealizing image of the human inquirer in thought and action. It should be evident that this "Socratic" ideal is essential to our apprehension of the *apodeictic* function of Socratic dialogue. For it is only against the background of our implicit conception of genuinely Socratic inquiry that we can take specific arguments deployed by Socrates as ad hominem, proleptic, or ironic.

But in the *Apology*, as I have suggested above, Socrates' deployment of the "Socratic" ideal seems to have, in addition, a specifically culturally therapeutic intent. In particular, his final "prophetic" speeches seem to be an attempt to add the name "Socrates" to the pantheon of mythic figures with whom he imagines himself conversing in Hades. First, Socrates claims, strangely and implausibly, that the Athenian citizens who voted to condemn him have called upon themselves a terrible elenctic punishment. Immediately upon his death, Socrates claims, they will be set upon by a great number of cross-examiners, younger and harsher than Socrates himself. It is only because Socrates had held them back while he was alive that they had not been perceived (*Ap.* 39c–d). Next, Socrates speaks to those whom he calls his judges, the men who voted to acquit him. He asks if they can remain with him until he must go, conversing with (or telling stories to) one another (διαμυθολογῆσαι πρὸς ἀλλήλους, 39e5). In this storytelling conversation, he imagines himself continuing his elenctic inquiries in a Hades populated wholly by mythic figures and myth-makers: Orpheus and Musaeus, Hesiod and Homer, Odysseus and Sisyphus. Socrates ends his speech by asking the men who are his judges to do something for him. He asks that they chastise and annoy his sons just as he has chastised and annoyed his fellow citizens. "If they seem to you to care more about money or anything more than excellence, and if they think they are something when they are really nothing, reproach them, just as I did with you. Say that they don't care about what they should, and that they believe they are something when they are worth nothing. If you do this, you will be treating us justly, myself and my sons" (*Ap.* 41e).

This image of a relentlessly chastising "Socrates" seems, on the evidence of the dialogues, every bit as fictitious as the elenctic Erinyes Socrates prophesies when speaking to those who voted to condemn him. With these two final addresses, Socrates seems intent on placing the character Socrates, on the one hand, alongside Palamedes and Ajax among those who have been unjustly condemned (*Ap.* 41b2) and, on the other hand, among the mythic figures of judgment, Minos and Rhadamanthys, Aeacus and Triptolemus (*Ap.* 41a3–4). He seems to have decided that if he will no longer be able to rouse individual Athenians from their sleep with his elenctic inquiries, as a mythic figure he will at least trouble their dreams until the god chooses to send them someone new.

Socrates begins his defense in the *Apology* by claiming that his real opponents are "the first accusers," his name for a cultural prejudice against "wise men" that used the name of "Socrates" as a paradigm of injustice (*Ap.* 18a–19d). In his final speech, Socrates poetically displaces these shadowy accusers. He chooses to become a paradigm of the wrongfully accused wise man, forever examining others and reproaching those who seem to care for anything more than the excellence of their souls. In Nietzsche's terms, Socrates chooses to become the "bad conscience" of his time. The success of Plato's Socrates in this venture is hard to dispute. One can nonetheless ask whether Socrates' choice to descend into the mythic underworld—Plato's choice to elevate the dying Socrates as a philosophic ideal—was a choice for the best. Nietzsche's critique of the philosophic moralism of the tradition that Socrates inspired argues that it was not.[3] To answer this aspect of Nietzsche's challenge, we would need to decide whether the arc of the history of Western philosophy following in the footsteps of this Socratic image was, on balance, worth the trouble. This is not a question addressed in this work, nor is it one to which Plato's Socrates can provide the answer.

---

3. See *Twilight of the Idols* 2.10, in Nietzsche 1968.

References

Adkins, A. W. H. 1960. *Merit and Responsibility: A Study in Greek Values.* Oxford: Clarendon Press.
———. 1973. "*Aretê, Technê,* Democracy, and Sophists: *Protagoras* 316b–328d." *Journal of Hellenic Studies* 93:3–12.
Aeschylus. 1922. *Prometheus Bound.* In *Aeschylus,* vol. 1, ed. and trans. Herbert Weir Smyth. London: William Heinemann; New York: G. P. Putnam's Sons.
Annas, Julia. 1981. *An Introduction to Plato's "Republic."* Oxford: Clarendon Press.
———. 1999. *Platonic Ethics, Old and New.* Ithaca: Cornell University Press, 1999.
Apollodorus. 1921. *The Library.* Trans. James George Frazer. 2 vols. Cambridge, Mass.: Harvard University Press; London: William Heinemann.
Aristophanes. 1907. *Aristophanis Comoediae.* Ed. F. W. Hall and W. M. Geldart. 2nd ed. Oxford: Clarendon Press.
Aristotle. 1935. "*The Metaphysics" X–XIV, "Oeconomica," and "Magna moralia."* Vol. 18 of *Aristotle in 23 Volumes.* Cambridge, Mass.: Harvard University Press.
———. 1962. *Nicomachean Ethics.* Trans. Martin Ostwald. New York: Macmillan.
———. 1995. *The Politics.* Trans. Ernest Barker. Oxford: Oxford University Press.
Ausland, Hayden Weir. 1987. "On the Dialogue-Proem to Plato's *Republic.*" Ph.D. diss., University of California, Berkeley.
———. 1997. "On Reading Plato Mimetically." *American Journal of Philology* 118, no. 3:371–416.
Baracchi, Claudia. 2001. *Of Myth, Life, and War in Plato's "Republic."* Bloomington: Indiana University Press.
Barnes, Jonathan. 1989. *The Presocratic Philosophers.* London: Routledge.
Barney, Rachel. 2004. "Callicles and Thrasymachus." In *Stanford Encyclopedia of Philosophy.* http://plato.stanford.edu/archives/fall2004/entries/callicles-thrasymachus.
Belfiore, Elizabeth. 1984. "A Theory of Imitation in Plato's *Republic.*" *Transactions of the American Philological Association* 114:123–24.
Benardete, Seth. 1964. "Sophocles' *Oedipus Tyrannos.*" In *Ancients and Moderns: Essays on the Tradition of Political Philosophy in Honor of Leo Strauss,* ed. Joseph Cropsey, 1–15. New York: Basic Books.
———. 1989a. *The Argument of the Action: Essays on Greek Poetry and Philosophy.* Chicago: University of Chicago Press.
———. 1989b. *Socrates' Second Sailing: On Plato's "Republic."* Chicago: University of Chicago Press.
———. 1991. *The Rhetoric of Morality and Philosophy.* Chicago: University of Chicago Press.

―――. 1994. *On Plato's "Symposium."* Munich: Carl Friedrich von Siemens Stiftung.

Berg, Steven. 1998. "Rhetoric, Nature, and Philosophy in Aristophanes' *Clouds*." *Ancient Philosophy* 18:1–19.

Bertram, Ernst. 1985. *Nietzsche: Versuch einer Mythologie.* Bonn: Bouvier Verlag.

Bett, Richard. 1989. "The Sophists and Relativism." *Phronesis* 34:139–69.

Beversluis, John. *Cross-Examining Socrates: A Defense of the Interlocutors in Plato's Early Dialogues.* Cambridge: Cambridge University Press, 2000.

Blondell, Ruby. 2002. *The Play of Character in Plato's Dialogues.* Cambridge: Cambridge University Press, 2002.

Bobonich, Christopher. 1994. "*Akrasia* and Agency in Plato's *Laws* and *Republic*." *Archiv für Geschichte der Philosophie* 76:3–36.

Bosanquet, Bernard. 1976. *A Companion to Plato's "Republic" for English Readers: Being a Commentary Adapted to Davies and Vaughan's Translation.* 2nd ed. Folcroft, Pa.: Folcroft Library Editions.

Brann, Eva. 1990. "The Music of the *Republic*." In "Four Essays on Plato's *Republic*," ed. David R. Lachterman. Special issue, *St. John's Review* 39:1–103.

Brickhouse, Thomas C., and Nicholas D. Smith. 1994. *Plato's Socrates.* New York: Oxford University Press.

Broadie, Sarah. 1991. *Ethics with Aristotle.* New York: Oxford University Press.

―――. 2001. "Theodicy and Pseudo-History in the *Timaeus*." *Oxford Studies in Ancient Philosophy* 21:1–28.

Burger, Ronna. 2008. *Aristotle's Dialogue with Socrates: On the "Nicomachean Ethics."* Chicago: University of Chicago Press.

Cairns, Douglas L. 1993. *Aidôs: The Psychology and Ethics of Honour and Shame in Ancient Greek Literature.* Oxford: Oxford University Press.

Cartledge, Paul. 1993. *The Greeks: A Portrait of Self and Others.* New York: Oxford University Press.

Casevitz, Michel. 1989. "L'humour d'Homère: Ulysse et Polyphème au chant 9 de l'Odyssée." In *Études homériques: Séminaire de recherche,* 55–58. Paris: Diffusion de Boccard.

Clay, Diskin. 1987. "Gaps in the 'Universe' of the Platonic Dialogues." In *Proceedings of the Boston Area Colloquium in Ancient Philosophy,* vol. 3, ed. J. J. Cleary, 131–57. Washington: University Press of America.

Coby, Patrick. 1982. "The Education of a Sophist: Aspects of Plato's *Protagoras*." *Interpretation* 10:139–58.

Consigny, Scott. 1992. "The Styles of Gorgias." *Rhetoric Society Quarterly* 22:43–53.

Cornford, Francis M. 1971. "The Doctrine of Eros in Plato's Symposium." In Vlastos 1971, 68–80.

Cross, R. C., and A. D. Woozley. 1964. *Plato's "Republic": A Philosophical Commentary.* London: St. Martin's Press.

Crowell, Steven. 2001. "Subjectivity: Locating the First-Person in Being and Time." *Inquiry* 44, no. 4:433–54.

Dannhauser, Werner J. 1974. *Nietzsche's View of Socrates.* Ithaca: Cornell University Press.

Davis, Michael. 1988. *Ancient Tragedy and the Origins of Modern Science.* Carbondale: Southern Illinois University Press.

―――. 1999. *The Poetry of Philosophy: On Aristotle's "Poetics."* South Bend, Ind.: St. Augustine's Press.

―――. 2000. "The Tragedy of Law: Gyges in Herodotus and Plato." *Review of Metaphysics* 53, no. 3:635–43.

Dawe, R. D. 1993. *The "Odyssey": Translation and Analysis.* Sussex: Book Guild.

Derrida, Jacques. 1978. "Structure, Sign, and Play in the Discourse of the Human Sciences." In *Writing and Difference,* trans. Alan Bass, 351–70. London: Routledge and Kegan Paul.

———. 1981. "Plato's Pharmacy." In *Dissemination,* trans. Barbara Johnson, 67–186. Chicago: University of Chicago Press.[1]

Diels, Hermann. 1952. *Die Fragmente der Vorsokratiker.* 6th ed., rev. Walther Kranz. 3 vols. Berlin: Weidmann.

Dihle, Albrecht. 1982. *The Theory of Will in Classical Antiquity.* Berkeley and Los Angeles: University of California Press.

Dodds, E. R. 1951. *The Greeks and the Irrational.* Berkeley and Los Angeles: University of California Press.

———. 1959. *Plato's "Gorgias."* Oxford: Oxford University Press.

Dover, Kenneth James. 1968. *Lysias and the Corpus Lysiacum.* Berkeley and Los Angele: University of California Press.

Engel, David Madison. 1997. "The Divided Self from Homer to Aristotle." Ph.D. diss., University of California, Berkeley.

Euripides. 1995. *Hippolytus.* In *Children of Heracles, Hippolytus, Andromache, Hecuba,* ed. and trans. David Kovacs. Loeb Classical Library 484, no. 2. Cambridge, Mass.: Harvard University Press.

Everson, Stephen, ed. 1990. *Epistemology.* Companions to Ancient Thought 1. Cambridge: Cambridge University Press.

Ferrari, G. R. F. 1989. "Plato and Poetry." In *The Cambridge History of Literary Criticism,* ed. George A. Kennedy, 92–148. Cambridge: Cambridge University Press.

———. 1990a. "*Akrasia* as Neurosis in Plato's *Protagoras.*" In *Proceedings of the Boston Area Colloquium in Ancient Philosophy,* vol. 6, 115–39. Lanham, Md.: University Press of America.

———. 1990b. *Listening to the Cicadas: A Study of Plato's "Phaedrus."* Cambridge: Cambridge University Press.

———. 2003. *City and Soul in Plato's Republic.* Chicago: University of Chicago Press.

———, ed. 2007a. *The Cambridge Companion to Plato's "Republic."* Cambridge: Cambridge University Press.

———. 2007b. "The Three-Part Soul." In Ferrari 2007a, 165–201.

Ferrarin, Alfredo. 2000. "Homo Faber, Homo Sapiens, or Homo Politicus? Protagoras and the Myth of Prometheus." *Review of Metaphysics* 54:289–319.

Fine, Gail. 1978. "Knowledge and Belief in *Republic* V." *Archiv für Geschichte der Philosophie* 60:121–39.

———. 1990. "Knowledge and Belief in *Republic* V–VII." In Everson 1990, 85–115.

Geertz, Clifford. 1973a. "Ethos, World View, and the Analysis of Sacred Symbols." In *The Interpretation of Cultures,* 126–41. New York: Basic Books.

———. "Religion as a Cultural System." In *The Interpretation of Cultures,* 87–125. New York: Basic Books.

Gerson, Lloyd P. 2004. *Knowing Persons: A Study in Plato.* Oxford: Oxford University Press.

———. 2006. *Aristotle and Other Platonists.* Ithaca: Cornell University Press.

Gill, Christopher. 1996. *Personality in Greek Epic, Tragedy, and Philosophy: The Self in Dialogue.* Oxford: Clarendon Press.

Gill, Christopher, and Mary Margaret McCabe, eds. 1996. *Form and Argument in Late Plato.* Oxford: Clarendon Press.

Goldberg, Larry. 1983. *A Commentary on Plato's "Protagoras."* New York: Peter Lang.

Goldhill, Simon. 1991. *The Poet's Voice: Essays on Poetics and Greek Literature.* Cambridge: Cambridge University Press.

Gonzalez, Francisco J., ed. 1995. *The Third Way: A New Direction in Platonic Studies.* Lanham, Md.: Rowman and Littlefield.

———. 1998. *Dialectic and Dialogue: Plato's Practice of Philosophic Inquiry.* Evanston: Northwestern University Press.

———. 2009. "Dialectic, Ethics, and Dialogue." In *Plato and Heidegger: A Question of Dialogue.* University Park: Pennsylvania State University Press.

Gould, Thomas. 1990. *The Ancient Quarrel Between Poetry and Philosophy.* Princeton: Princeton University Press.

Griffith, Mark. 1977. *The Authenticity of "Prometheus Bound."* Cambridge: Cambridge University Press.

Griswold, Charles L., Jr. 1981. "The Ideas and the Criticism of Poetry in Plato's *Republic,* Book 10." *Journal of the History of Philosophy* 19:135–50.

———. 1986. *Self-Knowledge in Plato's "Phaedrus."* New Haven: Yale University Press.

———. 1999. "E Pluribus Unum? On the Platonic 'Corpus.'" *Ancient Philosophy* 19:361–97.

———. 2005. "Plato on Rhetoric and Poetry." In *The Stanford Encyclopedia of Philosophy,* ed. Edward N. Zalta, Summer 2005 ed. http://plato.stanford.edu/archives/sum2005/entries/plato-rhetoric.

Guthrie, W. K. C. 1971. *The Sophists.* Cambridge: Cambridge University Press.

Haden, James. 1984. "Did Plato Refute Protagoras?" *History of Philosophy Quarterly* 1:223–40.

Hadot, Ilsetraut. 1991. "The Role of the Commentaries on Aristotle in the Teaching of Philosophy." In *Aristotle and the Later Tradition,* ed. Henry Blumenthal and Howard Robinson, 175–89. Oxford: Clarendon Press.

Hadot, Pierre. 1995a. "The Figure of Socrates." In Hadot (1995b), 147–78.

———. 1995b. *Philosophy as a Way of Life: Spiritual Exercises from Socrates to Foucault.* Ed. Arnold I. Davidson. Trans. Michael Chase. Oxford: Basil Blackwell.

Hall, Edith. 1989. *Inventing the Barbarian: Greek Self-Definition Through Tragedy.* Oxford: Oxford University Press.

Harlap, Shmuel. 1979. "Thrasymachus' Justice." *Political Theory* 7:347–70.

Hartog, Franç. 1988. *The Mirror of Herodotus: The Representation of the Other in the Writing of History.* Berkeley and Los Angeles: University of California Press.

Hays, Steven. 1990. "On The Skeptical Influence of Gorgias' On Not-Being." *Journal of the History of Philosophy* 28, no. 3:327–37.

Hegel, Georg Wilhelm Friedrich. 1977. *Phenomenology of Spirit.* Trans. Arnold V. Miller. Oxford: Oxford University Press.

———. 1983. *Lectures on the History of Philosophy.* Trans. E. S. Haldane and Frances H. Simson. 3 vols. Atlantic Highlands, NJ: Humanities Press. (Orig. pub. 1892.)

Heidegger, Martin. 1998. *Pathmarks.* Ed. William McNeill. Cambridge: Cambridge University Press.

Henderson, T. Y. 1970. "In Defense of Thrasymachus." *American Philosophical Quarterly* 7:218–28.

Herodotus. 1920. *The Histories.* Ed. and trans. A. D. Godley. Cambridge, Mass.: Harvard University Press.

Hobbes, Thomas. 1994. *Leviathan: With Selected Variants from the Latin Edition of 1668.* Ed. Edwin Curley. Indianapolis: Hackett.

Hobbs, Angela. *Plato and the Hero: Courage, Manliness, and the Impersonal Good.* Cambridge: Cambridge University Press, 2000.

Hourani, George F. 1962. "Thrasymachus' Definition of Justice in Plato's *Republic.*" *Phronesis* 7:110–20.

Howland, Jacob. 1993. *The "Republic": The "Odyssey" of Philosophy.* Boston: Twayne.

———. 1998. *The Paradox of Political Philosophy: Socrates' Philosophic Trial.* Lanham, Md.: Rowman and Littlefield.

Husserl, Edmund. 1973. *Cartesian Mediations.* Trans. Dorion Cairns. The Hague: Martinus Nijhoff.

———. 1983. *Ideas Pertaining to a Pure Phenomenology and to a Phenomenological Philosophy: First Book.* Trans. F. Kersten. The Hague: Martinus Nijhoff.

Hyland, Drew. 1995. *Finitude and Transcendence in the Platonic Dialogues.* Albany: SUNY Press.

Irwin, Terence. 1995. *Plato's Ethics.* Oxford: Oxford University Press.

Irwin, Terence, and Martha Craven Nussbaum, eds. 1994. *Virtue, Love, and Form: Essays in Memory of Gregory Vlastos.* Edmonton: Academic Printing and Publishing.

Isocrates. 1980. *Antidosis.* In *Isocrates,* vol. 2, trans. George Norlin. Loeb Classical Library 229. Cambridge, Mass.: Harvard University Press; London, William Heinemann.

Janaway, Christopher. 1995. *Images of Excellence: Plato's Critique of the Arts.* Oxford: Clarendon Press.

Jarratt, Susan. 1991. *Rereading the Sophists: Classical Rhetoric Refigured.* Carbondale: Southern Illinois University Press.

Jaspers, Karl. 1979. *Nietzsche: An Introduction to the Understanding of His Philosophical Activity.* Trans. Charles F. Wallraff and Frederick J. Schmitz. South Bend, Ind.: Regnery/Gateway.

Kahn, Charles. 1983. "Drama and Dialectic in Plato's *Gorgias.*" *Oxford Studies in Ancient Philosophy* 1:113–21.

———. 1993. "Proleptic Composition in the Republic, or Why Book 1 Was Never a Separate Dialogue." *Classical Quarterly* 43, no. 1:131–42.

———. 1996. *Plato and the Socratic Dialogue: The Philosophical Use of a Literary Form.* Cambridge: Cambridge University Press.

Kant, Immanuel. 1963. *Critique of Pure Reason.* Trans. Norman Kemp Smith. London: Macmillan.

Karamanolis, George E. 2006. *Plato and Aristotle in Agreement? Platonists on Aristotle from Antiochus to Porphyry.* New York: Oxford University Press.

Kaufmann, Walter. 1988. *Nietzsche: Philosopher, Psychologist, Antichrist.* Princeton: Princeton University Press.

Kerferd, G. B. 1947. "The Doctrine of Thrasymachus in Plato's *Republic.*" *Durham University Journal* 9:19–47.

———. 1953. "Protagoras' Doctrine of Justice and Virtue in the *Protagoras* of Plato." *Journal of Hellenic Studies* 73:42–45.

———. 1964. "Thrasymachus and Justice: A Reply." *Phronesis* 9:12–16

———. 1981a. *The Sophistic Movement.* Cambridge: Cambridge University Press.

———. 1981b. *The Sophists and Their Legacy.* Wiesbaden: Franz Steiner Verlag.

Klagge, James C., and Nicholas D. Smith, eds. 1992. *Methods of Interpreting Plato and His Dialogues.* Oxford: Clarendon Press.

Klein, Jacob. 1965. *A Commentary on Plato's "Meno."* Chapel Hill: University of North Carolina Press.

———. 1968. *Greek Mathematical Thought and the Origin of Algebra.* Trans. Eva Brann. Cambridge, Mass.: MIT Press.

————. 1985. "About Plato's *Philebus.*" In *Lectures and Essays by Jacob Klein,* ed. Robert Williamson and Elliott Zuckerman, 309–44. Annapolis: St. John's College Press.

Kofman, Sarah. 1998. *Socrates: Fictions of a Philosopher.* London: Athlone.

Kohut, Heinz. 1971. *The Analysis of the Self.* New York: International Universities Press, 1971.

————. 1986. "Forms and Transformations of Narcissism." In *Essential Papers on Narcissism,* ed. Andrew P. Morrison, 61–87. New York: New York University Press.

Kojève, Alexandre. 1991. "Tyranny and Wisdom." In Strauss 1991, 135–76.

Koziak, Barbara. 1999. *Retrieving Political Emotion: Thumos, Aristotle, and Gender.* University Park: Pennsylvania State University Press.

Kraut, Richard. 1992. *The Cambridge Companion to Plato.* Cambridge: Cambridge University Press.

Kube, Jörg. 1969. *TEXNH und APETH: Sophistisches und Platonisches Tugendwissen.* Berlin: Walter de Gruyter.

Lampert, Laurence. 2002. "Socrates' Defense of Polytropic Odysseus: Lying and Wrong-Doing in Plato's *Lesser Hippias.*" *Review of Politics* 64, no. 2:231–59.

Lane, Melissa. 2001. *Plato's Progeny.* London: Duckworth.

Lear, Jonathan. 1992. "Inside and Outside the *Republic.*" *Phronesis* 37:184–215.

————. 1994. "Plato's Politics of Narcissism." In Irwin and Nussbaum 1994, 137–59.

————. 1998. *Open Minded: Working Out the Logic of the Soul.* Cambridge, Mass.: Harvard University Press.

————. 2006a. "The Socratic Method and Psychoanalysis." In *The Blackwell Companion to Socrates,* ed. Sara Rappe and Rachana Kamtekar, 442–62. Oxford: Basil Blackwell.

————. 2006b. "Myth and Allegory in Plato's *Republic.*" In *The Blackwell Companion to Plato's "Republic,"* ed. Gerasimos Santas, 25–43. Oxford: Basil Blackwell.

Lévystone, David. 2005. "La figure d'Ulysse chez les Socratiques: Socrate polutropos." *Phronesis* 50, no. 3:181–214.

Liddell, Henry George, and Robert Scott. 1940. *A Greek-English Lexicon.* Rev. Henry Stuart Jones. Oxford: Clarendon Press.

Long, A. A. 1988. "Socrates in Hellenistic Philosophy." *Classical Quarterly* 38:150–71.

Longo, Angela. 2000. *La tecnica della domanda et le interrogazione fittizie in Platone.* Pisa: Scuola Normale Superiore.

Ludwig, Paul. 2007. "Eros in the *Republic.*" In Ferrari 2007a, 202–31.

Lycos, Kimon. 1987. *Plato on Justice and Power: Reading Book I of Plato's "Republic."* Albany: State University of New York Press.

Lysias. 1930. *Lysias.* Trans. W. R. M. Lamb. Cambridge: Harvard University Press; London: William Heinemann.

Maguire, Joseph P. 1971. "Thrasymachus . . . or Plato." *Phronesis* 16:142–63.

Marx, Karl. 1978a. *Economic and Philosophic Manuscripts of 1844: Selections.* In *The Marx-Engels Reader,* 2nd ed., ed. Robert C. Tucker, 66–125. New York: W. W. Norton.

————. 1978b. *The German Ideology: Part I.* In *The Marx-Engels Reader,* 2nd ed., ed. Robert C. Tucker, 146–202. New York: W. W. Norton.

McDowell, John Henry. 1998. "Two Sorts of Naturalism." In *Mind, Value, and Reality,* 167–97. Cambridge, Mass.: Harvard University Press.

McKirahan, Richard D., Jr. 1994. *Philosophy Before Socrates.* Indianapolis: Hackett.

McNeal, Richard. 1986. "Protagoras the Historian." *History and Theory* 25:299–318.

McNeill, David N. 2004. "On the Relationship of Alcibiades' Speech to Nietzsche's 'Problem of Socrates.'" In *Nietzsche and Antiquity: His Reaction and Response to the Classical Tradition,* ed. Paul Bishop, 260–75. Rochester: Camden House.

Moes, Mark. 2001. "Plato's Conception of the Relations Between Moral Philosophy and Medicine." *Perspectives in Biology and Medicine* 44, no. 3:353–67.

Monoson, S. Sara. 2000. *Plato's Democratic Entanglements: Athenian Politics and the Practice of Philosophy.* Princeton: Princeton University Press.

Moors, Kent. 1987. "The Argument Against a Dramatic Date for Plato's *Republic*." *Polis* 7, no. 1:6–31.

Moravcsik, Julius. 1992. *Plato and Platonism.* Oxford: Basil Blackwell.

Morgan, Kathryn A. 1998. "Designer History: Plato's Atlantis Story and Fourth-Century Ideology." *Journal of Hellenic Studies* 118:1–118.

———. 2000. *Myth and Philosophy from the Presocratics to Plato.* Cambridge: Cambridge University Press.

Morris, Herbert. 1976. *On Guilt and Innocence: Essays in Legal Philosophy and Moral Psychology.* Berkeley and Los Angeles: University of California Press.

Murphy, Neville Richard. 1951. *The Interpretation of Plato's "Republic."* Oxford: Oxford University Press.

Nails, Debra. 1998. "The Dramatic Date of Plato's *Republic*." *Classical Journal* 93, no. 4:383–96.

———. 2002. *The People of Plato.* Indianapolis: Hackett.

Natorp, Paul. 1994. *Platos Ideenlehre: Eine Einführung in den Idealismus.* Hamburg: Felix Meiner Verlag.

Nehamas, Alexander. 1985. *Nietzsche: Life as Literature.* Cambridge, Mass.: Harvard University Press.

———. 1998. *The Art of Living: Socratic Reflections from Plato to Foucault.* Berkeley and Los Angeles: University of California Press.

———. 1999. "Plato on Imitation and Poetry in *Republic* 10." In *Virtues of Authenticity: Essays on Plato and Socrates,* 251–78. Princeton: Princeton University Press.

Nietzsche, Friedrich Wilhelm. 1966. *Beyond Good and Evil.* Trans. Walter Kaufmann. New York: Random House.

———. 1967a. *The Birth of Tragedy.* Trans. Walter Kaufmann. In *"The Birth of Tragedy" and "The Case of Wagner."* New York: Random House.

———. 1967b. *Ecce Homo: How One Becomes What One Is.* Trans. Walter Kaufmann. In *"On the Genealogy of Morals" and "Ecce Homo."* New York: Random House.

———. 1967c. *On the Genealogy of Morals.* Trans. Walter Kaufmann and R. J. Hollingdale. In *"On the Genealogy of Morals" and "Ecce Homo."* New York: Random House.

———. 1967d. *The Will to Power.* Trans. Walter Kaufmann. New York: Random House.

———. 1968. *Twilight of the Idols.* Trans. Walter Kaufmann. In *The Portable Nietzsche,* ed. and trans. Walter Kaufmann. New York: Viking.

———. 1974. *The Gay Science: With a Prelude of Rhymes and an Appendix of Songs.* Trans. Walter Kaufmann. New York: Random House.

———. 1983. "On the Uses and Disadvantages of History for Life." In *Untimely Meditations,* trans. R. J. Hollingdale. Cambridge: Cambridge University Press.

———. 1988. *Sämtliche Werke: Kritische Studienausgabe.* Ed. Giorgio Colli and Mazzino Montinari. 15 vols. Berlin: Walter de Gruyter.

Nussbaum, Martha C. 1986. *The Fragility of Goodness.* Cambridge: Cambridge University Press.

O'Brien, Michael. 1967. *The Socratic Paradoxes and the Greek Mind.* Chapel Hill: University of North Carolina Press.

O'Connor, David. 2007. "Rewriting the Poets in Plato's Characters." In Ferrari 2007a, 55–89.

Osborne, Catherine. 1994. *Eros Unveiled: Plato and the God of Love.* Oxford: Clarendon Press.

Page, Carl. 1991. "The Truth About Lies in Plato's *Republic*." *Ancient Philosophy* 11:1–33.

Parry, Richard. 2003. "The Craft of Ruling in Plato's *Euthydemus* and *Republic*." *Phronesis* 48, no. 1:1–28.

Pears,[3] David F. 1978. "Aristotle's Analysis of Courage." In *Studies in Ethical Theory*, ed. Peter A. French, Theodore E. Uehling Jr., and Howard K. Wettstein, 273–85. Midwest Studies in Philosophy 3. Morris: University of Minnesota, Morris.

Penner, Terry. 1992. "Socrates and the Early Dialogues." In Kraut 1992, 121–69.

Peradotto, John. 1990. *Man in the Middle Voice: Name and Narration in the "Odyssey."* Princeton: Princeton University Press.

Piers, Gerhart, and Milton B. Singer. 1953. *Shame and Guilt: A Psychoanalytic and Cultural Study.* Springfield, Ill.: Charles C. Thomas.

Pindar. 2007. *The Complete Odes.* Ed. Stephen Instone. Trans. Anthony Verity. Oxford: Oxford University Press.

Plato. 1963. *The Republic.* Ed. James Adam. 2nd ed. Cambridge: Cambridge University Press.

———. 1967–68. *Platonis Opera.* Ed. John Burnet. 5 vols. Oxford: Clarendon Press. Orig. pub. 1900–1907.

———. 1969–70.[4] *The Republic.* Trans. Paul Shorey. Plato: In Twelve Volumes 5–6. Cambridge, Mass.: Harvard University Press.

———. 1984. *The Being of the Beautiful: Plato's "Theaetetus," "Sophist," and "Statesman."* Trans. Seth Benardete. Chicago: University of Chicago Press.

———. 1986. *Phaedrus.* Ed. and trans. Christopher J. Rowe. Warminster: Aris and Phillips.

———. 1987. *Gorgias.* Trans. Donald J. Zeyl. Indianapolis: Hackett.

———. 1988. *Republic 10.* Trans. Stephen Halliwell. Warminster: Aris and Phillips.

———. 1989. *Euthyphro, Apology, Crito, Meno, Gorgias, Menexenus.* Trans. R. E. Allen. Vol. 1 of *The Dialogues of Plato.* New Haven: Yale University Press.

———. 1991. *The Republic of Plato.* 2nd ed. Trans. Allan Bloom. New York: Basic Books.

———. 1995. *Phaedrus.* Ed. and trans. Alexander Nehamas and Paul Woodruff. Indianapolis: Hackett.

———. 1996. *Ion, Hippias Minor, Laches, Protagoras.* Trans. R. E. Allen. Vol. 3 of *The Dialogues of Plato.* New Haven: Yale University Press.

———. 2000. *The Republic.* Ed. G. R. F. Ferrari. Trans. Tom Griffith. Cambridge Texts in the History of Political Thought. Cambridge: Cambridge University Press.

Porter, James I. 1993. "The Seductions of Gorgias." *Classical Antiquity* 12, no. 2:267–99.

———. 2005. "Nietzsche and 'the Problem of Socrates.'" In *The Blackwell Companion to Socrates,* ed. S. Rappe and R. Kamtekar. Oxford: Basil Blackwell.

Press, Gerald A., ed. 1993. *Plato's Dialogues: New Studies and Interpretations.* Lanham, Md.: Rowman and Littlefield.

———. 1996. "The State of the Question in the Study of Plato." *Southern Journal of Philosophy* 34, no. 4:507–32.

———, ed. 2000. *Who Speaks for Plato? Studies in Platonic Anonymity.* Lanham, Md.: Rowman and Littlefield.

Price, Anthony W. 1989. *Love and Friendship in Plato and Aristotle.* Oxford: Clarendon Press.

Pucci, Pietro. 1987. *Odysseus Polutropos: Intertextual Readings in the "Odyssey" and the "Iliad."* Ithaca: Cornell University Press.

Rankin, H. D. 1964. *Plato and the Individual.* London: Methuen.

Redfield, James M. 1994. *Nature and Culture in the "Iliad": The Tragedy of Hector.* Expanded ed. Durham: Duke University Press.

Reeve, C. D. C. 1988. *Philosopher-Kings: The Argument of Plato's "Republic."* Princeton: Princeton University Press.

Robinson, John. 1973. "On Gorgias." In *Exegesis and Argument: Studies in Greek Philosophy Submitted to Gregory Vlastos,* edited by Edward N. Lee, Alexander P. D. Mourelatos, and Richard Rorty, 49–60. Phronesis Suppl. vol. 1. Assen: Van Gorcum.

Romilly, Jacqueline de. 1992. *The Great Sophists in Periclean Athens.* Trans. Janet Lloyd. Oxford: Clarendon Press.

Roochnik, David. 1996. *Of Art and Wisdom.* University Park: Pennsylvania State University Press.

———. 2003. *Beautiful City: The Dialectical Character of Plato's "Republic."* Ithaca: Cornell University Press.

Rorty, Amélie Oksenberg, ed. 1980. *Essays on Aristotle's Ethics.* Berkeley and Los Angeles: University of California Press.

Rosch, Eleanor. 1975. "Cognitive Representation of Semantic Categories." *Journal of Experimental Psychology* 104:192–233.

Rosen, Stanley. 1965. "The Role of Eros in Plato's *Republic.*" *Review of Metaphysics* 18:452–75.

———. 1987. *Plato's Symposium.* 2nd ed. New Haven: Yale University Press.

———. 1993. *The Question of Being: A Reversal of Heidegger.* New Haven: Yale University Press.

———. 2005. *Plato's Republic: A Study.* New Haven: Yale University Press.

Rowe, Christopher J. 2002. "Just How Socratic Are Plato's 'Socratic' Dialogues? A Response to Charles Kahn, *Plato and the Socratic Dialogue: The Philosophical Use of Literary Form.*" *Plato* 2 (January 2002), http://gramata.univ-paris1.fr/Plato/article30.html.[5]

Sallis, John. 1999. *Chorology: On Beginning in Plato's "Timaeus."* Bloomington: Indiana University Press.

Santos, Gerasimos. 1988. *Plato and Freud: Two Theories of Love.* Oxford: Basil Blackwell.

Schiappa, Edward. *Protagoras And Logos: A Study in Greek Philosophy and Rhetoric.* Columbia: U of South Carolina P, 1991.

Schmitt, Carl. 1996.[6] *The Concept of the Political.* Trans. George Schwab. Chicago: University of Chicago Press.

Sedley, David. 2005. *The Midwife of Platonism: Text and Subtext in Plato's "Theaetetus."* Cambridge: Cambridge University Press.

Smyth, Herbert Weir. 1920. *Greek Grammar.* Cambridge, Mass.: Harvard University Press.

Snell, Bruno. 1960. *The Discovery of the Mind: The Greek Origins of European Thought.* Trans. T. G. Rosenmeyer. New York: Harper and Row.

———. 1964. *Scenes from Greek Drama.* Berkeley and Los Angeles: University of California Press.

Sophocles. 1900. *The Antigone.* Vol. 3 of *Sophocles: The Plays and Fragments.* Ed. Richard Claverhouse Jebb. Cambridge: Cambridge University Press.

Stanford, William Bedell. 1954. *The Ulysses Theme: A Study in the Adaptability of a Traditional Hero.* Oxford: Basil Blackwell.

Stocks, J. L. 1915. "Plato and the Tripartite Soul." *Mind* 24, no. 94:207–21.

Strauss, Leo. 1953. *Natural Right and History.* Chicago: University of Chicago Press.

———. 1966. *Socrates and Aristophanes.* Chicago: University of Chicago Press.

———. 1978. *The City and Man.* Chicago: University of Chicago Press.

———. 1989. *The Rebirth of Classical Political Rationalism: An Introduction to the Thought of Leo Strauss: Essays and Lectures.* Ed. Thomas L. Pangle. Chicago: University of Chicago Press.

————. 1991. *On Tyranny.* Rev. ed. Edited by Victor Gourevitch and Michael S. Roth. New York: Free Press.

Szlezák, Thomas. 1985. *Platon und die Schriftlichkeit der Philosophie: Interpretationen zu den frühen und mittleren Dialogen.* Berlin: Walter de Gruyter, 1985.

————. 1993. *Platon Lesen.* Stuttgart: Verlag Fromman-Holzboog.

Taylor, Gabriele. 1985. *Pride, Shame, and Guilt: Emotions of Self-Assessment.* Oxford: Clarendon Press.

Thesleff, Holger. 1999. *Studies in Plato's Two-Level Model.* Helsinki: Societas Scientiarum Fennica.

Thucydides. 1942. *Thucydidis Historiae.* Ed. Henry Stuart Jones and John Enoch Powell. Oxford: Oxford University Press.

————. 1982. *The Peloponnesian War.* Trans. Richard Crawley, rev. T. E. Wick. New York: Modern Library.

Umphrey, Stewart. 1990. *Zetetic Skepticism.* Wolfeboro, N.H.: Longwood Academic Press.

————. 2002. *Complexity and Analysis.* New York: Lexington Books.

————. n.d. *"Natural Kinds and Genesis."*

Vander Waerdt, Paul A. 1994. "Socrates in the *Clouds.*" In *The Socratic Movement,* ed. Paul A. Vander Waerdt, 48–86. Ithaca: Cornell University Press.

Velleman, David. 2008. "The Way of the Wanton." In *Practical Identity and Narrative Agency,* edited by Kim Atkins and Catriona MacKenzie, 169–92. London: Routledge.

Vlastos, Gregory, ed. 1971. *Plato: A Collection of Critical Essays.* Vol. 2, *Ethics, Politics, and Philosophy of Art.* Garden City, NY: Anchor Books.

————. 1981. *Platonic Studies.* Princeton: Princeton University Press, 1981

————. 1991. *Socrates: Ironist and Moral Philosopher.* Ithaca: Cornell University Press.

Voegelin, Eric. 2000. *Plato and Aristotle.* Ed. Dante Germino. Vol. 3 of *Order and History.* Columbia: University of Missouri Press.

Wardy, Robert. 1998. *The Birth of Rhetoric: Gorgias, Plato, and Their Successors.* London: Routledge and Kegan Paul.

Watson, Gary. 1987. "Free Action and Free Will." *Mind* 96:148–49.

White, Nicholas P. *A Companion to Plato's "Republic."* Indianapolis: Hackett.

Wiggins, David. 1980. "Weakness of Will, Commensurability, and the Objects of Deliberation and Desire." In Rorty 1980, 241–65.

Williams, Bernard Arthur Owen. 1990. "Internal and External Reasons." In *Moral Luck: Philosophical Papers, 1973–1980,* 101–13. Cambridge: Cambridge University Press.

————. 1993. *Shame and Necessity.* Berkeley and Los Angeles: University of California Press.

Wittgenstein, Ludwig. 1958. *Philosophical Investigations = Philosophische Untersuchungen.* Trans. G. E. M. Anscombe. 2nd ed. Oxford: Basil Blackwell.

————. 1961. *Tractatus Logico-Philosophicus.* Trans. D. F. Pears and B. F. McGuinness. London: Routledge and Kegan Paul.

————. 1974. *Philosophical Grammar.* London: Basil Blackwell.

Xenophon. 1923. *"Memorabilia" and "Oeconomicus."* Trans. E. C. Marchant. Loeb Classical Library. Cambridge, Mass.: Harvard University Press; London: William Heinemann.

————. 1994. *Memorabilia.* Trans. Amy L. Bonnette. Ithaca: Cornell University Press.

Zahavi, Dan. 2006. *Subjectivity and Selfhood: Investigating the First-Person Perspective.* Cambridge, Mass.: MIT Press.

Zuckert, Catherine. 1996. *Postmodern Platos: Nietzsche, Heidegger, Gadamer, Strauss, Derrida.* Chicago: University of Chicago Press.

————. 2001. "Who's a Philosopher? Who's a Sophist? The Stranger v. Socrates," *Review of Metaphysics* 54: 65–97.
————. 2004. "The Socratic Turn." *History of Political Thought* 25:189–219.

General Index

abstraction
  the art of rule and, 99–103
  of capacity from its goal, 47–48
  Cephalus and, 24–26, 30
  ethical psychology and, 106–7
  geometry and, 236
  the good and, 18, 34
  injustice and, 103–6
  from interest, 158–59
  from interiority, 55–56
  the just man and, 289–92
  justice and, 282, 289–92, 294
  matter and, 135, 273
  money and, 31
  nature and, 122
  Polemarchus and, 34–35, 47–49
  politics and, 51
  from purpose, 32
  the self, and, 273, 289
  Thrasymachus and, 34, 98–99, 102
Achilles, 186, 246–52
  exteriority and, 251–52
  Odysseus and, 246–49
  as poet, 251–52, 275
  his relation to social world, 250–52
action. *See* agency
Adeimantus, 104, 144, 174, 186, 187, 214, 216, 255, 280–82, 292–30
  authority and, 294
  city-soul analogy and, 297
  ethical internalization and, 292–94
  guilt and, 280, 292–94
  the gods and, 293
  narcissism and, 297
  nature and, 298, 305
  his relation to Socrates, 294, 297–99

Adam, James, 69n28, 195n20, 187n12, 195n20, 214n17, 224n34
Adkins, Arthur W. H., 150n8, 252n15
Aeschylus, 152–53, 163n32
Agathocles, 156
Agathon, 21–22, 202
agency. *See also* responsibility
  causation and, 58–59, 241
  cave analogy and, 78–79
  contemplation and, 240–42
  epistemic problem of, 72, 78–82
  experience and, 226–35, 240–43, 278, 302
  the good and, 58–59
  hypothetical status of, 81–82
  indeterminacy of, 220
  interpretative activity and, 218–20
  (in)voluntary action and, 224, 241
  mimêsis and, 218–20
  the *polis* and, 68–69, 97
  practical problem of, 72–73
  problem of, 241
  psychological problem of, 72–78. *See also* akrasia
  self-ascription of agency and, 219
Aitia. *See* cause
akrasia (weakness of will), 73–74, 76
Alcibiades, 152, 198, 203, 205, 214, 269
Alcinous, 277–78
Allen, R. E., 1, 62n19, 127n9, 164n33, 168n39
Annas, Julia, 4n8, 30n43, 58, 60n15, 61n17, 63n20, 95n4, 98n9
antinaturalism, 122, 149–50, 160–62, 167–70, 173, 208–9. *See also* nature
Antiphon, *On Truth*, 121–22
Aporia, 92, 238
Apollodorus, 269

Apology, 3, 45, 47, 54, 57, 124, 188, 286, 304
  Socrates' self-presentation in, 203–4, 306–7
aretê (virtue, excellence)
  action and, 290
  the art of rule and, 100–103
  as cognitive capacities, 62, 69–72, 97
  denial of, 118–19, 125, 139
  as dispositions, 62, 97
  executive, 65, 73, 77
  harm and, 54–55, 57
  Homer and, 52
  human, 54–55, 68, 89–90
  images of, 213–15, 304–5
  instrumental reason and, 60–61
  justice and, 53, 61, 63, 65–66, 112,
    184–85n7
  knowledge and, 62, 182, 304–6
  pleasure and, 41
  the polis and, 30–31, 60, 65, 68, 84
  political virtue and, 150, 153, 158, 165–66,
    165–70
  recollection and, 189
  in *Republic*, 189
  rhetoric and, 116, 121–23, 127
  technê and, 62
  to thumoeides and, 265
  wealth and, 26–27, 30–31, 307
Aristophanes
  Archanians, 152
  Clouds, 152
  Frogs, 152, 172
Aristotle
  his account of action, 241
  courage and, 253
  communal life and, 270
  virtue and, 37, 65, 290
  hylomorphism and, 135
  justice and, 69
  matter and, 273
  mimêsis and, 240
  Nichomachean Ethics, 18, 37
  philosophy and, 40
  practical deliberation and, 233, 234n53, 253
  Poetics, 224
  Politics, 30–31
  practical syllogism, the, 78
  relation to Socrates, 3–4
  responsibility and, 68
  the three lives and, 18, 37
  irony and, 271
  technê and, 61

  virtue and the polis and, 30–31, 49, 65, 290
  wonder and, 199
Asclepius, 55, 61, 232
Athenian stranger, the, 130, 154, 230
Ausland, Hayden Weir, 6n11, 9n18, 44n58
authority
  calculation and, 260
  the crowd and, 140
  education and, 135–38, 140–41, 145, 157
  figure of, 294, 298
  the good and, 145
  guilt and, 294
  Homer as, 209
  the just man and, 50, 56
  as persuasion, 115, 135–38, 142, 145, 266
  of the philosopher, 39–41
  political, 50, 137
  poetic imitation and, 212–15
  religious poetic tradition and, 48–49, 62, 178
  representation and, 206
  rhetoric and, 123–24, 128–29
  of the ruler, 100–102, 113
  types of life and, 39–40

Baracchi, Claudia, 12n5
Barnes, Jonathan, 121n39
Barney, Rachel, 121–22
Benardete, Seth, 17n22, 26n36, 51, 65n21, 146n31,
    208n3, 212n11, 241n66, 302n1
  to thumoeides and, 263
Berg, Steven, 152n17
Bertram, Ernst, 11n1
Beversluis, John, 19n25, 28n41, 60n15, 63n20,
    70n29, 115n30
Bloom, Allan, 1, 61n17, 196n10, 187n12,
    226n39
Blondell, Ruby, 16n17, 18n23, 19n25, 25n36,
    115n29
Bobonich, Christopher, 261n28
body, the,
  care of, 143–45
  Cephalus and, 21, 25
  eros and, 201–2
  as "material" condition, 58–59, 273
  the soul and, 58–59, 256
  value of life and, 53–54
Boeckh, August, 16n15
Bosanquet, Barnard, 196n21
Brann, Eva, 12n5, 21, 33n50
Brickhouse, Thomas C., 81n37
Burger, Ronna, 3n7, 4n9, 84n39, 129n12
Broadie, Sarah, 20n27, 129n12

Cairns, Douglas L., 163n31, 281n2
calculation
    authority and, 260
    conditions of thought and, 196–97
    imaging relation and, 236–37
    mimêsis and, 221–22, 238, 242
    perception and, 221, 228
    to thumoeides and, 245, 258, 260–63, 268–70
    trust and, 221–23, 226
Callicles, 29, 44, 94, 109, 134, 138–41, 147, 174, 266
    his relation to Gorgias, 142–46
    natural justice and, 142
    persuasion and, 142
Cartledge, Paul, 15n12
Casevitz, Michel, 271n39
cause
    agency and, 58–59, 241, 273
    explanatory priority and, 58
cave analogy, 10, 32–33, 175–76, 193–95, 215
    artifice and, 193–95, 199, 206
    epistemic problem of agency and, 78–81
    function of, 79–80
    hypothesis of doxastic immanence and, 193–95, 206, 220–21
    the philosopher-ruler and, 194–95, 206
    idea of the good and, 80
Cephalus, 19–35, 44, 46–47, 82, 121–22, 262
    abstraction and, 24–26, 30
    the body and, 21, 25
    departure of, 33–34
    ethical world of, 29–30
    guilt and, 292–93
    justice and, 30
    madness and, 183–84
    piety and, 26–27
    poetic tradition and, 25–30, 33, 62
    political status of, 30
    symbolic function of, 19
    wealth and, 26–27, 30–31
Charmides, 62, 66, 129, 274
Cicero, 33
city-in-speech, the, 20, 24, 66, 72–73, 77, 79, 189, 210, 212, 267, 296, 301
    hypothesis of doxastic immanence and, 177–79, 184, 211
    as image of a human being, 176, 215
    mimêsis and, 214–16
    the philosopher-king and, 211–12
    the poet and, 186–87
    representation and, 175, 265

city-soul analogy
    philosopher-ruler in, 176
    psychological reorientation and, 295–99
    therapeutic role of, 297–99
    to thumoeides and, 244–45, 260–61
Clay, Diskin, 7n12
Cleitophon, 95
    his defense of Thrasymachus, 99–100
Cleon, 167
Coby, Patrick, 150n8
contemplation
    agency and, 240–42
    experience and, 216, 234–35, 237–40
    of idea of the good, 79–80
    life of, 18, 34, 37
    mimetic poetry and, 216, 238, 242, 278
    in *Phaedo*, 80–81, 81f
    Socratic dialogue and, 238, 242
    the tragic hero and, 230, 234–35, 239
    the transcendental *epochê* and, 240–42
Cornford, F. M., 9n16, 179n2
Critias, 20, 154, 166, 275
    making/doing distinction, 129
    Sisyphus, 154
Critias, 21, 24, 274
Crito, 38, 53, 188, 231
Cross, R. C., and A. D. Woozley, 60n15, 98n8
Crowell, Steven, 224n33, 239n60
culture, 15, 56–57, 149–50
    cultural decadence and,11–13, 17, 19, 32–35, 62, 178
    cultural relativism and, 15
    cultural roles and, 56
    human nature and, 161
    images of age and, 19–21
    representation and, 207
custom. See *nomos*

Daimonic, the
    eros and, 202–5, 270
    sign, 204
    Socrates and, 204–5
Dannhauser, Werner J., 11n1
Davis, Michael, 225n35, 241n65, 287nn11, 12
Dawe, R. D., 246n3
decline of the regimes, 13, 33, 75, 200, 261, 267–68
Delphic oracle, 1, 188
democracy
    Athenian, 14, 17, 20, 49, 84, 90, 166
    democratic rule and, 98–99

democracy (*continued*)
the democratic soul and, 26, 43, 67, 75, 84, 267, 298
Socrates' trial and, 14, 114
Protagoras and, 150, 170–71
context of *Republic* and, 17
Democritus
his relation to Protagoras, 149
Demodocus, 276–77
Derrida, Jacques, 208n3
desire, 18, 25–26, 38, 74
eros and, 179
mourning and, 229–31
politics and, 300–301
politicization of, 42
rational desires and, 181–82
to thumoeides and, 258
dialectics
critique of mimetic poetry and, 210
education and, 197–98, 267
Hegel and, 284
hypotheses and, 10, 236–38
knowledge and, 197–98, 237–38
in *Phaedrus*, 200–201
of social recognition, 240–42
dialogue, 174, 271–74. See also Plato's dialogues
apodeictic intent of, 52, 58, 82, 96, 303–6
Book I of *Republic* and, 9–10
dialogic practice and, 82–83, 96–97, 172–73
elenctic stage of, 64, 81, 83–87, 181–83, 238, 303
ethical inquiry and, 1–3
intentional misprision in, 28–29
the philosophic life and, 43–45
therapeutic stage of, 80, 87–92, 175, 297
within dialogue, 9
zetetic stage of, 83–84
dianoetic reflection, 235–37
calculation and, 238, 242
natural attitude and the, 235–36
geometry and, 236–37
Diomedes, 254
Diotima, 9, 200–203
discursive activity, 192–93, 206–7, 211. See also doxastic immanence, hypothesis of
relation to intelligible realm and, 180–81, 201
divided line, image of, 222, 236–37
Dodds, E. R., 14n8, 16n18, 128n10, 131n13, 133n15, 252n15
doxastic immanence, hypothesis of, 209–10, 245
cave analogy and, 193–95, 206, 220–21

the city-in-speech and, 177–79, 184, 211
eros and, 299
experientially understood, 206
mourning and, 231–32
orientation of *Republic* and, 177–81, 192–93, 195–98, 299–300
philosophic life and, 198
politics and, 178–79, 206–7, 219, 244
to thumoeides and, 265–66

education
of desires, 75–78
dialectical, 197–98, 267
eros and, 183–84
erotic, 201–2
gymnastic, 72–73, 264–65
the law and, 169, 264–65
madness and, 183–84, 198
mathematical, 189, 196–98, 206
musical, 50, 61, 75–77, 264–65
as persuasion, 132–46, 266
philosophic, 81–82, 205
poetry and, 152
the political art and, 157–59
political virtue and, 165–70
as redirection of vision, 278–79
rhetoric and, 102–3
Socratic, 300–301
types of soul and, 199–200, 203
to thumoeides and, 264–65
Engel, David M., 250n27
Epimetheus, 160–61
eros
daimonic, 202–5, 270
cave analogy and, 194
as divine, 179–81, 185
exclusion of, 184, 194, 198–99
and hypothesis of doxastic immanence, 179
in *Phaedrus*, 7, 179–80, 200–201
in *Republic*, 7, 179–81, 184
likeness to Socrates and, 202–4, 304
in *Symposium*, 7, 179–80, 201–5, 304
as tyrant, 179–81, 299
ethics. See also *arête*; practical deliberation
ethical exemplars and, 304–6
ethical internalization and, 244, 268–69, 291–94
ethical knowledge and, 78–79
recognition and, 290–91, 294–95, 306
Eumaeus, 186
Euripides, 116–17, 152n18, 207n1

Euthydemus, 9
Euthyphro, 158
Euthyphro, 45
excellence. See *aretê*
experience
abstraction from, 101–2
agency and, 226–35, 240–43, 278, 302
conditions of, 192–93, 197, 273
contemplation and, 238–40, 242
culture and, 11–12, 23, 34, 178
custom and, 228–35
dianoetic reflection and, 235–38
discursive activity and, 206, 211
of the good, 37–39
the intelligible realm and, 179–81, 195, 198, 221
limits of, 195–96
mathematical education and, 196–98
mimetic poetry and, 207–8, 216, 239–43, 273, 302
mimêsis and, 207–8
mourning and, 226–35
pleasure and, 38–41, 44
psychic conflict and, 73–74, 97
transcendence and, 183, 199
translation of *pathos*, 226n39
virtue and, 305–6
the visible and, 222–23
wonder and, 199

Ferrari, G. R. F., 1n1, 74, 196n11, 187n12, 227n42, 228n45, 257n24, 258n26, 269n36, 297n29
Ferrarin, Alfredo, 149n4, 150n8, 153n21, 160n27, 161n30
Fine, Gail, 192n16
Foot, Phillipa, 54n9
Fränkel, Herman, 250
Freud, Sigmund, 88–89, 282–83, 294, 295

Geertz, Clifford, 22–24
geometry, 235–37, 239
Gerson, Lloyd P., 4n9, 261n28
Gill, Christopher, 6n11, 79n36, 253
Glaucon, 33, 36, 37, 39, 109, 115, 183, 191, 210, 213, 214, 216–17, 219, 227, 230, 255–56, 258, 263, 274, 280–92, 294–301
abstract justice and, 289–92
being seen and, 284, 287–89
city-soul analogy and, 297
the good and, 198, 300–301

guilt and, 292
image and, 176
mathematical education and, 196–97
narcissism and, 297
nature and, 297–98, 300, 305
the philosophic life and, 40–41, 269
self-conception of, 284, 291
shame and, 280–82, 284–92, 296
his relation to the social world, 284, 288
his relation to Socrates, 80, 297–99
and restoration of Thrasymachus' argument, 147, 280, 284
God, the/the gods
character and, 188
death of, 12–13, 33–34
education and, 189
image-making and, 163–65
justice and, 293
likeness to, 164–65, 189, 201, 263–64, 288
obligation to, 30
punishment and, 24, 27, 164–65
representation of, 186–88, 220, 265
role of, 153–54
sacrifice and, 293
in *Republic*, 184
good, the
agency and, 58–59
contemplation and, 79–80
cultural death and, 34
as disclosive of beings, 238
eros and, 270
the good human being and, 205
hypothesis of, 242
idea of, 79–80, 175–76, 198, 268–69
images of, 81
madness and, 199–200
method of hypothesis and, 238
money and, 120
mourning and, 230–33
nature and, 18–19, 49, 52–55
orientation to, 278, 302
pleasure and, 36–41, 172
presentiment of, 195–96
rhetoric and, 131–32
representation of, 268–69
the rhetorician and, 123
the sun and, 199, 221, 224, 299
transgression and, 104–7
Goldberg, Larry, 152n16
Goldhill, Simon, 271n39
Gonzalez, Francisco J., 6n11, 192n16, 224n33

Gorgias, 66, 93–94, 97, 117, 123–46, 150, 173, 207, 209, 221, 262, 265–66, 274, 303
action/material production distinction and, 124, 128–30, 138, 145–46
his appropriation of rhetoric, 127
as author of his students, 124, 128, 136–38, 140–44
and authority, 124, 129, 131, 135–43
his relation to Callicles, 142–46
character of, 126
the crowd and, 133–34, 137, 140, 144
Defense of Palamedes, 126
his dependence on students, 145–46
divine power of rhetoric and, 123–24, 132, 144
Encomium to Helen, 125–26, 132, 221
flattery and, 144
functional level of arts and, 130–32
the good and, 131–32, 137, 145, 268
his hylomorphism, 135
the individual and, 133–34
injustice and, 138–39
justice and, 137–38, 140–41, 144
relation between nature and speech and, 126, 128
ontology of, 125, 128, 134–35
On What Is Not or On Nature, 125, 134
his relation to oratory, 127–28, 136, 139–40
pedagogic level of arts and, 130–31
persuasion and, 124–46, 219
his relation to the political community, 124
political justice and, 124, 137
his relation to Polus, 142–46
the rhetorical man and, 127, 134, 140, 212
relation of rhetoric to content and, 131
rhetoric as distinctive art and, 128–32
rhetoric as producing belief and, 131
self-persuasion and, 145
as teacher of rhetoric, 128, 132–33, 135–42
Socrates' critique of, 143–46
Socrates' dialogic intent toward, 126–27
Gorgias, 16–17, 29, 44, 66, 94, 100, 109, 120, 123–46, 173–74, 275
Gould, Thomas, 226n39
Griffith, Mark, 153n22
Griswold, Charles L., Jr., 2n4, 6n11, 7n12, 186n9, 211, 231n50
guardians, the
canine characteristics of, 256–57
education of, 10, 61, 72, 200
Glaucon's identification with, 297
gymnastic education of, 72–73, 264–65

lies and, 186, 266–67
mathematical education of, 61, 189, 193, 196–98
musical education of, 50, 61, 77–78, 182, 264–65
philosophical education of, 189, 198–99
their relation to philosopher-rulers, 266–67
to thumoeides and, 256–57
relation to the true philosopher and, 256–57
virtue and, 265
guilt, 280–85, 292–97
psychoanalytic theories of, 283
punishment and, 283, 292–94
Guthrie, W. K. C., 95n4

Hadot, Ilsetraut, 4n9
Hadot, Pierre, 4n8, 11n1, 303
Hall, Edith, 15n12
Halliwell, Stephen, 213n15, 226n39, 229
happiness
guilt and, 292
of others, 109
of the philosopher, 79
as transgression, 106
of the tyrant, 105–6
Harlap, Schmuel, 95n4
Hegel, G., 13
critique of abstract self-consciousness, 145
The Phenomenology of Spirit, 124, 284
Heidegger, Martin, 223–24, 240n61, 245
eidetic vision and, 223–24
Henderson, T. Y., 95n4
Herman, K. F., 10n19
Herodicus, 156
Herodotus
his account of Gyges, 287–88
Histories, 15
Hesiod, 175
Heteronomy
problem of, 42–44, 75, 105–6, 250
Hippias, 246–49
Hippocrates, 155–56, 266
Hobbes, Thomas, 49n4, 140n22, 141n23, 290n19
Hobbs, Angela, 245, 255n23
Homer, 29–30, 52, 154, 246–78, 281. See also Achilles, the critique of mimetic poetry, Odysseus
Iliad, 52, 186, 245–55, 275
mourning and, 229
Odyssey, 29, 154, 186, 245, 255, 275–78

poetic inspiration and, 186
psychology and, 250–55
Socrates' critique of, 213–16
Socrates' relation to, 207, 215
as Sophist, 156, 208–9
to thumoeides and, 245, 258–59
Honor, 261–62
Hourani, George F., 95n4
Howland, Jacob, 27n39, 255n23
Husserl, Edmund, 222–36, 238–40
the natural attitude and, 222–23, 235–36, 238
the transcendental epochê and, 238–42
Hyland, Drew, 185n7

images
cave analogy and, 80–82, 193–96, 206, 220, 223
contemplation and, 80–81, 273
daimonic character of, 279
of divided line, 222, 236–37
education and, 194, 278
of excellence, 213–15, 304–5
geometry and, 236–37
of the good, 81, 205, 238, 244–45, 268, 273, 302
of human being, 176, 212, 215, 267
of ideal inquirer, 299, 304
image-making and, 163–64, 173, 175–76, 273
the imaginary and, 89
imaging relation and, 236–37, 273
as incomplete, 278, 303
the intelligible realm and, 273, 278
of justice, 10, 176, 195, 295–96, 304–5
law and, 144
method of hypothesis and, 238
nature and, 148, 164, 173, 278
perspective and, 273, 278
the philosopher-ruler and, 175–76, 211–12, 264, 267
practical deliberation and, 222, 236
of reason, 267
of shame, 284, 286
speech and, 164
of Socrates, 202–4, 306–7
of Socrates' historical context, 5, 12, 17, 21, 178
Socrates' use of, 9, 174–75, 77, 80–82, 89, 213–15, 238, 244, 267, 273, 275, 278–79, 302–3
the Sophists and, 125, 148, 211–12, 275, 304
the soul and, 81, 176, 272

the sun and, 199, 221, 224, 299
of world, 22–23
indefinite, the, 134–35
the crowd and, 111, 115, 133–37, 139–40, 144, 175
intellect, the
awakening of, 221, 224
experience and, 24
perception and, 221–24
the self and, 272–73
intelligible, realm of the
discursive activity and, 177, 179, 181, 192, 200–204, 270
experience and, 193–95
images and, 278, 303
the intellect and, 241
the realm of the visible and, 207, 221–24, 236–37
in Republic, 184–85, 192, 195, 198
to thumoeides and, 245
the self and, 270, 273
interiority
abstraction from, 55–56
Odysseus and, 250, 252–55, 259–62, 271, 275
to thumoeides and, 245, 259–62
Irwin, T. H., 60n15, 139n21, 181, 261

Janaway, Christopher, 213n15
Jebb, Richard, 26n38
justice, 15, 28, 60–64, 84, 90, 96, 176
abstraction and, 282, 289–92, 294
as advantage of the stronger, 17, 93–95, 97–103
analogy with technê and, 60–72, 79, 83, 97
appeal to, 113–14, 119
appearance of, 137–39, 141, 166, 168, 171, 298, 305
the art of politics and, 66–67
authority and, 48–49
the body and, 53–54
as capacity, 61
community and, 119
as a compact, 147, 183, 305
as corrective, 86n40, 167–70
the crowd and, 144
difficulty of perceiving, 215
as disposition, 61
education and, 267
eros and, 184–85f
as gift of Zeus, 153, 163–65
the good and, 50, 120, 267, 294

justice (*continued*)
  the good of another and, 95, 103–7, 120
  guilt and, 292–94
  image of, 176, 195–96, 295–96, 304–5
  integrity and, 301
  the (un)just man and, 50–51, 64–65, 82–86,
    103–7, 112–19, 141, 176, 284–91
  madness and, 32–33, 166, 183
  nature and, 300
  natural, 44, 142
  nominalist account of, 98
  nomothetic account of, 98–99
  ownership, 301
  persuasion and, 131
  pleasure and, 38
  Polemarchus' account of, 46, 48–49, 82,
    87–88, 90
  as political, 137–38
  political community and, 50–53, 56–60, 63,
    65, 87, 219
  power and, 297–98
  punishment and, 165–68
  recognition and, 290–91
  retributive, 138, 143–44, 146
  reverence and, 163–65, 167
  rhetoric and, 115, 122, 137, 143–46
  shame and, 288–92
  social manifestations of, 282, 290–92
  social relations and, 301
  Thrasymachus' bifurcate account of, 95, 97, 113,
    121
  tradition and, 34
  virtue and, 112
justification, 11, 18, 35–37, 39, 271
  narratives of, 273–74, 302

Kahn, Charles, 3n6, 9n18, 10n19, 139n20, 141n25,
  182n6
Kant, Immanuel, 192–93, 196n22
  conditions of possibility and, 197–98
  The Critique of Pure Reason, 192
  and *Republic*, 192
Karamanolis, George E., 4n9
Kaufmann, Walter, 11n1
Kerferd, G. B., 95n4, 98n9, 125, 166n37
Klein, Jacob, 18n23, 44n57, 131n13, 208n3
knowledge
  action and, 74, 79
  authority and, 101–2, 135–36, 144–45, 266
  calculation and, 196–97
  as capacity, 189–92, 198

education and, 129–32, 300
eros and, 180, 201–8
ethical and, 60–61, 79
of the forms, 223
the good and, 198
and hypotheses, 238
hypothesis of doxastic immanence and,
  197–98, 300
imitation and, 213–15, 223–24
the individual and, 134
justified true belief and, 74, 191
mimetic poetry and, 213–14, 279
relation to opinion, 180–81, 189–92, 198
pleasures of, 40–41
as perception, 151, 171, 208–9
persuasion and, 132–35, 139, 145, 266
the political art and, 66–67
self-knowledge and, 1–2, 12, 120
as self-persuasion, 145–46
Socratic ignorance and, 273–74
virtue and, 62, 182, 304–6
wonder and, 201–2
Kofman, Sarah, 4n8
Kohut, Heinz, 282–83, 296
Kojève, Alexander, 109n18

Laches, 62, 158
Lampert, Laurence, 246n2, 255n23
Lane, Melissa, 4n8
law. See *nomos*
Laws, 21, 124, 130
Lear, Jonathan, 264
  idiopolis and, 88
  narcissism and, 295–96
  Socratic practice and, 181–82
legislative activity, 97, 102–3
  agency and, 68, 71–75, 97, 218–19, 295
  cave analogy and, 82
  the good and, 82
  mimêsis and, 207, 218–19, 223
  poetry and, 214, 262f
  of the philosopher-ruler, 184–85, 206–7, 213–14,
    223, 265, 267
  politics and, 66–68, 71, 83–84, 98, 98–99, 103,
    121, 125, 143–44, 148, 151, 171, 232
Lesser Hippias, 246–50
Lévystone, David, 246n2, 255n23
lies, 77, 186, 266
  the gods and, 187–88
  the lie of autochthony and, 77–78, 175
  manifest, 277–78

medicinal, 187–88
  Odysseus and, 29
  the true, 272–74, 278
Linguistic practice, 210–11
logos, 24, 132, 221
Long, A. A., 4n8
Longo, Angela, 9n17
Lysis, 16
Ludwig, Paul, 180n3, 217n20, 299n30
Lycos, Kimon, 94n2

madness
  divine, 182–85
  eros and, 179
  exclusion of in *Republic*, 183–87, 198–200
  the good and, 199–200
  justice and, 32–33, 166–67, 183
  the philosopher-ruler and, 183
  philosophic, 198–200
  Socratic philosophy and, 181–82
  transcendence and, 198–99
  types of, 185
Maguire, Joseph P., 95n4
McDowell, John, 54n9
Marcuse, Herbert, 297
Marx, Karl, 54n9, 68
  division of labor and, 124
materialism, 148–49
method of hypothesis, 238
McKirahan, Richard, 125
Meletus, 3, 57, 90
Menexenus, 16
Meno, 204
Meno, 191
mimêsis, 206–43, 246
  calculation and, 221–22
  the city in speech and, 214–16
  experience and, 207–8, 216, 230–31, 302
  graphic imitator and, 220–21
  graphic and poetic, 218–20
  logic of, 218
  the mimetic artist and, 220
  nature and, 211–13
  perception and, 221–24
  perspective and, 220–21, 225
  philosophic reflection and, 235, 241–44
  politics and, 207, 218–19, 225, 230–33, 235, 265
  practical deliberation, 224–28
  Socrates' dialogic practice and, 274
  as wholly determinate production, 207, 219, 221

mimetic poetry, 206–7
  agency and, 224–35, 240–43, 278, 302
  contemplation and, 216, 238, 242, 278
  customary roles and, 228–30, 235
  deception and, 213–15, 220–21
  experience and, 207–8, 216, 239–43, 273, 302
  as interpretively indeterminate, 219–20
  irony and, 218–20
  mourning and, 224–34
  philosophic reflection and, 235, 273
  the poet and, 186
  as resistant to exclusion, 218–19
  the transcendental *epochê* and, 239–42
mimetic poetry, the critique of, 206–34
  dialectics and, 210
  the divine craftsman and, 211–12
  Homer and, 209–10
  mourning and, 225–34
  Socrates self-presentation in, 216–19, 231
money, 26–27, 30, 36–37, 76–77, 84
  abstraction and, 31
Monoson, S. Sara, 30n43
Moes, Mark, 67n25
Moors, Kent, 16n14
morality. *See also* agency; *arête*; responsibility
  guilt and, 280–84
  shame and, 280–84
Moravcsik, Julius, 204
Morris, Herbert, 282–83
mourning, 224–35
  disclosure and, 226–29
  experience and, 230–31
  the good and, 232–34
  the law and, 226–34
  philosophic reflection and, 234
  politics and, 226–33
  practical deliberation and, 227–34
  role-playing and, 228–29
Murphy, Neville R., 221n27
myth, 159–60
  appropriation of, 173
  death of, 11–12, 24, 27, 34
  distrust of, 1
  of Er, 184, 277
  Homer and, 209
  the mythic tradition and, 1n1, 15, 32–35
  the philosopher and, 13, 150
  Protagoras', 159–68
  religion and, 15, 23–24
  Socrates' use of, 9, 138, 174–75, 184–85, 203, 209, 275, 303, 306–7

Nails, Deborah, 16n15, 17n19
narcissism, 296–97
  psychoanalytic theory of, 296–97
Natorp, Paul, 16n17, 193n17
nature, 49, 124–25, 188–89. *See also*
    antinaturalism
  abstraction from, 122
  Adeimantus' account of, 298, 305
  artifice and, 193–95
  disposition and, 255–56
  education and, 194, 278
  Glaucon's account of, 297–98, 300, 305
  the good and, 18–19, 49, 52–55
  homo mensura thesis and, 148–49
  human, 34, 43, 49, 54–55, 63, 68, 149, 161–64,
      167–70, 173, 194–95, 218, 298
  images and, 148, 164, 173, 278
  imitation and, 211–12
  justice and, 58
  law and, 124–25, 147–50
  mimêsis and, 211–13
  natural justice and, 140, 147
  naturalism and, 148–49
  occult qualities and, 298
  the philosopher-ruler and, 175–76
  political virtue and, 168–70
  politics and, 52–53, 63, 122, 161, 166
  Protagoras and, 148–50, 161, 170
  punishment and, 166–67
  in *Republic*, 175–76, 196
  second, 256–57
  Sophistic account of, 122, 123–24, 147–50,
      161–62
  speech and, 125–26
  as strife, 160–62
  as system of forces, 297–98
Nehamas, Alexander, 4n8, 8n15, 11n1, 200n20,
    221n27
Nietzsche, 4, 22–24, 91n46, 173, 231, 295, 307
  Beyond Good and Evil, 172, 266
  The Birth of Tragedy, 11, 19, 22–24
  his critique of Socrates, 4–5, 11–12, 14, 93,
      280–81
  cultural decadence and, 11–13, 19, 21, 33–35, 93
  the dionysian, 149–50
  ethical life and, 5
  The Gay Science, 32
  The Genealogy of Morality, 292
  Greek tragedy and, 22–23
  "On the Uses and Disadvantages of History
      for Life," 19

  philosophy as confession and, 271
  Protagoras and, 149–50, 152
  religion and, 23
  ressentiment and, 107–8, 111, 113, 118–19
  self-justification and, 273–74
  Socratic dialectic and, 5, 93
  Thrasymachus and, 107
  to thumoeides and, 266
  Twilight of the Idols, 5, 19, 173
  the will and, 245
  will to power and, 5, 93
nomos (law, custom)
  conformity and, 57–58, 84
  education and, 169, 264–65
  formative role of, 144, 149, 154–55, 161, 169–71,
      173, 264–65
  freedom from, 171
  ignorance of the good and, 231
  interest and, 98–99
  justice and, 98, 103
  lawlessness and, 153
  the legislative art and, 65–67, 84
  lies and, 188
  persuasion and, 228–29
  the polis and, 66–67
  money and, 31
  mourning and, 226–34
  natural justice and, 44, 142
  nature and, 150, 300
  punishment and, 154, 163–68
  reason and, 227–28
  Socrates and, 88, 96
  transgression and, 106, 121
  tyranny and, 153
Nussbaum, Martha, 155, 160n28, 162n31, 179n2

O'Brien, Michael, 14n8
O'Connor, David, 255n23
Oedipus, 225n35, 234n54, 241–42, 286
Odysseus, 29, 154, 186, 243, 245–78
  Achilles and, 246–50
  the Cyclops and, 270–71
  deception and, 249–50
  interiority and, 252–55, 258–60, 270–71
  mêtis and, 271
  mimetic capacity of, 249–50
  his poetic art, 275–78
  polutropos and, 246–47
  role-playing and, 274–75
  his relation to the social world, 250, 270–71
  to thumoeides and, 258–60, 262, 270

oligarchic man, the, 36, 76–77, 261–62
Orpheus, 153, 156
Osborne, Catherine, 203n30
Ostwald, Martin, 4n9

Page, Carl, 175n47
Parry, Richard, 60n15
pathos, 119, 227, 273. *See also* experience
Pears, David, 65n24
Penner, Terry, 181
Peradotto, John, 246n4
perception, 197, 241
    contradiction in, 242
    idealized perceptual experience and, 223, 225,
        236
    the intellect and, 221–24, 228
    knowledge and, 190–92, 208–9
    in *Theatetus*, 190–92
    trust and, 222–23
Pericles, 140, 158
persuasion, 50, 82, 115, 124–46, 175, 195, 209, 219,
    262–63, 264, 266. *See also* rhetoric
Phaedo, 58, 80–81, 188, 219, 231, 255–56, 273
Phaedrus, 111, 174, 225
Phaedrus, 1–2, 110, 115, 195
    daimonic sign in, 204
    distinctive conception of eros in, 179–80,
        200–201
    human character in, 188
    madness in, 182, 185, 199
    philosophic education in, 189
    rhetoric in, 200–201
    transcendent orientation of, 183, 188–89,
        199–201
    truth in, 195
Philebus, 44
philosopher, the. *See also* the philosopher-ruler
    ascent of, 79–80
    authority and, 39–41
    canine likeness of, 256
    the divine and, 201, 212
    education and, 13
    the good and, 268
    happiness of, 79
    madness and, 33, 183
    the philosophic life and, 38–41, 80–82, 201, 203
    pleasure and, 38–41
    the political community and, 10, 269
    the problem of action and, 79
    recollection and, 199
    self-sufficiency of, 269

Socratic philosophy and, 4, 4f
    the true philosopher and, 256–57, 304–5
    wonder and, 199
philosopher-ruler, the, 32, 73, 78
    cave analogy and, 78–79, 194–95
    in city-soul analogy, 176
    dialectical method of, 238
    calculation and, 176
    education and, 184
    as god-like, 176
    goodness of, 267
    his relation to guardians, 266–67
    Heidegger's interpretation of, 223–24
    as image, 176–77
    the image of human being and, 144, 211–12, 215,
        264
    legislative activity of, 184–85, 206–7, 213–14,
        223, 265–67
    madness and, 183
    mathematical education of, 221
    motivation of, 79
    philosophic education of, 214
    political community and, 211
    as Socratic artifact, 215
    Socrates' relation to, 274
    as distinct from sophist, 175–76
philosophic life, the, 38–41, 80–82, 201, 203
philosophical confusion, 302–3
Pindar, 27–28, 30
Piers, Gerhart, and Milton B. Singer, 282, 285
Piraeus, 14–15, 31, 50
Plato. *See also* Plato's dialogues; *Republic*
    his account of eros, 179–80
    discursive activity of, 204
    historical context and, 13–17, 19–21, 24
    philosophic education and, 205
    Platonism and, 5–6, 292
    his psychology, 280–82, 289, 295–96
    to thumoeides and, 245
    tradition and, 15
    his presentation of Socrates, 2–6, 8–10, 12–14,
        45, 79–80, 88, 95, 152–53, 174–77, 204–5,
        207n1, 214, 229–31, 255, 306–7
    the Sophists and, 95, 121, 123–25, 141–42,
        147–52, 173–75
    wonder and, 199
Plato's dialogues
    abstraction in, 31–32
    esotericism in, 127, 151, 151f
    function of interlocutor's in, 18, 43–48, 144,
        173–75, 269–70, 280, 302

Plato's dialogues (*continued*)
  madness in, 182–84, 199
  mimêsis and, 244–46, 302–3
  poetry in, 185–86
  relationship between, 6–7
  Socrates' authorship of, 8–9
pleasure, 35–42. *See also* desire
  as currency, 38
  freedom and, 44
  the good and, 37–39
  illusory pleasure and, 40–41
  justification and, 37–40
  the life of, 43–44
Plotinus, 159
poetry. *See* mimetic poetry; mimetic poetry,
    critique of
Polemarchus, 32–35, 46–92, 97, 99, 119, 122, 219,
    262, 274
  agency and, 58–60, 68–69
  his appropriation of Cephalus' argument, 48,
    50
  authority and, 48–50
  autonomy of the political and, 49, 52–53, 62
  conflicted commitments of, 87–88, 90
  conformity and, 57–58, 88, 90
  his dependence on Socrates, 92
  elenctic stage of dialogue and, 84–87
  ethical action and, 68–69
  force and, 50
  the friend/enemy distinction and, 51–53,
    82–87
  relation to the good and, 34, 63
  human nature and, 54–55
  imagined world of, 87
  interiority and, 56
  justice and, 46, 48–50, 56–66, 82–87, 90
  opening of *Republic* and, 49–50, 88
  the poetic tradition and, 48–49
  political community and, 51–57, 60–63
  political legislation and, 66–68, 83–84
  the political self and, 53–55
  reformation of vision and, 83, 88
  responsibility and, 68
  seeming/being distinction and, 85–87
  Socrates' alliance with, 82–91
  Socrates' apodeictic intent and, 52, 58, 82
  Socrates' dialogic intent and, 52, 58, 82–91
  species being and, 54–55, 68
  therapeutic stage of dialogue and, 87–91
  as unexceptional interlocutor, 47–48
  zetetic stage of dialogue and, 83–84

Polis, 30–31, 49, 51–57, 60, 84, 109
  as condition for ethical action, 68–69
  the good and, 65
  political activity, 7, 124, 129–30, 145–46, 148,
    149–51, 153
  political community, 50–53, 56–60, 63, 65, 87,
    219
politics
  agency and, 38, 60–65, 89, 97, 219
  the art of war and, 163, 165
  authority and, 48, 178, 260
  as autonomous, 43, 46, 48–49, 52–53, 62, 97,
    178, 300
  cave analogy and, 206
  conformity and, 57–58, 60, 62–63, 88–90, 92,
    97, 219, 231–33
  political courage and, 265
  education in, 157–59, 165, 168–72, 298
  eros and, 184–85f
  the good and, 51, 62
  human nature and, 162–65
  hypothesis of doxastic immanence and, 178–79,
    206–7, 219, 244
  justice and, 137–38
  legislative branch of, 66–68, 71, 83–84,
    98–99, 103, 121, 125, 143–44, 148, 151,
    171, 232
  mimêsis and, 207, 218–19, 225, 230–33, 235,
    265
  mourning and, 226–34
  Odysseus and, 250, 255, 262, 270, 275
  Plato's understanding of, 6, 13
  the political art and, 48, 157–59, 162–63,
    165–71
  political rule and, 95, 106–7
  the political self and, 272–74, 295–96, 301
  political virtue and, 150, 153, 158, 165–66,
    165–70
  rhetoric and, 123–24, 129–30, 137–38, 143–46,
    148, 149–51, 153
  self-interest and, 158–59
  Socrates and, 5, 17, 178, 203, 274–75
  to thumoeides and, 245, 257, 260–62, 265
  virtue and, 30–32, 49, 87, 120–21
  as zero-sum-game, 105, 107
politics, life of, 18, 34, 37, 46, 48, 79, 226–27
Polus, 29, 100, 138–41, 174
  his conventionalism, 142
  his relation to Gorgias, 142–46
  persuasion and, 142
Porter, James I., 5n10, 126n6

practical deliberation
custom and, 231–35, 234
mimêsis and, 224–28
Odysseus and, 252–53
to thumoeides and, 259–60, 263
pre-Socratics, the, 274
Priam, 252
Price, Anthony, 179n2
Prometheus, 153–54, 160–61
Protagoras, 21, 93–94, 97, 117, 145, 147–74, 177,
     194, 207–9, 211, 262, 265–66, 274–75
anthropology of, 162–68
Antilogies, 151
aristocracy and, 170
the art of war and, 163, 165
authority and, 157
his creation myth, 159–68
the cultural artists and, 149–50, 171
education and, 155, 168–71
esotericism of, 148–51, 150, 153–55, 157, 159,
     171–72
as foreigner, 155–57
Hippocrates and, 155–56, 171
homo mensura thesis and, 21–22, 148, 151, 171,
     208
human nature and, 161–62, 167–70, 173
husteron proteron and, 159–60
image-making and, 163–65
justice and, 163–68, 171
the legislative art and, 171
metaphysics of, 161–62
myth of Prometheus and, 153–54
Nietzsche and, 149–50, 173
On the Gods, 151
nature and, 160–61, 169–70, 173
poetic activity and, 149–50, 171, 303–4
poetry and, 152–53
the political art and, 48, 157–59, 162–63,
     165–71
political community and, 163–64
political virtue and, 150, 153, 158, 165–70
politics and, 150–51, 155
popular conception of, 148–49
Prometheus' theft of fire and, 162
Protagorean relativism and, 151
punishment and, 154, 164–70
as radical antinaturalist, 149–50
representation and, 164–65
reverence and, 163–66, 171
self-presentation of, 150, 155–57, 171
Socrates' critique of, 172

Socrates' imitation of, 209
Socrates' relation to, 153–54, 214
in *Theaetetus*, 148–49, 151
the tradition and, 173
his tripartite audience, 150, 171
Protagoras, 9, 74, 120, 145, 147–74, 275
Protrachus, 44
psychic conflict, 72–77, 93–94. *See also* mourning
psychology, 93, 146, 106–7. *See also* agency;
     interiority
of guilt, 282–84
Homeric, 250–51
problem of agency and, 72–78
of *ressentiment*, 107–8, 111, 113, 118–19
of shame, 282–84
Socratic, 2–3, 181–82
of the tyrant, 104–6
Pucci, Pietro, 246n3
punishment
capital, 164–65
corrective, 86–87, 167–70
fear of, 24, 27
the gods and, 24, 27
guilt and, 283, 292–94
justice and, 165–67
Protagoras and, 154, 166–70
purpose of, 165–68

reason
image of, 267
authority and, 267–68
representation and, 268
recognition, 290–91, 294–95
recollection, 183, 199
experience and, 226–34
Redfield, James, 248, 250–51
Reeve, C. D. C., 16n17, 25n36, 60n15, 61n18, 94n3,
     110n20, 181, 212
representation, 81, 175, 265. See also *mimêsis*
abstraction and, 274
as complete, 223–24
the gods and, 186–88, 220–21, 265
image-making and, 164–65
incompleteness of, 278
justice and, 176
painting and, 132–33
politics and, 274
reason and, 268
Sophistic account of, 173
Republic
date of, 16–17

Republic (*continued*)
  account of the good in, 198
  distinctive form of eros in, 7, 179–81, 180f
  education in, 184
  exclusion of divine poetry in, 185–87
  exclusion of eros in, 184, 194, 198–99
  exclusion of madness in, 183–87, 198–200,
    198–200
  exclusion of wonder in, 199
  the gods in, 184
  nature in, 175–76, 196
  philosophic orientation of, 79–80, 177, 183–84,
    188–89, 244
  setting of, 14–17
  role of *to thumoeides* in, 244–45
religion
  ritual and, 23
  death of, 23–24, 32–34, 46
  myth and, 15, 23–24
responsibility, 78–79, 90, 225. *See also* agency
  choice and, 58–59
  disavowal of, 67, 89–90
  guilt and, 292
  (in)voluntary action and, 241
  legislative activity and, 68–69
  political community and, 68–69
  tragedy and, 241
ressentiment, 107–8, 111, 113, 118–19
reverence, 163–66
rhetoric, 66, 115–20, 123–46
  appropriation of, 127
  art and technique distinction and, 110–11
  artist of, 123
  as distinct from other arts, 128–32
  authority and, 123–24, 128–31
  divine power of, 123–24, 132, 144
  education and, 128, 132–35, 135–42
  excellence and, 127
  flattery and, 144
  the good and, 123, 131–32
  innovation and, 116–18
  as imitative, 115–16
  justice and, 115, 122, 137, 143–46
  material terms of, 266–68
  in *Phaedrus*, 200–201
  persuasion and, 124–46
  political rule and, 95
  rhetorical man and, 127, 134, 140, 212
  relation to content and, 131
  Socrates' account of, 143
  supernatural power of, 123–24

Ring of Gyges, 286–87, 292
Romilly, Jacqueline de, 126n6
Roochnik, David, 14n10, 28nn41, 42
Rosch, Eleanor, 210n6
Rosen, Stanley, 9n16, 81n38, 180n3
Rousseau, J. J., 13
Rowe, Christopher J., 3n6
Ryle, Gilbert, 58

Sallis, John, 22n28
Santos, Gerasimos, 179n2
Schmitt, Carl, 51n5
Smith, Nicholas D., 6n11
Sedley, David, 208n3
Schopenhauer, Arthur, 245
Shorey, Paul, 31n45, 112n22
self, the
  nullity of, 272–73
  political and social, 272–74, 295–96, 301
self-consciousness
  political determination of, 260–62
  self-deception and, 272
  to thumoeides and, 260–62
Sextus Empiricus, 125
shame, 139–40, 142, 215–16, 253, 280–92, 296
  visibility and, 284–88
Simonides, 48–51, 151, 172
Snell, Bruno, 252–54
Socrates
  ad hominem argument and, 45, 211, 274, 278
  his relation to the cultural climate, 93, 178,
    273
  his "customary method," 210, 217
  as deceiver, 90–91, 215
  his dialogic activity, 174–75, 207, 242, 271,
    302–3
  his daimonic sign, 204
  dissemblance and, 96
  his elenctic method, 181, 238
  esoteric speech and, 127, 172
  care of human beings and, 143–44
  his comic critique of Protagoras, 172–73
  demagogic rhetoric and, 146
  idealized portrait of, 203–5
  idle talk accusation and, 94
  images and, 9, 77, 80–82, 89, 174–76,
    213–15, 238, 244, 267, 273, 275, 278–79,
    302–3
  imitative arts and, 144
  intellectualism and, 181–82
  his relation to interlocutors, 89–91, 271

irony and, 96, 216–19, 271, 275
his likeness to Eros, 202–4, 270, 304
midwifery and, 208–9
his mimetic activity, 150, 174–75, 274, 302–3
his use of myth, 9, 138, 174–75, 184–85, 203,
    209, 275, 303, 306–7
as narrator of *Republic*, 216–17, 275
his poetic activity, 12, 175–77, 275–79, 303
his philosophical activity, 93
his poetic rivalry with Protagoras, 214
his political activity, 178, 203
as politically threatened, 88, 90
the problem of, 5–7, 13, 80, 93, 127, 173, 176–77,
    214, 303
his account of rhetoric, 143
his second sailing, 58, 80–81, 200
self-imitation and, 216–19
self-knowledge and, 273, 304
his self-presentation, 231, 304–7
his self-sufficiency, 269–70
Socratic ignorance and, 273, 275, 302, 304
sons of, 306–7
Sophistic education and, 266
his relation to the Sophists, 173–77, 274, 303
his therapeutic activity, 175
the tradition and, 174–75
transference and, 88–89
his true political art, 178, 203, 274–75
Sophist, 183
Sophists, the. *See also* Gorgias; Protagoras;
    Thrasymachus
authority of, 157, 208–9
esotericism of, 148–51
creative activity and, 93–95, 142, 173, 178,
    211–12, 262
the critique of *mimêsis* and, 207, 218
Homer and, 208–9
image-making and, 163–64, 173, 211–12, 275
metaphysics of, 124–25, 148–50, 161–62, 173
nature and, 122, 123–24, 147–50, 161–62
Plato's account of, 95, 121, 123–25, 141–42,
    147–52, 173–75
political activity and, 7, 95, 124, 129–30, 145–46,
    148, 149–51, 153, 178, 211
reception of, 148
rhetoric and, 123–46, 171, 264, 266
Socrates' engagement with, 126–27, 274
virtue and, 139
Sophocles, 25–26, 30, 116, 281
soul, the. *See also* city-soul analogy; self-
    akrasia and, 73–74

cave analogy and, 195
conflict within, 76–77, 87–90, 93–94, 120,
    224–28, 240, 251, 267–69, 275
the body and, 58–59, 256
calculative aspect of. *See* calculation
the democratic soul and, 43, 84, 267
division of, 2, 18, 34–42
emptiness of, 272
eros and, 179
the good and, 195–96
gymnastic and, 73
harmony of, 35, 74–77, 262
image of, 176, 302, 306
inquiry and, 1–3, 5, 12, 80–81, 221–22
irascible aspect of, 226, 265
justice and, 66–67
the lie in, 272–74, 278
madness and, 179
midwifery and, 208
mimêsis and, 226–27, 244
perception and, 221–22
in *Phaedrus*, 200–201
politics and, 53–54, 56, 58, 87, 97, 143–44,
    295–96
social structure of, 295–96
speech and, 108, 176, 266
thumoeidic aspect of. *See to thumoeides*
trust and, 222
turning of, 41, 136, 196, 278, 300
space, 197
Stalley, R. F., 65n23
Stanford, William B., 249n8
Stocks, J. L., 18n24
Strauss, Leo, 12n5, 17n21, 65n21, 98n9, 114n28,
    124n2, 126n7, 127n8, 150n8, 152n17, 166n35,
    180n3, 184–85n7
Symposium, 7, 9, 21, 152, 198, 200–205, 214, 269,
    271, 279, 304
daimonic hypothesis of, 201–2
distinctive conception of eros in, 7, 179–80,
    201–4
Szlezák, Thomas, 151, 166n37

technê, 161
analogy with justice and, 60–72, 79, 83, 97
art and technique distinction and, 111
the good and, 63–64
Theaetetus, 148, 151, 192, 208–9
Theaetetus, 9, 21, 151, 187. *See also* Protagoras
intellectual paternity in, 208–9
wonder in, 199

Theages, 55
Theages, 204
Theodorus, 148
Themistocles, 26, 140
Thesleff, Holger, 10n19
Thrasymachus, 34–35, 39, 44, 47, 82, 83, 91,
    92–123, 124, 135, 139, 146–47, 150, 174, 175,
    262, 265–66, 274, 284
  abstraction and, 34, 98–99, 102
  his accusations against Socrates, 113–14
  Antiphon and, 121
  appeal to justice and, 113
  appearance of, 94
  the art of rule and, 98–103, 110, 115
  his bifurcate account of justice, 95, 97, 113,
      121
  character of, 92–96, 107–8, 114–15, 118–20
  Cleitophon's defense of, 99–100
  compared with Gorgias, 126–27
  as error theorist, 121
  his relation to ethical categories, 111–15
  ethical community and, 113–14, 118
  relation to the good and, 34
  his immoralism, 97, 104–7
  as impotent, 94–95
  the just and unjust man and, 103–7, 112–14, 117,
      117f
  justice as advantage of the stronger and, 17,
      93–95, 97–103
  justice as doing another's good and, 95, 103–7
  his legalism, 97–103
  material qualities of his rhetoric, 108
  his nomothetic account of justice, 98–99
  in the *Phaedrus*, 110–11, 115–16
  the political subject and, 102
  politics as zero-sum game and, 105, 107
  the polis and, 109
  practice of rhetoric and, 95
  precise speech and, 94, 100, 108, 126
  the psychology of the tyrant and, 103–9, 118,
      120
  ressentiment and, 107–8, 111, 113, 118–19
  as self-hating, 119–20
  as servant of rhetoric, 118–19
  Socrates' intent regarding, 47, 96, 108, 112–15
  as technician of rhetoric 111, 115–18, 120
  transgression and, 103–7
  tyranny and, 97, 99–100
  wage-earning and, 109–10, 112, 115, 116, 120
Thucydides, 15, 17, 167, 280
  History, 15

Timaeus, 135, 273
Timaeus, 20, 21, 24, 211
time, 197
Timocratic man, the, 36, 76, 267–69
to thumoeides, 6, 270, 246–78, 280
  calculation and, 245, 258–63, 268–70
  city-soul analogy and, 260–61
  definition of, 263
  desire and, 258
  dog-like nature and, 255–56
  eros and, 300–301
  the guardians and, 256–57
  honor and, 261–62
  hypothesis of doxastic immanence and, 265–66
  mimêsis and, 264
  Odysseus and, 245–46, 255
  self-consciousness and, 259–60
  strategy of *Republic* and, 244
  Socratic ignorance and, 274
  the will and, 245
tragic hero, the
  grief of, 230–31, 234–35
tragic poetry. *See* mimetic poetry
trust, 221–23, 235–36
truth, 223–24, 238
  experience of, 79
  coherence theories of, 192
tyranny, 99. *See also* tyrant, the
  law and, 153
  Zeus as, 153
tyrant, the, 97, 99
  eros and, 179, 299
  freedom and, 100
  psychology of the, 103–9, 118
  wealth and, 109–10

Umphrey, Stewart, 122n41, 273
unconscious, the, 88–89

Vander Waerdt, Paul A., 152n17
Velleman, David, 73n33
visible, the realm of the
  action and, 224–30, 241
  dianoetic reflection and, 236–37
  the realm of the intelligible and, 193, 207,
      221–24, 241
vision
  redirection of, 83, 278
  reformation of, 88–89
  perspectival character of, 220–21
  eidetic, 223–24

Vlastos, Gregory, 42, 181–82
Vogelin, Eric, 12n5

Wardy, Robert, 126n6
Watson, Gary, 73n33
Weber, Max, 23, 101
White, Nicholas, 61n18
Whitehead, A. N., 303
will, the, 6, 73–74, 93, 245
Wiggins, David, 38n54
Williams, Bernard, 225n35, 252
    Shame and Necessity, 280–81, 289–92, 294

Wittgenstein, Ludwig, 210, 237n56, 240n63
wonder, 199, 238, 256
    eros and, 201–2
Woodruff, Paul, 200n20

Xenophon, 263
    Memorabilia, 174, 181–82

Zahavi, Dan, 239n60
Zuckert, Catherine, 4n8, 11n1, 302n1

Index of Classical Passages

Antiphon
On Truth
  DK 88 44, A, 5–11   121
  DK 88 44, C, 1–21   121
Aristotle
De anima
  432a25   263n32
  433b4   263n32
Eudemian Ethics
  1243.22–23
Metaphysics
  1028a10–31   135n17
  1029a8–34   135n17
  1025a2–8   250n16
Nichomachean Ethics
  1094a1–a17   84n39
  1095b5–1096a10   37
  1095b13–19   18
  1096a111–17   4n9
  1105a25–b10   61
  1105b13–15   40
  1114b19   241
  1116a17–23   253n19
  1116a28–29   253
  1129b20–30   65n22
  1133a27–1134a22   31n46
  1139b9–11   233
  1140a1–4   129n12
Physics
  1.185a5–11   137n18
Poetics
  1453a6   228n44
  1448b5–20   240
  1449a8–30   116n33
Politics
  1252b7–32   49
  1276b30–33   65

  1280ab13–24   31
  1283a3   38n53
  1292a1–35   99n10
Rhetoric
  1375a35   288n14
Critias
Sisyphus
  DK 88 B 25   154
  DK 88 B 19   161n29
Cicero
Letters to Atticus
  4.16   33n49
Gorgias
On What is Not or On Nature
  DK 82 B3   125
Praise of Helen
  DK 82 B11   125
  DK 82 B11.8   132n14
Herodotus
Histories
  1.11.2–3   288n13
  2.121   247n5
  2.53.1   16n16
Homer
Illiad
  1.4–6   186
  2.245   260
  4.349–55   254
  4.401–18   254n20
  8.137–44   254
  8.77   253
  8.90–98   254
  9.157–59   249
  9.200–204   248
  9.371–72   248
  9.344   248
  9.378   248n6

Homer
  Illiad (continued)
    11.403–10   252
    16.33   249
    16.77   249n8
    16.201–8   251
    16.278–84   251
    16.799–801   251
    17.90–105   253
    21.552–70   253
    22.98–130   253
    22.300–305   251
    23.429–30   254n21
    24.507–51   252
  Odyssey
    1.3250n11
    8.306–12   276
    8.494   277
    9.407   277
    9.413   29
    11.363–69   277
    11.601   154
    14.29–38   257n25
    17.290–327   257n25
    17.383–5   186
    19.211–12   249
    20.17–18   255, 257
    20.9–25   252
    20.9–30   259
Pindar
  Complete Odes
    7.43–47   163n32
    11.45–46   27
    12.5–10   28
Plato
  Apology
    18a–19d   3, 307
    20d   2n5
    21b–23b   203n35
    21c   302n1
    21e   302n1
    22b   216
    22b1   286
    22c   185n8
    23a7–b1   306
    23c   204
    24d–25b   175n46
    26c–e   125
    29d–31b   203n30
    30c8–d5   54n7
    31c–d   204

    35b   203n30
    38a   231
    39c–d   306
    39e5   306
    41a3–4   307
    41b2   307
    41e   307
  Charmides
    153d   203n30
    155c   203n34
    155c–e   203n31
    156d–d7   203n34
    161b   25n36
    162d–163c   129
    166ff.   274
    170b   60
  Cratylus
    403a–b   220n24
    409c   229n49
    413a   148
  Critias
    109d1–3   24
  Crito
    47d–e   53
    47d–48a   231
    47e–48a   53
    49d   38
    50aff.   9
    50a–54e   203n30
    52c   229n49
  Euthydemus
    290b2ff   9
  Euthyphro
    2d–3a   45n59
    3d 114n28
    3d8–9   45n60
  Gorgias
    403e6   221n26
    447a   266
    447b7–8   142n28
    447c1–2   127
    448a7   142
    448b   142
    448c   135
    448e   138n19
    448c5–7   170n41
    449b1   128
    449c5   127
    449c6   127
    449c9–d1   128
    449d1–2   128

449d3	128	487b–c	143
449d4	128	488d–e	134
449d7–8	128	489b	94
449e1	128	490d–e	94
450a7–b2	130	492b5	144
450b–c	128	494a–495a	146
451d5–6	131	497b	143
451d5–8	131	497b8–10	146
451d7	131	519c	174
452b	66	521d	203n32
453b	145	521d6–7	17
453c	132	*Ion*	
453d	136	533e	185n8
453d11	133	535c	185n8
454b	137, 138	*Laches*	
454c5–7	133	194c	25n36
454e3–4	133	191a–c	70n30
455b–456a	135	198d	71n31
455d	138	*Laws*	
455d7	136	684e	26n38
456a	140	679c	21
456a5	123	843a	26n38
456a–b	132	871a–c	218n21
456b–c	137	913b	26n38
456b–457c	138	*Lesser Hippias*	
456b8–c1	134	363b	246
456b–c	127	363c	246
456c–457c	136	364e	247
458d7–8	139	365a–b	247
459a	136	370e	246
459a3–5	134	371e	249
460b–c	141	*Letters*	
461b–c	139	314c	205n40
461c–d	143	*Lysis*	
462a	142	206a	203n31
463a	139	*Meno*	
463a6–8	143	71a	9
464b–c	151n10	86b–c	227n43
467bff.	141	95c3–4	139
467b3	141	*Parmenides*	
470d–471d	142	128b–e	114n28
470e	104n15	*Phaedo*	
471a	142n27	62a	231
471e–472d	175n46	62b	148n3
473e–474b	175n46	69a–b	38n52
475e–476a	175n46	80d	220n24
478bff.	66	94d–c	256
478b–d	66	96a–100a	58
482b–c	175n46	96a–101b	302
482c–d	139	96e–97b	59
484a–b	140	99e5–100a2	81

Plato (*continued*)

  Phaedrus

228e	201n28
230a4–7	1
236d	229n49
241e	185n8
242b–c	204
242e	179
245a	185
246e–248e	188
249d	185n8
252c–253c	188
252e–253a	201
253a	185n8
257b	88n41, 200
260d–e	9, 201n27
263b–c	200
263e	201n27
265d–266b	189
266c	112n21
267d–e	110
268a–c	111
268b6–7	111
269b8–9	111
271b	200
275b	174
276a	201n27
276e–277a	201
279a	16n15

  Philebus

48c	1n2
63bff.	9

  Protagoras

311a	152
312b4	171
313a	155
313c	266
314b	266
315a–b	153
315b	154
315b2–3	153
316a	152
316c–317c	156
317c	229n49
318e	153
319a–320b	158
320d5–6	160
320e1–2	170
320e2	161n29
321a	160
321a7	161n29

321c	162
321d	162, 163
321d–e	162
322a	163
322c	163
323b	166
323c5	170
323d	170
324d	166
325b2	168
325c–d	169
326d1	169
326e–327a	169
333d	229n49
339a1	152
339a–347a	44
341a–b	71n31, 152n15
342a–343b	151
347c–d	152
353aff.	9

  Republic

328c2	21
329b7–c4	25
329d3–4	31
329e–330a	27
331c	32
331c1–5	28
331d	33
331d5	48
331d7	30
332a1	50
332a–b	50
332c5–d1	49
332d7–9	49
332e5	49
333e–334b	57n12
334d3	85
334d7	52
335b2–3	53
335c1–2	55n10
335c3	53
335d	56
336c	114, 114n28
336b8	94
336d6–8	64
337a	114
337b	114
337d	96, 114
338a	114
338d	98, 114, 114n28
340e	90, 102

341b5	129n11	360d	288
341d	114, 116	361d	176
341d7	122n41	362e5–363a2	292
342a6	116	363a6–7	293
342c	102	363d4–7	293
342e	90	364a	104
343c	90, 102	365b2–4	293
343c–d	105	366b	298
343c3–4	103	367c	105n16
343d	105	367d8	294
343e	107	367e1–5	293
343e7	107	368b4–5	10
344a	104	368c–d	213
344c2	106	370b	77
344c8	105	372a1–2	301
344d	266	372d3	301
344d1–2	108	374a–d	64
344d4	94	374c–375d	298
344d5	108	374e–376c	256, 260
345a–b	115	375b	90
345b	266	376a–b	90
345b4–6	108	376e	73
346b	70	377a–b	264
346d–e	117	379a	187
346e–347a	110	382a	272
347a–b	96	382a–c	272
347a–e	269	382b	272
347d5	122n41	382e	188
348d	97	389d	186
349–350c	117n35	390d	255
349a	112	391d1	288n14
349a–b	115	393a	186
350a	118	393c5–6	212n14
350b	118	398a–b	186
350c	117	400d–e	112n24
350d–e	112n24	401c–e	77
351d	119	401d–e	198n23
351e	119	401e–402a	57
352a	119	403c–404e	73
352a6	122n41	404a	257
352b	115	407d–408a	298
357a2	9	407e	61n16, 232
357b	38	410a	298
357d	41	410b–d	73
358b	115	410d	264, 298
358e3–4	300	411a–b	265
358e–359b	147	414e	77
359b	33, 183	416a	257
359b3	301	422b	64
359c	285	422d	257
359d	286	429a–430c	253n19

Republic (continued)

429c–d	265
430a–b	73, 265
435e–436e	36n51
439e7	287
439e–440a	258
440c–d	257, 258
440d	257
441a	258
441b	257
441b–c	255, 258
441e	260
450a	115
450b	115
451d	257
459a	257
459c–d	175
462b	77, 257
462c	77
466d	257
469d–e	257
474c–475c	299n31
477c	190
477c–d	189
477e2	191
478a	192
484c	223
485d4–7	25
487c	89n45
487e	175
488a–e	101
488a–489a	299
491a–3	298
491d	298
492–493	299
492a–494b	175n46
493a–b	144
495e	299
496c	204
498d	115
499c	15
500b–c	257, 269
500d	212
501a–b	144
501b	175
501b3	211
505b	37
505d–e	196, 196n21
506a	199
506b–d	294n21
506d	199
507e	193
509d	222

510b–c	236
514b	199
516b–c	195
516c	199
516d	196n21
517d–e	195n20
518b–e	41
518c8	300
518c–d	136
518d	278
519b–c	79
520b	79
520c	195n20
520d	269
521e	196, 196n21
522c	196
522e	197
523b–c	241
523b1	222
523d	222
523e	199
529d	197
531d	199
531e3	10
533b–c	197
535a	199
537c	189
538a–b	199
539b–d	36
540c	176
545a	36
545d–e	187
548d6	75n35
549c	269
549d	269, 287n11
550a–b	268
551a	261
553b–d	76, 261
554d	76
558d–559d	76
561a–e	75
561d	75
572e–573b	79
581d	39
581e–582a	37
582a	39
582c	41
582d	39
584d–e	40
584e–585a	40
585b	272
586a–b	41
587a	42

588b10–11	302	*Statesman*	
588b–589a	176	262a–e	15n13
592a	269	269d–274c	13
595b	207	*Theaetetus*	
595b–c	4n9	142c	16n15
595b9–c3	213	144b	208
595b10–c2	209	149d	203
595c9–10	222n28	149d–150b	208
596c–e	220, 275	151e	151
596c2	212n14	152c8–10	148
596d1	211n9	152e	209
597e	212	153c–d	209n4
598a	213	155d	199
598a–b	220	172b	148n2
598b–c	213	172b6–7	148
598d	213	181b	26n38
598d5	279	184c–185c	190
600a–b	156	185d	192
600e5–6	213	195d	229n49
602c	215n18	200b–c	9
602c4–5	220	201e–203c	187
602c7–11	220	*Timaeus*	
603a4	221	19d–e	203
603b10	219	22b–c	20
603c	213n15	29e	211
603c10	222n28	31b1	212n11
603e–604a	226	49c–52b	135n17
604b–c	226	Protagoras	
604b9–c3	227	*Antilogies*	
604d1–2	231	DK 80 B1	151n12
605a6–c4	222n44	*On the Gods*	
605b8	222n44	DK 80 B4	151n11
605d8–e1	229	Sophocles	
614b	270n38	*Antigone*	
615c1	222n28	51 286	
Sophist		1061	26n38
216c–d	183	*Oedipus Tyrannus*	
250c	196n21	1303–1306	234
Symposium		Thucydides	
174a	205n40, 229n49	2.65.8	17n20
174d	269, 287n11	2.65.12	17n21
175d	45n60	3.36–40	167n38
175d–e	175n46	3.38	167n37
177d–c	203n31	3.62.3	99n10
194b–d	175n46	4.21–22	167n38
201d–212b	302	6.82.3.8	129n11
202e	179n1	Xenophon	
203d8	221n26	*Memorabilia*	
210e	269n37	1.1.16	181
211b	202	1.2–3	174
219a	270	1.2.43–44	99n10
202a3	279	2.1.21	229n47
222a	215		